Julius Eggeling

The Satapatha-Brahmana, According to the Text of the Madhyandina School

Vol. XLI

Julius Eggeling

The Satapatha-Brahmana, According to the Text of the Madhyandina School

Vol. XLI

Reprint of the original, first published in 1891.

1st Edition 2023 | ISBN: 978-3-36863-597-8

Verlag (Publisher): Outlook Verlag GmbH, Zeilweg 44, 60439 Frankfurt, Deutschland
Vertretungsberechtigt (Authorized to represent): E. Roepke, Zeilweg 44, 60439 Frankfurt, Deutschland
Druck (Print): Books on Demand GmbH, In de Tarpen 42, 22848 Norderstedt, Deutschland

THE

SACRED BOOKS OF THE EAST

London

HENRY FROWDE

Oxford University Press Warehouse
Amen Corner, E.C.

New York

MACMILLAN & CO., 66 FIFTH AVENUE

THE

SACRED BOOKS OF THE EAST

TRANSLATED

BY VARIOUS ORIENTAL SCHOLARS

AND EDITED BY

F. MAX MÜLLER

VOL. XLI

Oxford

AT THE CLARENDON PRESS

1894

Oxford
PRINTED AT THE CLARENDON PRESS
BY HORACE HART, PRINTER TO THE UNIVERSITY

THE

SATAPATHA-BRÂHMANA

ACCORDING TO THE TEXT OF THE

MÂDHYANDINA SCHOOL

TRANSLATED BY

JULIUS EGGELING

PART III

BOOKS V, VI, AND VII

Oxford
AT THE CLARENDON PRESS
1894

CONTENTS.

SIXTH KÂ*N*D*A.

SEVENTH KÂ*N*D*A.

Agni-*k*ayana (continued).

INTRODUCTION.

THE first of the three Kâ*nd*as contained in the present volume continues the dogmatic discussion of the different forms of Soma-sacrifice, in connection with which two important ceremonies, the Vâgapeya and Râgasûya, are considered. From a ritualistic point of view, there is a radical difference between these two ceremonies. The Râgasûya, or 'inauguration of a king,' strictly speaking, is not a Soma-sacrifice, but rather a complex religious ceremony which includes, amongst other rites, the performance of a number of Soma-sacrifices of different kinds. The Vâgapeya, or 'drink of strength' (or, perhaps, 'the race-cup'), on the other hand, is recognised as one of the different forms (sa*m*sthâ) which a single Soma-sacrifice may take. As a matter of fact, however, this form hardly ever occurs, as most of the others constantly do, in connection with, and as a constituent element of, other ceremonies, but is almost exclusively performed as an independent sacrifice. The reason why this sacrifice has received a special treatment in the Brâhma*n*a, between the Agnish*t*oma and the Râgasûya, doubtless is that, unlike the other forms of Soma-sacrifice, it has some striking features of its own which stamp it, like the Râgasûya, as a political ceremony. According to certain ritualistic authorities[1], indeed, the performance of the Vâgapeya should be arranged in much the same way as that of the Râgasûya; that is, just as the central ceremony of the Râgasûya, viz. the Abhishe*k*anîya or consecration, is preceded and followed by certain other Soma-days, so the Vâgapeya should be preceded and followed by exactly corresponding ceremonies.

[1] See Kâty. *S*r. XIV, 1, 7; Lâ*t*y. *S*r. VIII, 11, 7-11.

The preceding Kâ*nd*a was chiefly taken up with a detailed discussion of the simplest form of a complete Soma-sacrifice, the Agnish*t*oma, serving as the model for all other kinds of one-day (ekâha) Soma-sacrifices; and it also adverted incidentally to some of the special features of such of the remaining fundamental forms of Soma-sacrifice as are required for the performance of sacrificial periods of from two to twelve pressing-days—the so-called ahîna-sacrifices—as well as for the performance of the sacrificial sessions (sattra) lasting from twelve days upwards. As the discussion of the Vâ*g*apeya presupposes a knowledge of several of those fundamental forms of Soma-sacrifice, it may not be out of place here briefly to recapitulate their characteristic features.

The ekâha, or 'one-day' sacrifices, are those Soma-sacrifices which have a single pressing-day, consisting of three services (or pressings, savana)—the morning, midday, and third (or evening) services—at each of which certain cups of Soma-liquor are drawn, destined to be ultimately consumed by the priests and sacrificer, after libations to the respective deities have been duly made therefrom. At certain stated times during the performance, hymns (stotra) are chanted by the Udgât*ri*s; each of which is followed by an appropriate recitation (*s*astra) of Vedic hymns or detached verses, by the Hot*ri* priest or one of his assistants. An integral part of each Soma-sacrifice, moreover, is the animal sacrifice (pa*s*ubandhu); the number of victims varying according to the particular form of sacrifice adopted. In the exposition of the Agnish*t*oma, the animal offering actually described (part ii, p. 162 seq.) is that of a he-goat to Agni and Soma, intended to serve as the model for all other animal sacrifices. This description is inserted in the Brâhma*n*a among the ceremonies of the day preceding the Soma-day; whilst, in the actual performance, the slaughtering of the victim, or victims, takes place during the morning service, and the meat-oblations are made during the evening service, of the pressing-day. The ritualistic works enumerate a considerable number of 'one-day' sacrifices, all of them with special features of their own; most of these sacrifices are, however, merely modifications of one or other of the fundamental forms of ekâhas. Of such forms or saṃsthâs—literally, 'completions,' being so called because the final chants or ceremonies are their most characteristic features—the ritual system recognises seven, viz. the Agnishṭoma, Atyagnishṭoma, Ukthya, Shoḍaśin, Vâgapeya[1], Atirâtra, and Aptoryâma.

The Agnishṭoma, the simplest and most common form of Soma-sacrifice, requires the immolation of a single victim, a he-goat to Agni; and the chanting of twelve stotras, viz. the Bahish-pavamâna and four Âgya-stotras at the morning service; the Mâdhyandina-pavamâna and four Pṛishṭha-stotras at the midday service; and the Tṛitîya (or Ârbhava)-pavamâna and the Agnishṭoma-sâman at the evening service. It is this last-named chant, then, that gives its name to this sacrifice which, indeed, is often explained as the 'Agnishṭoma-saṃsthaḥ kratuḥ[2],' or the sacrifice concluding with 'Agni's praise.' The term 'sâman,' in its narrow technical sense, means a choral melody, a hymn-tune, without reference to the words set thereto. Not unfrequently, however, it has to be taken in the wider sense of a chanted verse or hymn (triplet), a chorale; but, though the distinction is evidently of some importance for the ritual, it is not always easy to determine the particular sense in which the term is meant to be applied, viz. whether a specified sâman is intended to include the original text set to the respective tune, or whether some other verses to which that tune has been adapted are intended. In the case of the Agnishṭoma-sâman, however, the word 'sâman' cannot be taken in its narrow acceptation, but the term has to be understood in the sense of 'a hymn chanted in praise of Agni.' The words commonly used for this chant, are the first two verses of Rig-veda S. VI, 48, a hymn indeed

[1] In this enumeration the Vâgapeya is often placed between the Atirâtra and Aptoryâma; e.g. Lâṭy. V, 4, 24.

[2] Thus on Śat. Br. V, 1, 3, 1 Âgneyam agnishṭoma âlabhate, Sâyaṇa remarks, 'agniḥ stûyate 'sminn ity agnishṭomo nâma sâma, tasmin vishayabhûta âgneyam âlabhate, etena paśunâ 'smin vâgapeye 'gnishṭomasaṃsthaṃ kratum evânushṭhitavân bhavati.' In IV, 2, 4, 9 seq., also, the term 'agnishṭoma' would seem to apply to the final chant rather than to the whole sacrifice.

admirably adapted for the purpose of singing Agni's praises. For the first verse, beginning '*yag*ñâ-*yag*ñâ vo agnaye,' the chief tune-book, the Grâmageya-gâna, has preserved four different tunes, all of which are ascribed to the *Ri*shi Bharadvâ*g*a: one of them has, however, come to be generally accepted as the Ya*g*ñâya*g*ñiya-tune κατ' ἐξοχήν, and has been made use of for this and numerous other triplets[1]; whilst the other tunes seem to have met with little favour, not one of them being represented in the triplets arranged for chanting in stotras, as given in the Ûha and Uhya-gânas. Neither the Ya*g*ñâya*g*ñiya-tune, nor its original text, is however a fixed item in the chanting of the Agnish*t*omasâman. Thus, for the first two verses of Rig-veda VI, 48, the Vâ*g*apeya-sacrifice[2] substitutes verses nine and ten of the same hymn, and these are chanted, not to the Ya*g*ñâya*g*ñiya, but to the Vâravantîya-tune, originally composed for, and named after, Rig-veda I, 27, 1 (S. V. I, 17; ed. Calc. I, p. 121) 'a*s*va*m* na tvâ vâravantam.'

The Ukthya-sacrifice requires the slaughtering of a second victim, a he-goat to Indra and Agni; and to the twelve chants of the Agnish*t*oma it adds three more, the so-called Uktha-stotras, each of which is again followed by an Uktha-*s*astra recited by one of the Hotrakas, or assistants of the Hot*ri*. As the evening service of the Agnish*t*oma had only two *s*astras, both recited by the Hot*ri*, the addition of the three *s*astras of the Hotrakas would, in this respect, equalize the evening to the morning and midday savanas. The word 'uktha' is explained by later lexicographers either as a synonym of 'sâman,' or as a kind of sâman[3]; but it is not unlikely that that meaning of the word was directly derived from this, the most common use of the word in the term 'uktha-stotra.' The etymology of the word[4], at all events, would point to the

[1] Each Sâman-tune is usually chanted thrice, either each time on a special verse of its own, or so that, by certain repetitions of words, two verses are made to suffice for the thrice-repeated tune.

[2] So also does the Agnish*t*ut ekâha, cf. Tâ*nd*ya Br. XVII, 5, 7.

[3] Sâya*n*a, to *S*at. Br. IV, 3, 3, 2, explains it by 'stotra;' but see IV, 2, 3, 6-9 where it undoubtedly refers to the recited verses (*rik*), not to the sâman.

[4] Viz. from root 'va*k*' to speak. I cannot see the necessity for taking

meaning 'verse, hymn,' rather than to that of 'tune' or 'chant;' but, be that as it may, the word is certainly used in the former sense in the term 'mahad-uktha,' the name of the 'great recitation' of a thousand b*ri*hati verses[1], being the Hot*ri*'s *s*astra in response to the Mahâvrata-stotra at the last but one day of the Gavâm-ayana. And, besides, at the Agnish*t*oma a special 'ukthya' cup of Soma-juice is drawn both at the morning and midday pressings, but not at the evening savana. This cup, which is eventually shared by the three principal Hotrakas between them, is evidently intended as their reward for the recitation of their 'ukthas.' At the Ukthya-sacrifice, as might have been expected, the same cup is likewise drawn at the evening service. Though it may be taken for granted, therefore, that 'uktha' was an older term for '*s*astra,' it still seems somewhat strange that this term should have been applied specially to the additional *s*astras and stotras of the Ukthya-sacrifice. Could it be that the name of the additional Ukthya-cup, as a distinctive feature of this sacrifice, suggested the name for the *s*astras and stotras with which that cup was connected, or have we rather to look for some such reason as Ait. Br. VI, 13 might seem to indicate? This passage contains a discussion regarding the different status of the Hotrakas who have ukthas of their own, and those who have not; and it then proceeds to consider the difference that exists between the two first and the third savanas of the Agnish*t*oma in respect of the Hotrakas' ukthas. It is clear that here also, the term 'uktha' can hardly be taken otherwise than as referring to

---

'b*ri*had va*k*as' in Rig-veda VII, 96, 1 in the technical sense of B*ri*hat-tune, as is done by Prof. Hillebrandt, in his interesting essay, 'Die Sonnwendfeste in Alt-Indien,' p. 29, merely because it is used there in connection with Indra; whilst he himself is doubtful as to whether it should be taken in the same sense in III, 10, 5 where it occurs in connection with Agni. Though the B*ri*hat-sâman is no doubt frequently referred to Indra, and the Rathantara to Agni, the couplets ordinarily chanted to them (Rig-veda VI, 46, 1-2 and VII, 32, 22, 23) are both of them addressed to Indra. Both tunes are, however, applied to verses addressed to all manner of deities.

[1] See Catalogue of Sanskrit MSS. of the India Office, No. 434. In Kaush. Br. XI, 8, 'sadasy ukthâni *s*asyante,' also, the word has undoubtedly the sense of *s*astra, or (recited) hymn. In part i, p. 346, note 3 of this translation read 'great recitation or *s*astra,' instead of 'great chant.'

the *s*astras—though, no doubt, the stotra is sometimes said to belong to the priest who recites the *s*astra in response to it—and this paragraph of the Brâhma*n*a reads almost like the echo of an old discussion as to whether or not there should be recitations for the Hotrakas at the evening service of a complete Soma-sacrifice. If, in this way, the question of 'uktha or no uktha' had become a sort of catchword for ritualistic controversy, one could understand how the term came ultimately to be applied to the three additional stotras and *s*astras.

Not unfrequently, the Ukthya is treated merely as a redundant Agnish*t*oma, as an 'Agnish*t*oma*h* soktha*h*,' or Agnish*t*oma with the Ukthas[1]. Considering, however, that the term Agnish*t*oma, properly speaking, belongs only to a Soma-sacrifice which ends with the Agnish*t*oma (sâman), and that the addition of the Uktha-stotras also involves considerable modifications in the form of most of the preceding chants, a new term such as Ukthya, based on the completing and characteristic chants of this form of sacrifice, was decidedly more convenient. In regard to the composition of the preceding stotras, with the exception of the Mâdhyandina-pavamâna and the Agnish*t*oma-sâman, the Ukthya, indeed, may be said to constitute a parallel form of Sacrifice beside the Agnish*t*oma[2], the succeeding sa*m*sthâs following the model of either the one or the other of these two parallel forms.

The Sho*d*a*s*in-sacrifice requires, as a third victim, the

[1] See, for instance, Tâ*nd*ya Br. XX, 1, 1.

[2] Perhaps the most characteristic point of difference between these two forms in which the fundamental stotras are chanted is the first (or Hot*ri*'s) P*ri*sh*th*a-stotra at the midday service. Whilst the Agnish*t*oma here requires the Rathantara-tune chanted on the text, Sâma-veda S. II, 30, 31; the Ukthya, on the other hand, requires the text, S. V. II, 159, 160, chanted to the B*ri*hat-tune. Professor Hillebrandt, l. c., p. 22, has, indeed, tried to show that these two tunes play an important part in early India in connection with the celebration of the solstices. A similar alternation of sâmans to that of the Hot*ri*'s P*ri*sh*th*a-stotra obtains at the third, or Brâhma*n*â*kkh*a*m*sin's P*ri*sh*th*a-stotra; the Naudhasa-sâman (II, 35, 36) being used at the Agnish*t*oma, and the *S*yaita-sâman at the Ukthya-sacrifice. As regards the second (or Maitrâvaru*n*a's) and fourth (or A*kkh*âvâka's) P*ri*sh*th*a-stotras, on the other hand, the same sâman—viz. the Vâmadevya (II, 32-34) and Kâleya (II, 37, 38) respectively—is used both at the Agnish*t*oma and Ukthya.

immolation of a ram to Indra; and one additional chant, the shod*asi*-stotra, with its attendant *s*astra and Soma-cup. The most natural explanation of the name is the one supplied, in the first place, by Ait. Br. IV, 1 (as interpreted by Sâya*n*a)—viz. the sacrifice which has sixteen, or a sixteenth, stotra[1]. But, as the name applies not only to the sacrifice but also to the stotra and *s*astra, the Brâhma*n*a further justifies the name by the peculiar composition of the shod*asi*-*s*astra in which the number sixteen prevails[2]. Very probably, however, the name may have belonged to the sacrifice long before the *s*astra, for symbolic reasons, had assumed the peculiar form it now presents.

In this summary of the characteristic features of the forms of Soma-sacrifice presupposed by the Vâgapeya, no mention has yet been made of the Atyagnish*t*oma, or redundant Agnish*t*oma, which usually occupies the second place in the list of sa*m*sthâs. This form of sacrifice is indeed very little used, and there can be little doubt that it was introduced into the system, as Professor Weber suggests, merely for the sake of bringing up the Soma-sa*m*sthâs to the sacred number of seven. This sacrifice is obtained by the addition of the shod*asi*-stotra to the twelve chants of the Agnish*t*oma, as well as of the special Soma-cup and sacrificial victim for Indra, connected with that chant. It may thus be considered as a short form of the Shod*asi*n-sacrifice (though without the full complement of stotras implied in that name), which might have suited the views of such ritualists as held the *s*astras of the Hotrakas at the evening service to be superfluous[3].

The distinctive feature of the Atirâtra-sacrifice, as the name itself indicates, is an 'overnight' performance of chants and recitations, consisting of three rounds of four stotras and *s*astras each. At the end of each round

[1] This is also the explanation of the term given by Sâya*n*a in his commentary on Tâ*nd*ya Br. XII, 13, 1.

[2] See this translation, part ii, p. 402, note 1.

[3] See part ii, p. 402, note 2, where it is stated that the tenth and last day of the Da*s*arâtra is an Atyagnish*t*oma day, called Avivâkya, i.e. one on which there should be no dispute or quarrel.

(paryâya) libations are offered, followed by the inevitable potations of Soma-liquor. That the performance, indeed, partook largely of the character of a regular nocturnal carousal, may be gathered from the fact, specially mentioned in the Aitareya Brâhma*n*a, that each of the Hot*ri*'s offering-formulas is to contain the three words—'andhas,' Soma-plant (or liquor), 'pâ,' to drink, and 'mada,' intoxication. Accordingly, one of the formulas used is Rig-veda II, 19, 1 apâyy asyâ*s*ndhaso madâya, 'there has been drunk (by Indra, or by us) of this juice for intoxication.' The twelve stotras, each of which is chanted to a different tune, are followed up, at daybreak, by the Sandhi-stotra, or twilight-chant, consisting of six verses (Sâma-veda S. II, 99–104) chanted to the Rathantara-tune. This chant is succeeded by the Hot*ri*'s recitation of the Â*s*vina-*s*astra, a modification of the ordinary 'prâtar-anuvâka,' or morning-litany, by which the pressing-day of a Soma-sacrifice is ushered in[1]. The Atirâtra also requires a special victim, viz. a he-goat offered to Sarasvatî, the goddess of speech. As regards the ceremonies preceding the night-performance, there is again a difference of opinion among ritualists as to whether the sho*d*a*s*i-stotra, with its attendant rites, is, or is not, a necessary element of the Atirâtra[2]. Some authorities[3], accordingly, distinctly recognise two different kinds of Atirâtra,—one with, and the other without, the sho*d*a*s*in. In Kâtyâyana's Sûtra, there is no allusion to any difference of opinion on this point, but, in specifying the victims required at the different Soma-sacrifices, he merely remarks (IX, 8, 5) that, 'At the Atirâtra there is a fourth victim to Sarasvatî.' This would certainly seem to imply that there are also to be the three preceding victims, including the one to Indra peculiar to the Sho*d*a*s*in. Â*s*valâyana (V, 11, 1) also refers incidentally to the sho*d*a*s*in as part of the

[1] See part ii, p. 226 seq. On the present occasion the Prâtar-anuvâka is, however, to consist of as many verses as, counting their syllables, would make up a thousand b*ri*hatî-verses (of thirty-six syllables each). The three sections of the ordinary morning-litany from the body of the Â*s*vina-*s*astra which concludes, after sunrise, with verses addressed to Sûrya, the sun.

[2] Cf. Lâ*t*y. *S*r. VIII, 1, 16; IX, 5, 23 with commentary.

[3] Notably Tâ*nd*ya Br. XX, 1, 1 seq.

Atirâtra, though it is not quite clear from the text of the sûtra whether it is meant to be a necessary or only an optional feature of that sacrifice. The Aitareya Brahma*n*a (IV, 6), on the other hand, in treating of the Atirâtra, enters on a discussion with the view of showing that the night-performance of that sacrifice is in every respect equal to the preceding day-performance; and accordingly, as the three services of the day-performance include fifteen chants and recitations (viz. the twelve of the Agnish*t*oma, and the three Ukthas), so, during the night, the three rounds of in all twelve stotras, together with the sandhi-stotra, here counted as three stotras (triplets), make up the requisite fifteen chants. This Brâhma*n*a, then, does not recognise the sho*d*a*s*in as part of the Atirâtra, and, indeed, the manuals of the Atirâtra chants which I have consulted make no mention of the sho*d*a*s*i-stotra, though it is distinctly mentioned there among the chants of the Vâgapeya and the Aptoryâma. The passage in the Aitareya, just referred to, also seems to raise the question as to whether the Atirâtra is really an ekâha, or whether it is not rather an ahîna-sacrifice. On this point also the authorities seem to differ; whilst most writers take the Atirâtra, and the analogous Aptoryâma, to be 'one-day' sacrifices, the Tâ*n*dya Brâhma*n*a (XX) and Lâ*t*y. IX, 5, 6 class them along with the Ahînas[1]; and they may indeed be regarded as intermediate links between the two classes of Soma-sacrifice, inasmuch as, in a continued sacrificial performance, the final recitations of these sacrifices take the place of the opening ceremony of the next day's performance. Such, for instance, is the case in the performance of the Atirâtra as the opening day of the Dvâda*s*âha, or twelve days' period of sacrifice; whilst in the performance of the twelfth and concluding day, which is likewise an Atirâtra, the concluding ceremonies of the latter might be considered in

[1] The Aitareya Brâhma*n*a (VI, 18) in discussing the so-called sampâta hymns inserted in continued performances, with the view of establishing a symbolic connection between the several days, curiously explains the term 'ahîna,' not from 'ahas' day, but as meaning 'not defective, where nothing is left out' (a-hîna).

a manner superabundant. It is probably in this sense that Lâ*t*y. (IX, 5, 4) calls the overnight performance of the last day of an ahîna (e.g. the Dvâda*s*âha) the yag*ñ*apu*kkh*a, or tail of the sacrifice, which is to fall beyond the month for which, from the time of the initiation, the ahîna is to last.

The Aptoryâma-sacrifice represents an amplified form of the Atirâtra. It requires the sho*d*a*s*i-stotra and the ceremonies connected with it as a necessary element of its performance; whilst its distinctive feature consists in four additional (atirikta-) stotras and *s*astras, chanted and recited after the Â*s*vina-*s*astra, the concluding recitation of the Atirâtra. These four chants are arranged in such a manner that each successive stotra is chanted to a different tune, and in a more advanced form of composition, from the triv*ri*t (nine-versed) up to the ekavi*ms*a (twenty-one-versed) stoma. In the liturgical manuals, the Aptoryâma, moreover, performs the function of serving as the model for a sacrificial performance with all the 'p*ri*sh*th*as[1].' Though this mode of chanting has been repeatedly referred to in the translation and notes, a few additional remarks on this subject may not be out of place here. When performed in its 'p*ri*sh*th*a' form, the stotra is so arranged that a certain sâman (or chanted triplet) is enclosed, as the 'garbha' (embryo), within some other sâman which, as its 'p*ri*sh*th*a' (i.e. back, or flanks), is chanted a number of times before and after the verses of the central sâman. The tunes most commonly used for forming the enclosing sâmans of a P*ri*sh*th*a-stotra are the Rathantara and B*ri*hat; and along with these, four others are singled out to make up the six P*ri*sh*th*a-sâmans κατ' ἐξοχήν, viz. the Vairûpa (with the text Sâma-veda II, 212-13), Vairâ*g*a (II, 277-9), *S*âkvara[2] (chanted on the Mahânâmnî verses,

---

[1] From Â*s*valâyana's rule (IX, 11, 4), 'If they chant in forming the garbha (i.e. in the 'p*ri*sh*th*a' form), let him (the Hot*ri* or Hotraka) recite in the same way the stotriyas and anurûpas,' it seems, however, clear that the Aptoryâma may also be performed without the P*ri*sh*th*as.

[2] The original text of the *S*âkvara-sâman is stated (by Sâya*n*a on Aitar. Br. IV, 13; Mahîdhara on Vâ*g*. S. X, 14, &c.) to be Sâma-veda II, 1151-3, 'pro shv asmai purotatham,' but the Sâma-veda Gânas do not seem to give the tune

Aitar. Âr. IV), and Raivata[1] sâmans. These six sâmans are employed during the six days' sacrificial period called Prish*th*ya-sha*d*aha, in such a way that one of them, in the order in which they are here enumerated, is used for the first, or Hot*ri*'s, Pri*sh*t*h*a-stotra on the successive days of that period. In that case, however, these stotras are not performed in the proper 'prish*th*a' form[2], i. e. they have no other sâman inserted within them, but they are treated like any other triplet according to the particular stoma, or mode of composition, prescribed for them. But, on the other hand, in the Aptoryâma, when performed 'with all the P*ri*sh*th*as,' not only are a number of stotras chanted in the proper 'p*ri*sh*th*a' form, but the 'p*ri*sh*th*a' element asserts itself in yet another way, viz. by the appearance of all the six 'P*ri*sh*th*a-sâmans' in the course of the performance of the different stotras, in this way:—the Rathantara-tune forms the middlemost of the seven triplets of which the Madhyandina-pavamâna is composed;

with that text, but with the Mahânâmnî verses (ed. Bibl. Ind. II, p. 371). The Tâ*nd*ya Br. XIII, 4 (and comm.), gives minute directions as to the particular pâdas of the first three Mahânâmnî triplets which are singled out as of a *s*âkvara (potent) nature, and are supposed to form the three stotriyâ verses of the *s*âkvara-sâman, consisting of seven, six, and five pâdas respectively. The a*s*âkvara pâdas are, however, likewise chanted in their respective places, as is also the additional tenth verse, the five pâdas of which are treated as mere supplementary (or 'filling in') matter.

[1] That is, the Vâravantîya-tune adapted to the 'Revatî' verses. The Vâravantîya-tune is named after its original text, Rig-veda I, 27, 1, 'a*s*va*m* na tvâ vâravantam' (Sâma-veda, ed. Bibl. Ind. I, p. 121). When used as one of the P*ri*sh*th*a-sâmans it is not, however, this, its original text, that is chanted to it, but the verses Rig-veda I, 30, 13-15, 'revatîr na*h* sadhamâda' (Sâma-veda II, 434-6, ed. vol. iv, p. 56), whence the tune, as adapted to this triplet, is usually called Raivata. The Raivata-sâman, thus, is a signal instance of the use of the term 'sâman' in the sense of a chanted verse or triplet.

[2] The statement, in part ii, p. 403 note (and repeated in the present part, p. 6, note 2), that, while the P*ri*sh*th*a-stotras of the Abhiplava-sha*d*aha are performed in the ordinary (Agnish*t*oma) way, the P*ri*sh*th*ya-sha*d*aha requires their performance in the proper P*ri*sh*th*a form, is not correct. In both kinds of sha*d*aha, the P*ri*sh*th*a-stotras are performed in the ordinary way (viz. in the Agnish*t*oma or Ukthya way, see p. 4 note); but whilst, in the Abhiplava, the Rathantara and B*ri*hat sâmans are used for the Hot*ri*'s P*ri*sh*th*a-stotra on alternate days, the P*ri*sh*th*ya-sha*d*aha requires a different P*ri*sh*th*a-sâman on each of the six days. The two kinds of sha*d*ahas also differ entirely in regard to the sequence of stomas prescribed for the performance of the stotras.

the Brihat forms the 'garbha,' or enclosed sâman, of the Agnishtoma-sâman[1]; the Vairûpa the 'garbha' of the third, the Vairâga that of the first, the Sâkvara that of the second, and the Raivata that of the fourth, Prishtha-stotra. It is doubtless this feature which gives to certain Soma-days the name of 'sarvaprishtha,' or one performed with all the (six) Prishthas. Then, as regards the particular stotras that are chanted in the proper 'prishtha' form, these include not only the four so-called Prishtha-stotras of the midday service, but also the four Âgya-stotras of the morning service, as well as the Agnishtoma-sâman and the three Uktha-stotras of the evening service,—in short, all the first fifteen stotras with the exception of the three Pavamâna-stotras. Of the stotras which succeed the Ukthas, on the other hand—viz. the Shodasin, the twelve chants of the three night-rounds, the Sandhi-stotra, and the four Atirikta-stotras—not one is performed in the 'prishtha' form. How often the several verses of the 'prishtha-sâman,' and those of the 'garbha' are to be chanted, of course depends, in each case, not only on the particular stoma which has to be performed, but also on the particular mode (vishtuti) prescribed, or selected, for the stoma. Thus, while all the four Âgya-stotras are chanted in the pañkadasa, or fifteen-versed-stoma; the four Prishtha-stotras are to be performed in the ekavimsa (of twenty-one verses), the katurvimsa (of twenty-four verses), the katuskatvârimsa (of forty-four verses), and the ashtâkatvârimsa (of forty-eight verses) respectively. Now whenever, as in the case of the pañkadasa and the ekavimsa-stomas, the number of verses is divisible by three, one third of the total number of verses is usually assigned to each of the three parts of the stotra, and distributed over the respective (three or sometimes four) verses of that sâman[2].

[1] Either the Rathantara or the Brihat also forms the 'prishtha,' or enclosing sâman, of the first Prishtha-stotra.

[2] Whenever the stotra is not performed in the 'prishtha' form, but consists of a single sâman or triplet, the repetitions required to make up the number of verses implied in the respective stoma, are distributed over the three verses of the sâman in such a way that the whole sâman is chanted thrice, each time with various repetitions of the single verses. The usual form in which the

To illustrate this tripartite composition, the Hot*ri*'s P*r*ish*th*a-stotra, performed in the twenty-one-versed stoma, may be taken as an example. For the 'p*r*ish*th*a,' the manuals give the B*r*ihat-sâman, on its original text (Sâma-veda II, 159, 160, 'tvâm id dhi havâmahe,' arranged so as to form three verses), though the Rathantara may be used instead[1]. For the 'garbha,' or enclosed sâman, on the other hand, the Vairâga-sâman (with its original text, S. V. II, 277-9, 'pibâ somam indra mandatu tvâ') is to be used, a most elaborate tune[2], with long sets of stobhas, or musical ejaculations, inserted in the text. Of the twenty-one verses, of which the stoma consists, seven verses would thus fall to the share of the 'garbha,' and seven verses to that of the 'p*r*ish*th*a,' as chanted before and after the 'garbha.' Thus, in accordance with the formula set forth in p. xxii, note 2, the three verses (a, b, c) of the B*r*ihat would be chanted in the form aaa-bbb-c; then the verses of the Vairâga-sâman (as 'garbha') in the form a-bbb-ccc; and finally again the B*r*ihat in the form aaa-b-ccc. Stotras, the total number of verses of which is not divisible by three, of course require a slightly different distribution. Thus, of the third P*r*ish*th*a-stotra, the stoma of which consists of forty-four verses, the two parts of the 'p*r*ish*th*a' obtain fifteen verses each, whilst the 'garbha' has only fourteen verses for its share.

The Vâ*g*apeya, the last of the seven forms of a complete Soma-sacrifice, occupies an independent position beside the Atirâtra and Aptoryâma, whose special features it does not share. Like them, it starts from the Sho*d*a*s*in, to the characteristic (sixteenth) chant (and recitation) of which it adds one more stotra, the Vâ*g*apeya-sâman, chanted to the B*r*ihat-tune, in the Saptada*s*a (seventeen-versed) stoma, and followed by the recitation of the Vâ*g*apeya-*s*astra. The Saptada*s*a-stoma, indeed, is so characteristic of this sacrifice that—as has been set forth at p. 8 note

ekavi*m*sa is performed may be represented by the formula aaa-bbb-c; a-bbb-ccc; aaa-b-ccc, making together twenty-one verses.

[1] Â*s*val. *S*r. IX, 3, 4-5.

[2] It is given somewhat imperfectly in the ed. Bibl. Ind. V, p. 391.

below—all the preceding chants, from the Bahishpavamâna onward, are remodelled in accordance with it. Besides, over and above the three victims of the Sho*d*a*s*in-sacrifice, the Vâ*g*apeya requires, not only a fourth one, sacred to Sarasvatî, the goddess of speech, but also a set of seventeen victims for Pra*g*âpati, the god of creatures and procreation. As regards other rites peculiar to the Vâ*g*apeya, the most interesting, doubtless, is the chariot-race in which the sacrificer, who must be either of the royal or of the priestly order, is allowed to carry off the palm, and from which this sacrifice perhaps derives its name. Professor Hillebrandt[1], indeed, would claim for this feature of the sacrifice the character of a relic of an old national festival, a kind of Indian Olympic games; and though there is perhaps hardly sufficient evidence to bear out this conjecture, it cannot at least be denied that this feature has a certain popular look about it.

Somewhat peculiar are the relations between the Vâ*g*apeya and the Râ*g*asûya on the one hand, and between the Vâ*g*apeya and the B*ri*haspatisava on the other. In the first chapter of the fifth book, the author of this part of our Brâhma*n*a is at some pains to impress the fact that the Vâ*g*apeya is a ceremony of superior value and import to the Râ*g*asûya; and hence Kâtyâyana (XV, 1, 1–2) has two rules to the effect that the Râ*g*asûya may be performed by a king who has not yet performed the Vâ*g*apeya. These authorities would thus seem to consider the drinking of the Vâ*g*apeya-cup a more than sufficient equivalent for the Râ*g*asûya, or inauguration of a king; they do not, however, say that the Râ*g*asûya must be performed prior to the Vâ*g*apeya, but only maintain that the Vâ*g*apeya cannot be performed after the Râ*g*asûya. The Râ*g*asûya, according to the Brâhma*n*a, confers on the sacrificer royal dignity (râ*g*ya), and the Vâ*g*apeya paramount sovereignty (sâmrâ*g*ya). It might almost seem as if the relatively loose positions here assigned to the Râ*g*asûya were entirely owing to the fact that it is a purely Kshatriya ceremony to which the

[1] Vedische Mythologie, p. 247.

Brâhma*n*a has no right, whilst the Vâ*g*apeya may be performed by Brâhma*n*as as well as Kshatriyas. But on whatever grounds this appreciation of the two ceremonies may be based, it certainly goes right in the face of the rule laid down by Â*s*valâyana (IX, 9, 19) that, 'after performing the Vâ*g*apeya, a king may perform the Râ*g*asûya, and a Brâhma*n*a the B*ri*haspatisava.' With this rule would seem to accord the relative value assigned to the two ceremonies in the Taittirîya Sa*m*hitâ (V, 6, 2, 1) and Brâhma*n*a (II, 7, 6, 1), according to which the Vâ*g*apeya is a 'samrâ*t*sava,' or consecration to the dignity of a paramount sovereign, while the Râ*g*asûya is called a 'varu*n*asava,' i.e., according to Sâya*n*a, a consecration to the universal sway wielded by Varu*n*a[1]. In much the same sense we have doubtless to understand the rule in which Lâ*t*yâyana defines the object of the Vâ*g*apeya (VIII, 11, 1), viz. 'Whomsoever the Brâhma*n*as and kings (or nobles) may place at their head, let him perform the Vâ*g*apeya.' All these authorities, with the exception of the *S*atapatha-Brâhma*n*a and Kâtyâyana, are thus agreed in making the Vâ*g*apeya a preliminary ceremony, performed by a Brâhma*n*a who is raised to the dignity of a Purohita, or head-priest (so to speak, a minister of worship, and court-priest), or by a king who is elected paramount sovereign by a number of petty râ*g*as; this sacrifice being in due time followed by the respective installation and consecration ceremony, viz. the B*ri*haspatisava, in the case of the Purohita; and the Râ*g*asûya, in that of the king. In regard to the B*ri*haspatisava, which these authorities place on an equality with the Râ*g*asûya, our Brâhma*n*a finds itself in a somewhat awkward position, and it gets out of its difficulty (V, 2, 1, 19) by simply identifying the B*ri*haspatisava with the Vâ*g*apeya, and making the Vâ*g*apeya itself to be 'the consecration of B*ri*haspati;' and Kâtyâyana (XIV, 1, 2) compromises matters by combining the two ceremonies in this way that he who performs the Vâ*g*apeya is to perform the B*ri*haspatisava for a fortnight before and after the Vâ*g*apeya.

[1] Cf. *S*âṅkh. *S*r. XV, 13, 4, 'for it is Varu*n*a whom they consecrate.'

The Râgasûya, or inauguration of a king, is a complex ceremony which, according to the *S*rauta-sûtras, consists of a long succession of sacrificial performances, spread over a period of upwards of two years. It includes seven distinct Soma-sacrifices, viz. 1, the Pavitra, an Agnish*t*oma serving as the opening sacrifice, and followed, after an interval of a year (during which the seasonal sacrifices have to be performed), by 2, the Abhishe*k*anîya, an Ukthya-sacrifice, being the consecration (or anointing) ceremony. Then follows 3, the Da*s*apeya, or 'drink of ten,' an Agnish*t*oma, so-called because ten priests take part in drinking the Soma-liquor contained in each of the ten cups. After another year's interval[1], during which monthly 'offerings to the beams (i.e. the months)' are made, takes place 4, the Ke*s*avapaniya, or hair-cutting ceremony, an Atirâtra-sacrifice; followed, after a month or fortnight, by 5, and 6, the Vyush*t*i-dvirâtra, or two nights' ceremony of the dawning, consisting of an Agnish*t*oma and an Atirâtra; and finally 7, the Kshatra-dh*ri*ti, or 'the wielding of the (royal) power,' an Agnish*t*oma performed a month later. The round of ceremonies concludes with the Sautrâma*n*î, an ish*t*i the object of which is to make amends for any excess committed in the consumption of Soma-liquor.

The fifth book completes the dogmatic discussion of the ordinary circle of sacrifices, some less common, or altogether obsolete, ceremonies, such as the A*s*vamedha (horse-sacrifice), Purushamedha (human sacrifice), Sarvamedha (sacrifice for universal rule), being dealt with, by way of supplement, in the thirteenth book.

With the sixth Kâ*nd*a, we enter on the detailed explanation of the Agni*k*ayana, or building of the fire-altar, a very solemn ceremony which would seem originally to have stood apart from, if not in actual opposition to, the ordinary sacrificial system, but which, in the end, apparently by some ecclesiastical compromise, was added

[1] The Brâhma*n*a (V, 5, 2, 2), however, would rather seem to dispense with this interval by combining the twelve oblations so as to form two sets of six each.

on to the Soma ritual as an important, though not indispensable, element of it. The avowed object of this ceremony is the super-exaltation of Agni, the Fire, who, in the elaborate cosmogenic legend with which this section begins, is identified with Pragâpati, the lord of Generation, and the source of life in the world. As the present volume contains, however, only a portion of the Agni*k*ayana ritual, any further remarks on this subject may be reserved for a future occasion.

Since the time when this volume went to press, the literature of the Soma myth has been enriched by the appearance of an important book, the first volume of Professor A. Hillebrandt's Vedische Mythologie, dealing with Soma and cognate gods. As it is impossible for me here to enter into a detailed discussion of the numerous points raised in the work, I must content myself for the present with the remark that I believe Professor Hillebrandt to have fully established the main point of his position, viz. the identity of Soma with the Moon in early Vedic mythology.

SATAPATHA-BRÂHMA*N*A.

FIFTH KÂ*N*D*A*.

A. THE VÂ*G*APEYA.

FIRST ADHYÂYA. FIRST BRÂHMA*N*A.

1. Once upon a time the gods and the Asuras, both of them sprung from Pra*g*âpati, strove together. And the Asuras, even through arrogance, thinking, 'Unto whom, forsooth, should we make offering?' went on offering into their own mouths. They came to naught, even through arrogance: wherefore let no one be arrogant, for verily arrogance is the cause[1] of ruin.

2. But the gods went on making offerings unto one another. Pra*g*âpati gave himself up to them: thus the sacrifice[2] became theirs; and indeed the sacrifice is the food of the gods[3].

3. They then spake, 'To which of us shall this[4] belong?' They did not agree together, saying,

---

[1] Lit. 'the mouth,' i.e. the opening or beginning, of ruin. The St. Petersburg Dict. compares Prov. xvi. 18: 'Pride goeth before destruction, and an haughty spirit before a fall.'

[2] Pra*g*âpati (the lord of creatures or generation) is both the sacrifice and the year (time); see III, 2, 2, 4.

[3] See II, 4, 2, 1. To them (the gods) he (Pra*g*âpati) said, 'The sacrifice (shall be) your food, immortality your sustenance (ûrg), and the sun your light!'

[4] For the neuter idam—hardly here 'this universe,' or 'vâ-

'To me! to me!' Not being agreed, they said, 'Let us run a race for it: whichever of us shall win, to him it shall belong!'—'So be it!' so they ran a race for it.

4. Then Brihaspati hasted up to Savitri for his impulsion [1],—Savitri being the impeller (prasavitri) among the gods—saying, 'Impel this for me, (so that) impelled by thee, I may win this!' Then Savitri, as the impeller, impelled it for him, and impelled by Savitri, he won: he became everything here, he won everything here; for he won Pragâpati, and Pragâpati (the lord of creatures and procreation) indeed is everything here. By offering therewith he (Brihaspati) ascended to that upper region. Therefore who so knoweth, and who so knoweth not,—they say, 'That upper region belongeth to Brihaspati.'

5. Thus they who of old used to offer the Vâgapeya, ascended to that upper region. From there Aupâvi Gânasruteya descended again: thenceforward (all men) descend again.

---

gapeyam,' but rather 'this thing, it'—the Kânva text reads ayam 'he,' i.e. Pragâpati, or the sacrifice (yagña, masc.); cf. note on V, 1, 4, 15.

[1] For want of a simpler and more homely set of terms for the derivatives of the verb sû 'to animate' here used, those used in the preceding volumes are here generally adhered to, though, as there, somewhat reluctantly. The simple 'to bless, blessing, &c.' might sometimes fit quite well, though no doubt they imply an idea altogether foreign to the etymological meaning of this verb, and could not possibly be used, as is the case here, of the animating influence of the sun. Sometimes 'to speed' has been chosen, where the etymological connection with Savitri is not insisted upon; while in other passages 'to consecrate, consecration, &c.' might probably come nearer to the meaning of the original. Cp. Delbrück, Altindische Syntax, p. 256.

6. Indra offered that (Vâ*g*apeya),—he became everything here, he won everything here; for he won Pra*g*âpati, and Pra*g*âpati is everything here: by offering therewith he ascended to that upper region.

7. Thus they who of old used to offer the Vâ*g*apeya, ascended to that upper region. From there Aupâvi *G*âna*s*ruteya descended again: thenceforward (all men) descend again.

8. And whosoever offers the Vâ*g*apeya, he becomes everything here, he wins everything here; for he wins Pra*g*âpati, and Pra*g*âpati indeed is everything here.

9. Here now they say, 'One must not offer the Vâ*g*apeya; for he who offers the Vâ*g*apeya wins everything here,—for he wins Pra*g*âpati, and Pra*g*âpati is everything here,—he leaves nothing remaining here: his people (or offspring) is like to become worse (off).'

10. Let him none the less sacrifice: whatever (priests) thus know that sacrifice properly, in respect of the *Rik*, the Ya*g*us, and the Sâman, and such as are proficient, let them assist him in offering it; for verily this is the perfection of that sacrifice, when wise (priests) assist him in offering it: let him therefore sacrifice by all means.

11. Now truly this (the Vâ*g*apeya) is the Brâhma*n*a's own sacrifice, inasmuch as B*ri*haspati (the lord of prayer and devotion) performed it; for B*ri*haspati is the Brahman (priesthood, or priestly dignity), and the Brâhma*n*a is the Brahman. And it is also that of the Râ*g*anya, inasmuch as Indra performed it; for Indra is the Kshatra (nobility, or ruling power), and the Râ*g*anya is the Kshatra.

12. To the king (râgan) doubtless belongs the Râgasûya; for by offering the Râgasûya he becomes king; and unsuited for kingship is the Brâhmana. And, moreover, the Râgasûya is the lower, and the Vâgapeya the higher (sacrifice).

13. For by offering the Râgasûya[1] he becomes king, and by the Vâgapeya (he becomes) emperor (samrâg); and the office of king is the lower, and that of emperor the higher: a king might indeed wish to become emperor, for the office of king is the lower, and that of emperor the higher; but the emperor would not wish to become king, for the office of king is the lower, and that of emperor the higher.

14. Thus that (king) who, by performing the Vâgapeya, becomes emperor, possesses himself of everything here. Previously to each performance (of an ishti[2]) he offers that oblation to Savitri (the sun), with the text, 'O divine Savitri, impel (prosper) the sacrifice, impel Pragâpati for his portion!'

[1] Kâty. Sr. XV, 1, 1-2, lays down the rule that the Râgasûya is to be performed by a king who has not yet performed the Vâgapeya. Âsval. Sr. IX, 9, 19, on the other hand, rules: 'After performing it (the Vâgapeya) let a king perform the Râgasûya, a Brâhmana the Brihaspati-sava' (cf. V, 2, 1, 19). See also Kâty. XIV, 1, 2 seq. Cf. Lâty. Sr. VIII, 11, 1 seq.

[2] During the bright fortnights (of the waxing moon) preceding and following the Vâgapeya ceremony proper, the sacrificer has to perform a number of so-called pariyagña ('surrounding or enclosing sacrifices') consisting of one-day Soma-sacrifices of different kinds, each of which is preceded by a special dîkshâ, or initiation ceremony (cf. III, 1, 2, 1 seq.; Lâty. Sr. VIII, 11, 2). It is to the ishtis (dikshanîyeshti, prâyanîyeshti) of these pariyagñas that the above injunction regarding the performance of the Sâvitrî âhuti refers.

15. And even as then B*ri*haspati hasted up to Savit*ri* for his impulsion—Savit*ri* being the impeller among the gods—saying, 'Impel this for me, (so that) impelled by thee I may win it!' and Savit*ri*, as the impeller, impelled it for him; and impelled by Savit*ri* he won it: even so does this (sacrificing king) now haste up to Savit*ri* for his impulsion—Savit*ri* being the impeller among the gods—saying, 'Impel this for me: may I win it, impelled by thee!' and Savit*ri*, as the impeller, impels it for him, and he wins it impelled by Savit*ri*.

16. Wherefore he says (Vâ*g*. S. IX, 1), 'God Savit*ri*, speed the sacrifice, speed the lord of sacrifice unto his portion! May the heavenly, thought-cleansing Gandharva cleanse our thought! May the Lord of Speech render our meat palatable, hail!' For the Lord of Speech is Pra*g*âpati, and meat means food: 'May Pra*g*âpati this day make palatable this our food!' thus he thereby says. This same oblation he offers till the day before the Soma-feast, for thus that performance of his has been commenced; and he (Savit*ri*, the Sun) becomes serene during that sacrifice.

SECOND BRÂHMA*N*A.

1. He draws the A*ms*u[1] (graha), just for completeness' sake, for it is therefore that he draws

[1] Regarding this cup, or libation (consisting, it would seem, of imperfectly pressed Soma-plants in water), see part ii, p. 424, note 1. Here, and in the sequel, the author only refers to those points of ceremonial in which the performance differs from that of the ordinary Agnish*t*oma sacrifice, as described in part ii.

the A*m*su. After that he draws those recognised Agnish*t*oma cups[1] up to the Âgraya*n*a.

2. He then draws the P*r*ish*th*yas[2]: and whatever the gods (Agni, Indra, and Sûrya) won by them, even that he wins by them.

3. He then draws the Sho*d*a*s*in: and whatever Indra won thereby, even that he (the sacrificer) wins thereby.

4. He then draws those five Vâ*g*apeya cups (for Indra; the first) with the text (V. S. IX, 2), 'Thee, the firm-seated, the man-seated, the mind-seated! Thou art taken with a support[3]: I take thee, agreeable to Indra! This is thy womb[3] (i.e. thy home): thee, most agreeable to Indra!' therewith he deposits it; for of these

[1] Viz. the Upâ*m*su and Antaryâma; the Aindravâyava, Maitrâvaru*n*a and Â*s*vina; the *S*ukra and Manthin; and the Âgraya*n*a. Part ii, pp. 256 seq.

[2] That is, the three Atigrâhyas (part ii, p. 402, note 2), required for the P*r*ish*th*a-stotras at the midday feast, when performed in their proper 'p*r*ish*th*a' form, as they are at the P*r*ish*th*ya sha*d*aha, and at a Vi*s*va*g*it-ekâha with all the P*r*ish*th*as. See IV, 5, 4, 14. The authorities of the Black Ya*g*us adopt a somewhat different arrangement. The Vâ*g*apeya cups are likewise called by them Atigrâhyas (Taitt. S. I, 7, 12; T. B. I, 3, 9), and these are apparently drawn by them immediately after the second of the ordinary three Atigrâhyas, the one belonging to Indra (T. S. vol. i, p. 996,—but see ib. p. 1055, where it is stated that they are drawn immediately after the Âgraya*n*a,—that is, probably, if the ordinary Atigrâhyas are not required). Then follows (the third ordinary Atigrâhya?), then the Sho*d*a*s*in, and thereupon the seventeen cups for Pra*g*âpati.—Sâya*n*a remarks on our passage,—teshâm (atigrâhyâ*n*âm) prak*r*itigatâ tritvasa*m*khyaiva *s*âkhântaravat sa*m*khyântarânupade*s*ât. MS. I. O. 657.

[3] For an explanation of these notions, see part ii, p. 260, notes 1 and 2.

worlds this one, to wit the earth, is the firm one: this same world he thereby wins.

5. [The second with,] 'Thee, the water-seated, the ghee-seated, the ether-seated! Thou art taken with a support: I take thee, agreeable to Indra! This is thy womb: thee most agreeable to Indra!' therewith he deposits it; for among these worlds that ether (mentioned in the formula) is this air: he thereby wins this air-world.

6. [The third with,] 'Thee, the earth-seated, the air-seated, the sky-seated, the god-seated, the heaven-seated! Thou art taken with a support: I take thee, agreeable to Indra! This is thy womb: thee, most agreeable to Indra!' therewith he deposits it; for god-seated, heaven-seated indeed is yonder world of the gods: the world of the gods he thereby wins.

7. [The fourth with V. S. IX, 3.] 'The waters' invigorating essence, being contained in the sun,—that which is the essence of the waters' essence, that, the most excellent, I take for you! Thou art taken with a support: I take thee, agreeable to Indra! This is thy womb: thee, most agreeable to Indra!' therewith he deposits it; for the waters' essence is he that blows (or purifies) yonder (the wind), and he is contained in the sun, he blows from the sun: that same essence he thereby wins.

8. [The fifth with IX, 4.] 'Ye cups, of strengthening libations, inspiring the sage with thought,—I have gathered together the pith and sap of you, the handleless! Thou art taken with a support: thee, agreeable to Indra! This is thy womb: thee, most agreeable to

Indra!' therewith he deposits it;—pith means essence: it is the essence he thereby wins.

9. These, then, are five Vâgapeya cups he draws; for he who offers the Vâgapeya wins Pragâpati; and Pragâpati is the year, and there are five seasons in the year,—he thus wins Pragâpati: therefore he draws five Vâgapeya cups.

10. He (the Adhvaryu) then draws seventeen (other) cups of Soma, and (the Neshtri) seventeen cups of Surâ (spirituous liquor), for to Pragâpati belong these two (saps of) plants, to wit the Soma and the Surâ;—and of these two the Soma is truth, prosperity, light; and the Surâ untruth, misery, darkness: both these (saps of) plants he thereby wins; for he who offers the Vâgapeya wins everything here, since he wins Pragâpati, and Pragâpati indeed is everything here.

11. Now as to why he draws seventeen cups of Soma;—Pragâpati is seventeenfold, Pragâpati is the sacrifice[1]: as great as the sacrifice is, as great as is

[1] See I, 5, 2, 17, where the principal formulas used in making oblations are computed as consisting together of seventeen syllables. Pańk. Br. 18, 6 insists especially on the symbolic identity of Pragâpati and the Vâgapeya on the double ground that the Vâgapeya consists of seventeen stotras, and has for its characteristic mode of chanting the Saptadasa-stoma, or seventeen-versed hymn. That this is indeed so will appear from a glance at the chief chants. The Bahishpavamâna-stotra, which in the ordinary Agnishtoma is chanted in the trivrit-stoma, consisting of three triplets, or nine verses (see part ii, p. 310), is at the Vâgapeya made to consist of seventeen verses, by the insertion of eight verses (S.V. II, 180–82; 186–90) between the second and third triplets. Again, the Mâdhyandina-pavamâna, ordinarily chanted in fifteen verses (part ii, p. 333), here consists of seventeen, viz. II, 105–7 (sung twice in two tunes = six verses); II, 663 (one verse); II, 663–4 (sung as triplet, in two tunes = six verses); II, 665 (one verse); II, 821–23

its measure, with that much he thus wins its truth, its prosperity, its light.

12. And why he draws seventeen cups of Surâ;—Pragâpati is seventeenfold, Pragâpati is the sacrifice: as great as the sacrifice is, as great as is its measure, with that much he thus wins its untruth, its misery, its darkness.

13. These two amount to thirty-four cups; for there are thirty-three gods, and Pragâpati is the thirty-fourth: he thus wins Pragâpati.

14. Now when he buys the king (Soma), he at the same time buys for a piece of lead the Parisrut (immature spirituous liquor) from a long-haired man near by towards the south. For a long-haired man is neither man nor woman; for, being a male, he is not a woman; and being long-haired (a eunuch), he is not a man. And that lead is neither iron nor gold; and the Parisrut-liquor is neither Soma nor Surâ[1]: this is why he buys the Parisrut for a piece of lead from a long-haired man.

15. And on the preceding day they prepare two

(three verses)—making together seventeen verses. Similarly, the Ârbhava-pavamâna (chanted at the Agnishtoma also in the Saptadasa-stoma, cf. part ii, p. 315; but here with modifications) consists of II, 165-7 (sung twice in two tunes=six verses); II, 42, 44 (two verses); II, 47-9 (in two tunes=six verses); II, 720-23 (three verses)—making together seventeen verses. For the similarly constructed Vâgapeya hymn see page 11, note 1. See also Lâty. Sr. VIII, 11, 15 seq., where the number of officiating priests, as well as that of the various sacrificial fees, is fixed at seventeen. Similarly, Âsv. Sr. IX, 9, 2-3 says that there are either to be seventeen dikshâs, or the whole ceremony is to be performed in seventeen days.

[1] According to Sâyana, the difference between surâ and parisrut would seem to be that the former beverage is prepared from mature shoots (of rice, &c.), and the latter from such as are not quite ripe.

earth-mounds [1], the one in front of the axle, and the other behind the axle: 'Lest we should deposit together the cups of Soma, and the cups of Surâ,'—this is why, on the preceding day, they prepare two mounds, one in front, and the other behind the axle.

16. Now, when they take the Vasatîvarî water [2] (into the havirdhâna shed) by the front door, the Nesh*tri* takes in the Parisrut-liquor by the back door. From the south they bring in the drinking vessels. The Adhvaryu, seated in front of the axle, with his face towards the west, draws the cups of Soma; and the Nesh*tri*, seated behind the axle, with his face towards the east, draws the cups of Surâ. The Adhvaryu draws a cup of Soma, the Nesh*tri* a cup of Surâ; the Adhvaryu draws a cup of Soma, the Nesh*tri* a cup of Surâ: in this way they draw them alternately.

17. Neither does the Adhvaryu hold the Soma-cup beyond the axle towards the back, nor the Nesh*tri* the Surâ-cup beyond the axle towards the front, thinking, 'Lest we should confound light and darkness!'

18. The Adhvaryu holds the Soma-cup just over the axle, and the Nesh*tri* the Surâ-cup just below

[1] The mounds (khara) thrown up in the havirdhâna cart-shed, are used for placing the cups of Soma (and Surâ) after they are drawn, until they are used for the libations. See the plan of the sacrificial ground at the end of part ii; only that on the present occasion there is to be a second mound, for the placing of the Surâ-cups, under or just behind the axle of the southern Soma-cart (in the place where the Nârâ*s*a*m*sa cups to the Fathers were temporarily deposited at the Agnish*t*oma; see III, 6, 2, 25 with note). On this occasion a small door is also made in the southern wall of the cart-shed, by breaking through the hurdle.

[2] Part ii, p. 222 seq.

the axle, with (V. S. IX, 4), 'United ye are: unite me with happiness!' Thinking, 'Lest we should say "evil",' they withdraw them again, with, 'Disunited ye are: disunite me from evil!' Even as one might tear a single reed from a clump of reed-grass, so do they thereby tear him from out of all evil: there is not in him so much sin as the point of a grass-blade. They deposit the two (cups each time on the mounds).

19. Thereupon the Adhvaryu draws the Madhugraha (honey-cup) in a golden vessel, and deposits it in the middle of the Soma-grahas. He then draws the Ukthya, then the Dhruva. And when, at the last chant (of the evening press feast[1]), he has poured those Soma-grahas one by one into the cups of the officiating priests, they make offering and drink them. At the midday-pressing it is told regarding the honey-cup, and the cups of Surâ: thereof then[2].

THIRD BRÂHMANA.

1. At the Agnish*t*oma (Sâman[3]) he seizes a (victim) for Agni, for the Agnish*t*oma (i. e. 'Agni's

[1] The last chant (at the evening feast) of the Vâgapeya sacrifice is the so-called Vâgapeya-sâman, or B*r*ihat-stotra (Sâmav. II, 975-7), chanted, to the B*r*ihat tune, in the Saptadasa-stoma; the three verses being, by repetitions, raised to the number of seventeen.—'When he has poured . . . they offer it:' this is apparently a case of the absolute construction of the gerund in '-ya,' cf. Delbrück, Altindische Syntax, p. 108.

[2] On these cups, or libations, see V, 1, 5, 28.

[3] Of the seven fundamental forms (sa*m*sthâ) of Soma-sacrifice, each higher, or more complex, form is obtained by some additional ceremony, or ceremonies, being added on to one of the simpler forms of sacrifice. In the present paragraph, the author briefly reviews the lower forms of Soma-sacrifice, contained in the Vâga-

praise[1]) is Agni: he thereby wins Agni. For the Ukthas[2] he seizes one for Indra and Agni; for the hymns (uktha) relate to Indra and Agni[3]: the hymns he thereby wins. For the Shodasin he seizes one for Indra; for the Shodasin is Indra: the Shodasin (Indra) he thereby wins.

2. For the seventeenth (or seventeenfold) stotra[4] he seizes one for Sarasvatî: thereby, while there is no over-night performance[5], it is yet made like the night (performance); for he who offers the Vâga-

peya, with the view of enumerating the victims to be slaughtered at its performance; viz. the Agnishtoma with twelve chants and one victim; the Ukthya with fifteen stotras and two victims; and the Shodasin with sixteen chants and three victims. For further particulars, see part ii, p. 397, note 2.

[1] The Agnishtoma-sâman, the last (twelfth) and distinctive stotra of the Agnishtoma sacrifice, is in praise of Agni (see part ii, p. 368, note 2). At the Vâgapeya the ordinary (yagñâyagñîya) hymn is not chanted, but S.V. II, 973-4, sung to the Vâravantîya tune (Calc. ed., vol. v, p. 144), takes its place. Pañk. Br. 18, 6, 16.

[2] The three Uktha stotras (chants) and sastras (recitations) constitute the distinctive element of the Ukthya sacrifice; as the Shodasi-stotra and sastra (part ii, p. 401, note 3; p. 402, note 1) constitute that of the Shodasin sacrifice.

[3] On the important place assigned to these two deities in the traditional arrangement of the Rigveda-samhitâ, see the introduction to part i, p. xvi.

[4] That is the Vâgapeya-sâman, see note 1, p. 11.

[5] The author here alludes to another form of Soma-sacrifice, not contained in the Vâgapeya, viz. the Atirâtra, which is obtained by following up the Shodasin (with its sixteen chants) with the so-called râtri-paryâyâh, or night-rounds, consisting of three rounds of four chants each, or together twelve chants. These are succeeded, at day-break, by the Sandhi-stotra (or twilight chants), consisting of three chants. Although this night performance does not take place on the present occasion—the Vâgapeya-sâman taking its place—the author claims for this form of sacrifice also the moral benefits which would accrue to the sacrificer from the Atirâtra, for the reason that the same victim (a he-goat for Sarasvatî) is offered on both occasions.

peya wins Pragâpati, and Pragâpati is the year: by that (victim) for Sarasvati he now wins the night: hence, while there is no night performance, it is made like the night.

3. Thereupon he seizes a spotted sterile cow for the Victorious Maruts; for the spotted sterile cow is this (earth): whatever food, rooted and rootless, is here established on her, thereby she is a spotted cow. Now, he who offers the Vâgapeya wins food, for vâga-peya[1] doubtless means the same as anna-peya (food and drink); and the Maruts are the peasants, and the peasants are food (for the noble). 'To the Victorious (Maruts)!' he says, even for the sake of victory. It is difficult to obtain an invitatory and offering prayer containing the word 'victorious:' if he should be unable to obtain such as contain the word 'victorious,' any other two verses to the Maruts will do. Difficult to obtain also is a spotted sterile cow: if he cannot obtain a spotted sterile cow, any other sterile cow will do.

4. The course of procedure thereof (is as follows). When the Hot*ri* recites after the Mâhendra libation, then let them proceed with (the offering of) her omentum, for that, the Mâhendra[2], is Indra's special (nishkevalya) libation; and his also are the Nishkevalya-stotra and Nishkevalya-*s*astra. Now the sacrificer is Indra: thus he thereby puts strength into the sacrificer in the very middle (of the sacri-

[1] In Taitt. Br. I, 3, 2, 3, on the other hand, vâgapeya (which doubtless means 'drink of strength') is explained first by vâgâpya, 'that through which the gods wished to obtain (aipsan) strength (vâgam),' and then by 'drink of strength,' i.e. Soma 'by drinking (pitvâ) which one becomes strong (vâgin).'

[2] For this libation, and the accompanying Nishkevalya-*s*astra, at the midday Soma-feast, see part ii, pp. 338, 339, note 2.

fice): that is why they should proceed with her omentum at that particular time.

5. They cook the portions[1] in two lots. Of the one lot thereof, after making an 'under-layer' of ghee (clarified butter) in the *g*uhû spoon, he makes two cuttings from each (portion), bastes them once, and replenishes with ghee (the empty places of) the cuttings. Thereupon he makes one cutting from each into the upabh*ri*t spoon, bastes them twice, but does not replenish (the places of) the cuttings. Now, when of the one lot (of portions) he makes two cuttings from each, thereby that (sterile cow) becomes whole; and when he proceeds with those (portions), thereby he wins the divine race. He then presents the (other) half to the human kind: and thereby he wins the human kind (people, vi*s*).

6. But let him not do it in this wise; for verily he who departs from the path of the sacrifice, stumbles; and he who does it in this wise certainly departs from the path of the sacrifice. Hence when they proceed with the omenta of the other victims, only then let them proceed with the omentum of that (cow). They cook the portions in one lot, and do not present any to the human kind.

7. He then seizes seventeen victims for Pra*g*âpati. They are all hornless, all dark-grey[2], all (uncastrated) males; for he who offers the Vâ*g*apeya, wins Pra*g*âpati; but Pra*g*âpati is food, and the victim (cattle) is food: he thus wins Pra*g*âpati. And Pra*g*âpati is Soma, and the victim is the visible

[1] For particulars regarding the meat portions, see part ii, p. 204 seq.

[2] Or, black and white (*s*ukla-k*r*ish*n*a-var*n*a), as '*s*yâma' is explained by Sâya*n*a.

Soma: he thus wins the visible Pragâpati. There are seventeen (victims), because Pragâpati is seventeenfold: he thus wins Pragâpati.

8. Now, they are all hornless;—for man is nearest to Pragâpati, and he is hornless, unhorned; and Pragâpati also is hornless, unhorned; and these (victims) belong to Pragâpati: therefore they are all hornless.

9. They are all dark-grey. Now, the dark-grey has two forms, the light hair and the black; and a couple means a productive pair, and Pragâpati (the lord of generation) represents productiveness, and those (victims) belong to Pragâpati: therefore they are all dark-grey.

10. They are all males;—for the male means productiveness, and Pragâpati represents productiveness: hence they are all males. Difficult to obtain are victims with these perfections: if he cannot obtain them (all) with these perfections, even some with these perfections will do; for verily Pragâpati is everything here.

11. Now, some seize the last (victim) for Vâ*k* (Speech), thinking, 'If there be anything beyond Pragâpati, that is Speech: we thus win Speech.' But let him not do it in this wise; for Pragâpati is everything here,—these worlds and everything there is;—whatever speech speaks in these worlds, that speech he wins: therefore he need not heed this.

12. The course of procedure regarding these (victims is as follows). When the Maitrâvaru*n*a recites after the Vâmadevya [1], let them then proceed

[1] The Vâmadevya-sâman (Sâmav. II, 32–34) is the second P*ri*sh*th*a-stotra, after the chanting of which, at the midday feast.

with their omenta; for the Vâmadevya means productiveness, and Pragâpati means productiveness, and these (victims) belong to Pragâpati: therefore let them proceed with their omenta at that time.

13. And (when) the after-offerings have been performed, and the spoons have not yet been shifted (separated)[1], then they proceed with the (chief) oblations of those (victims). That (point in the performance) is the end, and Pragâpati is the end: thus he wins Pragâpati at the very end. But were he to proceed therewith sooner, it would be just as if a man had already gone the way he still intends to go,—and where would he be after that[2]?—there-

the first assistant of the Hotri, the Maitrâvaruna, has to recite his (the second) Nishkevalya-sastra; see part ii, p. 325, note 2; p. 339, note 2.—As regards the Hotri's Prishtha-stotra, the Rathantara-sâman (S. V. II, 30, 31) is used for it; while the Abhîvarta tune (S. V. ed. Bibl. Ind. III, p. 93) is employed in the chanting of the Brahma-sâman (S. V. II, 35, 36; see part ii, p. 434, note 1) instead of the ordinary Naudhasa tune. Pañk. Br. 18, 6, 11-14.

[1] On this ceremony with which the concluding rites of the ishti commence, see I, 8, 3, 1 seq.

[2] Or possibly, what would then become of him? The author's reasoning seems to be that, if the sacrificer were to offer any of the chief oblations at an earlier point in the performance, he would thereby anticipate the results he wants to obtain from the whole performance,—or, so to speak, he would then already reach the goal for the attainment of which the subsequent oblations are likewise intended. For the same reason the offering of the omentum of the sterile cow, previously to and independently of the omenta of the other victims, was discountenanced in paragraph 6. Our present passage is interpreted rather differently by Professor Delbrück in his Altindische Syntax, p. 550:—Wenn er vorher damit vorginge, so wäre das so, als ob er, nach Betretung des Pfades, den er zu betreten beabsichtigt, wo? wäre (d. h. in's Unglück geriethe): 'Were he to proceed therewith sooner, it would be just as if, after entering on the path he intends to enter upon, he would be where? (i.e. would get into trouble).'

fore they proceed with their (chief) oblations at that time.

14. But let him not do it in this wise; for he who departs from the path of the sacrifice stumbles; and he who does it in this wise certainly departs from the path of the sacrifice. Hence whenever they proceed with the omenta of the other victims, let them at the same time proceed with the omenta of these; and whenever they proceed with the (chief) oblations of the other victims, let them at the same time proceed with the oblations of these. There is but one invitatory prayer, and one offering prayer; for (these offerings) belong to one deity. He says (to the Maitrâvaruna), 'To Pragâpati'—saying this (name) in a low voice—'recite the invitatory prayer for the offering of the bucks!'—'To Pragâpati'—saying this in a low voice—'urge the ready-standing offering of the bucks!' and as the Vashat is uttered, he makes the offering.

FOURTH BRÂHMANA.

1. At the midday Soma-feast he consecrates (the Sacrificer) by sprinkling; and at the midday Soma-feast they run a race; for, verily, Pragâpati is that sacrifice[1] which is here performed, and from which these creatures have been produced,—and indeed, they are even now produced after this one: thus he thereby wins Pragâpati in the very centre (of the sacrifice).

2. The Mâhendra cup being not yet drawn,—for

[1] In the original, 'pragâpatih' is the predicate, not the subject, of the sentence; but considerations of construction seem to render the change desirable in English.

that, the Mâhendra, is Indra's special (nishkevalya) cup, and so also are his that Nishkevalya-stotra and Nishkevalya-*s*astra; and the Sacrificer is Indra: thus he consecrates him at his own dwelling-place. Hence, the Mâhendra cup being not yet drawn,—

3. He takes down the chariot[1], with (Vâ*g*. S. IX, 5), 'Thou art Indra's thunderbolt;' for the chariot is indeed a thunderbolt, and the sacrificer is Indra: therefore he says, 'Thou art Indra's thunderbolt;'—'a winner of wealth,' for the chariot is indeed a winner of wealth;—'May this one win wealth by thee!'—wealth means food: 'may this one gain food by thee,' is what he thereby says.

4. That chariot, seized by the pole, he turns (from left to right) so as to make it stand inside the vedi[2], with, 'In the winning of wealth, the great Mother'—wealth means food: 'in the winning of food, the great Mother'—is what he thereby says;—'Aditi by name, we praise with speech;' now Aditi is this earth: therefore he says, 'Aditi by name, we praise with speech,'—'whereon all this being hath settled;' for indeed thereon all being here is settled;—'thereon may the divine Savit*ri* prosper our stay!' whereby he means to say, 'thereon may the divine Savit*ri* prosper our Sacrificer!'

5. He then sprinkles the horses with water, either when being led down to be watered, or when brought

[1] The Adhvaryu takes it down from the vâhana, or car-stand.

[2] It is to be placed in the north-eastern part of the vedi, so as to be ready to start on the race northwards along the space between the *k*âtvâla (or pit) and the utkara (heap of rubbish); the horses thus being close to where the Brahman will have to mount a cart-wheel put up on the utkara (V, 1, 5, 2).

up after being watered. Now in the beginning the horse was produced from the water; while being produced from the water, it was produced incomplete, for it was indeed produced incomplete: hence it does not stand on all its feet, but it stands lifting one foot on each side. Thus what then was left behind of it in the water, therewith he now completes it, and makes it whole: therefore he sprinkles the horses with water, either when being led down to be watered, or when brought up after being watered.

6. He sprinkles them, with (Vâ*g*. S. IX, 6), 'Within the waters is ambrosia, in the waters is medicine: at the praises of the waters may ye wax strong, ye horses!' And with this also, 'O divine waters, what rushing, high-peaked, wealth-winning wave ye have, therewith may this one win wealth!' wealth is food: he thus says, 'May he thereby gain food!'

7. He then yokes (the team of) the chariot. The right horse he yokes (puts to) first; for in human (practice) they indeed put to the left horse first, but with the gods in this way.

8. He yokes it, with (Vâ*g*. S. IX, 7), 'Either the wind, or thought—' for there is nothing swifter than the wind, and nothing swifter than thought: therefore he says, 'Either the wind, or thought;'—'(or) the seven and twenty Gandharvas[1],

---

[1] Professor Weber (in his essay on the Nakshatras, II, 278; Abhandl. of Berlin Academy, 1861) takes this passage (=Taitt. S. I, 7, 7, 2; Kâ*th*aka 13, 14; Maitr. S. I, 11, 1) to contain the first allusion to the system of Nakshatras, or lunar mansions marking the daily stations occupied by the moon (masc.) during his circuit round the heavens.—In the ritual of the Black Yagus (Taitt. S.

they yoked the horse at first;' for the Gandharvas indeed yoked the horse at first: 'May they who yoked the horse at first yoke thee!' this he thereby says;—'they laid speed into him,'—he thereby says, 'May they who laid speed into it, lay speed into thee!'

9. He then yokes the left horse, with (Vâ*g*. S. IX, 8), 'Become thou swift as the wind, O courser, being yoked!'—thereby he says, 'Become quick as the wind, O courser, being yoked;'—'be thou as Indra's right (steed) in beauty!'—he thereby says, 'Even as Indra's right (steed) for beauty, so be thou that of the sacrificer for beauty!'—'May the all-knowing Maruts yoke thee!' he thereby says, 'may gods yoke thee!'—'May Tvash*tri* lay speed into thy feet!' in this there is nothing obscure. He then yokes the right side-horse; for in human (practice) they indeed yoke the left side-horse first, but with the gods in this way.

10. He yokes it, with (Vâ*g*. S. IX, 9), 'What speed hath been secretly laid into thee, O courser, and what (speed), bestowed on the eagle, went along in the wind;'—he thereby says, 'what speed of thine, O courser, is hidden away even elsewhere, therewith win this our sacrifice, Pra*g*âpati!'—'with that strength be thou strong and wealth-winning for us, O courser, and victorious at the gathering!'—wealth means food: he thus means to say, 'And be thou a food-winner for us at this our

I, 7, 7, 2) this formula runs thus: 'Either Vâyu, or Manu, or the Gandharvas, the twenty-seven, harnessed the horse at first, laid speed into him,'—which Sâya*n*a, however, interprets as meaning, 'Vâyu, and Manu, and the (twenty-five) Gandharvas,—these seven and twenty &c.'

sacrifice, at the gathering of the gods win thou this sacrifice, Pragâpati!'

11. Now only those three (horses) are yoked, for what is threefold belongs to the gods, and this (sacrifice is) with the gods. Alongside the yoke (laid) on the side-horse[1] goes a fourth (horse), for that one is human. When he is about to give that (chariot to the Adhvaryu), he gives it after yoking the fourth (horse) thereto. Hence also at any other sacrifice only those three (horses) are yoked; for what is threefold belongs to the gods, and this (sacrifice is) with the gods. Alongside the yoke of the side-horse goes a fourth (horse), for that one is human. When he is about to give that (chariot) away, he gives it after yoking the fourth (horse) thereto.

12. He now takes out material for a wild-rice pap of seventeen plates for B*ri*haspati; for he who offers the Vâgapeya wins food,—vâga-peya being doubtless the same as anna-peya (food and drink): thus whatever food he has thereby won, that he now prepares for him.

13. And as to why it belongs to B*ri*haspati:—B*ri*haspati won it in the beginning, therefore it belongs to B*ri*haspati.

14. And why it is prepared of wild rice:—B*ri*haspati is the Brahman (priesthood), and those wild-rice grains are cooked with the Brahman (prayer),—therefore it is of wild rice. It is one of seventeen plates,

[1] Or, of the leader, as would appear from Sâya*n*a to Taitt. S. I, 7, 8 (p. 1024),—'Between the right-hand and the left-hand horse he allows the shafts to project, and between them he puts the horse called "sapti" (in the text).' No fourth horse is, however, apparently mentioned in the ritual of the Black Yagus.

because Pragâpati is seventeenfold: he thus wins Pragâpati.

15. He makes the horses smell it, with 'Ye coursers—;' for horses are coursers (vâgin): therefore he says, 'Ye coursers,'—'wealth-winners,'—wealth is food: 'food-winners' he thereby says;—'starting upon the course;' for they are about to run a race;—'smell ye B*ri*haspati's portion!' for this indeed is B*ri*haspati's portion: therefore he says, 'smell ye B*ri*haspati's portion!' And why he makes the horses smell it: he thinks, 'may I win Him[1]!' therefore he makes the horses smell it.

Fifth Brâhma*n*a.

1. Now when they run a race, he thereby wins this same (terrestrial) world. And when the Brahman sings a Sâman on the cart-wheel set up on (a post) reaching to his navel, he thereby wins the air-world. And when he erects the sacrificial post, he thereby wins the world of the gods. Hence that threefold performance.

2. The Brahman mounts a cart-wheel, set up on (a post) as high as his navel[2], with (Vâg. S. IX, 10),

[1] That is, B*ri*haspati; unless 'lokam' has to be supplied to 'imam' ('this world'), as might appear probable from the next paragraph. See also V, 1, 5, 27–28.

[2] According to the Taittirîya ritualists, as quoted by Sâya*n*a (Taitt. S. I, 7, 8), the wheel after being mounted by the Brahman is to be turned round thrice in a sunwise motion;—the (pointed) end of the post being apparently inserted in the navel of the wheel, lying horizontally upon it. The turning wheel is there compared with the Vagra, or disk-shaped thunderbolt. While the wheel is turning round its axle, the Brahman sings the Sâman. Cf. also Lâ*t*y. *S*r. V, 12, 9 seq., according to which authority, however, the Brahman

'At the impulse (sava) of the god Savitri, of true impulsion, may I ascend unto the highest heaven of Brihaspati!' thus, if a Brâhmana sacrifices; for Brihaspati is the Brahman (priesthood, or sanctity), and the Brâhmana is the Brahman.

3. And if a Râganya sacrifices, (he does so) with, 'At the impulse of the divine Savitri, of true impulsion, may I ascend unto the highest heaven of Indra!' for Indra is the Kshatra (nobility, or power), and the Râganya is the Kshatra.

4. Thrice he sings the Sâman[1]. Having thrice sung it, he descends with, 'At the impulse of the divine Savitri, of true impulsion, I have ascended unto the highest heaven of Brihaspati!'—thus, if a Brâhmana sacrifices, for Brihaspati is the Brahman, and the Brâhmana is the Brahman.

5. And if a Râganya sacrifices,—with, 'At the impulse of the divine Savitri, of true impulsion, I have ascended unto the highest heaven of Indra!' for Indra is the Kshatra, and the Râganya is the Kshatra.

6. They put up seventeen drums along the edge of the altar, from the Âgnidhra backwards (towards

would seem only to put his arms on the wheel, and turn it round, while singing.

[1] Viz. the 'vâginâm sâman' (Tândy. Br. 18, 7, 12), Sâmav. I, 435, 'âvir maryâ â vâgam vâgino agman,' &c. 'The fiery steeds have gathered fiery mettle, the impulse of the god Savitri; win ye the heaven, O coursers!' Lâty. Sr. V, 12, 14. This singing of the Sâman takes place while the race lasts, the Brahman remaining all the time on the cart-wheel put up on a short post on (or near) the utkara, or heap of rubbish.—The author then anticipates in this and the next two paragraphs what the Brahman is to do when he descends from the wheel after the race is over. The placing of the drums next referred to must also be imagined as taking place whilst the Brahman is mounting the wheel.

the west); for he who offers the Vâgapeya wins Pragâpati; but Pragâpati is speech, and that doubtless is the supreme speech which is (the outcome) of seventeen drums: he thus wins the supreme speech, the supreme Pragâpati. Seventeen there are, because Pragâpati is seventeenfold: he thus wins Pragâpati.

7. One of these drums he (the Brahman) beats (while praying) with a sacrificial formula: thereby all of them become beaten with a sacrificial formula.

8. He beats it with (Vâg. S. IX, 11), 'O Brihaspati, win the race! lift ye up your voice unto Brihaspati: make ye Brihaspati win the race!' thus, if a Brâhmana sacrifices; for Brihaspati is the Brahman, and the Brâhmana is the Brahman.

9. And if a Râganya sacrifices, (he does so) with, 'O Indra, win the race! lift ye up your voice unto Indra: make ye Indra win the race!' for Indra is the Kshatra, and the Râganya is the Kshatra.

10. And when those race-running chariots[1] have come up again, he takes down one of those drums with a sacrificial formula; whereby they all become taken down with a formula.

11. He takes it down, with (Vâg. S. IX, 12), 'This hath been your true concord whereby ye (drums) have caused Brihaspati to win the race;—Brihaspati ye have caused to win the race: be released, ye wood-lords!' thus, if a Brâhmana

[1] Besides the Sacrificer's chariot inside the vedi, sixteen others, each drawn by four horses, have been got ready, outside the vedi, for the race to the udumbara branch, as its goal and turning-point. In paragraphs 10–12 the author again anticipates what is to be done with the drums after the race has taken place, just in order to deal with that item of the ceremonial as a whole.

sacrifices; for Brihaspati is the Brahman, and the Brâhmana is the Brahman.

12. And if a Râganya sacrifices, with, 'This hath been your true concord whereby ye have caused Indra to win the race;—Indra ye have caused to win the race: be released, ye wood-lords!' for Indra is the Kshatra, and the Râganya is the Kshatra.

13. A Râganya then[1] shoots seventeen arrow's ranges northwards from the edge of the altar; for as much as is one arrow's range, so much is Pragâpati crosswise; and as much as are seventeen arrow's ranges, so much is Pragâpati lengthwise.

14. And as to why a Râganya shoots,—he, the Râganya is most manifestly of Pragâpati (the lord of creatures): hence, while being one, he rules over many; and because 'pragâpati' has four syllables, and 'râganya[2]' also has four syllables, therefore a Râganya shoots. He shoots seventeen arrow's ranges, because Pragâpati is seventeenfold: he thereby wins Pragâpati.

15. And whichever (horse) he yokes with a formula, up to that the Sacrificer now steps[3], with (Vâg. S. IX, 13), 'At the impulse of the divine Savitri,

---

[1] That is, after (or at the same time when) the drums are put up. He is to shoot northwards through the space between the utkara and kâtvâla. At the end of the seventeenth arrow's range he plants an udumbara branch in the ground to serve as the goal round which the chariots are to turn sunwise on their way back to the sacrificial ground.

[2] Pronounce 'râ-ga-ní-a.'

[3] In the Taittirîya ritual (Taitt. S. I, 7, 7, 2; Taitt. Br. I, 3, 5, 4) the Sacrificer steps up to the chariot with the three Vishnu-strides, with appropriate formulas.

of true impulsion, may I win the race of the race-winning B*ri*haspati!'

16. And even as then B*ri*haspati hasted up to Savit*ri* for his impulsion,—Savit*ri* being the impeller among the gods—saying, 'Impel this for me: impelled by thee, may I win this!' and Savit*ri*, as the impeller, impelled it for him, and impelled by Savit*ri*, he won; in like manner does he thereby haste up to Savit*ri* for his impulsion,—Savit*ri* being the impeller among the gods,—saying, 'Impel this for me: impelled by thee, may I win!' and Savit*ri*, as the impeller, impels it for him, and impelled by Savit*ri* he wins.

17. And if a pupil of the Adhvaryu's or some (other) theological student were to know that prayer, stepping up he makes (the Sacrificer) say, 'O coursers!'—for horses are indeed coursers: therefore he says, 'O coursers'—'wealth-winners!' for wealth is food: 'food-winners' he thereby says;—'keeping the roads,' for they indeed run keeping (within) the roads;—'measuring the stages;' for measuring the stages they run over the course;—'go ye to the winning-post!' In order that the evil-doers, the Rakshas, may not hurt them midways, he thus says this.—They run the race, they beat the drums, and he (the Brahman) sings the Sâman.

18. He (the Adhvaryu) then[1] either offers or addresses (the horses) with those two *g*agati-verses: whether he offers, or whether he addresses (the

[1] That is, he does so whilst the cars are running; the offering or prayers being intended to make the Sacrificer's car win the race.

horses), the significance (of the performance) is the same.

19. He offers, with (Vâg. S. IX, 14; *Ri*k S. IV, 40, 4), 'That courser speedeth after the whip, fettered at the neck and shoulder and mouth: may Dadhikrâ win according to his power; may he run along the windings of the roads, hail!'

20. [Vâg. S. IX, 15; *Ri*k S. IV, 40, 3], 'And of him, the running, speeding, there fanneth like the wing of the eager bird,—as of the gliding eagle,—about the breast of Dadhikrâvan passing along with might, hail!'

21. He then either offers or addresses (the horses) with the following tristich: this is twofold, because he either offers or addresses. Whether he offers, or addresses (the horses), the significance is the same: he thereby speeds those running horses, imbues them with energy. There are here three earths, namely this one, and two beyond it: these he thereby wins.

22. He addresses (the horses, with Vâg. S. IX, 16; *Ri*k S. VII, 38, 7), 'Auspicious be the coursers unto us at the invocations in the divine service, running their measured course, with beautiful song; swallowing the dragon, the wolf, the evil spirits: may they ever keep away from us affliction!'

23. [Vâg. S. IX, 17; *Ri*k S. X, 64, 6], 'Those racers, wont to hear the calls, may they all hear our call, the coursers running their measured course: they, the winners of thousands, eager to win at the winning of oblations, who have carried off great gain in the contests.'

24. [Vâg. S. IX, 18; *Ri*k S. VII, 38, 8], 'In

every race, help us, ye racers, at the prizes, ye wise, immortal knowers of the divine law: drink of this mead, be gladdened, and satisfied walk ye on the paths trodden by the gods!'

25. He then[1] steps over against (the horses) with the Bârhaspatya pap, and touches it; for he who offers the Vâ*g*apeya wins food, since 'vâ*g*a-peya' is the same as 'anna-peya:' whatever food he has thus gained that he now, having reached that goal, brings in contact with himself, puts within himself.

26. He touches it, with (Vâ*g*. S. IX, 19), 'May gain of wealth come to me!' wealth means food: he thus says, 'May gain of food come (accrue) to me;'—'May these two, Heaven and Earth, the all-shaped, come to me!' for Pra*g*âpati is Heaven and Earth;—'May father and mother come to me!' for Pra*g*âpati is both father and mother;—'May Soma come to me with immortality!' for Pra*g*â-pati is Soma.

27. He makes the horses smell it, with, 'Ye coursers!' for horses are coursers: therefore he says, 'Ye coursers!'—'wealth-winners!' wealth is food: 'food-winners' he thereby says;—'having run the course—' for 'starting (upon the course)' he said before, as then they were indeed starting; but now he says, 'having run,' for they indeed have run (the race): therefore he says, 'having run;'—'smell ye B*ri*haspati's portion—' for this is B*ri*-haspati's portion: therefore he says, 'Smell ye B*ri*haspati's portion;'—'taking (it) in!' whereby he imbues the Sacrificer with energy. And as to why

[1] That is, after the cars have come back, that of the Sacrificer keeping ahead of the others.

he makes the horses smell,—he made them smell before, thinking, 'May I win this (world);' and now (he does so) thinking, 'I have won this (world):' that is why he makes the horses smell.

28. Now on one of those race-running (rival) chariots there has been standing either a Vaisya, or a Râganya; he now sits down on the northern hip of the altar. Thereupon the Adhvaryu and Sacrificer, taking the honey-cup, step out by the front door (of the cart-shed), and place it in the Vaisya's, or Râganya's, hand. And the Neshtri, taking the cups of Surâ, steps out by the back door. He walks round by the back of the hall, and placing one (of the cups) in the Vaisya's, or Râganya's, hand, he says, 'With this I buy Him of thee!' For the Soma is truth, prosperity, light; and the Surâ is untruth, misery, darkness: he thus imbues the Sacrificer with truth, prosperity, and light; and smites the Vaisya with untruth, misery, and darkness;—whatever benefit (or enjoyment) he desires, he obtains for himself by those (cups of Surâ). But that cup of honey he presents to the Brahman, together with the golden vessel. In presenting it to the Brahman, he imbues himself with immortal life; for gold is immortal life;—and whatsoever benefit he desires that he thereby obtains for himself.

SECOND ADHYÂYA. FIRST BRÂHMANA.

1. Thereupon, taking the dipping-spoon (sruva) and the pot for melting butter, he goes to the Âhavanîya fire. He either offers those twelve âptis[1], or makes (the Sacrificer) pronounce (the

[1] The term âpti, literally 'obtainment, gain,' is technically used

formulas). Whether he offers, or makes him pronounce (the formulas), the significance is the same.

2. He offers, with (Vâg. S. IX, 20), 'To the ally, hail!—To the good ally, hail!—To the after-born, hail!—To the purpose, hail!—To the Vasu, hail!—To the Lord of day, hail!—To the failing day, hail!—To the failing one, sprung from the evanescent, hail!—To the evanescent one, sprung from the terminal, hail!—To the terminal descendant of being, hail!—To the Lord of being, hail!—To the over-lord, hail!' These twelve âptis (obtainments) he offers, because there are twelve months in the year, and Pragâpati is the year, and the sacrifice is Pragâpati: hence whatever obtainment, whatever accomplishment there is for him[1], that he thereby wins, that he makes his own.

3. He then either offers six kliptis[2], or makes (the Sacrificer) pronounce them. Whether he offers, or makes him pronounce them, the significance is the same.

4. He makes him pronounce (Vâg. S. IX, 21), 'May the life prosper through sacrifice!—May the breath prosper through sacrifice!—May the eye prosper through sacrifice!—May the ear prosper through sacrifice!—May the back prosper through sacrifice!—May the sa-

for the twelve formulas, given in the next paragraph, as well as for the oblations made therewith. The first of these formulas is 'âpaye svâhâ,' whence the above term is probably derived.

[1] Or perhaps, 'there is of (belongs to) that (sacrifice).'

[2] This term, literally 'success, accomplishment,' is technically used to denote the succeeding formulas containing the verb 'klip,' to succeed, prosper, as well as the oblations made therewith.

crifice prosper through sacrifice!' These six k*l*iptis he makes him pronounce, because there are six seasons in the year, and Pragâpati is the year, and the sacrifice is Pragâpati: thus whatever success, whatever accomplishment there is for him, that he thereby wins, that he makes his own.

5. The sacrificial post is eight-cornered; for the Gâyatrî metre has eight syllables, and the Gâyatrî is Agni's metre: he thereby wins the world of the gods. The post is either wrapt up, or bound up, in seventeen cloths; for Pragâpati is seventeenfold: he thus wins Pragâpati.

6. There is a wheaten head-piece[1] on it; for man is nearest to Pragâpati, and he is skinless[2]. And among plants wheat comes nearest to man, (for) it has no skin: thus he thereby wins the world of men.

7. The post has a hollow (at the top), and is not pointed at the end; for the hollow is sacred to the Fathers: he thus gains the world of the Fathers. It is seventeen cubits long, for Pragâpati is seventeenfold: he thus wins Pragâpati.

8. Thereupon the Nesh*t*ri, being about to lead up the (Sacrificer's) wife, makes her wrap round herself, over the garment of consecration, a cloth, or skirt, made of Kusa grass[3]; for she, the wife, is the hind

---

[1] For the ordinary mortar-shaped top-piece fixed on the post, see part ii, p. 168, note 1. On the present occasion it is to be made of wheaten dough.

[2] According to a legend given at III, 1, 2, 13 seq., man had originally a (hairy) skin, or hide; but the gods having flayed him, put his skin on the cow.

[3] In the ceremonial of the Black Yagus (Taitt. Br. I, 3, 7, 1) the Sacrificer himself has to put on a 'târpya' garment, for which see note on V, 2, 5, 20.

part of the sacrifice[1]; and he wishes her, thus coming forward, to propitiate the sacrifice. But impure is that part of woman which is below the navel, and pure are the plants of (Ku*s*a) grass: thus having, by means of those plants of (Ku*s*a) grass, made pure whatever part of her is impure, he causes her to propitiate the sacrifice, while coming forward. This is why the Nesh*tri*, being about to lead up the wife, makes her wrap round herself, over the garment of consecration, a cloth, or skirt, made of Ku*s*a grass.

9. He then leans a ladder (against the post). He may ascend either from the south northwards, or from the north southwards; but let him rather ascend from the south northwards (udak), for thus it goes upwards (udak).

10. Being about to ascend, he (the Sacrificer) addresses his wife, 'Come, wife, ascend we the sky!'—'Ascend we!' says the wife. Now as to why he addresses his wife: she, the wife, in sooth is one half of his own self; hence, as long as he does not obtain her, so long he is not regenerated, for so long he is incomplete. But as soon as he obtains her he is regenerated, for then he is complete. 'Complete I want to go to that supreme goal,' thus (he thinks) and therefore he addresses his wife.

11. He ascends, with, 'We have become Pra*g*âpati's children;' for he who offers the Vâ*g*apeya indeed becomes Pra*g*âpati's child.

12. He then touches the wheat (top-piece)[2], with,

[1] Viz. because her ordinary seat is at the back, or west, end of the altar.

[2] According to the ritual of the Black Ya*g*us (Sây. on Taitt. S. I, 7, 9, vol. i, p. 1039), the Sacrificer, having ascended, lifts up his

'We have gone to the light, O ye gods!' for he who offers the Vâgapeya, indeed goes to the light.

13. And as to why he touches the wheat: wheat is food, and he who offers the Vâgapeya, wins food, for vâga-peya is the same as anna-peya (food and drink): thus whatever food he has thereby won, therewith now that he has gone to that supreme goal, he puts himself in contact, and possesses himself of it,—therefore he touches the wheat (top-piece).

14. He then rises by (the measure of) his head over the post, with, 'We have become immortal!' whereby he wins the world of the gods.

15. Thereupon, while looking in the different directions, he mutters (Vâg. S. IX, 22), 'Ours be your power, ours your manhood and intelligence, ours be your energies!' For he who offers the Vâgapeya wins everything here, winning as he does Pragâpati, and Pragâpati being everything here;—having appropriated to himself the glory, the power, and the strength of this All, he now lays them within himself, makes them his own: that is why he mutters, while looking in the different directions.

16. They throw up to him bags of salt; for salt means cattle, and cattle is food; and he who offers the Vagâpeya wins food, for vâga-peya is the same as anna-peya: thus whatever food he thereby has gained, therewith now that he has gone to the supreme goal, he puts himself in contact, and makes it his own,—therefore they throw bags of salt up to him.

17. They (the pieces of salt) are done up in asvattha

arms to heaven, praying, 'We have gone to the light, to the gods, we have become immortal; we have become Pragâpati's children!'

(ficus religiosa) leaves: because Indra on that (former) occasion called upon the Maruts staying on the A*s*vattha tree[1], therefore they are done up in a*s*vattha leaves. Peasants (vi*s*) throw them up to him, for the Maruts are the peasants, and the peasants are food (for the nobleman): hence peasants throw them up. There are seventeen (bags), for Pra*g*âpati is seventeenfold: he thus wins Pra*g*âpati.

18. Thereupon, while looking down upon this (earth), he mutters, 'Homage be to the mother Earth! homage be to the mother Earth!' For when B*ri*haspati had been consecrated, the Earth was afraid of him, thinking, 'Something great surely has he become now that he has been consecrated: I fear lest he may rend me asunder[2]!' And B*ri*haspati also was afraid of the Earth, thinking, 'I fear lest she may shake me off!' Hence by that (formula) he entered into a friendly relation with her; for a mother does not hurt her son, nor does a son hurt his mother.

19. Now the B*ri*haspati Soma-feast[3] is the same as the Vâ*g*apeya; and the earth in truth is afraid of that (Sacrificer), thinking, 'Something great

[1] See part ii, p. 334, with note 2. On the 'a*s*vattha devasadana' cp. also Ath.-veda V, 4, 3; Rig-veda I, 164, 20-22; A. Kuhn, Herabkunft des Feuers und des Göttertranks, p. 126 seq. (Mythol. Stud. i. p. 112 seq.).

[2] Or, 'I hope he will not rend me asunder.' For this construction—exactly corresponding to the German 'dass (or, wenn) er mich nur nicht aufreisst!' (cf. also the colloquial use of the French 'pourvu,'—'pourvu qu'il ne me déchire pas!')—see part ii, p. 31, note 1.

[3] The B*ri*haspatisava is performed by a Brâhma*n*a with a view to obtaining the office of Purohita (royal chaplain, or family priest). For Â*s*valâyana's rule, which places it on a level with the Râ*g*asûya sacrifice of a king, see p. 4, note 1.

surely has he become now that he has been consecrated: I fear lest he may rend me asunder!' And he himself is afraid of her, thinking, 'I fear lest she may shake me off!' Hence he thereby enters into a friendly relation with her, for a mother does not hurt her son; neither does a son hurt his mother.

20. He then descends (and treads) upon a piece of gold;—gold is immortal life: he thus takes his stand on life immortal.

21. Now (in the first place) he (the Adhvaryu) spreads out the skin of a he-goat, and lays a (small) gold plate thereon: upon that—or indeed upon this (earth) itself—he (the Sacrificer) steps.

22. They then bring a throne-seat for him; for truly he who gains a seat in the air[1], gains a seat above (others): thus these subjects of his sit below him who is seated above,—this is why they bring him a throne-seat.

23. It is made of udumbara wood,—the Udumbara tree being sustenance, (that is) food,—for his obtainment of sustenance, food: therefore it is made of udumbara wood. They set it down in front of the Havirdhâna (cart-shed), behind the Âhavanîya (fire).

24. He then spreads the goat-skin thereon; for truly the he-goat is no other than Pragâpati, for they, the goats, are most clearly of Pragâpati (the lord of generation or creatures);—whence, bringing forth thrice in a year, they produce two or three[2]: thus he thereby makes him (the Sacrificer) to be Pragâpati himself,—this is why he spreads the goat-skin thereon.

---

[1] The Sacrificer is supposed to have done so by the symbolical act of raising his head above the sacrificial post; see paragraph 14 above.

[2] See IV, 5, 5, 6; part ii, p. 407, note 3.

25. He spreads it, with, 'This is thy kingship[1]!' whereby he endows him with royal power. He then makes him sit down, with, 'Thou art the ruler, the ruling lord!' whereby he makes him the ruler, ruling over those subjects of his;—'Thou art firm, and stedfast!' whereby he makes him firm and stedfast in this world;—'Thee for the tilling!—Thee for peaceful dwelling!—Thee for wealth!—Thee for thrift!' whereby he means to say, '(here I seat) thee for the welfare (of the people).'

Second Brâhmana.

1. He now proceeds with the Bârhaspatya pap. Its svishtakrit remains yet unoffered, when he (the Adhvaryu) brings[2] him (the Sacrificer) some food; for he who offers the Vâgapeya wins food, vâgapeya being the same as anna-peya: thus whatever food he (the Sacrificer) has thereby gained, that he (the Adhvaryu) now brings to him.

2. In a vessel of udumbara wood—the Udumbara tree being sustenance, (that is) food—for the obtainment of sustenance, food: therefore it is in a vessel of udumbara wood. He first brings water, then milk, then (other) kinds of food, as they occur to him.

3. Now some bring seventeen kinds of food,

---

[1] Thus the formula 'iyam te rât' is interpreted by Mahîdhara (who, however, takes it to be addressed to the throne-seat, and not, as would seem preferable, to the king), and apparently also by our author. The word 'râg' would indeed seem to mean here something like the energy (sakti), or the symbol, of the king. The St. Petersburg dictionary, however, takes it here as the name of a female deity.

[2] He collects (sambharati), or provides food for him; this ceremony corresponding to that of equipping or provisioning the sacred fire with the so-called sambhâras, at the Agny-âdhâna; see II, 1, 1, 1 seq.; part i, p. 276, note 1.

saying, 'Seventeenfold is Pragâpati.' But let him not do so: surely all the food is not appropriated to Pragâpati[1], and, compared to him, what is man that he should appropriate to himself all food? Hence, while bringing every kind of food that occurs to him, let him not bring of some one (particular) kind of food.

4. And whatever food he does not bring to him, let him (the Sacrificer) forswear[2] that, and not eat of it as long as he lives: thus he does not go to the end, thus he lives long. Of all that food brought together he offers the (seven) Vâga-prasavanîya[3] oblations, cutting out (pieces) with the dipping-spoon. Thus to whatever deities he is now offering, they give an impulse to him, and impelled by them he

[1] Or 'from Pragâpati;' or perhaps, 'surely not all Pragâpati's food is appropriated.' The Kânva recension reads thus, VI, 2, 3, 3. He first brings water, then milk, then, as they occur to him (other) kinds of food. 'Let him bring those seventeen kinds of food,' they say, 'for Pragâpati is seventeenfold.' Nevertheless (tadu) let him bring whatever kinds of food he can either think of or obtain. 4. Of this his food that has been brought together, let him set aside (uddharet) one (particular kind of) food: let him forswear that (tad udbruvîta), and not eat of it as long as he lives (yâvag gîvet). By that much also (or, even so long, tâvad api vai prâgapateh sarvam annam anavaruddham) all the food of Pragâpati is not appropriated; and who is man (compared) to him, that he should appropriate to himself all food? Thus he does not go to the end, thus he lives long: that (food) is here left over for his offspring (or people).

[2] Sâyana explains 'tasya udbruvîta' by,—one ought to proclaim it, saying aloud 'such and such food has not been brought;'—na sambhritam ity ukkais tannâma brûyât.

[3] That is, oblations calculated to promote or quicken (pra-su) the strength (food,—vâga) by their prayers, the first three of which begin with 'vâgasya . . . prasavah.' See p. 2, note 1. In the Black Yagus ritual these oblations are called 'Annahomâh' or 'food-oblations.' Taitt. Br. I, 3, 8, 1. The Sûtras seem, however, likewise to use the term 'Vâgaprasavanîya' (or Vâgaprasavîya).

wins: therefore he offers the Vâgaprasavanîya oblations.

5. He offers with (Vâg. S. IX, 23–29), 'The impulse of strength impelled of old that king Soma in the plants, in the waters: may they be rich in honey for us! may we be wakeful in the kingdom, placed in the front, hail!'

6. 'The impulse of strength spread over this sky, and over all these worlds, as the all-ruler; knowing he causeth him to give gifts who wisheth not to give: may he bestow upon us wealth with the full muster of heroes, hail!'

7. 'Yea, the impulse of strength prevailed over all these worlds, on every side; from days of yore the king goeth about knowing, increasing the people, and the well-being amongst us, hail!'

8. 'To king Soma, to Agni we cling[1] for help, to the Âdityas, to Vishnu, to Sûrya, to the Brahman Brihaspati, hail!'

9. 'Urge thou Aryaman, Brihaspati, Indra to the giving of gifts, Vâk[2], Vishnu, Sarasvatî, and the vigorous Savitri, hail!'

10. 'O Agni, speak to us here, be thou gracious unto us! bestow blessings upon us, O winner of thousands, for thou art the giver of wealth, hail!'

11. 'May Aryaman bestow blessings upon us, and Pûshan, and Brihaspati! may the divine Vâk give us gifts, hail!'

12. With the remaining (offering material) he sprinkles him (the Sacrificer); he thereby sprinkles

[1] Rig-veda X, 141, 3 reads,—King Soma, Agni we invoke with our voices, the Âdityas, &c.

[2] Rig-veda X, 141, 5 has Vâta (Wind) instead of Vâk (Speech).

him with food, bestows food upon him: for this reason he sprinkles him with the remaining (material)[1].

13. He sprinkles with (Vâg. S. IX, 30), 'At the impulse of the divine Savitri, (I sprinkle) thee, by the arms of the Asvins, by the hands of Pûshan!' he thus sprinkles (consecrates) him by the hands of gods;—'I place thee in the leading of Sarasvati Vâk, the leader;' for Sarasvatî is Vâk (speech): he thus places him in the leading of Vâk, the leader.

14. Here now some say, 'I place thee in the leading of the leader of all the gods;' for all the gods are the All: he thus places him in the leading of the leader of the All. But let him not say so; let him rather say, 'I place thee in the leading of Sarasvatî Vâk;' for Sarasvatî is Vâk: he thus places him in the leading of Vâk.—'I consecrate thee, N. N., with the supreme rulership of Brihaspati!' therewith he mentions the (Sacrificer's) name: he thus makes him attain to the fellowship of Brihaspati, and to co-existence in his world.

15. He then says, 'All-ruler is he, N. N.! All-ruler is he, N.N.!' Him, thus indicated, he thereby indicates to the gods: 'Of mighty power is he who has been consecrated; he has become one of yours; protect him!' thus he thereby says. Thrice he says it, for threefold is the sacrifice.

[1] According to the Taittirîyas (Taitt. S., vol. i, p. 1049), the Sacrificer is made to sit on the black antelope skin, with his face to the east, with a small gold and silver plate placed on either side of him; and he is then sprinkled in front, on the head, so that the liquid runs down to his mouth, thus symbolizing the entering of food and strength into him.

16. He then either offers, or makes him pronounce (the formulas of) the Uggiti oblations[1]. Whether he offers or makes him pronounce (the formulas), the significance is the same.

17. He makes him say (Vâg. S. IX, 31-34), 'With the (word of) one syllable Agni won the breath: may I win that! — —[2] With the (metre of) seventeen syllables Pragâpati won the seventeenfold stoma: may I win that!' whatever those deities won by means of those (formulas), that he now wins by them. There are seventeen (formulas), for Pragâpati is seventeenfold: he thus wins Pragâpati.

18. Thereupon he says, 'Recite (the invitatory formula) to Agni Svishtakrit!' Now, as to why this rite is performed between two oblations. Pragâpati, truly, is that sacrifice which is here performed, and from which these creatures have been produced, —and, indeed, they are even now produced after this one: he thus wins Pragâpati in the very middle: therefore that rite is performed between two oblations. Having made (the Âgnidhra) utter the

[1] That is, oblations of 'victory,' with the formulas used therewith, containing each two forms of the verb ud-gi, 'to conquer.'

[2] The intervening formulas here understood, and given in the Vâg. Samhitâ, are to the effect that the Asvins, by two syllables, gained the two-footed men; Vishnu, by three, the three worlds; Soma, by four, the four-footed cattle; Pûshan, by five, the five regions (the four quarters and the upper region); Savitri, by six, the six seasons; the Maruts, by seven, the seven kinds of domestic animals; Brihaspati, by eight, the Gâyatrî metre; Mitra, by nine, the Trivrit stoma (hymn-tune); Varuna, by ten, the Virâg metre; Indra, by eleven, the Trishtubh metre; the All-gods, by twelve, the Gagatî metre; the Vasus, by thirteen, the thirteenfold stoma; the Rudras, by fourteen, the fourteenfold stoma; the Âdityas, by fifteen, the fifteenfold stoma; Aditi, by sixteen, the sixteenfold stoma.

*S*raushat, he says, 'Pronounce the offering-prayer to Agni Svish*t*akr*i*t!' and offers as the Vasha*t* is uttered.

19. He then puts the I*d*â on (the i*d*âpâtri). The I*d*â having been invoked[1], he, having touched water, draws the Mâhendra cup. Having drawn the Mâhendra cup, he sets the chant agoing[2]. He urges him (the Sacrificer) forward to the chant: he gets down (from the throne-seat); he is in attendance at the Stotra, in attendance at the *S*astra.

20. Here now some, having performed that, perform that[3]; but let him not do it thus; for the Stotra is his (the Sacrificer's) own self, and the *S*astra is his people (or offering): thereby then he ruins the Sacrificer; he goes astray, he stumbles;—hence having performed that, let him perform that:—

21. He puts the I*d*â on (the dish). The I*d*â having been invoked, he, having touched water, draws the Mâhendra cup. Having drawn the Mâhendra cup, he sets the (P*r*ish*th*a-) Stotra agoing. He urges him (the Sacrificer) forward to the chant: he gets down (from the throne-seat); he is in attendance at the chant (stotra), in attendance at the recitation (*s*astra).

[1] See I, 8, 1, 18 seq.

[2] That is, the (first or Hot*r*i's) P*r*ish*th*a-stotra, for which see above, p. 15, note 1; part ii, p. 339, note 2. Its chanting is followed by the Nishkevalya-*s*astra, recited by the Hot*r*i.

[3] That is to say, according to Sâya*n*a,—they make the Svish*t*akr*i*t, and the rising of the Sacrificer from the throne-seat, take place after the pronunciation of the 'uggiti' formulas, the drawing of the Mâhendra cup, and the performance of the Stotra and *S*astra.

B. THE RÂ*G*ASÛYA, OR INAUGURATION OF A KING.

SECOND ADHYÂYA. THIRD BRÂHMA*N*A.

1. He offers a full-offering[1]; for the full means the All: 'May I be consecrated after encompassing the All!' thus he thinks. At this (offering) he bestows a boon; for a boon means all: 'Having encompassed the All (the universe), may I be consecrated!' thus he thinks. He may perform this offering, if he chooses; or, if he chooses, he may disregard it.

2. And on the following day he prepares a cake on eight potsherds, as sacrificial food for Anumati[2]. And whatever portion of (the grains) being ground,—either flour or rice-grains,—falls down behind the pin, that he throws together into the dipping-spoon

---

[1] On the pûr*n*âhuti, or libation of a spoonful of ghee, see part i, p. 302 note. According to Kâty. *S*r. XV, 1, 4 seq., Âsv. *S*r. IX, 3, 2, and other authorities, this full-offering is preceded by the Pavitra (purificatory ceremony), a Soma-sacrifice with four dikshâs or initiation days (? commencing on the first day of the bright fortnight of Phâlguna), serving as the ordinary opening offering (anvârambha*n*îyesh*t*i). That it formed part of the ceremonial at the time of the composition of the Brâhma*n*a there can be little doubt (cf. Pa*ñk*av. Br. 18, 8, 1), but as it is an ordinary Agnish*t*oma, the author had no reason to refer to it.

[2] I. e. the approval or favour of the deities, personified.—According to Yâ*gñ*ika Deva (to Kâty. *S*r. XV, 1, 8), the ceremonies now beginning would commence on the 10th day of the bright half of Phalgunî; the fifth day's ceremony from this day, viz. the first of the four seasonal offerings, having to be performed on the Full-moon of that month; see p. 47, note 1.

(sruva)[1]. They take a firebrand from the Anvâhâr-yapakana (or southern) fire, and therewith go southward. And where he finds a self-produced hollow[2] or cleft,—

3. Having there made up a fire, he offers with (Vâg. S. IX, 35), 'This, O Nirriti, is thy portion: accept it graciously, hail!' For Nirriti is this (Earth); whomsoever she seizes upon with evil, him she seizes upon with destruction (nirriti): hence whatever part of this (Earth) is of the Nirriti nature, that he thereby propitiates; and thus Nirriti does not seize upon him, while being consecrated. And the reason why he offers in a self-produced hollow or

[1] The authorities of the Black Yagus prepare therewith a cake on one kapâla. Taitt. S. I, 8, 1.

[2] Sâyana, perhaps rightly, takes 'irina' here (and on Taitt. S. vol. ii, p. 6) in the sense of 'ûshara,' a spot of barren (or saline) soil. Cf. VII, 2, 1, 8: 'In whatever part of this (earth) there is produced (of itself) a cleft, or in whatever part of it plants are not produced, verily that part of it Nirriti seizes upon.'—Kausika-sûtra XIII, 28 (A. Weber, Omina und Portenta, p. 386) recommends the following propitiatory rites in case of a sudden cleft in the ground: 'If in the village, or house, or fire-house, or meeting-place, (the ground) should burst open, four cows are got ready, a white, a black, a red, and a one-coloured one. For twelve days he puts down the butter, milked together from these. In the morning of the twelfth, having made up a fire north of where there was that cleft, having swept and sprinkled it, and strewn sacrificial grass around it; and having mixed (the butter) with ghee from the white (cow), and addressed it (the spot) with the three verses, Ath.-veda XII, 1, 19–21 ("Agni is in the earth, in the plants, the waters carry Agni, Agni is in the flints, Agni is within men; in cows, in horses are Agnis," &c.), and touched it, let him then offer. In the same way on the south side; in the same way on the western side. Having concluded on the north side, let him offer with the (formulas addressed) to Vâstoshpati (the tutelary genius of the dwelling). Having poured the refuse in the cleft, and completed the oblations, he sprinkles the cleft with lustral water.'

cleft, is that that much of this (earth) is possessed with Nirriti.

4. They then return (to the sacrificial ground) without looking backward. He now proceeds with the cake on eight potsherds for Anumati. For Anumati is this (Earth); and whosoever knows to do that work which he intends to do, for him indeed she approves (anu-man) thereof: hence it is her he thereby pleases, thinking 'May I be consecrated, approved by that (genius of) approval!'

5. And as to why it is a (cake) on eight potsherds,—the Gâyatrî consists of eight syllables, and this earth is Gâyatrî. And as to why he offers of the same sacrificial food[1] both (oblations): thereby, indeed, both of it comes to be this latter one (viz. Anumati, or approval). A garment is the sacrificial fee for this (offering): for even as one clad in a garment does not venture into the forest, but having deposited that garment (somewhere) escapes (robbers), in like manner no assault befalls him while being consecrated.

6. And on the following day he prepares a cake on eleven potsherds for Agni and Vishnu, and offers it in the same way as the (regular) ishti: this indeed is just what that approved initiation-offering to Agni and Vishnu is there[2]. Now Agni is all the deities, since in Agni one offers to all deities; and Agni forsooth is the lower end, and Vishnu is the upper end: 'May I be consecrated, after thus encompassing all the deities, and after encompassing

[1] Though he has offered twice (to Nirriti and Anumati), he has only once taken out rice for oblation.

[2] Viz. at the ordinary Soma-sacrifice; for the Dîkshanîyeshti, see part ii, p. 12.

the whole sacrifice!' thus he thinks, and hence there is a cake on eleven potsherds to Agni and Vishnu. Gold is the sacrificial fee for this (offering); for to Agni belongs this sacrifice, and gold is Agni's seed. As to Vishnu, he is the sacrifice, and Agni forsooth is the sacrifice: nevertheless this is Agni's alone, therefore gold is the fee.

7. And on the following day he prepares a cake on eleven potsherds for Agni and Soma, and offers it in the same way as an (ordinary) ishti, for it was thereby Indra slew Vritra, and thereby he gained that universal conquest which now is his. And in like manner does this (king, the Sacrificer) thereby slay his wicked, hateful enemy, and in like manner does he gain the victory. 'May I be consecrated, when safety and security from evil-doers have been gained!' thus he thinks: hence there is a cake on eleven potsherds for Agni and Soma. For this (offering) a bull set at liberty is the sacrificial fee; for yonder moon[1] they slay while setting him at liberty[2]: to wit, by the full-moon offering they slay him, and by the new-moon offering they set him at liberty;—therefore a bull set at liberty is the fee.

8. And on the following day he prepares a cake on twelve potsherds for Indra and Agni, and offers it in the same way as an (ordinary) ishti. Now when

[1] On the identification of Vritra with the moon (and Soma), see I, 6, 3, 17. On the moon serving as food to the gods, see part ii, Introduction, p. xiii. According to a later conception, one kalâ (or sixteenth part of the moon's disc) was taken off each day during the period of the waning, and again added to it during the period of the waxing moon.

[2] Utsargam . . . ghnanti; perhaps the former has to be taken here as infinitive (in order to set him at liberty) rather than as gerund.

Indra slew Vritra, that vigour and energy of his went out of him, being frightened: by this offering he again possessed himself of that vigour and energy. And in like manner does this (Sacrificer) by this offering possess himself of vigour and energy; for Agni is fiery spirit, and Indra is vigour and energy: 'May I be consecrated, having embraced both these energies!' thus he thinks: hence there is a cake on twelve potsherds for Indra and Agni. A bull is the fee for this (offering), for by his shoulder he is of Agni's nature[1], and by his testicles he is of Indra's nature: therefore a bull is the fee for it.

9. Thereupon he performs the offering of first-fruits[2]; for verily he who performs the Râgasûya secures for himself (the benefits of) all sacrificial rites, all ishtis, even the spoon-offerings; and instituted by the gods, in truth, is that ishti, the Âgrayaneshti: 'May this also be offered by me! May I be consecrated by this (offering) also!' thus he thinks, and therefore he performs the offering of first-fruits. Moreover, it is for the plants that he who is consecrated, is consecrated; therefore he now makes the plants healthy and faultless, thinking, 'May I be consecrated for (the obtainment of) healthy, faultless plants (crops)!' A cow is the fee for this (offering).

10. Thereupon he performs the Seasonal offerings[3]; for verily he who performs the Râgasûya secures for himself (the benefits of) all sacrificial

[1] Cp. I, 1, 2, 9, '(Like) fire, verily, is the yoke of that cart: hence the shoulder of those (oxen) that draw it becomes as if burnt by fire.'

[2] For the Âgrayaneshti, see part i, p. 369 seq.

[3] For the four Kâturmâsya (enumerated in the next chapter), see part i, p. 383 seq.

rites, all ishtis, even the spoon-offerings; and instituted by the gods, in truth, is that sacrificial rite, the Seasonal offerings: 'May these also be offered by me! May I be consecrated by these (offerings) also!' thus he thinks, and therefore he performs the Seasonal offerings.

Fourth Brâhmana.

1. He offers the Vaisvadeva[1] (All-gods' offering); for by means of the Vaisvadeva, Pragâpati created abundance (of food) and creatures, thinking, 'May I be consecrated, after creating abundance and creatures!' And in like manner does this (Sacrificer) now, by the Vaisvadeva, create abundance and creatures, thinking, 'May I be consecrated, after creating abundance and creatures!'

2. He then offers the Varunapraghâsâh[2]; for by means of the Varunapraghâsâh Pragâpati delivered the creatures from Varuna's noose, and those creatures of his were produced healthy and faultless: 'May I be consecrated for healthy, faultless crea-

[1] This, the first of the Seasonal offerings, is to be performed on the full-moon of Phalgunî, the other three then following after intervals of four months each. During these intervals the ordinary fortnightly sacrifices are to be performed from day to day in this way that either the Full-moon and New-moon sacrifice are performed on alternate days, or the former on each day of the bright fortnights, and the latter on each day of the dark fortnights. Thus, according to Âsv. Sr. IX, 3, 6; while Kâty. XV, 1, 18 allows only the latter mode. The final Seasonal offering, or Sunâsirya, which ordinarily is performed a twelvemonth after the Vaisvadeva, or on the full-moon of Phâlguna, is on the present occasion to be performed just a year after the opening sacrifice, or Pavitra (p. 42, note 1), i.e. on the first day of the bright fortnight of Phâlguna, being immediately followed by the Pañkavâtîya.

[2] See part i, p. 391 seq.

tures!' he thought. And in like manner does this (Sacrificer) now, by the Varunapraghâsâh, deliver the creatures from Varuna's noose, and those creatures of his are produced healthy and faultless: 'May I be consecrated for healthy, faultless creatures!' so he thinks.

3. He then performs the Sâkamedhâh[1]; for by the Sâkamedhâh the gods slew Vritra, and gained that universal conquest which now is theirs. And in like manner does this (Sacrificer) thereby now slay his wicked, hateful enemy; and in like manner does he gain the victory, thinking, 'May I be consecrated, when safety and security are gained!'

4. He then performs the Sunâsîrya[2], thinking, 'May I be consecrated, having encompassed both essences!' Thereupon the Pañkavâtiya[3] (oblation to the five winds). Having poked the Âhavanîya fire asunder into five parts, he offers, cutting out butter with the dipping-spoon.

5. He offers in the forepart (of the fire), with (Vâg. S. IX, 35), 'To the Agni-eyed gods, the east-seated, hail!' He then offers in the southern part

---

[1] See part i, p. 408 seq.

[2] See part i, p. 444 seq., where the word is fancifully explained as composed of suna (prosperity) and sîra (=sâra, sap),—the two essences here referred to. Sâyana, following Yâska (and Sat. Br. II, 6, 3, 6–8?), identifies the two component elements with Vâyu, the wind, and Âditya, the sun; see part i, p. 445, note 3.

[3] The authorities of the Black Yagus (Taitt. Br. I, 7, 1, 5) call this oblation Pañkâvattîya, i.e. 'consisting of fivefold cut (or ladled)' ghee, which is offered without disturbing the fire. Prior to this oblation, Âpastamba (Taitt. S., vol. ii, p. 93), however, prescribes a so-called Pañkedhmîya, i.e. an oblation 'on five fire-brands,' the fire being, as here, poked about so as to form separate heaps in the four quarters and in the centre.

with, 'To the Yama-eyed[1] gods, the south-seated, hail!' He then offers in the hind part with, 'To the Vi*s*vadeva-eyed gods, the west-seated, hail!' He then offers in the northern part with either, 'To the Mitrâvaru*n*a-eyed gods,—or, To the Marut-eyed gods,—the north-seated, hail!' He then offers in the centre with, 'To the Soma-eyed gods, the above-seated, the venerable, hail!'

6. Having then poked (the fire) together, he offers with (Vâ*g*. S. IX, 36), 'The gods that are Agni-eyed, east-seated, to them hail!—The gods that are Yama-eyed, south-seated, to them hail!—The gods that are Vi*s*vadeva-eyed, west-seated, to them hail!—The gods that are Mitrâvaru*n*a-eyed—or, Marut-eyed—north-seated, to them hail!—The gods that are Soma-eyed, above-seated, venerable, to them hail!' Now as to why he thus offers.

7. Now when, by means of the Sâkamedhâ*h*, the gods were gaining that universal conquest, which now is theirs, they said, 'Verily the fiends, the Rakshas, suck out these (creatures) in the (four) quarters: come, let us throw the thunderbolt at them!' Now the ghee is a thunderbolt: with that thunderbolt, the ghee, they smote the fiends, the Rakshas, in the (four) quarters, and gained that universal conquest which now is theirs. And in like manner does this (Sacrificer) smite the fiends, the Rakshas, in the quarters, by that thunderbolt, the ghee; and thus he gains the victory, thinking, 'May

[1] Yama is the ruler of the departed ancestors, residing in the southern quarter.

I be consecrated, when safety and security have been gained!'

8. And as to why he offers those five latter oblations. Now when they poke the Âhavanîya asunder into five parts, thereby they wound and tear some of the fire; and hereby now he heals it: therefore he offers those five latter oblations.

9. For this (offering) a carriage and pair, with a side horse, is the priest's fee. Three horses, the warrior, and the charioteer,—these are five breaths, and the breath is the same as the wind: and because that is the fee for this sacrifice, therefore it is called Pa*ñk*avâtîya (belonging to the five winds).

10. He may also heal (some disease[1]) with this (offering): For yonder blower (or purifier, the wind) is this breath; and the breath is the same as the vital energy. Now he (the wind) blows as one only, but on entering into man, he is divided tenfold; and ten are those oblations he offers: thus he (the priest) endows him with the ten vital airs, with the whole, entire vital energy; and were he now even as one whose vital spirit has departed, verily by this (offering) he (the priest) brings him round again.

11. Thereupon the Indraturîya[2].—There is a cake on eight potsherds for Agni, a barley pap for Varu*n*a, a pap of gavedhukâ seed (coix barbata) for Rudra; and a mess of sour curds from a yoke-

[1] Tenâpy etena vish*t*âvrâ*g*e (v. l. vish*t*âbrâ*g*e) bhishagyet. Ka*n*va rec.

[2] That is, the ceremony in which the fourth oblation belongs to Indra. While the Mâdhyandinas perform this ceremony on the same day (the pratipad of the bright fortnight of Phalgunî), the Kâ*n*vas do so on the following day; the Apâmârgahoma being then likewise shifted on another day.

trained cow for Indra: this Indraturiya he offers. Now Indra and Agni on that occasion consulted with each other: 'Verily the fiends, the Rakshas, suck out these (creatures) in the (four) quarters: come, let us throw the thunderbolt at them!'

12. Agni then spake, 'Let there be three shares for me, one for thee!'—'So be it!'—By that offering those two smote the fiends, the Rakshas, in the (four) quarters, and gained that universal conquest which now is theirs. And in like manner does this (Sacrificer) by that offering smite the fiends, the Rakshas, in the quarters; and gain the victory, thinking, 'May I be consecrated, when safety and security have been gained!'

13. Now what cake on eight potsherds there is for Agni, that is one of Agni's shares; and what barley pap there is for Varu*n*a—Varu*n*a being the same as Agni—that is Agni's second share; and what pap of gavedhuká seed there is for Rudra—Rudra being the same as Agni—that is Agni's third share. And as to why it is prepared of gavedhukâ seed: that god surely is (the recipient) of refuse (remains of offering)[1], and gavedhukâ grass is refuse,—hence it is prepared of gavedhukâ seed. And what mess of sour curds there is from a yoke-trained cow for Indra, that is the fourth share (being that) of Indra—turiya being the same as *k*aturtha (fourth)—hence the name Indraturiya. That same yoke-trained cow is the fee for this (offering); for by her shoulder she is of Agni's nature, since her shoulder is, as it were, fire-burnt; and in that, being a female, she improperly draws (the cart), that is her Varu*n*ic

[1] On Rudra's epithet vâstavya, see I, 7, 3, 1. 8.

nature; and in that she is a cow, she is of Rudra's nature[1]; and in that Indra's sour curds (come) from her, thereby she is of Indra's nature. Indeed that (cow) commands all that: therefore that same yoke-trained cow is the fee.

14. Thereupon he performs the Apâmârgahoma; for by means of apâmârga plants (achyranthes aspera) the gods wiped away (apa-marg) the fiends, the Rakshas, in the quarters, and gained that universal conquest which now is theirs. And in like manner does this (Sacrificer) now by means of apâmârga plants wipe away the fiends, the Rakshas, in the quarters; and in like manner does he gain the victory, thinking, 'May I be consecrated, when safety and security have been gained!'

15. He takes apâmârga grains in a dipping-spoon of either palâsa (butea frondosa) or vikaṅkata (flacourtia sapida) wood. They take a firebrand from the Anvâhâryapa*k*ana (southern) fire; and proceed therewith eastward or northward; and there having made up a fire he offers.

16. He takes the firebrand with (Vâg. S. IX, 37; *Ri*k S. III, 24, 1), 'Encounter the arrays, Agni!'—arrays means battles: 'encounter the battles!' he thereby says;—'Repel the evil-wisher!'—the evil-wisher is the enemy: 'beat off the enemy!' he thereby says;—'Unconquerable, conquering the evil-doers!'—unconquerable he is indeed, by the Rakshas, the fiends; and conquering the evil-doers, for he conquers every evil:

[1] Rudra rules over the beasts (III, 6, 2, 20), whence he is also called the lord of beasts (pasûnâm pati, I, 7, 3, 8; Pasupati V, 3, 3, 7). Pûshan, the genius of thrift and prosperity, is also (like the Greek Pan) regarded as the protector of cattle; see V, 2, 5, 8.

therefore he says, 'conquering the evil-doers;'—'Bestow glory upon the offerer of sacrifice!'—'bestowing blessing on the Sacrificer,' is what he thereby says.

17. Thereupon making up the fire he offers with (Vâg. S. IX, 38), 'At the impulse of the God Savitri I offer with the arms of the Asvins, with the hands of Pûshan, with the strength of the Upâmsu!' for the Upâmsu[1] (cup of Soma) is the mouth (or opening) of the sacrifice: thus he slays the fiends, the Rakshas, by the mouth of the sacrifice;—'Slain is the Rakshas, hail!' thus he slays the fiends, the Rakshas.

18. If the dipping-spoon is of palâsa wood,—the palâsa being the Brahman—it is with the Brahman that he slays the fiends, the Rakshas; and if it is of vikaṅkata wood,—the vikaṅkata being the thunderbolt—it is with the thunderbolt that he slays the fiends, the Rakshas: 'For the slaughter of the Rakshas (I take) thee!' therewith he slays the fiends, the Rakshas.

19. If he offers after going eastward, he throws the spoon towards the east; and if he offers after going northward, he throws the spoon towards the north, with, 'We have slain the Rakshas!' thus he slays the fiends, the Rakshas.

20. Thereupon they return (to the sacrificial ground) without looking back. Now by this (ceremony) also he may make for himself a counter-charm[2]. In whatever direction from there (his evil-wisher) is,

[1] See part ii, p. 248.

[2] Viz. an amulet consisting of a band running back into itself. The Kânva text has,—Tena hâpy etena vishâvrâge pratisaram kurvîta.

looking back thither he offers; for the Apâmârga is of a backward effect: whosoever does anything to him there, him indeed he thereby pitches backward. Let him indicate the name of that one, saying, 'We have slain so and so! So and so is slain!' thus he slays the fiends, the Rakshas.

Fifth Brâhmana.

1. He prepares a cake on eleven potsherds for Agni and Vishnu, a pap for Indra and Vishnu, and either a cake on three potsherds, or a pap, for Vishnu. He performs that Trishamyukta[1] offering. Therewith the gods came by men, and in like manner does this (king) now thereby come by men.

2. Now as to why there is that cake on eleven potsherds for Agni and Vishnu;—Agni is the giver, and men are Vishnu's: thus Agni, the giver, gives him (the king) men.

3. And as to why there is a pap for Indra and Vishnu;—Indra is the Sacrificer, and men are Vishnu's: thus Agni, the giver, gives him (the

[1] That is, 'the triply connected,' the ceremony being made up of three rounds, each of which consists of three separate oblations, viz.:—

1. Âgnâvaishnava cake, Aindrâvaishnava pap, Vaishnava pap;
2. Âgnâpaushna cake, Aindrâpaushna pap, Paushna pap;
3. Agnîshomîya cake, Aindrâsaumya pap, Saumya pap.

In this way one of the three divinities for whom the offering is intended,—viz. Vishnu, Pûshan, and Soma,—is each time connected with the two head-gods, Agni and Indra.—In the Black Yagur-veda, this set of offerings (not, however, called there by this name), is preceded by another ceremony consisting of five oblations to Dhâtri, Anumati, Râkâ, Sinîvâlî, and Kuhû. Taitt. S. I, 8, 8. Cf. Sat. Br. IX, 5, 1, 38.

Sacrificer) men; he now puts himself in contact with them, makes them his own.

4. And as to why there is either a cake on three potsherds, or a pap, for Vishnu;—whatever men Agni, the giver, gives him, among them he thereby finally establishes him (the king); and whatever work he wishes to do with his men, that he is able to do. Thus he thereby approaches the men, thinking, 'May I be consecrated, and possessed of men!' A dwarfish bull is the sacrificial fee for this (offering), for the dwarf belongs to Vishnu[1].

5. He then performs another Trishamyukta offering. He prepares a cake on eleven potsherds for Agni and Pûshan, a pap for Indra and Pûshan, and a pap for Pûshan: this Trishamyukta he offers. Thereby the gods obtained cattle; and in like manner does this (king) thereby obtain cattle.

6. Now as to why there is that cake on eleven potsherds for Agni and Pûshan;—Agni is the giver, and the cattle are Pûshan's: thus Agni, the giver, gives him cattle.

7. And as to why there is a pap for Indra and Pûshan;—Indra is the Sacrificer, and the cattle are Pûshan's: whatever cattle Agni, the giver, gives him, therewith he now puts himself in contact, those he makes his own.

8. And why there is a pap for Pûshan;—whatever cattle Agni, the giver, gives him, therewith he thereby finally establishes him, and whatever work he wishes to do with his cattle, that he is able

[1] See the legend, I, 2, 5, 1 seq., which represents Vishnu as a dwarf, who obtained from the Asuras as much ground for the gods, as he lay upon.—'Tad dhi pasushu vaishnavam rûpam yad vâmanasya goh.' Kânva rec.

to do: thus he comes by cattle, thinking, 'May I be consecrated, possessed of cattle!' A dark-grey[1] bull is the fee for this (offering), for such a dark-grey one is of Pûshan's nature: there are two forms of the dark-grey, the white hair and the black; and 'two and two' means a productive pair, and Pûshan represents productiveness, for Pûshan is cattle, and cattle means productiveness: thus a productive pair is obtained,—hence a dark-grey bull is the sacrificial fee.

9. He then performs another Trisha*m*yukta offering. He prepares a cake on eleven potsherds for Agni and Soma, a pap for Indra and Soma, and a pap for Soma: this Trisha*m*yukta (triply connected) he offers:—Thereby the gods attained glory; and in like manner does this (king) thereby attain glory.

10. Now as to why there is that cake on eleven potsherds for Agni and Soma;—Agni is the giver, and Soma is glory: thus Agni, the giver, gives him glory.

11. And as to why there is a pap for Indra and Soma;—Indra is the Sacrificer, and Soma is glory: whatever glory Agni, the giver, gives him, therewith he now puts himself in contact, that he makes his own.

12. And why there is a pap for Soma;—whatever glory, Agni, the giver, gives him, therein he now finally establishes him; and whatever work he, the glorious, wishes to do, that he is able to do. Thus he thereby attains glory,—thinking, 'May I be consecrated, endowed with glory!' for the inglorious one has no concern with success. A brown bull is

[1] See V, 1, 3, 9.

the fee for this (offering); for such a brown one is of Soma's nature.

13. And on the following day he prepares a cake on twelve potsherds for (Agni) Vais*v*ânara, and a barley pap for Varu*n*a. These two offerings he performs either on days following one another, or so as to use the same barhis[1].

14. And as to why there is that (cake) for Vais*v*ânara;—Vais*v*ânara ('belonging to all men') truly is the year, and Pra*g*âpati is the year; and Pra*g*âpati indeed thereby created abundance and creatures, thinking, 'May I be consecrated, having created abundance and creatures!' And in like manner does that (king) thereby create abundance and creatures, thinking, 'May I be consecrated, having created abundance and creatures!'

15. And why it is one on twelve potsherds;—twelve months there are in the year, and Vais*v*ânara is the year: this is why it is one on twelve potsherds.

16. And as to why there is a barley pap for Varu*n*a; he thereby frees the creatures from every snare of Varu*n*a, from all that comes from Varu*n*a[2];

[1] That is to say, he is either to perform the Vais*v*ânara on one, and the Vâru*n*a one on the next—in which case a different barhis, or altar-covering of sacrificial grass, would be needed—or he may perform them both on one and the same day, with the same barhis serving for both.

[2] See III, 8, 5, 10 where I translated, 'from all (guilt) against Varu*n*a;' varu*n*ya, doubtless, implies both the guilt incurred by the infringement of Varu*n*a's sacred laws, and the punishment inflicted by him. As regards the 'swearing by Varu*n*a (?)' there referred to, see *Ri*k S. X, 97, 16 where the conjurer mutters: 'May they (the plants) free me from the (evil) resulting from the curse and from Varu*n*a;'—mu*ñk*antu mâ *s*apathyâd atho varu*n*yâd uta.

and those creatures of his are produced sound and faultless: 'May I be consecrated for sound and faultless creatures (or subjects)!' he thinks.

17. A bull is the fee for the Vaisvânara (oblation); for Vaisvânara is the year, and Pragâpati is the year; and the bull is the Pragâpati (lord of creatures or generation) among cows: therefore a bull is the fee for the Vaisvânara. A black cloth for the Vâruna (oblation), for what is black belongs to Varuna. If he cannot obtain a black one, any kind of cloth will do: it is by its knots that the cloth belongs to Varuna, for the knot is sacred to Varuna.

Third Adhyâya. First Brâhmana.

1. Having taken up both (the Gârhapatya and Âhavaniya) fires on the two kindling-sticks[1], he goes to the house of the Commander of the army, and prepares a cake on eight potsherds for Agni Anîkavat; for Agni is the head (anîka) of the gods, and the commander is the head of the army: hence for Agni Anîkavat. And he, the commander, assuredly is one of his (the king's) jewels[2]: it is for

[1] Each of the two 'aranis' is held for a moment to one of the two fires, which are thereby supposed to become inherent in them till they are 'churned out' again for the new offering fire required. For this 'mounting' of the fire see part i, p. 396.

[2] Ratna, jewel, precious thing; whence the eleven offerings described in this section are called ratna-havis, or ratninâm havîmshi; the recipients of these sacrificial honours, on the part of the newly-consecrated king, being called ratninah, 'possessed of the Jewel (offering).'—In the ritual of the Black Yagus (Taitt. S. I, 8, 9; Taitt. Br. I, 7, 3) the order of the Ratninah, at whose houses these oblations are performed on successive days, is as follows:—1. Brahman priest (a pap to Brihaspati); 2. Râganya (a cake of eleven kapâlas to Indra); 3. Consecrated Queen (pap to

him that he is thereby consecrated (or quickened), and him he makes his own faithful (follower). The sacrificial fee for this (jewel-offering) consists in gold; for Agni's is that sacrifice, and gold is Agni's seed: therefore the sacrificial fee consists in gold.

2. And on the following day, he goes to the house of the Purohita (the king's court chaplain), and prepares a pap for *Bri*haspati; for *Bri*haspati is the Purohita of the gods, and that (court chaplain) is the Purohita ('praepositus') of that (king): hence it is for *Bri*haspati. And he, the Purohita, assuredly is one of his (the king's) jewels: it is for him that he is thereby consecrated, and him he makes his own faithful follower. The sacrificial fee for this is a white-backed bullock; for to *Bri*haspati belongs that upper region, and there above lies that path of Aryaman (the sun)[1]: therefore the fee for the Bârhaspatya (oblation) is a white-backed (bullock).

3. And on the following day he prepares a cake on eleven potsherds for Indra at the dwelling of him who is being consecrated (the king); for Indra is the Kshatra (ruling power), and he who is consecrated is

Aditi); 4. The king's favourite wife (pap to Bhaga); 5. A discarded wife (pap to Nir*ri*ti); 6. Commander of the army (cake of eight kap. to Agni); 7. Sûta (charioteer, Sây.—cake of ten kap. to Varu*n*a); 8. Grâma*n*î (cake of seven kap. to Maruts); 9. Kshatt*ri* (chamberlain, or superintendent of seraglio, Sây.—cake of twelve kap. to Savit*ri*); 10. Sa*m*grahît*ri* (treasurer, Sây.—cake of two kap. to A*s*vins); 11. Bhâgadugha (collector of taxes, Sây.—pap to Pûshan); 12. Akshâvâpa (dyûtakâra, superintendent of gambling, Sây.—gavîdhuka pap to Rudra).—Finally the king offers in his own house two cake-oblations (of eleven kapâlas) to Indra Sutrâman (the good protector) and Indra A*m*homu*k* (the deliverer from trouble).

[1] Whence the back of that upper region is white, or bright.

the Kshatra: hence it is for Indra. The sacrificial fee for this is a bull, for the bull is Indra's own (animal).

4. And on the following day, he goes to the dwelling of the Queen, and prepares a pap for Aditi; for Aditi is this Earth, and she is the wife of the gods; and that (queen) is the wife of that (king): hence it is for Aditi. And she, the Queen, assuredly is one of his (the king's) jewels: it is for her that he is thereby consecrated, and he makes her his own faithful (wife). The sacrificial fee, on her part, is a milch cow; for this (earth) is, as it were, a milch cow: she yields to men all their desires; and the milch cow is a mother, and this (earth) is, as it were, a mother: she bears (or sustains) men. Hence the fee is a milch cow.

5. And on the following day, he goes to the house of the Sûta (court-minstrel and chronicler), and prepares a barley pap for Varu*n*a; for the Sûta is a spiriter (sava), and Varu*n*a is the spiriter of the gods: therefore it is for Varu*n*a. And he, the Sûta, assuredly is one of his (the king's) jewels: it is for him that he is thereby consecrated; and him he makes his own faithful (follower). The sacrificial fee for this one is a horse, for the horse is Varu*n*a's own.

6. And on the following day, he goes to the house of the Headman (Grâma*n*î[1]), and prepares a cake

[1] The exact function of this officer is not clearly defined. Though the term is also used of an ordinary village headman (Patel, Adhikârin, Adigar), this could hardly apply here. Sâya*n*a, on one passage, indeed explains the term by 'Grâma*m* nayati,' but elsewhere he explains it by 'Grâmâ*n*â*m* netâ;' and some such meaning it may perhaps have here,—the head of communal administration, either for a district (like one of Manu's lords of a hundred, or a

on seven potsherds for the Maruts; for the Maruts are the peasants, and the headman is a peasant: therefore it is for the Maruts. And he, the headman, assuredly is one of his (the king's) jewels: it is for him that he is thereby consecrated, and him he makes his own faithful follower. The sacrificial fee for this (jewel) is a spotted bullock, for in such a spotted bullock there is abundance of colours; and the Maruts are the clans (or peasants), and the clan means abundance; therefore the sacrificial fee is a spotted bullock.

7. And on the following day he goes to the house of the Chamberlain (kshatt*ri*), and prepares a cake on either twelve, or eight, potsherds for Savit*ri*; for Savit*ri* is the impeller (prasavit*ri*) of the gods, and the chamberlain is an impeller: hence it is for Savit*ri*. And he, the chamberlain, assuredly is one of his (the king's) jewels: it is for him that he thereby is consecrated, and him he makes his own faithful (follower). The sacrificial fee for this (jewel) is a reddish-white draught-bullock; for Savit*ri* is he that burns yonder, and he (the sun) indeed moves along; and the draught-bullock also moves along, when yoked. And as to why it is a reddish-white one;—reddish-white indeed is he (the sun) both in rising and in setting: therefore the sacrificial fee is a reddish-white draught-bullock.

8. And on the following day he goes to the house

thousand villages), or for the whole country. If, however, the headman of a single village be intended (as the coupling of the office with the Maruts might lead one to suppose), he would probably be a hereditary territorial proprietor residing near the place where the inauguration ceremony takes place. Cf. V, 4, 4, 18; and Zimmer, Altindisches Leben, p. 171.

of the Charioteer (samgrahitri), and prepares a cake on two potsherds for the Asvins; for the two Asvins are of the same womb; and so are the chariot fighter[1] and the driver (sârathi) of the same womb (standing-place), since they stand on one and the same chariot: hence it is for the Asvins. And he, the charioteer, assuredly is one of his (the king's) jewels: it is for him that he is thereby consecrated, and him he makes his own faithful follower. The sacrificial fee for this (jewel) is a pair of twin bullocks, for such twin bullocks are of the same womb. If he cannot obtain twins, two bullocks produced by successive births (of the same cow) may also form the sacrificial fee, for such also are of the same womb.

9. And on the following day he goes to the house

[1] Savyashthri (otherwise savyeshthri, savyeshtha;—savyastha, Kânva rec.) is explained by the commentaries as a synonym of sârathi, charioteer (with which it is compounded in savyeshtha-sârathî, Taitt. Br. I, 7, 9, 1, where Sâyana makes them the two charioteers standing on the left and right side of the warrior), but it seems more probable that the former terms refer to the warrior (παραβάτης) himself (as savyashthâ, Atharva-veda VIII, 8, 23, undoubtedly does), who stands on the left side of the driver (sârathi, ἡνίοχος); the change of meaning being perhaps due to caste scruples about so close an association between the Kshatriya warrior and his Sûdra servant, as is implied in this and other passages. (Cf. V, 3, 2, 2 with note.)—On Taitt. S. I, 8, 9, Sâyana explains samgrahitri as the treasurer (dhanasamgrahakartâ kosâdhyakshah), but on I, 8, 16 optionally as treasurer or charioteer; while the Sûta is I, 8, 9 identified by him with the charioteer (sârathi). It is more probable, however, that at the time of the Brâhmana the Sûta occupied much the same position as that assigned to him in the epics, viz. that of court-bard and chronicler. The connection of the samgrahîtri with the Asvins can also scarcely be said to favour the interpretation of the term proposed by Sâyana (who, moreover, is himself compelled, on Taitt. S. I, 8, 15; Taitt. Br. I, 7, 10, 6, to take it in the sense of charioteer).

of the Carver (bhâgadugha[1]), and prepares a pap for Pûshan, for Pûshan is carver to the gods; and that (officer) is carver to that (king): therefore it is for Pûshan. And he, the carver, assuredly is one of his (the king's) jewels: it is for him that he is thereby consecrated, and him he makes his own faithful follower. The sacrificial fee for this (jewel) is a dark-grey bullock: the significance of such a one being the same as at the Trisha*m*yukta[2].

10. And on the following day, having brought together gavedhukâ (seeds) from the houses of the Keeper of the dice (akshâvâpa[3]) and the Huntsman (govikartana[4]), he prepares a gavedhukâ pap for Rudra at the house of him who is consecrated. These two, while being two jewels (of the king), he makes one for the purpose of completeness. And as to why he performs this offering,—Rudra is hankering after that (cow) which is killed here in this hall;

[1] The meaning 'tax-gatherer, collector of tithes (or rather, of the sixth part of produce)' assigned to the term by Sâya*n*a, both here, and on Taitt. S. I, 8, 9, might seem the more natural one, considering the etymology of the term. See, however, the explanation given of it in our Brâhma*n*a I, 1, 2, 17:—'Pûshan is bhâgadugha (distributor of portions) to the gods, who places with his hands the food before them.' This clearly is Homer's *δαιτρός*,—Od. I, 141-2:

δαιτρὸς δὲ κρειῶν πίνακας παρέθηκεν ἀείρας
παντοίων, παρὰ δέ σφι τίθει χρύσεια κύπελλα.

[2] See V, 2, 5, 8.

[3] 'The thrower, or keeper, of the dice,' according to Sâya*n*a. At V, 4, 4, 6 the verb â-vap is used of the throwing the dice into the hand of the player; and it is perhaps that function of the keeper of the dice which is meant to be expressed by the term ('der Zuwerfer der Würfel').

[4] Literally, the cutter up of cows, the (beef-) butcher. But according to Sâya*n*a, this official was the constant companion of his master in the chase.

now Rudra is Agni (fire), and the gaming-board being fire, and the dice being its coals, it is him (Rudra) he thereby pleases. And verily whosoever, that knows this thus, performs the Râgasûya, in his house that approved (cow) is killed. And he, the keeper of dice, and the huntsman, are (each of them) assuredly one of his (the king's) jewels: it is for these two that he is thereby consecrated, and these two he makes his own faithful followers. The sacrificial fee for this (jewel) is a bicoloured bullock—either one with white fore-feet, or a white-tailed one,—a claw-shaped knife, and a dice-board[1] with a horse-hair band[2]; for that is what belongs to those two[3].

11. And on the following day he goes to the house of the Courier, and having taken ghee in four ladlings, he offers the ghee to the way, with, 'May the way graciously accept of the ghee, hail!' For the courier is to be dispatched, and when dispatched goes on his way: therefore he offers the ghee to the way. And he, the courier, assuredly is one of his (the king's) jewels: it is for him that he is thereby consecrated, and him he makes his own faithful follower. The sacrificial fee for this (jewel) consists in a skin-covered bow, leathern quivers, and a red turban, for that is what belongs to him.

12. These are the eleven jewels (ratna) he completes; for of eleven syllables consists the Trish/ubh, and the Trish/ubh is vigour: it is for the sake

[1] Or, a dice-box, as 'akshâvapanam' is explained by some commentaries,—akshâ upyante ssminn ity akshâvapanam aksha(?aksha-dyûta-)sthânâvapanapâtram, Sây.

[2] Or, fastened with a hair-chain (romasragâ prabaddham, Sây.).

[3] That is to say, the knife and the dice-board are the objects those two officials have chiefly to do with.

of vigour that he completes the (eleven) jewels. Then as to why he performs the oblations of the Ratnins: it is their king he becomes; it is for them that he thereby is consecrated, and it is them he makes his own faithful followers.

13. And on the following day he goes to the house of a discarded (wife), and prepares a pap for Nirriti;—a discarded wife is one who has no son. He cooks the pap for Nirriti of black rice, after splitting the grains with his nails. He offers it with (Vâg. S. IX, 35), 'This, O Nirriti, is thy share: accept it graciously, hail!' For a wife that is without a son, is possessed with Nirriti (destruction, calamity); and whatever of Nirriti's nature there is in her, that he thereby propitiates, and thus Nirriti does not take possession of him while he is consecrated. The fee for this (oblation) consists of a black, decrepit, diseased cow; for such a one also is possessed with Nirriti. He says to her (the wife), 'Let her not dwell this day in my dominion[1]!' thus he removes evil from himself.

SECOND BRÂHMANA.

1. After the 'jewels' he offers (a pap) to Soma and Rudra. It is cooked in milk from a white (cow) which has a white calf. And as to why, after the 'jewels,' he offers (a pap) to Soma and Rudra.

2. Now, once upon a time, Svarbhânu, the Âsura, struck the sun with darkness, and stricken with darkness he did not shine[2]. Soma and Rudra

[1] According to the commentary on Kâty. Sr. XV, 3, 35 she has to betake herself to a Brâhman's house, where the king has no power.

[2] According to Rig-veda V, 40, 5–9 (cf. Sat. Br. IV, 3, 4, 23

removed that darkness of his; and freed from evil he burns yonder. And in like manner does that (king) thereby enter darkness,—or darkness enters him,—when he puts those unworthy of sacrifice[1] in contact with the sacrifice; and he does indeed now put those unworthy of sacrifice—either *S*ûdras or whomever else—in contact with the sacrifice. It is Soma and Rudra who remove that darkness of his; and freed from evil he becomes consecrated. And as to why it is cooked in milk from a white (cow) which has a white calf,—darkness is black: that darkness he removes. The sacrificial fee for this (oblation) is a white (cow) which has a white calf.

3. Even he who, while being qualified for fame, is not yet famous, may perform that offering. Now he who is learned (in the Veda), while being qualified for fame, is not famous; and he who is not famous, is covered with darkness: that darkness of his Soma and Rudra thereby remove; and freed from evil he becomes a very light by his prosperity and renown.

4. Thereupon he prepares a pap for Mitra and B*ri*haspati[2]. For verily he who departs from the

with note) it was Atri who restored the light of the sun. Professor Ludwig (Bohemian Academy of Sciences, Sitzungsber., May, 1885) has tried to prove that solar eclipses (partly available for chronological purposes) are referred to in this and some other passages of the hymns. Compare also Professor Whitney's remarks thereon, Proceedings of Am. Or. Soc., Oct. 1885, p. xvii.

[1] That is, some of those officials of his to whom the ratnahavis were offered; Sâya*n*a specifying 'the Commander of the army and others' as *S*ûdras; and the 'Huntsman and others' as of whatsoever (low) caste.

[2] According to the Taittirîya ritualists this double oblation forms part of the dîkshâ, or initiation ceremony (V, 3, 3, 1). See Taitt. S., vol. ii, p. 108.

path of the sacrifice stumbles; and he does indeed depart from the path of the sacrifice, when he puts those unworthy of sacrifice in contact with the sacrifice, and he does indeed now put those unworthy of sacrifice—either *S*ûdras or whomever else—in contact with the sacrifice. And the path of the sacrifice is Mitra and B*ri*haspati; for Mitra is the Brahman, and the Brahman is the sacrifice; and B*ri*haspati is the Brahman, and the Brahman is the sacrifice. Thus he returns again to the path of the sacrifice; and as soon as he has returned to the path of the sacrifice he is consecrated: therefore he prepares a pap for Mitra and B*ri*haspati.

5. The course of this (is as follows). Any a*s*vattha branch broken off by itself, either on the eastern or on the northern side (of the tree), from that he makes a vessel (to hold the pap) for Mitra; for that which is hewn by the axe belongs to Varu*n*a; but that which is broken off by itself belongs to Mitra: therefore he makes the vessel for Mitra from a branch broken off by itself.

6. Thereupon having curdled the (milk into) curds, and poured it into a leathern bag; and having put (the horses) to the cart, and fastened (the bag on the cart), he tells it to 'fly away.' This is that (kind of) fresh butter which is self-produced[1]; for that which is churned belongs to Varu*n*a, and that which is self-produced belongs to Mitra: therefore it is self-produced butter.

7. They divide the rice-grains into two parts: the smaller and broken ones belong to B*ri*haspati,

[1] That is, produced in the leathern bottle without further direct human agency, and by the mere motion of the cart.

and the larger and unbroken ones to Mitra. For Mitra injures no one, nor does any one injure Mitra; neither a kusa stalk nor a thorn pricks him, nor has he any scar; for Mitra is every one's friend (mitram).

8. He then puts the pap for Bri*haspati on (the fire), covers it with the vessel for Mitra's (pap), pours the butter (into the latter), and throws in the (larger) rice-grains. It is cooked merely by the hot steam[1]; for what is cooked by fire belongs to Varu*n*a, and what is cooked by hot steam belongs to Mitra: therefore it is cooked by hot steam. Making cuttings from both these sacrificial dishes, he says, 'Pronounce the invitatory prayer to Mitra and Bri*haspati!' Having called for the *S*raushat, he says, 'Pronounce the offering-prayer to Mitra and Bri*haspati!' and offers as the Vashat is uttered.

THE ABHISHE*K*ANÎYA[2], OR CONSECRATION CEREMONY.

THIRD BRÂHMANA.

1. He performs the initiation ceremony. On the day of preparation he seizes the victim for Agni

[1] That is, by the steam rising from the Bri*haspati pap in the bottom vessel.

[2] The Abhishe*k*anîya (or Abhisheka, literally 'the sprinkling'), the Consecration ceremony (corresponding to the Anointment of modern times), requires for its performance five days, viz. one dikshâ (initiation ceremony), three upasads, and one sutyâ or Soma-day, the particular form of Soma-sacrifice being the Ukthya (part ii, p. 325, note 2). The Dîkshâ is performed immediately after the expiration of the dark fortnight following the full-moon of Phalgunî, that is to say, on the first day of *K*aitra (about the middle of March).—According to Kâty. XV, 3, 47 both the Abhishe*k*anîya and Da*s*apeya require special offering-places, the latter being north of the former. Cf. note on V, 4, 5, 13.—As regards

and Soma. Having performed the offering of the omentum thereof, he prepares a cake on eleven potsherds for Agni and Soma[1]. Thereupon the offerings of the Divine Quickeners (Devasû) are prepared.

2. For Savit*ri* Satyaprasava (of true impulse) he prepares a cake from fast-grown (plâ*s*uka) rice[2], on either twelve, or eight, potsherds; for Savit*ri* is the impeller (prasavit*ri*) of the gods: 'May I be quickened[3], impelled by Savit*ri*!' thus (he thinks). And as to (its being) of fast-grown rice: 'May they quickly impel me!' he thinks.

3. For Agni G*ri*hapati (the house-lord) he then prepares a cake on eight potsherds from quick-grown (â*s*u) rice[4]; for the house-lord's position means prosperity: as much as he (the king) rules over, over

the chants (stotra) of the Consecration ceremony, the Pavamâna-stotras are chanted in the thirty-twofold, the Âg*y*a-stotras in the fifteenfold, the P*ri*sh*th*a-stotras in the seventeenfold, and the Agnish*t*oma-sâman and Uktha-stotras in the twenty-onefold mode of chanting (stoma). Pa*ñk*. Br. 18, 10, 9. The Bahishpavamâna is specially constructed so as to consist of the following parts,—Sâma-veda II, 978–80; further six so-called sambhâryâ verses; further II, 125–27; II, 4–6; II, 431–3; II, 128–30; II, 555–59; II, 7–9; II, 981–83; see Pa*ñk*. Br. 18, 8, 7 seq.—The Taittirîya ritual (Taitt. Br. I, 8, 7 seq.), on the other hand, prescribes for the Pavamâna-stotras, the thirty-four-versed stoma, commencing the Bahishpavamâna by II, 920; II, 431, &c.

[1] This is the ordinary Pa*s*u-puro*d*â*s*a, or cake of animal (offering). See part ii, p. 199, note 2 (where read Agni and Soma, instead of Indra and Agni).

[2] That is, according to Sâya*n*a, rice which has sprung up again and ripens very rapidly. Taitt. S. I, 8, 10 has 'â*s*u' instead, for which see next paragraph.

[3] Or, consecrated (sû).

[4] That is, according to Sâya*n*a, rice ripening in sixty days. The Taitt. S. prescribes a cake of black rice for Agni.

that Agni, the house-lord, leads him to hold the position of a master of the house. And as to its being of quick-grown rice: 'May they quickly lead me!' so he thinks.

4. For Soma Vanaspati (the wood-lord or tree) he then prepares a pap of *s*yâmâka millet: thereby Soma, the wood-lord, quickens him for the plants. And as to its being prepared of *s*yâmâka,—they, the *s*yâmâkas among plants doubtless are most manifestly Soma's own: therefore it is prepared of *s*yâmâka grain.

5. For B*ri*haspati Vâ*k*[1] (speech) he then prepares a pap of wild rice: thereby B*ri*haspati quickens him for speech. And as to its being prepared of wild rice,—B*ri*haspati is the Brahman, and they, the wild rice-plants, are ripened by the Brahman[2]: hence it is prepared of wild rice.

6. For Indra *G*yesh*th*a (the most excellent) he then prepares a pap of red rice-grains (hâyana)[3]: thereby Indra, the most excellent, leads him to excellence (or, lordship). And as to its being prepared of red rice: outstanding doubtless are those plants, the red rice, and outstanding is Indra: therefore it is prepared of red rice.

7. For Rudra Pa*s*upati (lord of beasts) he then prepares a Raudra pap of gavedhukâ seeds (coix barbata): thereby Rudra, the lord of beasts, quickens

[1] B*ri*haspati Vâkpati (lord of speech), according to the Black Yagus, where the order of the 'Divine Quickeners' is moreover somewhat different.

[2] ? Or cooked by the Brahman, that is by Brâhmans, when living the life of hermits or ascetics.

[3] The Taitt. S. prescribes a cake prepared of large rice (mahâvrîhi).

him for cattle. And as to its being prepared of gavedhukâ seed;—that God is (the recipient of) refuse (remains of offering), and gavedhukâ seeds are refuse: therefore it is (prepared) of gavedhukâ seed.

8. For Mitra Satya (the True) he then prepares a pap of Nâmba[1] seed: thereby Mitra the True quickens him for the Brahman. And as to its being prepared of Nâmba seed,—to Varu*n*a, no doubt, belong those plants which grow in ploughed ground; but those, the Nâmba plants, belong to Mitra: therefore it is (prepared) of Nâmba seed.

9. For Varu*n*a Dharmapati (the lord of the law) he then prepares a Varu*n*a pap of barley: thereby Varu*n*a, the lord of the law, makes him lord of the law; and that truly is the supreme state, when one is lord of the law; for whosoever attains to the supreme state, to him they come in (matters of) law: therefore to Varu*n*a Dharmapati.

10. He then proceeds with the cake for Agni-Soma. The Svish*t*ak*ri*t of that (oblation) remains yet unoffered, when he proceeds with those (other) oblations.

11. Thereupon, taking hold of him (the Sacrificer) by the right arm, he mutters (Vâg. S. IX, 39, 40), 'May Savit*ri* quicken thee for (powers of) quickening (ruling)[2], Agni for householders, Soma for trees, B*ri*haspati for speech, Indra for lordship, Rudra for cattle, Mitra for truth, Varu*n*a for the lord of the law.'

12. 'Quicken him, O gods, to be unrivalled!'

---

[1] The Taitt. S. and Br. read 'âmba' instead, 'a kind of grain,' according to Sâya*n*a.

[2] Or, perhaps, 'on the part of the quickeners (rulers, savânâm).'

—he thereby says, 'Quicken him, O gods, so as to be without an enemy;'—'for great chiefdom, for great lordship!' in this there is nothing obscure;—'for man-rule!' 'for the ruling of men,' he thereby says;—'for Indra's energy!' 'for vigour' he means to say when he says, 'for Indra's energy;'—'him, the son of such and such (a man), the son of such and such (a woman),'—whatever be his parentage, with reference to that he says this;—'of such and such a people,' that is to say, of the people whose king he is;—'this man, O ye (people)[1], is your king, Soma is the king of us Brâhmans!' He thereby causes everything here to be food for him (the king); the Brâhman alone he excepts: therefore the Brâhman is not to be fed upon, for he has Soma for his king.

13. Now those gods have the power of quickening, whence their name 'devasû' (Divine Quickeners). It is those gods who now quicken him thus, and quickened (consecrated) by them he will be consecrated on the morrow.

14. They are double-named, for a coupling means strength: 'May the strong quicken (him),' thus he thinks, and therefore they are double-named.

15. He now says, 'Pronounce the invitatory prayer to Agni Svish*t*ak*ri*t.' And as to why that ceremony is performed here between two offerings[2],—verily Pragâpati is that sacrifice which is here performed, and from which all these creatures were produced,—

[1] Here the name of the people, e.g. 'O ye Kurus, O ye Pañ*k*âlas!' is inserted. The Taitt. S. reads, 'O ye Bharatâ*h*.'

[2] That is to say, the oblations to the 'Divine Quickeners,' which were inserted between the chief oblation of the (Agnishomîya) pa*s*upurodâ*s*a and the Svish*t*ak*ri*t of it; see above, parag. 10.

and so they are even now produced after this one. Thus he places him (the Sacrificer) in the very middle of that Pragâpati, and quickens him in the middle: this is why that ceremony is performed between two offerings. Having called for the Sraushat, he says, 'Urge for Agni Svishtakrit!' and offers as the Vashat is pronounced.

FOURTH BRÂHMANA.

1. He collects (various kinds of) water. The reason why he collects water, is that—water being vigour—he thereby collects vigour, the essence of the waters.

2. In a vessel of udumbara wood,—the udumbara (ficus glomerata) being sustenance, (that is) food—for the obtainment of sustenance, food: hence in an udumbara vessel (he mixes the different liquids).

3. He first takes (water)[1] from the (river) Sarasvatî, with (Vâg. S. X, 1), 'The gods took honey-sweet water,'—whereby he says, 'the gods took water full of essence;'—'sapful, deemed king-quickening,'—by 'sapful' he means to say, 'full of essence;' and by 'deemed king-quickening' he means to say, '(water) which is recognised as king-quickening:'—'wherewith they anointed Mitra and Varuna,' for therewith they did anoint (sprinkle) Mitra and Varuna;—'wherewith they guided

[1] This water gathered from an adjacent river and pond, with some admixture of genuine water from the sacred river Sarasvatî—whence the whole water is also called 'sârasvatya âpah'—is to be used partly in the place of the ordinary Vasatîvarî water, and partly for the consecration or anointment (sprinkling) of the king. The different kinds of water or liquids are first taken in separate vessels of palâsa (butea frondosa) wood, and then poured together into the udumbara vessel.

Indra past his enemies,' for therewith they indeed guided Indra past the fiends, the Rakshas. Therewith he sprinkles him,—Sarasvatî being (the goddess of) Speech: it is with speech he thereby sprinkles him. This is one kind of water: it is that he now brings.

4. Thereupon the Adhvaryu, having taken ghee in four ladlings, steps down into the water, and takes the two waves which flow away (in different directions) after an animal or a man has stept (or plunged) into it.

5. The one which rises in front of him he catches up with (Vâg. S. X, 2), 'Thou art the male's wave, a bestower of kingship: bestow kingship on me, hail!—Thou art the male's wave, a bestower of kingship: bestow kingship on N. N.!'

6. He then catches up that (wave) which rises up behind him with, 'Thou art the lord of a host of males, a bestower of kingship: bestow kingship on me, hail!—Thou art the lord of a host of males, a bestower of kingship: bestow kingship on N. N.!' With that (water) he sprinkles; for indeed that is the vigour of the water which rises when either beast or man plunges into it: it is with vigour he thus sprinkles him. This is one kind of water: it is that he now brings.

7. He then takes flowing (water) with (Vâg. S. X, 3), 'Task-plying ye are, bestowers of kingship: bestow ye kingship on me, hail!—Task-plying ye are, bestowers of kingship: bestow ye kingship on N. N.!' With that (water) he sprinkles; for with vigour these (waters) flow, whence nothing stops them flowing along: it is

with vigour he thus sprinkles him. This is one kind of water: it is that he now brings.

8. He then takes such (water) as flows against the stream of the flowing water with, 'Powerful ye are, bestowers of kingship: bestow ye kingship on me, hail!—Powerful ye are, bestowers of kingship: bestow ye kingship on N. N.!' With that (water) he sprinkles, for with vigour indeed those (waters) flow against the stream of the flowing ones: it is with vigour he thus sprinkles him. This is one kind of water: it is that he now brings.

9. He then takes (water) that flows off (the main current) with, 'Overflowing waters ye are, bestowers of kingship: bestow ye kingship on me, hail!—Overflowing waters ye are, bestowers of kingship: bestow ye kingship on N. N.!' With that (water) he sprinkles. Now that (flow of water), after separating itself from that (main current), comes to be that again [1]; and so there is in his kingdom even one belonging to some other kingdom, and even that man from another kingdom he absorbs: thus he (the Adhvaryu) bestows abundance upon him (the king), and it is with abundance that he thus consecrates him. This is one kind of water: it is that he now brings.

10. He then takes the lord of rivers (sea-water) with, 'Thou art the lord of waters, a bestower of kingship: bestow thou kingship on me, hail!—Thou art the lord of waters, a bestower of kingship: bestow thou kingship on N. N.!'

[1] That is to say, it ultimately flows back and mingles again with the main current.

With that (water) he sprinkles him; and that lord of rivers (the ocean) being the same as the lord of waters, he thereby makes him (the king) the lord of the people. This is one kind of water: it is that he now brings.

11. He then takes (water from) a whirlpool with, 'Thou art the offspring of the waters, a bestower of kingship: bestow thou kingship on me, hail!—Thou art the offspring of the waters, a bestower of kingship: bestow thou kingship on N. N.!' With that (water) he sprinkles. Now the waters enclose the offspring (embryo): he thus makes him the offspring of the people. This is one kind of water: it is that he now brings.

12. Then what standing pool of flowing water there is in a sunny spot, that (water) he takes with (Vâg. S. X, 4), 'Sun-skinned ye are, bestowers of kingship: bestow ye kingship on me, hail! —Sun-skinned ye are, bestowers of kingship: bestow ye kingship on N. N.!' With that (water) he sprinkles: it is with lustre he thereby sprinkles him, and makes him sun-skinned. Now it is to Varuna that those waters belong which, (whilst being part) of flowing water, do not flow; and Varuna's quickening (sava) is that Râgasûya: therefore he sprinkles him therewith. This is one kind of water: it is that he now brings.

13. He then catches such (water) as it rains while the sun shines, with, 'Lustrous as the sun ye are, bestowers of kingship: bestow ye kingship on me, hail!—Lustrous as the sun ye are, bestowers of kingship: bestow ye kingship on N. N.!' With this (water) he sprinkles: it is with lustre he thereby sprinkles him, and lustrous

as the sun he thereby makes him. And pure indeed is such water as it rains while the sun shines, for before it has reached this (earth), he catches it: he thus makes him pure thereby. This is one kind of water: it is that he now brings.

14. He then takes (water) from a pond with, 'Pleasing ye are, bestowers of kingship: bestow ye kingship on me!—Pleasing ye are, bestowers of kingship: bestow ye kingship on N. N.!' With that (water) he sprinkles: he thereby makes the people steady and faithful to him. This is one kind of water: it is that he now brings.

15. He then draws (water) from a well with, 'Fold-dwellers ye are, bestowers of kingship: bestow ye kingship on me, hail!—Fold-dwellers ye are, bestowers of kingship: bestow ye kingship on N. N.!' With this (water) he sprinkles. He thereby brings (some of) the water which is beyond this (earth), and also (he does so) for the completeness of the waters, this is why he sprinkles him therewith. This is one kind of water: it is that he now brings.

16. He then takes dew-drops[1] with, 'Devoted[2]

[1] Sâya*n*a explains 'prushvâ' by 'nîhârâ*h*' (mist water), the commentators on Kâty. XV, 4, 38, by 'hoar-frost.'

[2] It is difficult to see in what sense the author takes vâ*s*a. While Mahîdhara (Vâ*g*. S. X, 4) explains it by 'pleasing' or 'desirable' (u*s*yante *g*anai*h* kâmyante*s*nnanishpattihetutvât); Sâya*n*a leaves a choice between that meaning (sarvai*h* kâmyamânâ) and that of 'obedient, submissive' (yadvâ va*s*yâ stha, nîhâro hi nadîpravâhavan manushyâdigatim na pratibadhnâti, ato va*s*yatvam prushvâ*n*âm annâdyâtmakatvam upapâdayati; MS. I. O. 657). The St. Petersburg dictionary gives the meaning 'submissive,' but leaves it doubtful whether it may not be derived from va*s*a, 'fat, grease.'

ye are, bestowers of kingship: bestow ye kingship on me, hail!—Devoted ye are, bestowers of kingship: bestow ye kingship on N. N.!' With that (water) he sprinkles: it is with food he thereby consecrates him, and food he thereby bestows upon him. For even as this fire burns up (the wood) so does that sun yonder, even in rising, burn up the plants, the food. But those waters coming down, quench that (heat), for if those waters were not to come down, there would be no food left remaining here: it is with food he thus sprinkles him. This is one kind of water: it is that he now brings.

17. He then takes honey with, 'Most powerful ye are, bestowers of kingship: bestow ye kingship on me, hail!—Most powerful ye are, bestowers of kingship: bestow ye kingship on N. N.!' With this (water) he sprinkles, and it is by the essence of the waters and plants that he thereby sprinkles him. This is one kind of water: it is that he now brings.

18. He then takes embryonic (waters) of a calving cow with, 'Mighty ye are, bestowers of kingship: bestow ye kingship on me, hail!—Mighty ye are, bestowers of kingship: bestow ye kingship on N. N.!' With that (water) he sprinkles: it is with cattle he thereby consecrates him. This is one kind of water: it is that he now brings.

19. He then takes milk with, 'Man-supporting ye are, bestowers of kingship: bestow ye kingship on me, hail!—Man-supporting ye are, bestowers of kingship: bestow ye kingship on N.N.!' With that (water) he sprinkles:

it is with cattle he thereby consecrates him. This is one kind of water: it is that he now brings.

20. He then takes clarified butter with, 'All-supporting ye are, bestowers of kingship: bestow ye kingship on me, hail!—All-supporting ye are, bestowers of kingship: bestow ye kingship on N. N.!' With that (water) he sprinkles: it is with the essence of cattle he thereby consecrates him. This is one kind of water: it is that he now brings.

21. Having then caught up (moist) sun-motes with the hollow of his hands, he mixes them (with the other kinds of water), with, 'Self-ruling waters ye are, bestowers of kingship: bestow ye kingship on N. N.!' For those sun-motes are indeed self-ruling waters, since they are flowing, as it were, and, not yielding to one another's superiority, keep being now higher now lower: he thus thereby bestows self-ruling power upon him. This is one kind of water: it is that he now brings.

22. These then are seventeen (kinds of) water he brings together, for Pragâpati is seventeenfold, and Pragâpati is the sacrifice: that is why he brings together seventeen kinds of water.

23. Now sixteen kinds of water are those he offers upon; and he offers sixteen oblations: that makes thirty-two. On two of them he does not offer, viz. on the water from the Sarasvatî and on the sun-motes: that makes thirty-four. For three and thirty are the gods, and Pragâpati is the thirty-fourth: he thus makes him to be Pragâpati (the lord of creatures).

24. And as to why he takes (water) each time after offering,—the ghee, to be sure, is a thunder-

bolt: having won them, one by one, by means of that thunderbolt, the ghee, and made them his own, he takes them.

25. And as to why he does not offer on the (water) from the Sarasvatî,—Sarasvatî, to be sure, is (the goddess of) Speech, and the ghee is a thunderbolt: 'Lest I should injure (the goddess of) Speech!' thus (he thinks, and) therefore he does not offer on the water from the Sarasvatî.

26. And as to why he does not offer on the sun-motes: 'Lest I should offer that oblation in a doubtful way[1]!' thus (he thinks, and) therefore he does not offer on the sun-motes.

27. He pours them together into an udumbara vessel with, 'Let the honey-sweet mix with the honey-sweet!'—'Let those full of essence mix with those full of essence!' he thereby says;—'Winning great power (kshatra) for the Kshatriya!' in saying this he prays in a covert way for power to the Sacrificer.

28. He deposits them in front of the Maitrâvaruna's hearth, with, 'Unimpaired rest ye, the strengthful!'—'unimpaired by the Rakshas rest ye!' he thereby says; and by 'strengthful' he means to say 'powerful;' 'bestowing great power on the Kshatriya;'—in saying this he prays in an overt way for power to the Sacrificer.

Fifth Brâhmana.

1. He consecrates him at the midday Soma-feast. Now Pragâpati is that sacrifice which is here performed, and whence these creatures have been

[1] On account of the doubtful nature of the watery sun-motes.

produced,—and so they are even now produced after this one: he thus places him in the very middle of that Pragâpati, and consecrates him in the middle.

2. Before the Mâhendra (cup) has been drawn,—for that Mâhendra cup is Indra's special (nishkevalya) cup, and so is that Nishkevalya Stotra (hymn) and Nishkevalya *S*astra (recitation); and the Sacrificer is Indra: he thus consecrates him in his own resting-place. Hence before the Mâhendra (cup) has been drawn,—

3. He spreads a tiger-skin in front of the Maitrâvaru*n*a's hearth[1], with (Vâg. S. X, 5), 'Thou art Soma's beauty.' For because when Soma flowed through Indra he (Indra) thereupon became a tiger, therefore he is Soma's beauty: this is why he says, 'Thou art Soma's splendour;'—'may my beauty become like unto thine!' He thus bestows the tiger's beauty on him: therefore he says, 'May my beauty become like unto thine!'.

4. He then offers the Pârtha oblations. Now P*ri*thin Vainya was consecrated first of men. He desired that he might appropriate to himself all food. They offered up for him those (oblations), and he appropriated to himself all the food here on earth. They would even call forest beasts to him, saying, 'Come hither thou (beast) so and so, the king wants to cook thee!' Thus he appropriated all food here on earth; and verily he appropriates to himself all food for whom that knows this those (oblations) are offered.

5. There are twelve of them,—for there are

[1] Viz. before the 'waters' deposited there, according to V, 3, 4, 28.

twelve months in the year: therefore there are twelve of them.

6. Six he offers before, and six after, the consecration: he thereby places him in the very middle of that Pragâpati, and consecrates him in the middle.

7. Now of those which he offers before the consecration, B*ri*haspati is the last (recipient), and of those which he offers after the consecration, Indra is the first;—but B*ri*haspati is priestly dignity (brahma), and Indra is might, vigour: with these two kinds of vigour he thus encloses him on both sides.

8. Those which he offers before the consecration, he offers (resp.) with, 'To Agni hail!'—Agni is brightness (te*g*as): with brightness he thus sprinkles (endows) him;—'To Soma hail!'—Soma is princely power (kshatra): with princely power he thus sprinkles him;—'To Savit*ri* hail!'—Savit*ri* is the impeller of the gods: impelled by Savit*ri* he thus consecrates him;—'To Sarasvatî hail!'—Sarasvatî is Speech: he thus sprinkles him with Speech;—'To Pûshan hail!'—Pûshan is cattle: with cattle he thus sprinkles him;—'To B*ri*haspati hail!'—B*ri*haspati is priestly dignity: with priestly dignity he thus sprinkles him. These he offers before the consecration: these are called the Agni-named ones.

9. Those which he offers after the consecration, he offers (resp.) with, 'To Indra hail!'—Indra is vigour: with vigour he thus sprinkles him;—'To the roar hail!'—roar means vigour: with vigour he thus sprinkles him;—'To the noise hail!'—noise means vigour: with vigour he thus sprinkles him;—'To A*m*sa hail!'—A*m*sa is vigour: with vigour he thus sprinkles him;—'To Bhaga hail!'—Bhaga is vigour: with vigour he thus sprinkles

him;—'To Aryaman hail!'—he thus makes him the friend (aryaman) of everything here. These he offers after the consecration: these are called the Âditya-named[1] ones.

10. In front of the Maitrâvaruna's hearth are the (four) consecration vessels in which that consecration water is contained[2].

11. There is a palâsa (butea frondosa) one: with (the water of) that (vessel) a Brâhman sprinkles;—the Palâsa tree is priestly dignity (brahman): it is with priestly dignity that he sprinkles (endows) him.

12. There is an udumbara (ficus glomerata) one: therewith one of his own (kinsmen, or brothers) sprinkles. The udumbara tree means sustenance, (that is) food, and the 'own' means sustenance, for as far as a man's own goes, so far he does not hunger: thereby his 'own' is sustenance, and therefore one of his own (kinsmen) sprinkles with an udumbara (vessel).

13. There is one made of the foot (stem) of the nyagrodha (ficus indica): therewith a friendly (mitrya) Râganya sprinkles: for by its feet[3] the

[1] Viz. because three of the recipients of these libations—Amsa, Bhaga and Aryaman—belong to the deities called Âdityas, or sons of Aditi.

[2] The water in the Udumbara vessel is now distributed into these four (smaller) vessels.

[3] That is, by its pendant branches. It is well known that the ficus indica, or banyan-tree, as it is ordinarily called, has the habit of bending its branches down to the ground, which then strike root and develop new secondary trunks, so that a single tree may in course of time form a large grove. Hence the name here used for the tree (nyag-rodha, the downward-growing one). 'A family tends to multiply families around it, till it becomes the centre of a tribe, just as the banyan tends to surround itself with a forest of its own offspring.' Maclennan, Primitive Marriage, p. 269.

nyagrodha tree is supported, and by the friend (mitra) the Râganya (nobleman or king) is supported: therefore a friendly Râganya sprinkles with (the water of a vessel) made of the foot of a nyagrodha.

14. There is an asvattha (ficus religiosa) one: therewith a Vaisya sprinkles. Because Indra on that (former) occasion called upon the Maruts staying on the Asvattha tree[1], therefore a Vaisya sprinkles with an asvattha (vessel). These are the consecration vessels.

15. He then prepares two strainers (pavitra), with (Vâg. S. X, 6), 'Purifiers ye are, Vishnu's own;'—the significance is the same (as before[2]). He weaves gold (threads) into them. With them he purifies those consecration waters. As to why he weaves gold (threads) in,—gold is immortal life: that immortal life he lays into these (waters), and hence he weaves gold (threads) in.

16. He purifies with, 'By the impulse of Savitri I purify you with a flawless purifier, with the rays of the sun.' The significance is the same (as before[3]). 'Not downfallen thou art, the friend of Speech, born of heat,'—'unimpaired by the Rakshas' he means to say when he says, 'not downfallen;'—'the friend of Speech' —as long as there is water in the vital airs, so long (man) speaks with speech: therefore he says, 'the friend of Speech.'

[1] See above, p. 34, note 1. The Maruts are constantly identified with the Vis, or people (peasants, &c.) generally, whilst Indra is taken as the divine representative of the ruling class (the king and nobleman).

[2] See I, 1, 3, 1 (part i, p. 19).

[3] See I, 1, 3, 6 (part i, p. 21).

17. 'Born of heat' he says, for from fire springs smoke, from smoke the cloud, from the cloud rain,—it is from fire that these are produced: hence he says, 'born of heat.'

18. 'Soma's portion thou art;' for when they consecrate him with those (waters), then there is an oblation: therefore he says 'Soma's portion thou art;'—'Hail, spiriters of kings!'—it is with 'Hail' that he thus purifies them.

19. He distributes them over those (consecration) vessels, with (Vâg. S. X, 7), 'Playmates are these glorious waters;'—'not overbearing' he means to say, when he says 'playmates;' and by 'these glorious waters' he means to say 'the powerful ones;'—'unimpaired, active, enveloping,' he thereby means to say 'ye are unimpaired by the Rakshas;'—'In the habitations Varuna hath made a home;'—the habitations are the people (clans): 'in the people Varuna has made a support' he thereby says;—'he, the child of the waters, in the best of mothers;'—for he who performs the Râgasûya is indeed the child of the waters: therefore he says, 'the child of the waters, in the best of mothers.'

20. He then makes him (the king) put on garments. There is that one called târpya[1]; therein are

[1] This is variously explained, by Kâtyâyana and Sâyana, as a linen one, or simply one soaked in ghee, or a tripâna one—i. e. one made of triparna plants, or a thrice saturated one (with ghee)—or one woven out of materials derived from the tripâ plant. It is quite evident that they did not exactly know what to make of it. Indeed, it would almost seem as if the author of the Brâhmana himself was already doubtful as to the meaning of the term. Goldstücker (s.v. abhishekaniya) perhaps rightly takes it to mean a silk under-garment.

wrought[1] all forms of sacrifice: that he makes him put on, with (Vâg. S. X, 8), 'Thou art the inner caul of knighthood (kshatra)!' He thus causes him to be born from out of what is the inner caul (amnion) of knighthood.

21. He then makes him put on one of undyed wool, with, 'Thou art the outer caul of knighthood!' He thus causes him to be born from what is the outer caul (chorion) of knighthood.

22. He then throws over the mantle, with, 'Thou art the womb of knighthood!' He thus causes him to be born from what is the womb of knighthood.

23. He then draws the head-band together, and conceals it (tucks it under) in front[2], with, 'Thou art the navel of knighthood!' He thus places him in what is the navel of knighthood.

24. Now some wind it quite round about (the navel) saying, 'that (band) is his navel, and this navel goes all round.' But let him not do this, but let him merely tuck it under in front, for this navel is in front. And as to why he makes him put on the garments;—he thereby causes him to be born[3],

---

[1] According to the commentators, figures of sacrificial spoons, cups, &c., are sewn in by means of a needle.

[2] The commentators do not seem to be quite in accord in regard to this particular item of the ceremonial. The most natural explanation, however, seems to be this: the head-band (turban, ushnîsha) is wound (? once) round the head and tied behind; the ends being then drawn over the shoulders so as to hang down from the neck in the manner of a brahmanical cord (or like the ribbon of an order); and being finally tucked in under the mantle somewhere near the navel.

[3] Viz. inasmuch as the garments are intended to symbolically represent the vestures of the embryo and stages of birth.

thinking, 'I will anoint him when born:' that is why he makes him put on the garments.

25. Now some put off those garments[1], and make him put on again the garment of initiation. But let him not do this; for, the limbs[2] being his natural vestments, they deprive him of his limbs, of his native bodily form. The garment of initiation belongs to Varuna. Let him put on one of those same garments: he (the priest) thereby causes him to be furnished with his limbs, his native bodily form. The garment of initiation belongs to Varuna: he thus saves him from the Varunic garment of initiation.

26. And when he enters the bath[3] they throw it into (the water). This is a congruous[4] performance. After putting on one of those same garments he comes out (of the bath). Let him give away those (garments) either when the omentum of the barren cow has been offered[5], or at the completing oblation[6].

27. He (the Adhvaryu) then strings the bow, with, 'Thou art Indra's Vritra-killer;' for the bow

[1] This change of garments takes place optionally when the Mâhendra libation is about to be offered. Kâty. XV, 5, 16; 7, 23-26.

[2] That is, according to Sâyana, the skin, &c.

[3] That is, at the end of the Râgasûya. In case of the change of garments before the Mâhendra libation, the king keeps on the initiation garment in entering and coming out of the bath. This paragraph is of course put in here by anticipation, merely in order to state all that relates to the garments.

[4] Viz. inasmuch as it is in accordance with what is done at an ordinary Soma-sacrifice, at the end of which the Sacrificer and his wife enter the bath and come forth with fresh garments. See part ii, p. 385. In the present case the king is to enter the bath clothed in one of those three garments, and in coming out he is to put on another of them.

[5] See part ii, pp. 391-2.

[6] For the Udavasânîyâ-ishti, see ib. p. 389.

is indeed a V*ri*tra-killer, and the Sacrificer is Indra. —he is Indra in a twofold way, both as a Kshatriya, and as Sacrificer: therefore he says, 'Thou art Indra's V*ri*tra-killer.'

28. He then strokes the two arms[1], with, 'Mitra's thou art,—Varu*n*a's thou art;' for the bow is within the two arms, and by his two arms the Râ*g*anya pertains to Mitra and Varu*n*a: therefore he says, 'Mitra's thou art, Varu*n*a's thou art.' He hands it to him, with, 'May he slay V*ri*tra by thee!' whereby he means to say, 'May he slay by thee his spiteful enemy!'

29. He then hands him three arrows. That first one by which he pierces on shooting[2], that is one, that one is this earth, that one is called 'd*ri*bâ.' And the one by which (the enemy) being pierced lies either living or dead, that is the second, that is this air, that is called 'ru*g*â.' And the one with which he misses (his aim)[3], that is the third, that is yonder sky, that is called 'kshumâ.' For these are the three (kinds of) arrows: therefore he hands him three arrows.

30. These he hands to him with, 'Protect ye him in front[4]!—Protect ye him from behind! —Protect ye him from the side!—Protect ye

[1] Viz. the arms of the king, as it would seem, according to Sâya*n*a; but the arms (or ends) of the bow, according to Karka and Mahîdhara.

[2] Literally, on fixing (the arrow on the string); or perhaps, on hitting (the enemy).

[3] Sâya*n*a takes apa-râdhnoti in the sense of 'he hurts (or hits)' the enemy. In the Kâ*n*va text (Grantha MS.) the three arrows are called ru*g*â, d*ri*vâ, and kshupâ resp.

[4] Or perhaps,—whilst (he is) moving forward,—whilst moving backward,—whilst moving sideways.

him from (all) quarters!' Thus he makes all the quarters safe from arrows for him. And as to why he hands the bow to him;—this, the bow, truly is the nobleman's strength: it is because he thinks, 'I will consecrate him when endowed with strength!' that he hands the weapon to him[1].

31. Thereupon he makes him pronounce the âvid formulas[2] (Vâg. S. X, 9), 'In sight, ye mortals!' This is mysterious, for mysterious is Pragâpati: he thus announces him to Pragâpati, and this one approves of his consecration; and approved by him he is consecrated.

32. 'Present is Agni, the house-lord;'—Agni is the priesthood (brahman); he thus announces him to the priesthood; and it approves of his consecration, and approved by it he is consecrated.

33. 'Present is Indra, the far-famed;'—Indra is the nobility: he thus announces him to the nobility; and it approves of his consecration, and approved by it he is consecrated.

34. 'Present are Mitra and Varu*n*a, the upholders of the law;'—Mitra and Varu*n*a are the out-breathing and in-breathing: he thus announces him to the out-breathing and in-breathing, and they approve of his consecration, and approved by them he is consecrated.

35. 'Present is Pûshan, the all-possessing;'

---

[1] For a sham fight with arrows forming part of the ceremony in the Black Yagus ritual, see p. 100, note 1.

[2] That is, as would seem, the formulas of information (or perhaps of announcement, introduction); the first of these formulas beginning with âvis (in sight), the others with the participle âvitta, i.e. 'obtained, present;' Sâya*n*a and Mahîdhara, however, taking it in the sense of 'informed,'—a meaning which, indeed, the word may perhaps have been intended to convey in these formulas.

Pûshan is (the lord of) cattle: he thus announces him to the cattle, and they approve of his consecration; and approved by them he is consecrated.

36. 'Present are Heaven and Earth, the all-propitious;'—he thus announces him to those two, the heaven and the earth, and they approve of his consecration; and approved by them he is consecrated.

37. 'Present is Aditi, of wide shelter;'—Aditi is this earth: he thus announces him to this earth, and she approves of his consecration, and approved by her he is consecrated. Thus to whatever deities he announces him, they approve of his consecration, and approved by them he is consecrated.

Fourth Adhyâya. First Brâhmana.

1. He puts a piece of copper[1] into the mouth of a long-haired man, with (Vâg. S. X, 10), 'Removed by sacrifice are the mordacious.' For verily he who performs the Râgasûya escapes all kinds of death, all murderous blows, and old age alone is his death: hence whatever kind of death, whatever murderous blow there is, past that he now guides him, as past the mordacious ones.

2. And as to why it is of a long-haired man,—such a long-haired man is neither woman nor man; for being a male, he is not a woman, and being long-haired (a eunuch), he is not a man. And copper (or bronze) is neither iron nor gold; and those mordacious ones (snakes) are neither worms nor non-worms. And as to its being copper,—reddish

[1] Lohâyasa, literally, 'red metal,' apparently either copper, or an alloy of copper and some other metal.—The eunuch is sitting in the Sadas.

to be sure are mordacious ones: therefore (he throws it in the face) of a long-haired man.

3. He then makes him ascend the regions, with (Vâg. S. X, 10-14), 'Ascend thou the East! May the Gâyatrî (metre) protect thee, the Rathantara-sâman, the threefold stoma, the spring season, the Priesthood, that precious treasure!'

4. 'Ascend thou the South! May the Trish*t*ubh protect thee, the B*ri*hat-sâman, the fifteenfold stoma, the summer season, the Knighthood, that precious treasure!'

5. 'Ascend thou the West! May the *G*agatî protect thee, the Vairûpa-sâman, the seventeenfold stoma, the rainy season, the Peasantry, that precious treasure!'

6. 'Ascend thou the North! May the Anush*t*ubh protect thee, the Vairâ*g*a-sâman, the twenty-onefold stoma, the autumn season, fruit, that precious treasure!'

7. 'Ascend thou the upper region! May the Pańkti protect thee, the *S*âkvara and Raivata-sâmans, the thrice-ninefold and the three and thirtyfold stomas, the winter and dewy season, spiritual lustre, that precious treasure!'

8. And as to why he makes him ascend the quarters,—that is a form of the seasons: it is the seasons, the year, that he thereby makes him ascend; and having ascended the seasons, the year, he is high, high above everything here, and everything here is below him.

9. On the hind part of the tiger's skin[1] a piece of

[1] This was spread out in front of the Maitrâvaru*n*a's hearth, see V, 3, 5, 3.

lead is laid down. He kicks it off with his foot, with (Vâg. S. X, 14), 'Kicked off is Namu*k*i's head!' Now there was once an Asura, Namu*k*i by name. Indra knocked him down, and trod with his foot upon him. And in that he, thus trodden upon, bulged out, that (is the origin of) a rupture. He tore off his head with his foot, and therefrom sprang a goblin (Rakshas). That one kept calling out to him, 'Whither art thou going? Where wilt thou rid thyself of me?'

10. He beat it off with (a disk of) lead: hence lead is soft, for it has lost its spring, as it beat off (the goblin) with all its might. Hence also, while being like gold, it is not worth anything; for it has lost its spring, as it beat off (the goblin) with all its might. And so, indeed, he (Indra) thereby beat off the fiends, the Rakshas; and in like manner this one (the king) thereby beats off the fiends, the Rakshas.

11. He then makes him step upon the tiger's skin, with (Vâg. S. X, 15), 'Thou art Soma's beauty;'—For because when Soma flowed through Indra, he (Indra) thereupon became a tiger, and therefore he is Soma's beauty: this is why he says, 'Thou art Soma's beauty;'—'May my beauty be like unto thine!'—The tiger's beauty he thereby bestows upon him: therefore he says, 'May my beauty be like unto thine!'

12. Below (the king's foot) he throws a (small) gold plate, with, 'Save (him) from death!'—Gold is immortal life: he thus takes his stand on immortal life.

13. Then there is (another) gold plate, perforated either with a hundred, or with nine, holes. If with

a hundred holes,—man here lives up to a hundred (years), and has a hundred energies, a hundred powers; therefore it is perforated with a hundred holes. And if with nine holes,—there are in man those nine vital airs: therefore it is perforated with nine holes.

14. That (gold plate) he lays upon his head, with, 'Might thou art, victory thou art, immortality thou art!' Gold being immortal life, he thus lays immortal life into him. And as to why there are gold plates on both sides,—gold being immortal life,—he thus encloses him on both sides with immortal life: this is why there are gold plates on both sides.

15. He then lifts up his arms, with (Vâg. S. X, 16[1]), 'Golden-bodied, ye two lords rise like the sun: mount ye the chariot, O Mitra and Varu*n*a, and thence behold Aditi and Diti!' Mitra and Varu*n*a verily are the two arms, and the chariot (-seat) is the man: therefore he says, 'Mount ye the chariot, O Mitra and Varu*n*a!'—'thence behold Aditi and Diti!' By this he means to say, 'See ye your own (property) and that of others!'

16. Let him not lift up (the king's arms) with that one, but let him rather lift them up with, 'Thou art Mitra, thou art Varu*n*a;' for Mitra-Varu*n*a are the two arms, and by his arms the Râganya belongs to Mitra and Varu*n*a: let him therefore lift up his arms with, 'Thou art Mitra, thou art Varu*n*a.'

[1] In *Ri*k S. V, 62, 8 the verse runs as follows:—At the glow of the dawn, at the rising of the sun, ye, O Mitra and Varu*n*a, mount your golden-formed, iron-pillared chariot; thence ye behold Aditi and Diti (? the boundless space and the bounded).

17. And as to why he anoints him (standing) with upstretched arms;—those arms in truth are the Râganya's power, and power also is that collected essence of the waters wherewith he now anoints him: 'Lest that power, the collected essence of the waters, weigh down (paralyze) this power of mine, the arms,' thus he thinks, and therefore he anoints him (standing) with upstretched arms.

SECOND BRÂHMANA.

1. He (the king) is anointed (sprinkled) whilst standing with his face turned towards the east. A Brâhman—either the Adhvaryu, or he who is his (the king's) court chaplain—sprinkles him in front, from behind;—

2. With (Vâg. S. X, 17), 'With Soma's glory I sprinkle thee,'—'with vigour' he thereby says;—'With Agni's glow ...[1],'—'with vigour' he thereby says;—'With Sûrya's splendour ...,'—'with vigour' he thereby says;—'With Indra's energy ...,'—'with vigour' he thereby says;—'Be thou the chieftain of chiefs!'—'be thou the supreme king of kings' he thereby says;—'Guard (him)[2] against darts!'—darts meaning arrows, it is past murder by arrows that he thus guides him: therefore he says, 'guard him against darts!'

3. [Vâg. S. X, 18] 'Quicken him, O gods, to

[1] While the preceding formula is used by the priest, the present and two succeeding ones (each with the words '... I sprinkle thee; guard him against darts!') are pronounced by the other three persons specified in V, 3, 5, 12–14, each sprinkling the king with the water in his respective vessel.

[2] Mahîdhara explains: 'O Soma, protect him, the Sacrificer, in overcoming the enemy's missiles.'

be unrivalled!'—he thereby says, 'Quicken him, O gods, so as to be without an enemy;'—'For great chiefdom, for great lordship!'—in this there is nothing obscure;—'For man-rule!'—'for the ruling of men' he thereby says;—'For Indra's lordly sway!'—'for power' he means to say, when he says, 'for Indra's lordly sway!'—'Him, the son of such and such (a man), the son of such and such (a woman),'—whatever be his parentage regarding that he says this;—'of such and such a people'—that is to say, of the people whose king he is;—'This man, O ye (people), is your king, Soma is the king of us Brâhmans!'—he thereby causes everything here to be food for him (the king); the Brâhman alone he excepts: therefore the Brâhman is not to be fed upon, for he has Soma for his king[1].

4. He (the king) then rubs the sprinkled water

[1] Either at this juncture, or after the game at dice, the Hotri recites the legend of Sunahsepha, as given Ait. Br. VII, 13-18.—'King Harischandra, of the race of Ikshvâku, being childless, made a vow that if he obtained a son he would sacrifice him to Varuna. A son was born, who received the name of Rohita, but the father postponed, under various pretexts, the fulfilment of his vow. When at length he resolved to perform the sacrifice, Rohita refused to be the victim, and went out into the forest, where he lived for six years. He then met a poor Brâhman Rishi called Agigarta, who had three sons, and Rohita purchased from Agîgarta, for a hundred cows, the second son, named Sunahsepha, to be the substitute for himself in the sacrifice. Varuna approved of the substitute, and the sacrifice was about to be performed, the father receiving another hundred cows for binding his son to the sacrificial post, and a third hundred for agreeing to slaughter him. Sunahsepha, however, saved himself by reciting verses in honour of different deities, and was received into the family of Visvâmitra, who was one of the officiating priests.' Dowson, Dict. of Hindu Mythology.

over himself with the horn of a black antelope; for that collected essence of the waters wherewith he now anoints him means vigour: 'May this vigour of mine spread through my whole self,' thus he thinks, and therefore he rubs it all over himself.

5. He rubs it over himself, with (Vâg. S. X, 19), 'Forth from the back of the mountain, of the bull,'—even as the mountain stands out here, even as the bull stands out beyond the cattle, so does he who performs the Râgasûya stand out beyond everything here, and everything here is below him: therefore he says, 'Forth from the back of the mountain, of the bull,'—'The ships keep moving, the self-pouring; they, the upwards bent, have turned back downwards, flowing after the dragon of the deep[1].'

6. He then makes him step the (three) Vish*n*u-steps within (the extent of) the tiger's skin, with, 'Vish*n*u's outstepping thou art! Vish*n*u's outstep thou art! Vish*n*u's step thou art!' Now Vish*n*u's outstepping (vikrama*n*a), Vish*n*u's outstep (vikrânta), and Vish*n*u's step (krânta)[2] are these (three) worlds: thus having ascended these worlds, he is high above everything here, and everything here is below him.

7. He then pours the remainders (of the water) together into the Brâhman's vessel: he thereby makes the Brâhman an object of respect after the king, whence the Brâhman is an object of respect after the king.

---

[1] Ahi Budhnya, the Πύθων ὄφις of Hellenic mythology (St. Petersburg dict.).

[2] In the Black Yagus ritual the three steps are called 'krama, krânta, and vikrânta.'

8. And to him who is his (the king's) dearest son, he hands that vessel, thinking, 'May this son of mine perpetuate this vigour of mine!'

9. He then returns to the Gârhapatya fire, (his son) holding on to him behind, and offers, with (Vâ*g*. S. X, 20), 'O Pra*g*âpati, than thee none other hath encompassed all these forms: for whatsoever object we sacrifice, let that accrue unto us!—This one is the father of N. N.!'—him who is the son, he makes the father, and him who is the father, he makes the son[1]: he thereby links together the vigour of both of them.—'N. N. is the father of this one!' him who is the father, he makes the father, and him who is the son, he makes the son: after linking together the vigour of these two, he puts it again in the proper way,—'May we be the lords of riches, hail!'—this is the blessing of that ceremony: a blessing he thereby invokes.

10. And any residue that is left over, he offers in the Âgnîdhrîya; for redundant is that residue, and redundant also is the Âgnîdhriya,—in the Gârhapatya they cook the oblations, and in the Âhavanîya they offer, but that one is redundant: thus he puts the redundant to the redundant. He offers it on the north part (of the hearth), for that is the region of that god (Rudra): hence he offers it on the north

[1] By way of illustration, Mahîdhara explains what would have happened at the inauguration of king Da*s*aratha (of Ayodhyâ), the father of Râma; viz. in that case the first formula would run,—'Râma is the father of Da*s*aratha;' and the second—'Da*s*aratha is the father of Râma.' According to the ceremonial of the Black Ya*g*us the offering of the residue takes place at the house (first of the favourite son, according to Âpastamba, and then) of the queen. Taitt. S., vol. ii, p. 154.

part. He offers with, 'O Rudra, whatever potent[1], highest name is thine, therein thou art an offering, thou art a home-offering, hail!'

THIRD BRÂHMANA.

1. North of the Âhavanîya he places a hundred, or more than a hundred, cows of that relative of his. The reason why he does so is this:

2. When Varuna was consecrated, his energy, his vigour departed from him. Probably[2] that collected essence (life-sap) of the waters wherewith they were sprinkling him, drove out his energy, his vigour. He found it in the cattle, and because he found it in them, therefore cattle are an object of respect. And having found it in the cattle, he again took to himself his energy, his vigour. And in like manner this one;—that energy does not indeed depart from him, but he does it (thinking), 'This Râgasûya is Varuna's consecration, and Varuna did so.'

3. He takes down the chariot (from the stand[3]); for whatever turns away from the warrior (râganya) that he overtakes with his chariot: for this reason he takes down the chariot.

4. He takes it down with (Vâg. S. X, 21), 'Thou art Indra's thunderbolt!' The chariot is indeed a thunderbolt; and the Sacrificer is Indra;—he is Indra for a twofold reason, namely because he is a

[1] The meaning of krivi (krayi, Taitt. S.) is doubtful. Mahîdhara derives it from 'kar' (to make or injure), in the sense of either 'efficacious,' or 'destructive.'—A Grantha MS. of the Kânva text reads kavi, 'wise.'

[2] I am now inclined to think that some such meaning as 'probably, perhaps' (more nearly, German 'wohl'), fits all the passages (in the Brâhmanas at all events) where sasvat occurs.

[3] See above, V, 1, 4, 3 seq.

Kshatriya, and because he is a Sacrificer: therefore he says, 'Indra's thunderbolt thou art.'

5. Having turned it (so as to stand) inside the Vedi, he yokes it with, 'I yoke thee by the direction of Mitra and Varuna, the directors[1];' for Mitra and Varuna are the two arms, and by his arms the Râganya belongs to Mitra and Varuna: that is why he says, 'I yoke thee by direction of Mitra and Varuna, the directors.'

6. He yokes it with four (horses). He passes along by the same way as that on which the dakshinâs[2] go,—behind the Sadas, and in front of the hall. He stops it behind the kâtvâla, and in front of the Âgnidhra.

7. He mounts it with, 'For unfeebleness (I mount) thee, for svadhâ[3] (I mount) thee!'—by 'for unfeebleness thee' he means to say, 'for a state free from afflictions (I mount) thee;' by 'for svadhâ thee' he means to say, 'for life-sap (I mount) thee;'—'I, the unharmed Arguna!' Now Indra is called Arguna, which is his mystic name; and this (king) is Indra for a twofold reason, namely because he is a Kshatriya, and because he is a Sacrificer: therefore he says, 'the unharmed Arguna.'

8. He then goads on the right yoke-horse, with, 'Conquer thou by the impulse of the Maruts!' For the Maruts are the clansmen, and it is by his

[1] Prasâstri, 'the director,' is also another name for the Maitrâvaruna priest.

[2] That is, the cows given to priests as sacrificial fee. For particulars regarding the passage by which they are driven to their destination, see part ii, p. 344, note 1.

[3] Probably here 'for well-being;' the author, however, evidently takes it here in the sense of 'invigorating potion,' the drink offered to the deceased ancestors.

clan that the chieftain wins what he desires to win: therefore he says, 'Conquer thou by the impulse of the Maruts!'

9. He then stops (the chariot) in the midst of the cows[1], with, 'May we obtain by the mind!' For it is by the mind that everything here (that is obtained) is obtained; and by the mind therefore he now obtains everything: therefore he says, 'May we obtain by the mind!'

10. He then touches a cow with the end of the bow, with, 'Together with energy!'—energy means vigour, kine: it is energy, vigour, he thereby takes to himself. And he adds, 'I overpower them, I seize them!'

11. Now as to why he stops amidst the cows of his relative,—whatever is tending away from a man, be it either fame, or anything else, that passes over to his relative foremost of all;—that energy, or vigour, he now takes again from his relative to himself: that is why he stops amidst the cows of his relative.

12. In return he presents to him just as many (cows)[2], or more. For assuredly he, the Sacrificer,

---

[1] In the ceremonial of the Black Yagus a sham-fight takes place here. East or north of the sacrificial ground a Râganya has posted himself with bow in hand. The king discharges the arrows at him, with, 'Obtained is the mind!' and having thus, as it were, overpowered the enemy, he wheels round in a sunwise direction, with, 'I (have become endowed) with energy, with vigour!' He then puts on shoes of boar's skin, with, 'Thou art the mettle of cattle,' gets down from the chariot, and puts on ornaments of silver, copper (as Sâyana here interprets audumbara), and gold (afterwards to be given to the Brahman). Then follow the oblations relating to the unyoking of the chariot. Taitt. S. I, 8, 15, with commentary.

[2] Viz. as many as he has taken from him, a hundred or more.

is not capable of a cruel deed; but cruelly indeed he acts when he says, 'I overpower them, I seize them;' and thus that is done by him without cruelty: this is why, in return, he presents to him just as many (cows) or more.

13. He then pulls the right-side (horses, or reins). He passes along on the same way as that on which the dakshi*n*â (cows) go,—in front of the sacrificial post, and along the south of the Vedi. Behind the Sadas, and in front of the hall, he stops that (car).

14. [Vâg. S. X, 22], 'Lest, O Indra, overpowerer of the mighty, we be wanting thee, heedless through ungodliness,—mount thou, O divine wielder of the thunderbolt, the chariot which thou restrainest (as well as its) well-horsed reins[1].' With this (verse) he stops (the chariot);—reins (ra*s*mi[2]) means bridle (abhî*s*u): therefore he says, 'Thou restrainest the well-horsed reins.' Thereupon he offers the (four oblations) relating to the unyoking of the chariot. 'Well-pleased the chariot shall be when unyoked,' he thinks, and therefore he offers the (oblations) relating to the unyoking of the chariot.

15. He offers with (Vâg. S. X, 23), 'To Agni, the House-lord, hail!' He thereby pleases the part of the chariot relating to Agni; and it is the shoulder-pieces of the chariot that relate to Agni: it is the shoulder-pieces (of the yoke) he thereby pleases. And the house-lord's position means prosperity: as much as he (the king) rules over, for

[1] For a different version of this somewhat awkwardly constructed verse, see *Ri*k S. V, 33, 3.

[2] The explanation is given because the word has also the meaning 'ray.'

the prosperity, the house-lordship, of that his kingship is thereby rendered free (unopposed).

16. 'To Soma, the wood-lord (tree), hail!' There are two kinds of (objects) coming from trees, the wheels of chariots and waggons, for both of these he thereby ensures safety. And the wood-lord (tree) being Soma,—whatever part of the chariot comes from the tree, that he thereby pleases. Now the parts of the chariot coming from trees are the wooden pieces of the chariot: hence it is the wooden pieces he thereby pleases. And Soma being the nobility, it is over the nobility that his kingship is thereby rendered free.

17. 'To the strength of the Maruts, hail!' He thereby pleases the part of the chariot belonging to the Maruts,—there are four horses, the chariot the fifth, and the warrior (chariot-fighter) and charioteer two—these are seven, and the host of the Maruts consists of (troops of) seven each: he thereby pleases the whole chariot; and the Maruts being the peasants, it is over the peasantry that his kingship is thereby rendered free.

18. 'To Indra's energy, hail!' He thereby pleases the part of the chariot that belongs to Indra. Now the warrior relates to Indra, and it is the warrior he thereby pleases. And Indra's energy (indriya) means the vigour in Indra[1]: it is in regard to energy, vigour, that his kingship is thereby rendered free.

19. He then puts on shoes of boar's skin. Now the gods once put a pot of ghee on the fire. Therefrom a boar was produced: hence the boar is fat,

[1] ? Or, means vigour, Indra.

for it was produced from ghee. Hence also cows readily take to a boar: it is indeed their own essence (life-sap, blood) they are readily taking to. Thus he firmly establishes himself in the essence of the cattle: therefore he puts on shoes of boar's skin.

20. Looking down on this (earth) he then mutters, 'O mother Earth, injure me not, nor I thee!' For the Earth was once afraid of Varuna, when he had been consecrated, thinking, 'Something great surely has he become now that he has been consecrated: I fear lest he may rend me asunder!' And Varuna also was afraid of the Earth, thinking, 'I fear lest she may shake me off! Hence by that (formula) he entered into a friendly relation with her; for a mother does not injure her son, nor does a son injure his mother.

21. Now this Râgasûya is Varuna's consecration; and the Earth is afraid of him, thinking, 'Something great surely has he become now that he has been consecrated: I fear lest he may rend me asunder!' And he also is afraid of her, thinking, 'I fear lest she may shake me off.' Hence he thereby enters into a friendly relation with her; for a mother does not injure her son, nor does a son injure his mother: therefore he mutters thus.

22. He steps down (from the chariot), muttering this ati*kh*andas verse (Vâg. S. X, 24; *Ri*k S. IV, 40, 5), 'The swan dwelling in the light, the Vasu dwelling in the air, the priest seated on the altar, the guest dwelling in the retreat (house), —the man-dwelling, the space-dwelling[1], the law-dwelling, the sphere-dwelling, the water-

[1] Or perhaps, 'in the best place (vara).' See VI, 7, 3, 11.

born, cow-born, law-born, rock-born (is) the great truth.' For that ati*kh*andas (or excessive metre) comprises all the metres: thus evil does not descend along with him.

23. Let not the charioteer get down along with (or, after) him, lest he should descend on the same world on which the anointed (king) has just descended. They put him up, along with the chariot, on the car-stand. Thence he leaps down: thus he does not descend on the same world on which the anointed has just descended[1].

24. North of the Âhavanîya is the original fire, taken up (from the hearth[2]). Behind the right hind-wheel of the cart-stand he fastens two round *s*atamânas[3].

25. He then hides an udumbara (ficus glomerata) branch (in the wheel-track). He touches one of those two (plates), with (Vâ*g*. S. X, 25), 'So great thou art, life thou art: bestow life upon me! A yoke-mate thou art, lustre thou art: bestow lustre upon me!' He thereby takes life and lustre to himself.

26. He then touches the udumbara branch, with, 'Sustenance thou art: bestow sustenance upon me!' He thereby takes sustenance (strength) to himself. Those same two round *s*atamânas are the fee for this ceremony. He gives them to the

---

[1] According to Taitt. Br. I, 7, 9, 6, the king, on returning to the Vedi, is supposed to have ascended to the heavenly world (suvarga-loka), from which the charioteer is to be excluded by this expedient.

[2] The Âhavanîya of the hall (the so-called 'hall-door fire') has been lifted and placed on a cart.

[3] Or, two round (gold) plates, weighing a hundred mâna (or berries of Gu*ñg*â, or Abrus Precatorius, the average weight of which is stated to be $1\frac{5}{16}$ grains Troy).

Brahman priest, for the Brahman protects the sacrifice from the south: therefore he gives them to the Brahman.

27. In front of the Maitrâvaruna's hearth the dish of curds for Mitra and Varuna has been deposited. He draws down to it his (the Sacrificer's) two arms[1], with, 'I draw you down, the arms of Indra, the doer of mighty deeds.' Now curds are the essence of cattle: hence it is to the essence of cattle that he thereby brings down his (the Sacrificer's) arms. And as to its being for Mitra-Varuna, it is because Mitra and Varuna are the two arms.

Fourth Brâhmana.

1. He proceeds with the curds for Mitra-Varuna. Whilst the Svishtakrit of it remains yet unoffered, they bring a throne-seat for him (the king); for truly he who gains a seat in the air, gains a seat above (others): thus these subjects of his sit below him who is seated above,—that is why they bring him a throne-seat. It is of khadira (acacia catechu) wood, and perforated, and bound with thongs as that of the Bhâratas.

2. He places it (on the tiger's skin), in front of the Maitrâvaruna's hearth, with (Vâg. S. X, 26), 'Thou art pleasant, thou art soft-seated!'—he thereby renders it kindly and auspicious.

3. He then spreads a mantle over it, with, 'Thou art the womb (seat) of knighthood!'—he thus

[1] Whilst this is done, the king stands on the tiger's skin, and the Adhvaryu hands him his bow and arrows. Thereupon the dish of curds is taken to the uttaravedi to be proceeded with. Kâty. Sr. XV, 6, 34-35.

makes it (the king's throne) the very womb of knighthood.

4. He then makes him sit down on it, with, 'Seat thee on the pleasant one! seat thee on the soft-seated!'—whereby he says, 'Seat thyself on the kindly and auspicious (seat)!'—'Seat thee in the womb of knighthood!'—thus he places him in what is the very womb of knighthood.

5. Having touched him on the chest, he then mutters (Vâ*g*. S. X, 27; *Ri*k S. I, 25, 10), 'He hath sat down, the upholder of the sacred law,'—the king indeed is the upholder of the sacred law, for he is not capable of all and every speech, nor of all and every deed; but that he should speak only what is right, and do what is right, of that he, as well as the *S*rotriya (the Brâhman versed in sacred writ), is capable; for these two are the upholders of the sacred law among men: therefore he says, 'He hath sat down, the upholder of the sacred law;'—'Varu*n*a, in the home-steads,'—the home-steads are the peasants (clans, people): 'among the peasants' he means to say;—'for supreme rule, he the wise!'—'for kingship' he means to say when he says, 'for supreme rule, he the wise.'

6. He then throws the five dice[1] into his hand,

[1] The allusions to the game of dice in the early literature are not sufficiently definite to enable us to form a clear idea as to the manner in which the game was played. Sâya*n*a, on our passage (as on Taitt. S. I, 8, 16), remarks that the dice here used consisted either of gold cowries (shells) or of gold (dice shaped like) Vibhîtaka nuts. That the (brown) fruit of the Vibhîtaka tree (Terminalia Bellerica)—being of about the size of a nutmeg, nearly round, with five slightly flattened sides—was commonly used for this purpose in early times, we know from the Rig-veda; but we do not know in what manner the dice were marked in those days. Accord-

with (Vâg. S. X, 28), 'Dominant thou art: may these five regions of thine prosper!'—now that

ing to the commentators, the game is played with five dice, four of which are called kṛita, whilst the fifth is called kali; and if all the dice fall uniformly (ekarûpa)—i. e. with the marked sides either upwards or downwards—then the player wins, and in that case the kali is said to overrule the other dice. In this case the kali would seem to represent the king. Kâty. Sr. XV, 7, 18-19, however, admits of another mode of playing, by which the kali represents the sagâta (tribesman), whilst the king and those that come after him (in the enumeration in paragraphs 15-20) play the kṛita, &c. To understand this mode, we have probably to turn to Khândog. Up. IV, 1, 4, where it is said of the saint Raikva, that everything good fell to him, just as the lower dice (or casts) submit to the conquering kṛita. Here the commentators assign the names kṛita, tretâ, dvâpara, and kali to different sides of the die, marked respectively with 4, 3, 2, and 1 marks (añka).—In Taitt. Br. I, 7, 10 the game at dice, at the Râgasûya, is referred to as follows:—With, 'This king has overcome the regions,' he hands (to the king) five dice; for these are all the dice: he thereby renders him invincible. They engage (to play) for a dish of rice (odana), for that is (a symbol of) the chief: he thus makes him obtain every prosperity. He addresses them (with the epithets of) 'far-famed, most prosperous, true king.' The Commentary and Sûtras then supply the following explanations:—The keeper of the dice (akshâvâpa), having (marked off and) raised the gambling-ground (by means of the wooden sword), and sprinkled it, throws down more than a hundred—or more than a thousand—gold dice. From them he takes five dice and hands them to the king: these, as representing the five regions, are taken to include all those dice. These explanations, so far from clearing up the doubtful points, seem rather to add to them. It may be noted, however, that in the well-known hymn, Rik S. X, 34, in which the gambler's state of mind is pictured in very expressive language, the dice of the game are apparently spoken of as tripañkâsa vrâta, or 'the troop of fifty-three' (or thrice five, according to Ludwig's rather improbable conjecture). For other particulars see R. Roth, Zeitsch. d. deutsch. morg. Ges. II, p. 122; A. Weber, Ind. Stud. I, p. 284. According to Goldstücker (s.v. abhishekanîya) this game of dice is intended to symbolize the victory of the present age, or kali-yuga, over the former ages; but the commentator rather takes it as symbolizing the king's dig-vigaya, or victorious sway in every quarter.

one, the Kali, is indeed dominant over the (other) dice, for that one dominates over all the dice: therefore he says, 'Dominant thou art: may these five regions of thine prosper!' for there are indeed five regions, and all the regions he thereby causes to prosper for him.

7. They (the Adhvaryu and his assistants) then silently strike him with sticks on the back;—by beating him with sticks (da*nd*a) they guide him safely over judicial punishment (da*nd*abadha): whence the king is exempt from punishment (ada*nd*ya), because they guide him safely over judicial punishment.

8. Thereupon he chooses a boon; and, verily, whatsoever boon he who has been anointed chooses, that is completely fulfilled for him: therefore he chooses a boon.

9. 'O Brahman!' thus he addresses (the priest) the first time[1], thinking, 'I will first utter the (word)

[1] If it were not for the clear and unmistakable interpretation of the commentators on the Brâhma*n*a and Kâtyâyana, one might feel inclined to translate, 'thus he addresses the first—the second,' &c., so as to bring it into accord with the practice of the Black Yagus. This practice is as follows (Taitt. S. I, 8, 16, with commentary).—The priest moves the previously uplifted arms of the Sacrificer down to the Vais*v*adeva dish of curds (cf. above, V, 4, 3, 27), with, 'Thou art Mitra!—thou art Varu*n*a!' He then places the khâdira throne-seat on the vedi, covers it with a leathern (or fur) cover, with, 'Thou art the navel of the Kshatra, the womb of the Kshatra,' and makes the king sit down with, 'Seat thee on the pleasant one, seat thee on the soft-seated!' The king sits down, with, 'May it not injure thee! may it not injure me!' The priest then addresses him, with, 'He hath sat down, the upholder of the sacred law, Varu*n*a in the home-steads, for supreme rule, he the wise!' The priests and Ratnins (see V, 3, 1, 1 seq.) then sit down in a circle round the king in order to do homage to him,—the Adhvaryu being seated towards the east, the Brahman towards the south, the Hot*ri*

Brahman, I will speak speech sped by the Brahman:' this is why he first addresses him with 'O Brahman!' The other answers, 'Thou art Brahman! Thou art Savit*ri* of true impulsion!'—he thereby lays vigour into him, and causes Savit*ri* to be of true impulsion.

10. 'O Brahman!' thus he addresses him the second time. The other answers, 'Thou art Brahman! Thou art Varu*n*a of true power!'—he thereby lays vigour into him, and causes Varu*n*a to be of true power.

11. 'O Brahman!' thus he addresses him the third time. The other answers, 'Thou art Brahman! Thou art Indra, mighty through the people[1]!'—he thereby lays vigour into him, and causes Indra to be mighty through the people.

12. 'O Brahman!' thus he addresses him the

---

towards the west, the Udgât*ri* towards the north. The king then addresses the Adhvaryu, with, 'O Brahmân, (Om)!' That priest replies, 'Thou, O king, art Brahman, thou art Savit*ri* of true impulsion.' In the same way the king addresses the Brahman, 'O Brahmăn!' and that priest replies, 'Thou, O king, art Brahman, thou art Indra, of true energy!' Then the Hot*ri*, who replies, '... thou art Mitra, the most kindly!'—the Udgât*ri*: '... thou art Varu*n*a, of true laws!' Thereupon the Brahman hands the sacrificial sword to the king, with, 'Indra's thunderbolt thou art!' He then hands to him five dice, with, 'This king has overcome the regions!' see next note.—The charioteer, treasurer, and chamberlain are invited by the king (to the game?) by auspicious epithets ('far-famed one,' 'most prosperous one,' 'true king'). Thereupon the Hot*ri* recites the story of *S*una*h*s*e*pa, whereupon follows the offering of the svish*t*ak*ri*t of the cake of the Maruts, and the dish of curds to the Visve Devâ*h*.

[1] Or, he whose strength is the people (vi*s*, vi*s*a),—that is, the Maruts, in the case of Indra, and the subjects or peasantry in that of the king. Sây.

fourth time. The other answers, 'Thou art Brahman! Thou art Rudra, the most kindly!'—he thereby lays into him (the king) those former energies, and he appeases him (Rudra); and he, Rudra, therefore, is gracious to every one, because he (the priest) appeases him.

13. 'O Brahman!' thus he addresses him the fifth time. The other answers (undefinedly), 'Thou art Brahman!'—undefined means unlimited: thus heretofore he laid limited vigour into him; but now he answers undefinedly; and undefined meaning unlimited, he thereby lays complete, unlimited vigour into him: therefore he answers here undefinedly.

14. He then hails him as one bearing auspicious names,—'Much-worker, better-worker, more-worker[1]!' Whoever bears such names speaks auspiciously even with a human voice.

15. A Brâhma*n*a then hands to him the sacrificial (wooden) sword,—either the Adhvaryu, or he who is his (the king's) domestic chaplain—with, 'Indra's thunderbolt thou art: therewith serve me!'—the sacrificial sword being a thunderbolt, that Brâhma*n*a, by means of that thunderbolt, makes the king to be weaker than himself; for indeed the king who is weaker than a Brâhma*n*a, is stronger than his enemies: thus he thereby makes him stronger than his enemies.

16. The king hands it to the king's brother, with, 'Indra's thunderbolt thou art: therewith serve me!' Thereby the king makes his brother to be weaker than himself.

17. The king's brother hands it either to the

[1] That is, increaser of the prosperity of himself and his people.

Sûta (minstrel and chronicler), or to the Governor, with, 'Indra's thunderbolt thou art: therewith serve me!' Thereby the king's brother makes the Sûta, or the Governor, to be weaker than himself.

18. The Sûta, or the Governor, hands it to the Grâma*n*i (village-headman[1]), with, 'Indra's thunderbolt thou art: therewith serve me!' Thereby the Sûta, or the Governor, makes the headman to be weaker than himself.

19. The Grâma*n*i hands it to a tribesman[2], with, 'Indra's thunderbolt thou art: therewith serve me!' Thereby the headman makes the tribesman to be weaker than himself. And as to why they mutually hand it on in this way, they do so lest there should be a confusion of classes, and in order that (society) may be in the proper order.

20. Thereupon the tribesman and the Pratiprasthât*ri*[3], with that sacrificial sword, prepare the gaming-ground, (close) by the original fire[4], with the puroru*k* verse of the *S*ukra[5]. The *S*ukra is the eater: he thereby makes (him) the eater.

21. With the puroru*k* verse of the Manthin[6] they then put up a shed (vimita). The Manthin cup is

---

[1] See p. 60, note.

[2] The sagâta would seem to be one of the peasant proprietors or 'sharers' constituting the village 'brotherhood' ruled over by the headman, and often actually belonging to the same family as the latter (Gaugenosse, clansman).

[3] The first assistant of the Adhvaryu.

[4] That is, north of the Âhavanîya fire, where the cart stands, containing the original (hall-door) fire.

[5] For this verse (Vâg. S. VII, 12; *Ri*k S. V, 44, 1), preceding the ordinary formula with which the Soma-cups are drawn, see IV, 2, 1, 9 (part ii, p. 280).

[6] Vâg. S. VII, 16; *Ri*k S. X, 123, 1; see IV, 2, 1, 10.

he that is to be eaten,—thus having first made (him) the feeder, they now make for him one to be fed upon: that is why they put up a shed with the puroru*k* verse of the Manthin cup.

22. The Adhvaryu then takes clarified butter in four ladlings, places a piece of gold on the gaming-ground, and offers with (Vâ*g*. S. X, 29), 'May ample Agni, the lord of rites, delighted,—may ample Agni, the lord of rites, accept of the butter, hail!'

23. He (the Adhvaryu) throws down the dice, with, 'Hallowed by Svâhâ, strive ye with Sûrya's rays for the middlemost place among brethren!' For that gaming-ground is the same as 'ample Agni,' and those dice are his coals, thus it is him (Agni) he thereby pleases; and assuredly in the house of him who offers the Râ*g*asûya, or who so knows this, the striking[1] of that cow is approved of. On those dice he says, 'Play for the cow!' The two draught oxen of the original (hall-door) fire are the sacrificial fee.

24. He then says, 'Pronounce the invitatory prayer to Agni Svish*t*ak*ri*t!' And as to why that ceremony is performed between two oblations,—verily, Pra*g*âpati is that sacrifice which is here performed, and from which these creatures have been produced,—and, indeed, they are even now produced after this one;—thus he places him (the Sacrificer) in the very middle of that Pra*g*âpati, and consecrates him in the very middle: that is why that ceremony is performed between two oblations.

[1] Thus (not the slaying) according to the commentary on Kâty. *S*r. XV, 7, 20, hantis *k*âhananamâtro na mâra*n*ârtha*h*.—The cow is the one staked by the tribesman (sa*g*âta).

Having called for the *S*rausha*t*, he says, 'Pronounce the offering-formula to Agni Svish*t*ak*ri*t,' and offers as the Vasha*t* is uttered.

25. He then puts the i*d*â on (the fire). After the invocation of I*d*â, he touches water and draws the Mâhendra cup. Having drawn the Mâhendra cup, he sets the chant agoing. He urges him (the Sacrificer) forward to the chant: he gets down (from the throne-seat); he is in attendance at the chant (stotra), in attendance at the recitation (*s*astra).

THE DA*S*APEYA.

FIFTH BRÂHMA*N*A.

1. Now when Varu*n*a was consecrated, his lustre departed from him,—lustre means vigour: that Vish*n*u, the Sacrifice, it was he that departed from him,—probably that collected essence of the waters wherewith he is anointed on that occasion, drove out his lustre.

2. He stole after it with those deities[1],—with Savit*ri*, the impeller (prasavit*ri*); with Sarasvatî, speech; with Tvash*t*ri, the forms of being; with Pûshan, cattle; with Indra, on the part of him[2] (the Sacrificer); with B*ri*haspati, holiness; with Varu*n*a, might; with Agni, fiery spirit; with Soma, the King;

[1] In the Black Yagus ritual the order of deities to whom the 'sa*m*s*ri*pâ*m* havî*m*shi' are offered is as follows,—Agni, Sarasvatî, Savit*ri*, Pûshan, B*ri*haspati, Indra, Varu*n*a, Soma, Tvash*t*ri, Vish*n*u. Cf. Taitt. S. I, 8, 17; Taitt. Br. I, 8, 1.

[2] Or, with Indra, for (the lost vigour) itself. Hardly, 'for us.' The Kâ*n*va text has 'indre*n*âsmai,' and so Sâya*n*a (MS. I. O. 657): asmai apas*ri*tâya vîryâya tadadhînakara*n*ârtham indre*n*a; yad vâ vibhaktivyatyaya*h*, anena vîrye*n*a vîryavatâ indre*n*a.

—but only through Vish*n*u[1], the tenth deity, he found it.

3. And because he there stole after (anu-sam-s*ri*p) with those deities, hence the name Sa*m*s*ri*pa*h*. And because he becomes consecrated on the tenth day, therefore (this ceremony is called) Da*s*apeya[2]. And because each time ten (men) steal along[3] after each cup, therefore also it is called Da*s*apeya.

4. Here now they say,—'Let him steal forth after enumerating ten Soma-drinking grandfathers[4]: it is thus that he obtains for himself the Soma-draught of this (Da*s*apeya), for it is a "drinking of ten."' But that is an overburdening[5], for people (will

[1] It seems rather strange that Varu*n*a and Vish*n*u should be included amongst the deities, with whose help Varu*n*a sought to recover his vigour, or Vish*n*u the sacrifice; but—'Twere to consider too curiously, to consider so.

[2] That is, da*s*a (ten) and peya (drink, beverage).

[3] For an explanation of the noiseless mode of moving with bent bodies, called sarpa*n*am, 'creeping,' see part ii, pp. 299, 450. It is in this way they are to move when they betake themselves to the respective fire-places for performing the sa*m*s*ri*p oblations; as they also do when betaking themselves to the Sadas to drink the cups of Soma at the Soma-feast on the next day. When libations of Soma-juice are made from the ten cups (*k*amasa, see part ii, p. 287), each cup is to be followed by ten Brâhmans who then take part in consuming the liquor in the Sadas—there being thus altogether one hundred Brâhmans taking part in these potations. The contents of the Sacrificer's cup, on the other hand, may be drunk by ten Râ*g*anyas (i.e. himself and nine others). See Kâty. XV, 8, 18-20; Taitt. S., vol. ii, p. 179.

[4] Sâya*n*a takes this literally as meaning that he is to call out the name of the Sacrificer's grandfather, then the grandfather of that one and so on. The commentary on Kâty. XV, 8, 16, on the other hand, apparently takes it to mean ten forefathers of the Sacrificer who have performed Soma-sacrifices, from the grandfather upwards.

[5] That is, an excessive demand, or, a weighing down, or crushing of the Sacrificer, making it impossible for him to perform the ceremony at all.

be able to) obtain only two or three Soma-drinking grandfathers: hence let him steal forth after enumerating those same deities[1].

5. For, surely, it was by those same deities that Varuna obtained the Soma-draught of that (Consecration-ceremony); and in like manner does this one now obtain the Soma-draught of that (ceremony): let him therefore steal forth after enumerating those same deities. Now as soon as the completing oblation[2] of that Consecration-ceremony comes to an end,—

6. He prepares those (samsrip) oblations,—a cake on twelve, or eight, potsherds for Savitri; for Savitri is the impeller of the gods: impelled by Savitri, Varuna on that occasion stole along; and in like manner does this one now steal along impelled by Savitri. At this (oblation) he presents one lotus-flower[3].

7. He then prepares a (rice) pap for Sarasvatî,—for Sarasvatî is speech, and it was with speech that Varuna on that occasion stole along; and in like manner does this one now steal along with speech. At this (oblation) he presents one lotus-flower.

8. He then prepares a cake on ten potsherds for Tvashtri,—for Tvashtri (the fashioner, creator) rules over living forms, and with Tvashtri, the living forms, Varuna on that occasion stole along; and in

[1] That is to say, after pronouncing the mantra, Vâg. S. X, 30, agreeing partly with paragraph 2 above, viz. beginning, 'By Savitri, the impeller; by Sarasvatî, speech,' . . . and ending, 'by Vishnu, the tenth deity, impelled I steal forth.'

[2] For the Udavasânîyâ ishti, see part ii, p. 389.

[3] The lotus-flowers presented on this occasion are gold ones, according to Sâyana, or optionally ordinary white or gold ones, according to Kâty. XV, 8, 5-6.

like manner does this one now steal along with Tvash*t*r*i*, the living forms. At this (oblation) he presents one lotus-flower.

9. He then prepares a pap for Pûshan;—for Pûshan is cattle, and with cattle Varu*n*a on that occasion stole along; and in like manner does this one now steal along with cattle. At this (oblation) he presents one lotus-flower.

10. He then prepares a cake on eleven potsherds for Indra;—for Indriya means energy, vigour, and with vigour Varu*n*a on that occasion stole along; and in like manner does this one now steal along with energy, with vigour. At this (oblation) he presents one lotus-flower.

11. He then prepares a pap for B*ri*haspati;—for B*ri*haspati means holiness, and with holiness Varu*n*a on that occasion stole along; and in like manner does this one now steal along with holiness. At this (oblation) he presents one lotus-flower.

12. He then prepares a barley pap for Varu*n*a;—with what vehemence Varu*n*a seized the creatures, with that vehemence Varu*n*a on that occasion stole along; and in like manner does this one now steal along with vehemence. At this (oblation) he presents one lotus-flower.

13. The deities of the Upasad are the (eighth, ninth, and) tenth [1]. At these (oblations) he presents

[1] For the Upasad, or preliminary oblations of ghee to Agni, Soma, and Vish*n*u, to be performed twice daily for (usually) three days preceding an ordinary Soma-sacrifice, see part ii, p. 104. At the Da*s*apeya, the ten Sa*m*s*ri*p-oblations take as it were the place of the ordinary Upasads, the latter being performed on the last three preliminary days along with, and to the same deities as, the last three Sa*m*s*ri*p-oblations; or, according to some authorities,

five lotus-flowers. That wreath of twelve lotus-flowers he puts on himself; that is the initiation: by that initiation he initiates himself.

14. And as to why there are twelve (flowers),—there being twelve months in the year, and the year being All, it is by the All that he thus initiates him: what flowers there are of the lotus, they are a form (an image) of the sky, they are a form of the stars; and what seed-stalks there are, they are a form of the air; and what suckers there are, they are a form of this (earth): thus he initiates him (to rule) over these worlds.

15. And having bought the King (Soma)[1], and

being substituted for them. There seems also some difference of opinion as to the exact time when the other preliminary ceremonies—the procession and entrance of king Soma, the guest-meal, &c.—are to take place, see paragraph 15.—According to Kâty. XV, 8, 14, these ceremonies are to take place on the seventh day (which the commentator, however, takes to mean the seventh day of the light fortnight of *K*aitra; the first seven Sa*m*s*ri*p-oblations being, according to him, performed on the day before). The Kâ*n*vas, however, perform these offerings on separate days.—The Taittirîya authorities seem also to be at variance with each other as to the exact relation of the Upasads and the last three Sa*m*s*ri*p-oblations, the deities of the two being, according to their scheme, only partly identical. According to Âpastamba (and Taitt. Br.) the first seven Sa*m*s*ri*ps are performed on so many days and, moreover, one Dîkshâ on the seventh day. Then on the last three days the Sa*m*s*ri*ps and Upasads are combined in this way, that the eighth day's Sa*m*s*ri*p is performed previous to, the ninth between, the tenth after the two daily Upasad-performances.—Each of the ten oblations also requires a special set of fires for its performance, the first being laid down immediately north of the one used for the Abhishe*k*anîya ceremony, the second immediately north of the first, &c.; the last Sa*m*s*ri*p-oblation being performed in the fire-shed (*s*âlâ) of the Dasapeya proper. Kâty. XV, 8, 2–3; cf. Taitt. S., vol. ii, p. 176.

[1] Namely, at the beginning of the Abhishe*k*aniya, or Consecration-ceremony, when Soma-plants are purchased sufficient to last

tied him up in two parts, they drive him around. Having then placed one-half on the throne-seat, he proceeds therewith. Having then placed on the throne-seat that portion which was deposited in the Brahman's house, he proceeds with the guest-meal. Whilst he is proceeding with the guest-meal, he performs the Upasads. Whilst he is performing the Upasads,—

16. He prepares those (three) oblations,—a cake on eight potsherds for Agni; a pap for Soma; and a cake on three potsherds, or a pap, for Vishnu. Thus he performs the sacrifice in this way, if it pleases him.

17. But let him not do it in this way; for he who departs from the path of the sacrifice stumbles, and he who departs from the path of the Upasads certainly departs from the path of the sacrifice: let him therefore not depart from the path of the Upasads.

18. Now when he offers to Agni, he steals along with Agni, with fiery spirit; and when he offers to Soma, he steals along with Soma, the King; and when he offers to Vishnu,—Vishnu being the sacrifice,—he visibly obtains the sacrifice, and having visibly obtained it, he makes it his own (or, takes it in).

19. This same (Dasapeya) is an Agnishtoma sacrifice (performed) with the seventeenfold (stoma)[1]; for Pragâpati is seventeenfold, and Pragâpati is the

for both that ceremony and the succeeding Dasapeya; the portion destined for the latter ceremony being meanwhile deposited in the Brahman's house.

[1] All the chants (stotra) of the Dasapeya are to be executed in the seventeenfold mode of chanting, or Saptadasa-stoma; for an example of which see part ii, p. 315, note 1.

sacrifice[1]: thus he visibly obtains the sacrifice, and having visibly obtained it, he makes it his own.

20. Twelve heifers with first calf are the sacrificial fee for this (sacrifice); for twelve months there are in the year, and the year is Pragâpati, and Pragâpati is the sacrifice: thus he visibly obtains the sacrifice, and having visibly obtained it, he makes it his own.

21. These (heifers) have twelve embryo calves,—that makes twenty-four; for twenty-four half-moons there are in the year, and the year is Pragâpati, and Pragâpati is the sacrifice: thus he visibly obtains the sacrifice, and having visibly obtained it, he makes it his own.

22. He gives them to the Brahman, for the Brahman guards the sacrifice from the south: therefore he gives them to the Brahman. To the Udgât*ri* (chanter) he gives the gold wreath, to the Hot*ri* the gold plate, to the two Adhvaryus two golden mirrors, to the Prastot*ri* (precentor) a horse, to the Maitrâvaru*n*a a sterile cow, to the Brâhma*n*â*kkh*a*m*sin a bull, to the Nesh*t*i and Pot*r*i two garments, to the A*kh*âvâka (a cart) laden with barley, and yoked (with an ox) on one side, to the Agnidh an ox[2].

23. Now there are here either twelve or thirteen[3] presents,—for either twelve or thirteen are there months in the year, and the year is Pragâpati, and Pragâpati is the sacrifice: thus he visibly obtains the sacrifice, and having visibly obtained it he makes it his own.

---

[1] See p. 8, note.

[2] The text has 'gâm agnîdhe,' i.e. either 'a bull,' or 'a cow.' So also Kâty. XV. 8, 27. Sâya*n*a, however, refers to another authority,—ana*d*vâham agnîdha iti sûtritam, . . . vahnir vâ ana*d*vân iti hi taittirîyakam.

[3] That is, according to Sâya*n*a, counting the unborn calves.

FIFTH ADHYÂYA. FIRST BRÂHMANA.

1. There is a cake on eight potsherds for Agni: this he places on the eastern part (of the Vedi). There is either a cake on eleven potsherds for Indra, or a rice-pap for Soma: this he places on the southern part. There is a pap for the Visve Devâh (All-gods): this he places on the western part. There is a dish of curds for Mitra-Varuna: this he places on the north part. There is a pap for Brihaspati: this he places in the middle. This is the five-holed pap[1];—what five sacrificial dishes (havis) there are, for them there are five holes: hence the name 'five-holed pap.'

2. And as to why the performer of the Râgasûya should perform this offering: because he (the priest) makes him ascend the regions, the seasons, the hymns and metres, he now redeems him therefrom by this (offering). But were the performer of the Râgasûya not to perform this offering, then verily he would become intoxicated (with pride)[2] and would fall down headlong: that is why the performer of the Râgasûya performs this offering.

3. And why he proceeds with the cake on eight

[1] According to Sâyana (MS. I. O. 657) the term 'Pañkabila' is derived from the circumstance that the vessel (pâtrî) on which the five sacrificial dishes are placed when taken about to be 'deposited' on the vedi, contains five holes or openings for the dishes to be taken out. The Pañkabila oblations are to be performed during the light fortnight succeeding the performance of the Dasapeya,—that is to say, during the fortnight commencing with the new moon of Vaisâkha, or in the latter part of April. The Taittirîya ceremonial calls these oblations the 'Disâm aveshtayah,' i.e. 'Sacrifices performed for the appeasement of the regions.'

[2] Or, would become giddy (in flying through space), cf. Taitt. Br. I, 8, 3, 1.

potsherds for Agni,—because he makes him ascend the eastern region, the seasons, the hymns and metres, he now redeems him therefrom by this (oblation). The remains of it he pours on the B*ri*haspati pap.

4. And why he proceeds with the cake on eleven potsherds for Indra, or with the pap for Soma,—because he makes him ascend the southern region, the seasons, the hymns and metres, he now redeems him therefrom by this (oblation). The remains he pours on the B*ri*haspati pap.

5. And why he proceeds with the pap to the All-gods,—because he makes him ascend the eastern region, the seasons, the hymns and metres, he now redeems him therefrom by this (oblation). The remains he pours on the B*ri*haspati pap.

6. And why he proceeds with the dish of curds for Mitra-Varu*n*a,—because he makes him ascend the northern region, the seasons, the hymns and metres, he now redeems him therefrom by this (oblation). The remains he pours on the B*ri*haspati pap. And in that he pours those remains on the B*ri*haspati pap, he thereby bestows food upon him[1] (the Sacrificer); and hence food is brought to the king from every quarter.

7. And why he proceeds with the B*ri*haspati pap,—because he makes him ascend the upper region, the seasons, the hymns and metres, he now redeems him therefrom by this (oblation).

8. And what cake on eight potsherds there is for Agni, the priest's fee for that is gold; for that offering is for Agni, and gold is Agni's seed: there-

[1] Or, puts food into him.

fore the fee is gold. He gives it to the Agnîdh; for he, the Âgnîdhra, is really the same as Agni: therefore he gives it to the Agnîdh.

9. And what cake on eleven potsherds there is for Indra, the fee for that is a bull, for the bull is Indra. And if there be a pap for Soma, then the fee for that is a brown ox, for the brown one is sacred to Soma. He gives it to the Brahman, for the Brahman guards the sacrifice from the south: therefore he gives it to the Brahman.

10. And what pap there is for the All-gods, the fee for that is a piebald bullock; for abundance of forms (marks) there is in such a piebald bullock, and the Visve Devâ*h* are the clans, and the clans mean abundance: therefore a piebald bullock is the fee. He gives it to the Hot*ri*, for the Hot*ri* means abundance: therefore he gives it to the Hot*ri*.

11. And what dish of curds there is for Mitra-Varu*n*a, the fee for that is a sterile cow, for that one is sacred to Mitra-Varu*n*a. If he cannot procure a sterile cow, any unimpregnated one will do; for every sterile cow is indeed unimpregnated. He gives it to the two Adhvaryus; for the Adhvaryus are the out-breathing and the in-breathing, and the out-breathing and in-breathing are Mitra-Varu*n*a: therefore he gives it to the two Adhvaryus.

12. And what pap there is for B*ri*haspati, the fee for that is a white-backed bullock; for to B*ri*haspati belongs that upper region[1], and above that there is that path of Aryaman[2]: therefore a white-backed (bullock) is the fee for the B*ri*haspati (pap). He gives it to the Brahman, for B*ri*haspati is the

[1] Or rather, that upward direction.

[2] That is, the region of light, of the sun. See V, 3, 1, 2 with note.

Brahman of the gods, and this one is his (the Sacrificer's) Brahman: therefore he gives it to the Brahman. Even a vish*th*âvrâ*g*in[1] who is desirous of food may perform this offering: he (the priest) thereby bestows food upon him from all quarters, and verily he becomes an eater of food.

Second Brâhma*n*a.

1. He performs the oblations of teams (prayu*g*â*m* havi*m*shi). The reason why he performs the oblations of teams, is that the anointed thereby yokes the seasons, and thus yoked those seasons draw him along, and he follows the seasons thus yoked: therefore he performs the oblations of teams.

2. There are twelve of these (oblations), for there are twelve months in the year: that is why there are twelve. 'Let him make offering month by month,' they say. Who knows about (the life of) man[2]? Let him therefore not make offering month by month. Moving eastward he offers six of them each at the distance of the yoke-pin's throw from the other[3]; and then turning backward he offers six, each at a yoke-pin's throw from the other.

---

[1] The meaning of this compound is unknown. Sâya*n*a explains it as meaning 'one who does not move from one spot, one who always remains in one and the same place.' Hence the St. Petersburg dictionary conjectures: 'One whose herd (or cattle-pen, vra*g*a, vrâ*g*a) is stationary.' Similarly, Prof. Weber, in Böhtlingk's Dictionary. See, however, the Kâ*n*va reading above, p. 50, note 1, according to which the word would seem to mean one afflicted with a certain malady (?cholera or dysentery). The 'Pañ*k*abila' offering may be performed as a special ish*t*i, independently of the Râ*g*asûya.

[2] 'But who (knows if he) will live a year?' Taitt. Br. I, 8, 4, 3.

[3] In that case, he could offer them as distinct ish*t*is, each with its special barhis, and moving eastwards from the Âhavanîya fire.

3. But let him not do it thus. He prepares those first six so as to have a common barhis[1], after the manner of those deities (of the first six oblations); even as in early spring they[2] would yoke their team and go onward until the rainy season, so does he now yoke the six seasons, and thus yoked the six seasons draw him forward and he follows the six seasons thus yoked until the rainy season. Two of the (oxen) drawing the original (hall-door) fire are the sacrificial fee.

4. He prepares the last six oblations so as to have a common barhis, after the manner of those (six) deities. Even as they would return again towards the rainy season, so does he yoke the six seasons, and thus yoked the six seasons draw him towards the rainy season, and he follows the six seasons thus yoked, in the rainy season. Two of the (oxen) drawing the original fire are the sacrificial fee. And as to why the (oxen) drawing the original fire are the sacrificial fee,—the consecrated (king) now yokes the seasons, and it being oxen that (actually) draw (and thus represent the seasons), therefore the (oxen) drawing the original fire are the sacrificial fee.

5. Now as to this the Kurupa*ñk*âlas used formerly to say, 'It is the seasons that, being yoked, draw us, and we follow the seasons thus yoked.' It was because their kings were performers of the Râ*g*asûya that they spake thus.

[1] That is to say, the first six oblations are to be combined and performed together as a single offering, without changing the covering of sacrificial grass on the altar.

[2] Sâya*n*a supplies 'kings,' and refers to Taitt. Br. I, 8, 4, 1, where the Kurupa*ñk*âla (kings) are said to issue forth in the dewy season (on a raid over the eastern country), and to return with their booty at the end of the hot season. See paragraph 5.

6. There is a cake on eight potsherds for Agni, a pap for Soma, a cake on twelve or eight potsherds for Savit*ri*, a pap for B*ri*haspati, a cake on ten potsherds for Tvash*t*ri, and one on twelve potsherds for (Agni) Vais*v*ânara—these are the first six oblations.

7. The six last are paps,—a pap for Sarasvati, a pap for Pûshan, a pap for Mitra, a pap for Kshetrapati (the Landlord or Lord of the manor), a pap for Varu*n*a, and a pap for Aditi,—these are the last six paps.

8. Thereupon they seize [1] a reddish-white (cow) which is clearly with calf, (as a victim) for Aditi. The mode of procedure regarding her is the same as that of the eight-footed barren cow [2]. Now, Aditi being this earth, it is her embryo (child) he thereby causes him (the king) to be. The sacrificial fee for this (cow-offering) is just such a reddish-white cow that is clearly with calf.

9. They then seize a dappled one, which is clearly with calf, (as a victim) for the Maruts. The mode of procedure regarding this one is the same. The Maruts being the clans, he thereby makes him the embryo [3] of the clans. The sacrificial fee for this (cow-offering) is just such a dappled (cow) that is clearly with calf.

[1] In the Taittiriya ceremonial this animal sacrifice precedes the 'prayugâ*m* havi*m*shi;' being itself succeeded in the first place by the 'sâtyadûtânâ*m* havi*m*shi.'

[2] On the course of procedure regarding the 'ash*t*âpadi,' or (supposed) barren cow, found ultimately to be impregnated, see part ii, p. 391 seq.

[3] That is, he causes him to spring forth from the midst of the people, and be protected by them on all sides.

10. These two animal victims, whilst being such, are seized (by some) in a different way. The one that is seized for Aditi, (some) seize for the Âdityas,—the Âdityas being the All, he (the priest) thereby makes him the embryo of the All (universe). And the one that is seized for the Maruts, (some) seize for the All-gods,—the All-gods being the All, he thereby makes him the embryo of the All.

THE KESAVAPANÎYA.

Third Brâhmana.

1. When he has performed the Consecration-ceremony (Abhishekanîya), he does not shave his hair. The reason why he does not shave his hair (is this):—that collected essence of the waters wherewith he is then sprinkled (anointed) is vigour, and it is the hair (of his head) that it reaches first when he is sprinkled; hence were he to shave his hair, he would cause that glory to fall off from him, and would sweep it away: therefore he does not shave his hair.

2. He does not shave his hair for a year[1],—religious observance is of equal measure with the year, hence he does not shave for a year: the Kesavapaniya[2], namely, is a (day of) praise-

[1] He is, however, allowed to shave his beard. According to Lâty. Sr. IX, 2, 20 seq., he is to pass his nights during the year in the fire-house on a tiger's skin; he is never to enter the village, and is constantly to keep up the fire. Nor is any one in his kingdom, except a Brâhman, to get his hair cut, and even the horses are to remain unclipped.

[2] The Kesavapanîya, or 'hair-cutting' (sacrifice), the fourth of the seven Soma-sacrifices enjoined for the inauguration of a king, is to be performed on the full-moon of Gyeshtha (about

singing (stoma) with the view of the termination of the religious performance.

3. Twenty-onefold is (each stotra of) its Morning-service, seventeenfold (of) the Midday-service, fifteen-fold (of) the Evening-service, together with the Uktha (stotras), the Shodasin, and (the twelve stotras of) the Night-service.

4. The Twilight (hymn)[1] is (performed in the) Trivrit (stoma), and with the Rathantara (tune). For the twenty-onefold (stoma) is he that burns yonder (the sun); from that twenty-onefold one he (the Sacrificer) parts, and descends again to the seventeenfold one; from the seventeenfold one to the

May 1), a twelvemonth after the Abhishekanîya, and is to take the form of the Atirâtra-Gyotishtoma. As usual, the author only alludes to any special peculiarities from the ordinary performance. The ordinary ascending scale of stomas—viz. the Trivrit-stoma for the Bahishpavamâna-stotra, the Pañkadasa for the Âgya-stotras and the Mâdhyandina-pavamâna; the Saptadasa for the Prishtha-stotras, and the Tritîya-pavamâna; and the Ekavimsa-stoma for the Agnishtoma-sâman—prescribed for the twelve stotras of the Agnishtoma (part i, p. 310 seq.), is to be reversed on the present occasion, and the scale of stomas is to be a descending one. The succeeding stotras—viz. (13-15) the three Uktha-stotras; (16) the Shodasin; and (17-28) the three rounds of the night service requiring four stotras each—are likewise to be performed in the Pañkadasa (or fifteen-versed) stoma, employed for the hymns of the evening pressing.

[1] The Sandhi-stotra, or Twilight hymn, Sâma-veda II. 99-104, is the final stotra of the Atirâtra (part ii, p. 398). Each of the three couplets is, as usual, sung as a triplet, the three thus producing the nine verses of the Trivrit-stoma. The Rathantara tune, to which the couplets are to be sung, is given in the Uhyagâna (Sâma-veda, vol. v, p. 381), but with different verses, viz. Sâma-veda I, 30, 31 (abhi tvâ sûra nonumo), the verses most commonly sung to that famous tune. The chanters' manuals of the Atirâtra (e.g. Ind. Off. MS. 1748) accordingly adapt the tune to the verses here required (enâ vo agnim namaso).

fifteenfold one; and from the fifteenfold one he plants his foot on this firm footing, the Triv*ri*t (stoma).

5. The Rathantara is the P*ri*sh*th*a (stotra)[1] of this (sacrifice); for the Rathantara is this (earth): it is on her, as on a firm footing, he thereby plants his feet. It is an Atirâtra (sacrifice),—the Atirâtra is a firm footing: therefore it is an Atirâtra.

6. He only cuts down his hair, but does not shave it; for that collected essence of the waters with which he is sprinkled is vigour, and it is the hair that it reaches first when he is sprinkled. Thus were he to shave off his hair he would cause that glory to fall off from him, and would sweep it away. But when he cuts it down, he attaches that glory to his own self: therefore he only cuts down his hair, but does not shave it. This is for him a religious observance: as long as he lives he does not stand on this (earth with bare feet[2]).

7. From the throne-seat he slips into the shoes; and on shoes (he stands), whatever his vehicle may be, whether a chariot or anything else. For verily he who performs the Râ*g*asûya is high above everything here, and everything here is beneath him;—therefore this is for him a religious observance: as long

[1] The first (or Hot*ri*'s) P*ri*sh*th*a-stotra at the midday-service is either the Rathantara, Sâma-veda II, 30, 31 (as for instance at the Agnish*t*oma), or B*ri*hat-sâman II, 159–160 (as at the Ukthya sacrifice). The B*ri*hat is also ordinarily chanted at the Atirâtra, but on the present occasion the Rathantara is to be substituted for it.

[2] Sâya*n*a interprets this passage so as to imply two separate injunctions:—'For as long as he lives this (cutting down of his hair) is a religious observance for him; and he does not stand on the ground (without shoes).' The repetition in the next paragraph, however, renders this interpretation very improbable.

as he lives he does not stand on the earth (with bare feet).

THE SAUTRÂMANÎ.

FOURTH BRÂHMANA.

1. There is a reddish-white (he-goat as the victim) for the Asvins [1], for the Asvins are reddish-white. There is an ewe with teats in the dewlap [2] for Sarasvatî; and a bull he seizes for Indra Sutrâman (the good protector) [3]. Difficult to obtain are beasts with such perfections; if he cannot obtain any

[1] The last three Soma-sacrifices of the Inauguration-ceremony are not even alluded to by the author, their performance involving no features different from those of the normal Soma-sacrifice. The Vyush*t*i-dvirâtra, or 'two nights' ceremony of the dawn,' consists of an Agnish*t*oma and an Atirâtra Soma-sacrifice, to be performed a month after the Kesavapanîya (or, according to Taitt. Br. I, 8, 10, a fortnight after, viz. on the new-moon, and the first day of the light fortnight respectively). Finally, the Kshatra-dh*ri*ti, or 'wielding of the ruling-power,' an Agnish*t*oma, is performed a month later, or on the full-moon of *S*râva*n*a (about 1 August). Some authorities, however, allow the Soma-sacrifices of the Inauguration-ceremony to conclude with the Kesavapanîya Atirâtra (Kâty. *S*r. XV, 9, 26), perhaps for the very reason that no mention is made in the Brâhma*n*a of the remaining three Soma-days. The final Soma-sacrifice is followed, in the succeeding fortnight of the waxing moon, by the performance of the Sautrâma*n*î, some peculiar features of which the author now proceeds to consider. This ceremony (one of the objects of which is the expiation of any excess committed in the consumption of Soma-juice) is considered in the sacrificial system as the last of the seven forms of Haviryag*ñ*a; being a combination of the ish*t*i with the animal sacrifice. As this ceremony is also performed after the Agni*k*ayana, or construction of the fire-altar, it is more fully dealt with by the author later on (Kâ*n*da XII, 7 seq.).

[2] Prof. R. Wallace's 'India in 1887' (plate 39) contains a photographic representation of an Indian goat with pendicles like teats.

[3] In the case of the 'somâtipavita,' not the 'somavâmin,' the Taittirîyas slaughter a fourth victim to B*ri*haspati.

with such perfections, they may slaughter only goats, for they are easier to cook. And if they seize only goats, that for the A*s*vins is a red one. Then as to why he performs this sacrifice.

2. Now Tvash*t*ri had a three-headed, six-eyed son[1]. He had three mouths; and because he was thus shapen, he was called Vi*s*varûpa ('All-shape').

3. One of his mouths was Soma-drinking, one spirit-drinking, and one for other food. Indra hated him, and cut off those heads of his.

4. And from the one which was Soma-drinking, a hazel-cock sprang forth; whence the latter is of brownish colour, for king Soma is brown.

5. And from the one which was spirit-drinking, a sparrow sprang; whence the latter talks like one who is joyful, for when one has drunk spirits, one talks as one who enjoys himself.

6. And from the one which was for other (kinds of) food, a partridge sprang; whence the latter is exceedingly variegated: ghee drops indeed have, as it were, dropped on his wings in one place, and honey-drops, as it were, in another; for suchlike was the food he consumed with that (mouth).

7. Tvash*t*ri was furious: 'Has he really slain my son?' He brought Soma-juice withheld from Indra[2]; and as that Soma-juice was, when produced, even so it remained withheld from Indra.

---

[1] This portion of the legend is but a repetition from I, 6, 3, 1 seq. A few alterations are, however, made here in the translation.

[2] Or, 'Soma from which Indra was excluded' (apendra), as formerly translated; a closer rendering of the succeeding clause making this change desirable;—even as Indra was excluded from the Soma-juice when produced, so he remained excluded from it (when it was offered up).

8. Indra thought within himself: 'There now, they are excluding me from Soma!' and even uninvited he consumed what pure (Soma) there was in the tub, as the stronger (would consume the food) of the weaker. But it hurt him: it flowed in all directions from (the openings of) his vital airs; only from his mouth it did not flow. Hence there was an atonement; but had it flown also from his mouth, then indeed there would have been no atonement.

9. For there are four castes, the Brâhma*n*a, the Râ*g*anya, the Vai*s*ya, and the *S*ûdra; but there is not one of them that vomits Soma; but were there any one of them, then indeed there would be atonement.

10. From what flowed from the nose a lion sprang; and from what flowed from the ears a wolf sprang; and from what flowed from the lower opening wild beasts sprang, with the tiger as their foremost; and what flowed from the upper opening that was the foaming spirit (parisrut). And thrice he spit out: thence were produced the (fruits called) 'kuvala, karkandhu, or badara[1].' He (Indra) became emptied out of everything, for Soma is everything.

11. Being thus purged by Soma, he walked about as one tottering. The A*s*vins cured him by this (offering), and caused him to be supplied with everything, for Soma is everything. By offering he indeed became better.

12. The gods spake, 'Aha! these two have saved him[2], the well-saved (sutrâta):' hence the name Sautrâma*n*i.

[1] The berries of three different species of the Zizyphus jujuba, or jujube-tree.

[2] The MS. of Sâya*n*a's commentary reads 'atrâsâtâm.'

13. Let him also cure by this (ceremony) one purged by Soma;—he whom Soma purges is indeed emptied out of everything, for Soma is everything. He now causes him to be supplied with everything, for Soma is everything; and by offering he indeed becomes better: let him therefore cure thereby also one purged by Soma.

14. And as to why the performer of the Râgasûya performs this offering. He who performs the Râgasûya assuredly gains for himself all sacrificial rites, all offerings, even the spoonful-oblations; and instituted by the gods indeed is this offering, the Sautrâmanî: 'May offering be made by me with this one also! may I be consecrated by this one also!' thus (he thinks, and) therefore the performer of the Râgasûya performs this offering.

15. And as to why there is (a victim) for the Asvins,—it was the Asvins who cured him; and in like manner does he (the priest) now cure him through those same Asvins: that is why there is (a victim) for the Asvins.

16. And why there is one for Sarasvatî,—Sarasvatî assuredly is speech, and it was by speech that the Asvins cured him; and in like manner does he now cure him by speech: that is why there is one for Sarasvatî.

17. And why there is one for Indra,—Indra assuredly is the deity of the sacrifice, and it is by this (offering) that he now heals him: this is why there is one for Indra.

18. On (the meat-portions of) those victims he throws hairs of a lion, hairs of a wolf, and hairs of a tiger, for that was what sprang therefrom, when Soma flowed right through him. He now supplies

him therewith, and makes him whole: therefore he throws those (hairs) thereon.

19. But let him not do it so; for he who throws them on the (portions of) the victims, urges the animals on from behind with a clawed (prickly) fire-brand. Let him therefore rather throw them into the fermented liquor (parisrut[1]),—thus he does not urge on the animals from behind with a clawed fire-brand; and thus alone he supplies him therewith, and makes him whole: let him therefore throw it rather into the spirituous liquor.

20. Now on the day before, he mixes the spirituous liquor (while muttering, Vâg. S. X, 31), 'Get done for the Asvins! get done for Sarasvati! get done for Indra, the good protector!' When that liquor is (done) he proceeds with that (offering).

21. They take up two fires; on the northern altar[2] (they lay down) the northern (fire), and on a raised (mound) the southern one, thinking, 'Lest we should offer together the Soma-libations, and the Surâ (liquor) -libations:' therefore they take up two fires, and on the northern altar (they lay down) the northern (fire), and on a raised (mound) the southern one. And when he proceeds with the omenta, then he proceeds with that spirituous liquor.

22. He purifies it with stalks of Darbha-grass, thinking, 'Let it be pure,'—with (Vâg. S. X, 31), 'The inviting[3] Soma, purified by the purify-

[1] On the preparation of the parisrut or surâ, see XII, 7; Weber, Ind. Studien, X, p. 349.

[2] The two new fireplaces, to the east of the Âhavanîya, are to be constructed on the model of those of the Varunapraghâsâh, see part i, p. 392.

[3] This doubtful interpretation of 'vâyu' is adopted from the St.

ing (strainer), has overflown backwards, Indra's mated friend.' He then pours in flour of 'kuvala, karkandhu, and badara' berries, for when he (Indra) spit out thrice, that was what was produced therefrom: therewith he now supplies him and makes him whole,—therefore he pours in that (flour).

23. He then draws either one or three cups[1],—but only one should be drawn, for there is one puroruk-formula, one invitatory prayer, and one offering prayer; therefore only one (cup) should be drawn.

24. He draws it with (Vâg. S. X, 32), 'Yea, even as the owners of barley cut their barley, spreading it asunder in due order, so hither, hither, bring thou the nourishments of them that offer up the devotional invocation of the Barhis[2]!—Thou art taken with a support—thee for the Asvins, thee for Sarasvatî, thee for Indra, the good protector!' And if he draw three (cups), let him draw them with that same (verse); but let him in that case draw them with separate 'supports[3].' He then says, 'Recite the

Petersburg dictionary, where, however, it is only applied to two passages of the Rig-veda. Sâyana here explains it by 'pâtrâni gakkhan vâyuvak khigragâmî vâ bhûtvâ pratyan adhovartî pâtrâbhimukhah san.' In the Taitt. S. this verse is preceded by another (Rik S. IX, 1, 6). 'May Sûrya's daughter purify thy foaming (parisrut) Soma with the never-failing horse-tail (strainer).'

[1] According to the ritual of the Taittirîyas, three cups of Surâ are drawn.

[2] Rik S. X, 131, 2, and Taitt. S. I, 8, 21 read—'hither, hither bring the nourishments of them that have not gone to the devotional up-pulling (cutting) of the barhis-grass' (but differently Sâyana,—'that have not gone to the neglect of the devotion of the barhis').

[3] That is to say, he is to repeat the formula, 'Thou art taken

invitatory prayer to the Asvins, to Sarasvatî, and to Indra Sutrâman!'

25. He recites (Vâg. S. X, 33; Rik S. X, 131, 4), 'Ye, O Asvins, lords of splendour, having quaffed the cheering (Soma) together with Namuki, the Âsura, helped Indra in his deeds!' Having called for the Sraushat, he says, 'Pronounce the offering prayer to the Asvins, to Sarasvatî, and to Indra Sutrâman!'

26. He prays (Vâg. S. X, 34; Rik S. X, 131, 5), 'As the parents (stand by) their son, so the two Asvins have stood by thee, O Indra, with wise plans and wonderful deeds; when thou quaffedst the cheering (Soma), Sarasvatî cured thee, O Lord, by her services.' Twice the Hotri utters the Vashat, twice the Adhvaryu offers and fetches drink. And if he draw three (cups of liquor), then after the offering of that one the other two are offered.

27. Now there is a pitcher perforated either with a hundred, or with nine, holes. If it is one with a hundred holes,—man lives up to a hundred (years), and has a hundred energies, and a hundred powers: therefore it is perforated with a hundred holes. And if with nine holes,—there are in man those nine vital airs: therefore it is perforated with nine holes.

28. This (pitcher), hung up by a sling, they hold just over the Âhavanîya[1]. He pours into it what spirituous liquor has been left over, and whilst it is

with a support,' each time followed by a special dedication, 'thee for the Asvins!' &c.

[1] That is, over the southern one of the two new fires, the one laid down on a raised mound.

trickling through, he stands by worshipping with the three verses[1] of the Pitara*h* Somavanta*h* (the Fathers accompanied by Soma), with three verses of the Pitaro Barishada*h* (the Fathers seated on the barhis), and with three verses of the Pitaro Agnishvâttâ*h* (the Fathers consumed by the fire). And as to why he thus stands by worshipping,—when Soma flowed through Indra, what part of it then went to the Fathers—there being three kinds of Fathers—therewith he now supplies him and makes him whole: therefore he thus stands by worshipping.

29. He then prepares those oblations[2],—a cake on twelve or eight potsherds for Savit*ri*, a barley pap for Varu*n*a, and a cake on eleven potsherds for Indra.

30. And why there is one for Savit*ri*,—Savit*ri* is the impeller of the gods, and impelled by Savit*ri* he now heals[3]: therefore there is one for Savit*ri*.

---

[1] These triplets to the Fathers are given Vâg. S. XIX, 49-51; 55-57; 58-60.—The Taitt. ritual here has a curious variation. After the remainder of the (pure) liquor has been offered to the Fathers, a Brâhman is to be bought over to drink the dregs; and if such an one cannot be found (willing to do it), they are to be poured away on an ant-hill. This is to be done for the sake of atonement.

[2] That is, according to Kâtyâyana (XV, 10, 19) and Sâya*n*a, the pa*s*u-puro*d*â*s*a, or cakes of the animal offering. The performance of these is irregular, inasmuch as their deities are not the same as those of the animal sacrifice (the A*s*vins, Sarasvatî, and Indra Sutrâman). Taitt. Br. I, 8, 6, 1, however, explains that in this case the animal sacrifices are without 'animal cakes,' the libations of liquor, which indeed are offered to the same deities, being in lieu of them.

[3] The object of the Sautrâma*n*î offering is to heal or 'make whole' the Sacrificer.

31. And why there is one for Varu*n*a,—Varu*n*a is the injurer, and he thus heals him even by him who is the injurer: therefore there is one for Varu*n*a.

32. And why there is one for Indra,—Indra is the deity of the sacrifice, and he thus heals him by him who is the deity of the sacrifice: therefore there is one for Indra.

33. And if by that (Sautrâma*n*i-offering) he would heal one purged by Soma[1], then—(after) the after-offering (of the animal sacrifice) has been performed, and the two spoons separated—he proceeds with those (three) oblations[2]. For it is towards the back part that Soma flows through, and at the back part (of the sacrifice) he thus closes him up by that sacrificial essence. Let him in that case prepare a cake on two potsherds for the A*s*vins; and when he proceeds with the offering of the omenta, then he also proceeds with that two-kapâla cake for the A*s*vins.

34. Let him, however, not do it in this way; for verily whosoever departs from the path of the sacrifice stumbles, and he who does this indeed departs from the path of the sacrifice. Hence at the very time when they proceed with the omenta of those victims, let them then proceed also with those (three) oblations, and let him not then prepare a two-kapâla cake for the A*s*vins.

35. A castrated bull is the sacrificial fee for this

[1] That is to say, if it is performed, independently of the Râga-sûya, as a special offering with a view to expiating any excess committed at a Soma-sacrifice.

[2] A glance at the list of contents prefixed to part ii will show how this shifting of the Pa*s*u-puro*d*â*s*a would alter the regular order of procedure.

(sacrifice);—the castrated bull is neither female nor male; for being a male it is not a female, and being a female (unmanned) it is not a male: therefore a castrated bull is the fee. Or a draught-mare;—the draught-mare is neither male nor female; for in that it pulls the cart it is not a female; and being a female, it is not a male: therefore a draught-mare (may be) the fee.

Fifth Brâhmana.

1. He prepares a cake on twelve potsherds for Indra and Vishnu. Now as to why he makes this offering. Of old, everything here was within Vritra, to wit, the *Rik*, the Yagus, and the Sâman. Indra wished to hurl the thunderbolt at him.

2. He said to Vishnu, 'I will hurl the thunderbolt at Vritra, stand thou by me!'—'So be it!' said Vishnu, 'I will stand by thee: hurl it!' Indra aimed the thunderbolt at him. Vritra was afraid of the raised thunderbolt.

3. He said, 'There is here a (source of) strength: I will give that up to thee; but do not smite me!' and gave up to him the Yagus-formulas. He (Indra) aimed at him a second time.

4. He said, 'There is here a (source of) strength: I will give that up to thee; but do not smite me!' and gave up to him the *Rik*-verses. He aimed at him a third time.

5. 'There is here a (source of) strength: I will give that up to thee; but do not smite me!' and gave up to him the Sâman-hymns (or tunes). Therefore they spread the sacrifice even to this day in the same way with those (three) Vedas, first with the

Yagus-formulas, then with the *R*ik-verses, and then with the Sâman-hymns; for thus he (V*ri*tra) at that time gave them up to him.

6. And that which had been his (V*ri*tra's) seat, his retreat, that he shattered, grasping it and tearing it out[1]: it became this offering. And because the science (the Veda) that lay in that retreat was, as it were, a threefold (tridhâtu) one, therefore this is called the Traidhâtavi (ish*t*i).

7. And as to why the oblation is one for Indra and Vish*n*u, it is because Indra raised the thunderbolt, and Vish*n*u stood by him.

8. And why it is (a cake) on twelve potsherds,—there are twelve months in the year, and the offering is of equal measure with the year: therefore it is one of twelve potsherds.

9. He prepares it of both rice and barley. He first puts on (the fire) a ball of rice, that being a form (symbol) of the Yagus-formulas; then one of barley, that being a form of the *R*ik-verses; then one of rice, that being a form of the Sâman-hymns. Thus this is made to be a form of the triple science: and this same (offering) becomes the Udavasânîyâ-ish*t*i (completing oblation) for the performer of the Râgasûya.

10. For, verily, he who performs the Râgasûya gains for himself (the benefit of) all sacrificial rites, all offerings, even the spoonful-oblations; for him the sacrifice becomes as it were exhausted, and he, as it were, turns away from it. Now the whole sacrifice is just as great as that triple Veda; and this (offering) now is made a form of that (Veda, or

[1] Cf. III, 2, 1, 28.

sacrifice); this is its womb, its seat: thus he commences once more the sacrifice by means of that triple Veda; and thus his sacrifice is not exhausted, and he does not turn away from it.

11. And, verily, he who performs the Râgasûya gains for himself all sacrificial rites, all offerings, even the spoonful-oblations; and this offering, the Traidhâtavî (ish*t*i), is instituted by the gods: 'May this offering also be performed by me, may I be consecrated by this one also!' thus he thinks, and therefore this is the completing offering for him who performs the Râgasûya.

12. And also for him who would give (to the priests) a thousand (cows) or more[1], let this be the completing offering. For he who gives a thousand or more becomes as it were emptied out; and that triple Veda is the thousandfold progeny of Vâ*k* (speech): him who was emptied out he thus fills up again with a thousand; and therefore let it be for him also the completing offering.

13. And also for those who would sit through (perform) a long sacrificial session[2], for a year or more, let this be the completing offering. For by those who sit through a long sacrificial session, for a year or more, everything is obtained, everything conquered; but this (offering) is everything: let it therefore be for them also the completing offering.

14. And indeed one may also practise magic by this (offering); for it was thereby that Âra*n*i be-

[1] For a (three days') Soma-sacrifice with a sacrificial fee of a thousand cows, the Trirâtra Sahasradakshi*n*a, see part ii, p. 414.

[2] See part ii, pp. 426, 440 seq.

witched Bhadrasena Âgâtasatrava[1]: 'Quick, then, spread (the barhis)!' thus Yâgñavalkya used to say. And by this (offering) indeed Indra also shattered Vritra's retreat; and, verily, he who therewith practises magic shatters thereby the retreat (of his enemy): therefore one may also practise magic with this (offering).

15. And, indeed, one may also heal thereby; for, verily, whomsoever one would heal by a single *rik*, by a single yagus, by a single sâman, him he would indeed render free from disease; how much more so by the triple Veda! Therefore one may also heal by this (offering).

16. Three gold pieces of a hundred mânas[2] each are the sacrificial fee for this (offering). He presents them to the Brahman; for the Brahman neither performs (like the Adhvaryu), nor chants (like the Udgâtri), nor recites (like the Hotri), and yet he is an object of respect. And with gold they do nothing[3], and yet it is an object of respect: therefore he presents to the Brahman three gold pieces of a hundred mânas each.

---

[1] Apparently the son of Agâtasatru, king of Kâsî, who is mentioned as having been very proficient in speculative theology, and jealous, in this respect, of king Ganaka of Videha.

[2] According to Sâyana, these 'satamânas' are similar to the round plate worn by the king during the Consecration-ceremony; see p. 104, note 2. These plates (as the 'rukmas' generally, VI, 7, 1, 1 seq.) were apparently used for ornament only, not as coins.

[3] Sâyana explains this to mean that gold is not used for actual consumption, but only indirectly, as for vessels on which food is served, or in traffic, as a medium of barter;—the gold thus never losing its appearance, its 'glory.' See II, 1, 1, 5, 'Hence also one does not cleanse oneself with it (?), nor does one do anything else with it.'

17. Three milch cows (he gives) to the Hot*ri*;—for three milch cows mean abundance, and the Hot*ri* means abundance: therefore (he gives) three milch cows to the Hot*ri*.

18. Three garments (he gives) to the Adhvaryu;—for the Adhvaryu 'spreads' the sacrifice, and the garments spread themselves (over the body)[1]: therefore (he gives) three garments to the Adhvaryu. A bullock (he gives) to the Agnîdh[2].

19. Now there are here either twelve, or thirteen gifts[3], and there are either twelve or thirteen months in the year;—the offering thus is of equal measure with the year: that is why there are either twelve or thirteen sacrificial gifts.

---

[1] Or, people spread the clothes (either in weaving them, or in putting them on). 'To spread the sacrifice' is the regular term for the ceremonial practice of spreading the sacrificial fire from the Gârhapatya (or household fire) over the other two hearths, and thus for the performance of the sacrifice generally.

[2] See p. 119, note 2.

[3] That is, taking the calves of the three milch cows into account; and optionally counting the gift to the Âgnîdhra.

SIXTH KÂNDA.

THE AGNIKAYANA, OR BUILDING OF THE FIRE-ALTAR.

CREATION OF THE UNIVERSE.

FIRST ADHYÂYA. FIRST BRÂHMANA.

1. Verily, in the beginning there was here the non-existent[1]. As to this they say, 'What was that non-existent?' The *Ri*shis, assuredly,—it is they that were the non-existent[2]. As to this they say, 'Who were those *Ri*shis?' The *Ri*shis, doubtless, were the vital airs: inasmuch as before (the existence of) this universe, they, desiring it, wore themselves out (rish) with toil and austerity, therefore (they are called) *Ri*shis.

2. This same vital air in the midst doubtless is Indra. He, by his power (indriya), kindled those (other) vital airs from the midst; and inasmuch as he kindled (indh), he is the kindler (indha): the kindler[3] indeed,—him they call 'Indra' mystically

---

[1] Or, perhaps, In the beginning this (universe) was indeed non-existent. Thus J. Muir, Or. S. T. IV, p. 22, of which translation of this cosmogonic myth considerable use has been made here. It need scarcely be remarked that 'idam' is constantly used in an adverbial sense in the Brâhma*n*a.

[2] In the original, 'the non-existent' is the subject of the clause, not the predicate as would appear from the translation. A similar transposition seems often advisable in English, for the sake of emphasis, and on other grounds. Muir's rendering, 'The Rishis say that in the beginning there was non-existence,' is a mistake.

[3] The nominative here is striking, and vivid, cf. paragraph 11 below. In corresponding passages of the preceding books, the accusative would stand here; e.g. II, 1, 2, 4, saptarshîn u ha sma vai purarkshâ ity â*k*akshate; similarly III, 1, 2, 3.

(esoterically), for the gods love the mystic. They (the vital airs), being kindled, created seven separate persons[1] (purusha).

3. They said, 'Surely, being thus, we shall not be able to generate: let us make these seven persons one Person!' They made those seven persons one Person: they compressed two of them[2] (into) what is above the navel, and two of them (into) what is below the navel; (one) person was (one) wing (or side), (one) person was (the other) wing, and one person was the base (i.e. the feet).

4. And what excellence, what life-sap (rasa) there was in those seven persons, that they concentrated above, that became his head. And because (in it) they concentrated the excellence (*s*rî), therefore it is (called) the head (*s*iras). It was thereto that the breaths resorted (*s*ri): therefore also it is the head (*s*iras). And because the breaths did so resort (*s*ri) thereto, therefore also the breaths (vital airs, and their organs) are elements of excellence (*s*rî). And because they resorted to the whole (system) therefore (this is called) body (*s*arîra).

5. That same Person became Pra*g*âpati (lord of generation). And that Person which became Pra*g*âpati is this very Agni (fire-altar), who is now (to be) built.

6. He verily is composed of seven persons, for this Person (Agni) is composed of seven persons[3],

---

[1] That is, living beings or souls, individualities, which, in their combined form, are here imagined to take the shape of a bird. Muir's rendering, 'males,' can scarcely commend itself.

[2] Literally, 'those two.'

[3] The fire-altar is usually constructed so as to measure seven

to wit, the body (trunk) of four, and the wings and tail of three; for the body of that (first) Person (was composed of) four, and the wings and tail of three. And inasmuch as he makes the body larger by one person, by that force the body raises the wings and tail.

7. And as to the fire which is deposited on the built (altar),—whatever excellence, whatever life-sap there was in those seven persons, that they now concentrate above, that is his (Pragâpati's) head. On that same (head) all the gods are dependent (*s*rita), for it is there that offering is made to all the gods: therefore also it is the head (*s*iras).

8. Now this Person Pragâpati desired, 'May I be more (than one), may I be reproduced!' He toiled, he practised austerity. Being worn out with toil and austerity, he created first of all the Brahman (neut.), the triple science. It became to him a foundation: hence they say, 'the Brahman (Veda) is the foundation of everything here.' Wherefore, having studied (the Veda) one rests on a foundation; for this, to wit, the Veda, is his foundation. Resting on that foundation, he (again) practised austerity.

9. He created the waters out of Vâ*k* (speech, that is) the world; for speech belonged to it[1]: that was

---

man's lengths square; the particular length being that of the Sacrificer. This, however, is the smallest size allowed for an altar, there being altogether ninety-five different sizes specified, varying between seven and 101 man's lengths square.

[1] Or, perhaps, to him (Pragâpati). Sâya*n*a merely says,—vâg evâsya sâs*r*i*g*yata, vâk sahakâri rasanam abhavat, tad as*r*i*g*yatety artha*h*; sâ vâk sahakâri rasanam prâgâpatya(*m*) s*r*ish*t*a*m* sad ida*m* sarvam âpnot.—On the part which Vâ*k* (the personification of the Brahman or Veda) takes by the side of Pragâpati in the creation

created (set free). It pervaded everything here; and because it pervaded (âp) whatsoever there was here, therefore (it is called) water (âpa*h*); and because it covered (var), therefore also it (is called) water (vâr).

10. He desired, 'May I be reproduced from these waters!' He entered the waters with that triple science. Thence an egg arose. He touched it. 'Let it exist! let it exist and multiply!' so he said. From it the Brahman (neut.) was first created, the triple science. Hence they say, 'The Brahman (n.) is the first-born of this All.' For even before that Person the Brahman was created[1]: it was created as his mouth. Hence they say of him who has studied the Veda, that 'he is like Agni;' for it, the Brahman (Veda), is Agni's mouth.

11. Now the embryo which was inside was created as the foremost (agri): inasmuch as it was created foremost (agram) of this All, therefore (it is called) Agri: Agri, indeed, is he whom they mystically call[2] Agni; for the gods love the mystic. And the tear (asru, n.) which had formed itself[3] become the 'asru' (m.): 'asru' indeed is what they mystically call 'asva' (horse), for the gods love the

of the universe, and the parallelism between Vâ*k* and λόγος, see Weber, Ind. Stud. IX, p. 473 seq.; Muir, Or. S. T. V, p. 391. Thus Pa*ñk*. Br. XX, 14, 2, 'Pragâpati alone existed here. He had Vâ*k* indeed as his own, as a second to him.'

[1] Muir takes this differently,—Further, (as) the Veda was first created from that Male, therefore it was created his mouth. This translation, however, takes no account of the particle 'hi.'

[2] For the construction, see above, paragraph 2, with note.

[3] Literally, which had flowed together. It is explained as the embryonic liquid in the amnion, or innermost membrane enveloping the foetus.

mystic. And that which, as it were, cried[1] (ras), became the ass (râsabha). And the juice which was adhering to the shell (of the egg) became the he-goat (aga[2]). And that which was the shell became the earth.

12. He desired, 'May I generate this (earth) from these waters!' He compressed it[3] and threw it into the water. The juice which flowed from it became a tortoise; and that which was spirted upwards (became) what is produced above here over the waters. This whole (earth) dissolved itself all over the water: all this (universe) appeared as one form only, namely, water.

13. He desired, 'May it become more than one, may it reproduce itself!' He toiled and practised austerity; and worn out with toil and austerity, he created foam. He was aware that 'this indeed looks different, it is becoming more (than one): I must toil, indeed!' Worn out with toil and austerity, he created clay, mud, saline soil and sand, gravel (pebble), rock, ore, gold, plants and trees: therewith he clothed this earth.

14. This (earth), then, was created as (consisting of) these same nine creations. Hence they say, 'Threefold (three times three) is Agni;' for Agni is this (earth), since thereof the whole Agni (fire-altar) is constructed.

15. 'This (earth) has indeed become (bhû) a foundation!' (he thought): hence it became the earth (bhûmi). He spread it out (prath), and it

[1] ? Or, that part (of the egg) which made a noise (in cracking).

[2] The word 'aga' is apparently fancifully taken here in the sense of 'unborn (a-ga).'

[3] That is, the earth when as yet in the form of the egg-shell.

became the broad one (or earth, p*ri*thivî). And she (the earth), thinking herself quite perfect[1], sang; and inasmuch as she sang (gâ), therefore she is Gâyatrî. But they also say, 'It was Agni, indeed, on her (the earth's) back, who thinking himself quite perfect, sang; and inasmuch as he sang (gâ), therefore Agni is Gâyatra.' And hence whosoever thinks himself quite perfect, either sings or delights in song[2].

SECOND BRÂHMA*N*A.

1. That Pra*g*âpati desired, 'May it multiply, may it be reproduced!' By means (or, in the form) of Agni he entered into union with the Earth: thence an egg arose. He touched it: 'May it grow! May it grow and multiply!' he said.

2. And the embryo which was inside was created as Vâyu (the wind). And the tear which had formed itself became those birds. And the juice which was adhering to the shell became those sun-motes. And that which was the shell became the air.

3. He desired, 'May it multiply, may it reproduce itself!' By means of Vâyu he entered into union with the Air: thence an egg arose. He touched it, saying, 'Bear thou glory!' From it yonder sun was created, for he indeed is glorious. And the tear which (a*s*ru) formed itself became that variegated pebble (a*s*man); for 'a*s*ru' indeed is what

[1] Abhimâninîstrîvigrahâ yasmâd agâyad tasmâd iya*m* Gâyatrî, Sây.—'Because, like a haughty woman, she (the earth) sang, therefore she is Gâyatrî.'

[2] On this illustration, which might either be taken as applying to men in easy circumstances, not troubled with cares;—or, perhaps, to a new-born child which cries out lustily, and likes to be sung to,—Sâya*n*a only remarks,—tasmâd u haitad iti svabhâvânuvâda*h*, kâryadharme*n*a kâra*n*adharmânupâdanâya.

they mystically call 'asman,' for the gods love the mystic. And the juice which was adhering to the shell became those sunbeams. And that which was the shell became the sky.

4. He desired, 'May it multiply, may it reproduce itself!' By means of the Sun he entered into union with the Sky: thence an egg arose. He touched it, saying, 'Bear thou seed!' From it the moon was created, for he (the moon) is seed. And the tear which formed itself became those stars. And the juice which was adhering to the shell became those intermediate quarters; and that which was the shell became those (chief) quarters (points of the compass).

5. Having created these worlds, he desired, 'May I create such creatures as shall be mine in these worlds!'

6. By his Mind (manas) he entered into union with Speech (vâk): he became pregnant with eight drops. They were created as those eight Vasus[1]: he placed them on this (earth).

7. By his Mind he entered into union with Speech: he became pregnant with eleven drops. They were created as those eleven Rudras[2]: he placed them in the air.

8. By his Mind he entered into union with Speech: he became pregnant with twelve drops. They were created as the twelve Âdityas[3]: he placed them in the sky.

---

[1] As here, this class of deities—whose sphere of action are the terrestrial regions—was associated with Agni, the guardian of the earth, at III, 4, 2, 1.

[2] Another class of (storm) deities, here associated with Vâyu, the wind, the guardian of the air-region.

[3] This class of deities (of light) are here associated with the

9. By his Mind he entered into union with Speech: he became pregnant. He created the All-gods: he placed them in the quarters.

10. And so they say, 'After Agni having been created, the Vasus were created: he placed them on this (earth);—after Vâyu, the Rudras: (he placed) them in the air;—after the sun, the Âdityas: (he placed) them in the sky;—after the moon, the All-gods[1]: he placed them in the quarters.'

11. And so they say, 'Pragâpati, having created these worlds, was firmly established on the earth. For him these plants were ripened[2] into food: that he ate. He became pregnant. From the upper vital airs he created the gods, and from the lower vital airs the mortal creatures.' In whatever way he created thereafter, so he created; but indeed it was Pragâpati who created everything here, whatsoever exists.

12. Having created creatures he, having run the whole race, became relaxed[3]; and therefore even now he who runs the whole race becomes indeed

---

Sun, who indeed is called the Âditya in paragraphs 4 and 10 (instead of Sûrya).

[1] Professor Weber (Ind. Stud. XIII, p. 268) has drawn attention to the discrepancy between this passage and III, 4, 2, 1, where the Visve Devâh (with Brihaspati) are denied the privilege of forming a special class of deities,—this being one of many points of difference, doctrinal as well as linguistic, between Books 1–5 and 6–10.

[2] Professor Delbrück, Altind. Synt. p. 147, reads 'apakanta,'—the plants matured fruit.

[3] Literally, he fell asunder, or to pieces, became disjointed. Hence, when the gods 'restored' Pragâpati (the lord of generation, identified with the sacrifice, and with Agni, the fire), the verb used is *samskri*, 'to put together;' and this putting together, or restoration, of Pragâpati is symbolically identified with the building up of the fire-altar.

relaxed. From him being thus relaxed, the vital air went out from within. When it had gone out of him the gods left him.

13. He said to Agni, 'Restore me!'—'What will then accrue to me?' said he.—'They shall call me after thee; for whichever of the sons succeeds (in life), after him they call the father, grandfather, son, and grandson: they shall call me after thee,—restore me, then!'—'So be it!' so (saying) Agni restored him: therefore, while being Pragâpati, they call him Agni; and verily, whosoever knows this, after him they call his father, grandfather, son, and grandson.

14. He said, 'Whereon shall we set thee up[1]?'—'On the hita (set, or suitable, good)!' he said: the vital air is indeed something good, for the vital air is good for all beings. And inasmuch as he set him up on the hita, therefore one says, 'I shall set up, I am setting up, I have set up[2].'

15. As to this they say, 'What is hita, and what is upahita?' The vital air, forsooth, is the 'hita,' and speech is the 'upahita,' for it is on the vital air that this speech is based (upa-hitâ). The vital air, again, is the 'hita,' and the limbs are the 'upahita,' for on the vital air these limbs are indeed based.

16. This, then, was his (Pragâpati's) '*k*itya' (Agni to be set up on an altar-pile); for he had to be built up (*k*i) by him, and therefore was his '*k*itya.' And

[1] Upa-dhâ. Paragraphs 14 and 15 involve a double meaning of the word hita, the past participle of dhâ, to put,—viz. put, set, or suitable, beneficial.

[2] Or, 'I shall put on,' &c., upa-dhâ, the verb used of the putting on of bricks in building up the altar. Cf. II, 1, 2, 15.

so indeed he now is the Sacrificer's '*k*itya;' for he is to be built up by him, and therefore is his '*k*itya.'

17. Now it was those five bodily parts (tanu) of his (Pra*g*âpati's) that became relaxed,—hair, skin, flesh, bone, and marrow,—they are these five layers (of the fire-altar); and when he builds up the five layers, thereby he builds him up by those bodily parts; and inasmuch as he builds up (*k*i), therefore they are layers (*k*iti).

18. And that Pra*g*âpati who became relaxed is the year; and those five bodily parts of his which became relaxed are the seasons; for there are five seasons, and five are those layers: when he builds up the five layers, he thereby builds him up with the seasons; and inasmuch as he builds up (lays down), therefore they are layers.

19. And that Pra*g*âpati, the year, who became relaxed, is that very Vâyu (wind) who blows yonder. And those five bodily parts of his, the seasons, which became relaxed, are the regions (or quarters)[1]; for five in number are the regions, and five those layers: when he builds up the five layers, he builds him up with the regions; and inasmuch as he builds up, therefore they are layers.

20. And the Fire that is laid down on the built (altar), that is yonder Sun;—that same Agni is indeed (raised) on the altar, and that just because Agni had restored him (Pra*g*âpati).

21. But they say,—Pra*g*âpati, when relaxed, said to the gods, 'Restore me!' The gods said to Agni, 'In thee we will heal this our father Pra*g*âpati.'—

[1] That is, the four quarters, or cardinal points of the compass; and the upper region, or rather the upward (or perpendicular) direction.

'Then I will enter into him, when whole,' he said.—'So be it!' they said. Hence, while being Pragâpati, they yet call him Agni.

22. In the fire the gods healed him by means of oblations; and whatever oblation they offered that became a baked brick and passed into him. And because they were produced from what was offered (ishta), therefore they are bricks (ishtakâ). And hence they bake the bricks by means of the fire, for it is oblations they thus make.

23. He spake, 'Even as much as ye offer, even so much is my happiness:' and inasmuch as for him there was happiness (ka) in what was offered (ishta), therefore also they are bricks (ishtakâ).

24. Here now Âktâkshya used to say, 'Only he who knows abundant bricks possessed of (special) prayers, should build up the fire (altar): abundantly indeed he then heals Father Pragâpati.'

25. But Tândya used to say, 'Surely the bricks possessed of prayers are the nobility, and the space-fillers[1] are the peasants; and the noble is the feeder, and the peasantry the food; and where there is abundant food for the feeder, that realm is indeed prosperous and thrives: let him therefore pile up abundant space-fillers!' Such then was the speech of those two, but the settled practice is different therefrom.

26. Now that father (Pragâpati) is (also) the son:

[1] In contradistinction to the yagushmatî (prayerful) bricks, which bear special names, and have special formulas attached to them; lokam-prinâ (space-filling ones) is the technical term for those bricks which have no special prayers belonging to them, but are piled up with a common formula (Vâg. S. XII, 54; Sat. Br. VIII, 7, 2, 1 seq.), beginning 'lokam prina khidram prina,' 'fill the space, fill the gap!'

inasmuch as he created Agni, thereby he is Agni's father; and inasmuch as Agni restored him, thereby Agni is his (Pragâpati's) father; and inasmuch as he created the gods, thereby he is the father of the gods; and inasmuch as the gods restored him, thereby the gods are his fathers.

27. Twofold verily is this,—father and son, Pragâpati and Agni, Agni and Pragâpati, Pragâpati and the gods, the gods and Pragâpati—(for) whosoever knows this.

28. He builds up with[1], 'By that deity'—that deity, doubtless, is Vâ*k* (speech),—'Aṅgiras-like,'—Aṅgiras, doubtless, is the breath;—'lie thou steady!' —that is, 'lie thou firm;' or 'lie thou firmly established.' It is both with speech and with breath that he builds; for Agni is speech, and Indra is the breath; and the fire (agni) relates to Indra and Agni: as great as Agni is, as great as is his measure, by so much he thus builds him up. And again, Indra and Agni are all the gods, (for) Agni belongs to all deities: thus as great as Agni is, as great as is his measure, by so much he thus builds him up.

29. Here now they say, 'Wherefore is Agni (the fire-altar) built of this (earth)?' But, surely, when that deity (Pragâpati) became relaxed (fell asunder), he flowed along this (earth) in the shape of his life-sap; and when the gods restored him (put him together), they gathered him up from this earth: this earth then is that one brick[2], for Agni is this earth, since

[1] This is the formula (Vâg. S. XII, 53) with which the so-called 'sâdanam' or 'settling' of the bricks is performed. See VII, 1, 1, 30.

[2] That is, the first brick which the wife of the Sacrificer herself forms, and which is called Ashâ*dh*â. See VI, 3, 1, 1; 5, 3, 1.

it is thereof[1] that the whole Agni is built up. Now this earth is four-cornered, for the quarters are her corners: hence the bricks are four-cornered; for all the bricks are after the manner of this earth.

30. As to this they say, 'But if he (Agni) thus consists of one brick, how then (comes he to be) a five-bricked[2] one?' Now surely the first brick of clay is this earth,—whatever made of clay he places on that (altar) that is that one brick. And when he puts thereon the heads of the animal victims[3], that is the animal-brick. And when he puts on the gold plate and man[4], when he scatters gold shavings thereon, that is the golden brick. And when he puts on two spoonfuls (of ghee)[5], when he puts on the mortar and pestle[6], and fire-sticks, that is the wood-brick. And when he puts on a lotus-leaf (petal), a tortoise[7], sour curds, honey, ghee, and whatever other food he puts on, that is the fifth brick, the food. Thus, then, it is a five-bricked (Agni).

31. As to this they say, 'On which side is the head of the brick?'—'Where he touches it and says a prayer,' so say some, 'on one end of the naturally perforated (brick)[8] alone indeed should he

---

[1] Viz. by means of the clay bricks, and the loose soil put between the layers.

[2] Sâyana only refers here to the fact that the sacrifice (yagña) is called 'pâñkta,' 'the fivefold.'

[3] See VII, 5, 2, 1 seq.

[4] See VII, 4, 1, 15 seq.

[5] See VII, 4, 1, 32 seq.

[6] See VII, 5, 1, 12 seq.

[7] See VII, 5, 1, 1 seq.

[8] Apparently some kind of porous stone. Three such perforated stones or 'bricks' are used in the construction of the fire-altar; viz. one which is laid on the gold man in the centre of the bottom layer (a sâman relating to bhûs, the earth, being pronounced

say a prayer while touching it, but thus all those (bricks) of his are turned towards the naturally perforated one.' Let him not do so, for those bricks doubtless are his (Agni's) limbs, his joints; and it would be just as if he were to put a head on each limb, on each joint. But indeed, the fire which is deposited on the pile, that is the head of all those (bricks).

32. Here they say, 'How many animal victims are laid upon the fire (altar)?'—Let him say 'Five,' for he does lay thereon those five victims.

33. Or, 'One,' he may say; 'a ewe;' for a ewe (avi) is this earth, since she favours (av) all these creatures. And the fire (altar) also is this earth, for the whole fire (altar) is built up thereof: hence he may say, 'One.'

34. Or, 'Two,' he may say, 'two sheep;' for sheep, indeed, are both this (earth) and that (sky), since these two favour all these creatures;—what clay (there is in the brick) that is this earth; and what water there is that is that sky; and the bricks consist of clay and water: therefore he may say, 'Two.'

35. Or he may say, 'A cow (or bullock, go);'—the cow forsooth means these worlds, for whatever walks (gam) that walks in these worlds[1]; and that

on it while touching it); the second in the centre of the third layer; and the third one being laid upon the centre of the completed fifth layer. They are meant to represent the three worlds, the holes being intended to afford to the Sacrificer (represented by the gold man) a passage to the highest regions. See VI, 2, 3, 1 seq.

[1] It is not quite clear whether the author indulges in etymological trifling (go—gû). The Bombay MS. of Sâyana reads,—imâmstallokân gakkhatîti kavana(?gavana)karmasâdhanam gosabdam darsayati.

fire also is these worlds: therefore he may say, 'A cow.'

36. As to this they say, 'For what object is this fire (altar) built?'—'Having become a bird, he (Agni) shall bear me to the sky!' so say some; but let him not think so; for by assuming that form, the vital airs became Pragâpati[1]; by assuming that form, Pragâpati created the gods[2]; by assuming that form, the gods became immortal: and what thereby the vital airs, and Pragâpati, and the gods became, that indeed he (the Sacrificer) thereby becomes.

THIRD BRÂHMANA.

1. Verily, Pragâpati alone was here in the beginning. He desired, 'May I exist, may I reproduce myself!' He toiled, he practised austerity (or, became heated). From him, worn out and heated, the waters were created: from that heated Person the waters are born.

2. The waters said, 'What is to become of us?'—'Ye shall be heated,' he said. They were heated; they created foam: hence foam is produced in heated water.

3. The foam (m.) said, 'What is to become of me?'—'Thou shalt be heated!' he said. It was heated, and produced clay; for indeed the foam is heated, when it floats on the water, covering it; and when one beats upon it, it indeed becomes clay.

4. The clay (f.) said, 'What is to become of me?'—'Thou shalt be heated!' he said. It was heated,

[1] See VI, 1, 1, 2 seq., where the seven vital airs are represented as assuming the form of a bird—the Purusha Pragâpati.

[2] See paragraphs 7–11.

and produced sand; for this clay becomes indeed heated when they plough it; and if only they plough very fine then it becomes, as it were, sandy. So much, then, as to that 'What is to become of me? what is to become of me[1]?'

5. From the sand he created the pebble: whence sand finally indeed becomes a pebble;—from the pebble the stone: whence the pebble finally indeed becomes a stone;—from the stone metal ore: whence from stone they smelt ore;—from ore gold: whence ore much smelted comes, as it were, to have the appearance of gold.

6. Now that which was created was flowing; and inasmuch as it was flowing (aksharat), a syllable (akshara) resulted therefrom; and inasmuch as it flowed eight times, that octosyllabic Gâyatrî was produced.

7. 'This has indeed become (bhû) a foundation (resting-place),' so he thought: whence it became the earth (bhûmi). He spread it out (prath): it became the broad (earth, p*ri*thivî). On this earth, as on a foundation, the beings, and the lord of beings, consecrated themselves for a year: the lord of beings was the master of the house[2], and Ushas (the Dawn) was the mistress.

8. Now, those beings are the seasons; and that lord of beings is the year; and that Ushas, the mistress, is the Dawn. And these same creatures, as well as the lord of beings, the year, laid seed

[1] He means to say that he will leave this to be supplied in the enumeration of the subsequent creations.

[2] At sacrificial sessions the Sacrificer is called G*ri*hapati. On this, see IV, 6, 8, 3-5.

into Ushas[1]. There a boy (kumâra) was born in a year: he cried.

9. Pragâpati said to him, 'My boy, why criest thou, when thou art born out of labour and trouble?' He said, 'Nay, but I am not freed from (guarded against) evil; I have no name given me: give me a name!' Hence one should give a name to the boy that is born, for thereby one frees him from evil;—even a second, even a third (name), for thereby one frees him from evil time after time.

10. He said to him, 'Thou art Rudra[2].' And because he gave him that name, Agni became suchlike (or, that form), for Rudra is Agni: because he cried (rud) therefore he is Rudra. He said, 'Surely, I am mightier than that: give me yet a name!'

11. He said to him, 'Thou art Sarva.' And because he gave him that name, the waters became suchlike, for Sarva is the waters, inasmuch as from the water everything (sarva) here is produced. He said, 'Surely, I am mightier than that: give me yet a name!'

12. He said to him, 'Thou art Pasupati.' And because he gave him that name, the plants became suchlike, for Pasupati is the plants: hence when cattle (pasu) get plants, then they play the master[3] (patiy). He said, 'Surely, I am mightier than that: give me yet a name!'

13. He said to him, 'Thou art Ugra.' And

---

[1] On the legend regarding Pragâpati and his daughter Ushas, see I, 7, 4, 1 seq.

[2] On this and several of the other names, see part i, p. 201.

[3] As, when a horse gets much corn, it becomes spirited, 'masterful.' The St. Petersburg dictionary suggests the meaning, 'they become strong.' It might also mean, 'they lord it (over the plants).'

because he gave him that name, Vâyu (the wind) became suchlike, for Ugra is Vâyu: hence when it blows strongly, they say 'Ugra is blowing.' He said, 'Surely, I am mightier than that: give me yet a name!'

14. He said to him, 'Thou art A*s*ani.' And because he gave him that name, the lightning became suchlike, for A*s*ani is the lightning: hence they say of him whom the lightning strikes, 'A*s*ani has smitten him.' He said, 'Surely, I am mightier than that: give me yet a name!'

15. He said to him, 'Thou art Bhava.' And because he gave him that name, Par*g*anya (the rain-god) became suchlike; for Bhava is Par*g*anya, since everything here comes (bhavati) from the rain-cloud. He said, 'Surely, I am mightier than that: give me yet a name!'

16. He said to him, 'Thou art Mahân Deva*h* (the Great God).' And because he gave him that name, the moon became suchlike, for the moon is Pra*g*âpati, and Pra*g*âpati is the Great God. He said, 'Surely, I am mightier than that: give me yet a name!'

17. He said to him, 'Thou art Î*s*âna (the Ruler).' And because he gave him that name, the Sun became suchlike, for Î*s*âna is the Sun, since the Sun rules over this All. He said, 'So great indeed I am: give me no other name after that!'

18. These then are the eight forms of Agni. Kumâra (the boy) is the ninth: that is Agni's threefold state[1].

19. And because there are eight forms of Agni—

[1] That is, his state of being triv*ri*t, or three times three.

the Gâyatrî consisting of eight syllables—therefore they say, 'Agni is Gâyatra.' That boy entered into the forms one after another; for one never sees him as a mere boy (kumâra), but one sees those forms of his [1], for he assumed those forms one after another.

20. One ought to build him (Agni, the fire-altar) up in (the space of) a year, and recite for a year. 'For two (years),' however, say some; 'for in one year they laid the seed, and in one year that boy was born, therefore let him build for two (years), and recite for two (years).' Let him, however, build for a year only, and recite for a year; for the same seed which is laid is brought forth; it then lies changing and growing: hence let him build for a year only, and recite for a year. To him (Agni) when built up (*k*ita) he gives a name: whereby he keeps away evil from him. He calls him by a bright (*k*itra) name [2], saying, 'Thou art bright;' for Agni is all bright things.

THE ANIMAL SACRIFICE [3].

SECOND ADHYÂYA. FIRST BRÂHMA*N*A.

1. Pragâpati set his mind upon Agni's forms. He searched for that boy (Kumâra) who had entered

---

[1] Tata*s* *k*a tatprabh*ri*ti tam Agnim kumârarûpa*m* na kva*k*ana pa*s*yanti ki*m*tv etâny etaggvalanâdîni rûpâ*n*y apurushavidhâni pa*s*yanti, Sây.

[2] Or, he calls him by the name of *K*itra (bright), that being the name by which he is actually to address the fire on the altar at the end of the performance. Kâty. XVIII, 6, 23.

[3] This is the so-called ish*t*akâ-pa*s*u, or animal sacrifice performed with regard to the bricks; the heads of the victims being used in building up the altar, whilst some of the blood is mixed with the clay of which the bricks are made.

into the (different) forms. Agni became aware of it,—'Surely, Father Pragâpati is searching for me: well then, let me be suchlike that he knows me not.'

2. He saw those five animals,—the Purusha (man), the horse, the bull, the ram, and the he-goat. Inasmuch as he saw (pa*s*) them, they are (called) cattle (pa*s*u).

3. He entered into those five animals; he became those five animals. But Pragâpati still searched for him.

4. He saw those five animals. Because he saw (pa*s*) them, therefore they are animals (pa*s*u); or rather, because he saw him (Agni) in them, therefore they are animals.

5. He considered, 'They are Agni: I will fit them unto mine own self[1]. Even as Agni, when kindled, glares, so their eye glares; even as Agni's smoke rises upwards, so vapour rises from them; even as Agni consumes what is put in him, so they devour; even as Agni's ashes fall down, so do their faeces: they are indeed Agni; I will fit them unto mine own self.' He meant to slaughter them for different deities: the Purusha (man) for Vi*s*vakarman, the horse for Varu*n*a, the bull for Indra, the ram for Tvash*t*ri, the he-goat for Agni.

6. He considered, 'For different deities, indeed, I mean to slaughter now; but I myself desire (kam)

[1] Or, I will make them part of mine own self.—Similarly St. Petersburg dictionary, 'I will change them into myself.' But differently Professor Delbrück, Altind. Synt., p. 239, 'I will make myself to be these, change myself into these.' This is on account of the middle form of the verb, which, however, is quite justified also in the former interpretation. Cf. VI, 8, 2, 1, where there is no question of changing the whole sacrifice into a heap of ashes, but of taking over the ashes, or some of it, to form part of the sacrifice.

Agni's forms: well then, I will slaughter them for the Agnis, as for the (object of my) desire.' He slaughtered them for the Agnis, as for (his) desire, —to wit, 'for the Agnis,' because many were the forms of Agni he had set his mind upon; and 'for the desire,' because it was with a desire that he slaughtered them. Having appeased them and carried the fire round them, he led them northwards and slew them.

7. He considered, 'Those glories (signs of excellence[1]) upon which I have set my mind are contained in the heads: well then, I will only put on the heads[2].' He cut off the heads and put them on (himself, or the altar). The remaining trunks he then let float on the water[3], and brought the sacrifice to its completion by means of (the offering of) a he-goat, thinking, 'Lest my sacrifice be pulled to pieces.' After performing that animal sacrifice, Pragâpati saw that he had not yet reached the end of Agni (the fire-altar).

8. He considered, 'I must search for that body[4] which I let float on the water.' He searched for it; and what (part) of those (bodies) cast into the water had settled therein, that water he gathered; and what (had settled) in this earth, that clay (he gathered)[5]. And having gathered both that clay

[1] See VI, 1, 1, 4.

[2] That is, on the fire-altar, or (which is the same thing) on himself, Pragâpati, the sacrifice. The heads of the five victims are placed in (a dish introduced into) the bottom layer of the altar so as to impart stability to it. See VII, 5, 2, 1 seq.

[3] Or, he washed them, cleaned them, in water.

[4] Literally, that self, i.e. that part of mine own self, the sacrifice (?).

[5] It seemed desirable here to leave the construction of the original text unchanged.

and water, he made a brick: hence a brick consists of these two, clay and water.

9. He considered, 'Surely, if I fit[1] this (matter) such as it is unto mine own self, I shall become a mortal carcase, not freed from evil: well then, I will bake it by means of the fire.' So saying, he baked it by means of the fire, and thereby made it immortal; for the sacrificial food which is baked by fire is indeed immortal (or, ambrosia). Hence they bake the bricks with fire: they thereby make them immortal.

10. And inasmuch as he saw them after offering (ish*t*vâ) the animal, therefore they are bricks (ish*t*akâ). Hence one must make the bricks only after performing an animal sacrifice; for those which are made before (or, without) an animal sacrifice are 'anish*t*akâ[2].' And, moreover, there is this other (consideration).

11. As to those glories, they are these same heads of the victims; and those (headless) trunks are these five layers (of the fire-altar): thus when he builds up the layers after putting on the heads of the victims, he thereby unites those trunks with those heads.

12. And because Agni is all those animal victims, therefore animals delight (being) near the fire[3],—

---

[1] Sâya*n*a explains 'abhisa*m*skarishye' by 'âdhiyag*ñ*ike *s*arîra upadhâsyâmi,' 'if I were to put this (clay and water) on the sacrificial body.'

[2] A play on the word which may mean either 'non-bricks,' or 'being without oblation (ish*t*a).'

[3] Sâya*n*a seems to take this to mean, that animals (cattle) delight, or sport, when the sacrificial fire is established; that is to say, they feel at home and increase wherever a new household is established (?);—tasmâd agnâv âhite pa*s*avo ramante, âtmany eva sâ prîtir ity abhiprâya*h*. Adhunâ*s*gne*h* pa*s*ushv âtmabhûteshu prîti*m*

there animals sport with animals. Hence the (sacrificial) fire is set up with him who possesses cattle: for inasmuch as Agni (was) the same as cattle, therefore Pragâpati (the lord of creatures or generation) became Agni.

13. Here now some say, 'It is at this (point of the performance) that he should offer up all those (five) victims; for had Pragâpati then offered up all of them, he would certainly have reached the end of the fire (altar): hence were he (the Sacrificer) now to offer up all those (victims) he would certainly reach the end of the fire (altar).' Let him not do so: he thus would stray from where the gods have gone, he would stray from the path;—and what would he then gather[1]? For those same bodies, those layers, he gathers: let him therefore not do so.

14. Now when he slaughters those animals, he prepares a home for Agni; for nowhere but in his home does one enjoy himself. But the home means food: it is that he lays down in front, and when Agni sees that, he turns unto him.

15. There are a man, a horse, a bull, a ram, and a he-goat; for such are all the animals (used for sacrifice). Animals are food: he thus lays down in front whatever food there is; and seeing that, Agni turns unto him.

16. There are five; for there are those five Agnis,

---

darsayann âha, yasmâd agnir esha yat pasavas tasmâd yasya manushyasya pasavo bhavanti tasminn etad agnir âdhîyate, tatra hi sa âtmabhûtai*h* pasubhi ramate nânyatra: evam yad agnyâtmikâ*h* pasavas tatas tam agnim âtmâ*bhisa*m*skr*i*tya pragâpatir agnir abhavat.

[1] That is, what 'sambhâras' or equipments of the fire should he then collect? Cf. part i, p. 276.

to wit, the five layers (of the fire-altar): for them he thus lays down five homes; and seeing that, Agni turns unto him.

17. And when (he offers) 'to the Agnis,'—it is because there are here many Agnis, to wit, those layers; and when (he offers) 'to the desire,' it is in order that the Sacrificer may obtain the object for which he performs that ceremony.

18. A man (purusha) he slaughters first, for man is the first of animals; then a horse, for the horse comes after man; then a bull, for the bull (or cow) comes after the horse; then a ram, for the sheep comes after the cow; then a he-goat, for the goat comes after the sheep: thus he slaughters them according to their form, according to their excellence.

19. Their ropes may be unequal; that of the man being the longest, then shorter and shorter: thus he makes the ropes according to the form of the animals, to avoid confusion between good and bad. But let them be all alike, all similar; for all these victims are alike, all similar, for they are (all) called Agnis, they are called food: hence they are alike and similar.

20. Here now they say, 'How is that complete five-bricked fire of his gained in the animals?'—Well, in the kapâlas of the sacrificial cakes that first brick, the earthen one, is obtained; and when he slaughters the animal, thereby the animal brick is obtained, and when two gold chips are (placed) on both sides of the omentum, thereby the gold brick is obtained; and what firewood, stake, and enclosing sticks there are, thereby the wooden brick is obtained; and what ghee, sprinkling-water, and cake there are, thereby the fifth brick, the food, is

obtained: thus then that complete five-bricked fire of his is gained in the animals.

21. For these (victims) there are twenty-four kindling-verses[1]; for the year consists of twenty-four half-moons, and Agni is the year: as great as Agni is, as great as is his measure, by so much he thus kindles him.

22. And, again, why there are twenty-four,—the Gâyatrî consists of twenty-four syllables, and Agni is Gâyatra[2]: as great as Agni is, as great as is his measure, by so much he thus kindles him.

23. And, again, why there are twenty-four,—man (purusha) doubtless is twenty-fourfold: ten fingers of the hands, ten toes, and four limbs; and Pragâpati is the Purusha, and Pragâpati is Agni: as great as Agni is, as great as is his measure, by so much he thus kindles him.

24. He recites both gâyatrî and trishtubh verses; for the gâyatrî metre is the vital air, and the trishtubh is the body (self): by the gâyatrî verses he thus kindles his vital air, and by the trishtubh ones the body. The trishtubh verses are in the middle, and the gâyatrî verses on both sides thereof; for this body is in the middle, and the (organs of) the vital airs are on the sides thereof. He pronounces more gâyatrî verses before, and fewer after (the

[1] For the eleven gâyatrî verses, used as sâmidhenis at an ordinary ishti—and raised to the number of fifteen by repetitions of the first and last verses—see part i, p. 102. The present animal sacrifice (ishtakâ-pasu) adds to these verses nine trishtubh verses (Vâg. S. XXVII, 1–9), which (according to Kâty. XVI, 1, 11) are to be inserted between the two verses containing the words 'samidhyamâna' (being kindled) and 'samiddha' (kindled) respectively,—that is, between the ninth and tenth of the normal or gâyatrî kindling-verses (cf. I, 4, 1, 38). [2] See VI, 1, 1, 15; 3, 19.

trish/ubh verses); for there are more (organs of the) vital airs in front, and fewer behind.

25. He recites (Vâg. S. XXVII, 1), 'May the months[1], O Agni, may the seasons make thee grow!' When Agni restored the relaxed Pragâpati, he (Pragâpati) said to him, 'What kindling-verses there are equal to me (in measure), with them kindle me!'

26. He (Agni) saw these (verses), 'May the months, O Agni, may the seasons make thee grow!' that is, 'May both the months, O Agni, and the seasons make thee grow!'—'The years, the *Ri*shis, whatsoever truths' that is, 'May the years, and the *Ri*shis, and the truths make thee grow!'—'With heavenly brightness do thou shine!'—the heavenly brightness doubtless is yonder sun: thus 'together with that do thou shine!'—'lighten up the whole four regions!' that is, 'lighten up all the four regions!'

27. These (verses) have one and the same explanation regarding him (Agni-Pragâpati): how one would make him complete, how he would restore and produce him. They relate to Agni and Pragâpati: to Agni, inasmuch as Agni saw (them); to Pragâpati, inasmuch as he (Agni) kindled Pragâpati.

---

[1] This is the meaning assigned here to 'samâ*h*' by Mahîdhara, a doubtful meaning indeed. Besides the ordinary meaning 'year,' the St. Petersburg dictionary also allows to 'samâ' that of 'half-year' in some passages of the Atharva-veda. In the present passage, the dictionary refers 'samâ*h*' to the adjective 'sama,' hence 'the equal seasons.' This cannot, however, have been the meaning assigned to the word by the author of this part of the Brâhma*n*a, whatever it may originally have been in this verse of the Sa*m*hitâs. Sâya*n*a, Taitt. S. IV, 1, 7, takes 'samâ*h*' in the sense of 'the years,' but remarks that 'the months and half-months' have to be understood by it in this verse.

28. Twelve Âprî (propitiatory) verses[1] there are,—twelve months are a year, and the year is Agni: as great as Agni is, as great as is his measure, with so much he thus propitiates (or gratifies) him.

29. And, again, why there are twelve,—of twelve syllables consists the *G*agatî, and the *G*agatî is this earth, for on her there is everything that moves (*g*agat) here. And Agni also is this earth, for it is out of her that the whole fire (altar) is built up: as great as Agni is, as great as is his measure, by so much he thus propitiates him.

30. And, again, why there are twelve,—of twelve syllables consists the *G*agatî, and the *G*agatî is all the metres, and all the metres are Pra*g*âpati (the sacrifice), and Pra*g*âpati is Agni: as great as Agni is, as great as is his measure, by so much he thus propitiates him.

31. Those 'kindling-sticks of his (Agni) are upright.' When Agni restored the relaxed Pra*g*âpati, he said to him, 'What Âprî-verses there are equal to me, with them propitiate me!'

32. He saw these (verses)[2]:—'Upright are his kindling-sticks,' for upright indeed are the kindling-sticks of him when kindled;—'upwards tending the bright flashes of Agni,' for tending upwards are his bright flashes, his flames;—'they, the most brilliant,' that is 'the most powerful;'—'of the fair-looking son,' for fair-looking indeed Agni is on all sides; and inasmuch as he (the Sacrificer) produces him thereby he (Agni) is his son.

[1] For the purport of these verses which form the offering-prayers at the fore-offerings of the animal sacrifice, see part ii, p. 185, note 1.

[2] Vâg. S. XXVII, 11 seq.

33. These (verses) have one and the same explanation regarding him (Agni-Pragâpati): how one would make him complete, how he would restore and produce him. They relate to Agni and Pragâpati, —to Agni, inasmuch as Agni saw (them); to Pragâpati, inasmuch as he (Agni) propitiated Pragâpati.

34. They are unequal, and consist of unequal feet, and unequal syllables; for the metres are unequal: whatever unequal limbs there are at his (Agni's) body, those (limbs) of his he propitiates by these (verses).

35. The animal cake belongs to (Agni) Vaisvânara—Vaisvânara being all the fires—for the obtainment of all the fires.

36. As to why it belongs to Vaisvânara;—those layers (of the altar) no doubt are the seasons, for the seasons are the fires; and the seasons are the year, and the year is Vaisvânara (belonging to all men). Were it (offered) to Agni (Vaisvânara), he would cause it (the formula) to be redundant. It is one on twelve potsherds: twelve months are a year, and the year is Vaisvânara. The offering and invitatory formulas relate to Agni, for the obtainment of Agni's forms. They contain the word 'kâma' (desire), for the obtainment of his desires.

37. Now some, having in that way[1] obtained those heads, put them on (the fire-altar), thinking, 'Either way[2] are they animals.' But they (who do this) become mortal carcases, for unpropitiated are

---

[1] That is, according to Sâyana, somehow or other, in some worldly manner, as by buying or begging them, without performing the animal sacrifice.

[2] That is to say, whether they are consecrated or unconsecrated, in either case they are 'pasavah' or animal (victims). Sây.

those (heads) of theirs. In this way, indeed, they did put them on for Ashâdhi Sausromateya[1]; but quickly indeed he died after that.

38. Some, however, make gold ones, saying, 'They are immortal bricks (amriteshtakâ).' But indeed those are false bricks (anriteshtakâ), those are no heads of victims.

39. Some, again, make earthen ones, thinking, 'Passed away, forsooth, are these animals, and this earth is the shelter of all that has passed away: thus whither those animals have gone, from thence we collect them.' Let him not do so, for whoso knows not both the practice and theory of these (victims), for him let them be passed away. Let him slaughter those very five victims, as far as he may be able to do so; for it was these Pragâpati was the first to slaughter, and Syâparna Sâyakâyana the last; and in the interval also people used to slaughter them. But nowadays only these two are slaughtered, the one for Pragâpati, and the one for Vâyu. The theory of these two is now (to be) told.

Second Brâhmana.

1. The Karakas slaughter (a he-goat) for Pragâpati, saying, 'Pragâpati, having built up the fire-altar (agni), became Agni. When he slaughters that one, then indeed he reaches the end of Agni (the fire-altar).'

2. It is a dark grey one; for the grey has two kinds of hair, the white and the black; and two make a productive pair: that is its Pragâpati-characteristic. It is a hornless one, for Pragâpati is hornless.

[1] The son of Ashâdha and Susromatâ, according to Sâyana.

3. For this (animal sacrifice) there are twenty-one kindling-verses[1];—twelve months, five seasons, these three worlds, and yonder sun,—that is the twenty-onefold Pragâpati; and Pragâpati is Agni: as great as Agni is, as great as is his measure, by so much he thus kindles him.

4. And, again, why there are twenty-one;—man (purusha) doubtless is twenty-onefold, ten fingers of the hand, ten toes, and the body (make) the twenty-onefold man Pragâpati; and Pragâpati is Agni: as great as Agni is, as great as is his measure, by so much he thus kindles him.

5. He recites both gâyatrî and trishṭubh verses: their significance has been told; and (what applies to) the order of the verses has been told. The libation of ghee[2] he makes with the verse containing (the name) Hiraṇyagarbha[3]; for Hiraṇyagarbha

[1] Viz. the eleven ordinary gâyatrî verses raised, by repetitions, to the number of fifteen; with six special trishṭubh inserted (p. 167, note 1). Kâty. XVI, 1, 34.

[2] On the two libations of ghee, see part i, p. 124 note; p. 128, n. 2. It is doubtful which of the two libations is intended here; whether the first which in any case belongs to Pragâpati, but is usually made with a different formula from the one prescribed here, or the second. The later ritualists themselves seem to have been doubtful on this point; but Kâtyâyana (XVI, 1, 35–37) leans to the opinion, that the second libation must be intended; both libations thus being made to Pragâpati on this occasion. Sâyaṇa remarks,—hiraṇyavatyâ ṛikâ 'hiraṇyagarbhaḥ samavartatety' ata uttaraṃ samaprakam (? samaprakâram) âghâram âghârayati; pragâpatir vai hiraṇyagarbhaḥ sa kâgnis tam evam tarpayitvâpnotîty abhiprâyaḥ.

[3] That is, Vâg. S. XXV, 10 (XIII, 4; Ṛik S. X, 121, 1, 'Hiraṇyagarbhaḥ samavartatâgre'), 'Hiraṇyagarbha (the golden child) came first into existence; he was born as the only lord of all being; he sustained this earth and sky: what god (or the god Ka) shall we serve with offering.'

is Pragâpati, and Pragâpati is Agni. There are twelve Âpri-verses: their significance has been told; and (what applies to) the order of the verses has been told. The animal cake belongs to Pragâpati, for the relation of the victim is also that of the animal cake[1]. It is one on twelve potsherds: twelve months are a year, and the year is Pragâpati. The offering and invitatory formulas contain the word 'Ka,' for Pragâpati is Ka[2].

6. He then slaughters for Vâyu Niyutvat (the wind, driving a team of horses) that white, bearded (he-goat). When Pragâpati had produced living beings, he looked about him, and from exceeding delight his seed fell: it became that white, hornless, bearded he-goat (aga, 'unborn'); for seed is life-sap, and as far as there is life-sap, so far extends the self. And when he slaughters that one, then indeed he reaches the end of Agni (the fire-altar). It is a white one, because seed is white. It is hornless, because seed is hornless. It belongs to Vâyu, because Vâyu (the wind) is the out-breathing; and to Niyutvat, because the teams (niyut[3]) are the in-breathing: the out-breathing and in-breathing he thus lays into him.

[1] See III, 8, 3, 1 seq.

[2] See I, 1, 1, 13 with note.—The above verse, *Ri*k S. X, 121, 1, and following five verses,—each of which ends with, 'what god (or the god Ka) shall we serve with offering,'—are used with the omentum, the animal cake (pasupuro*d*âsa), and the animal oblations respectively; viz. the first three verses as invitatory formulas (anuvâkyâ) and the last three as offering formulas (yâgyâ). Âsv. *S*r. III, 8, 1.—Vâg. S. XXV, 10–13, only the first four verses are given together; whilst Sâya*n*a, in accordance with Âsvalâyana, remarks,—vapâ puro*d*âsapasûnâ*m* 'hira*n*yagarbha*h* samavartatâgra' ity âdaya*h* syu*h*.

[3] Probably 'niyuta*h*' here with allusion to 'niyuta,' shut in.

7. And, again, why he slaughters that white, hornless (he-goat);—when the gods restored the relaxed Pragâpati, they, by means of this victim, put into him that out-breathing which had gone out of him; and in like manner this one now puts it into him. It belongs to Vâyu, because Vâyu is the out-breathing; and to Niyutvat, because the teams are the in-breathing: he thus puts the out-breathing and in-breathing into him. It is white, because Vâyu (the wind) is white; and it is hornless, because Vâyu is hornless.

8. For this (animal sacrifice) there are seventeen kindling-verses[1]; for the year is seventeenfold—there are twelve months and five seasons—Pragâpati is the year, and Pragâpati is Agni: as great as Agni is, as great as is his measure, by so much he thus kindles him.

9. And, again, why there are seventeen,—man is seventeenfold,—there are ten vital airs, four limbs, the body the fifteenth, the neck-joints the sixteenth, and the head the seventeenth,—Pragâpati is the Person (or man, purusha), and Pragâpati is Agni: as great as Agni is, as great as is his measure, by so much he thus kindles him.

10. He recites both gâyatrî and trish*t*ubh verses: their significance has been told; and (what applies to) the order of the verses has been told. There are twelve Âprî-verses: their significance has been told; and (what applies to) the order of the verses has been told. The animal cake belongs to Pragâpati: 'Therein then that wish was obtained,'

[1] That is, only two additional trish*t*ubh verses are to be inserted between the 11 (or 15) gâyatrî ones.

Mâhitthi once said,—'which the *K*arakâs say is in the victim to Pra*g*âpati.'

11. And as to why the victim belongs to Vâyu, and the animal cake to Pra*g*âpati;—one half of Pra*g*âpati doubtless is Vâyu, and one half is Pra*g*âpati: thus, were they both to belong to Vâyu, or both to Pra*g*âpati, then only one half of him (Pra*g*âpati) would be made up, and one half would not (be made up). But in that the victim belongs to Vâyu, and the animal cake to Pra*g*âpati, thereby he puts together (restores) him, Pra*g*âpati, wholly and entirely.

12. And, again, why the victim belongs to Vâyu, and the animal cake to Pra*g*âpati;—when the gods restored the relaxed Pra*g*âpati, they, by means of this victim, put into him that out-breathing which had gone out of him; and by means of this cake they restored that body (trunk) of his. And as to why it belongs to Pra*g*âpati, it is because the body (self) is Pra*g*âpati; and (why it is) one on twelve potsherds,—twelve months are a year, and Pra*g*âpati is the year. One of the offering prayers and one of the invitatory prayers[1] contain (the word) 'ka,' for Pra*g*âpati is Ka.

[1] The three chief oblations of the Animal Sacrifice, requiring each an invitatory prayer (anuvâkyâ) and an offering prayer (yâgyâ), are the omentum-oblation (vapâ), the animal cake (pasu-puro*d*âsa), and the meat oblations (pasu-havis). This is the order on the present occasion, whilst usually the cake-oblation succeeds the offering of meat portions. Now the first of the three invitatory prayers (that of the omentum), viz. Vâg. S. XXVII, 26 (*Ri*k S. X, 121, 8), and the last of the three offering prayers (that of the meat portions), viz. Vâg. S. XXVII, 25 (*Ri*k S. X, 121, 7), end with the refrain, 'what god (or, the god Ka) should we serve with offering.' Thus, then, the first and the last of the six formulas would be

13. Now when in the first place he offers the omentum, he thereby puts into him (Pragâpati) that vital air which is here in front. And when they proceed with that (cake) in the middle, it is because this trunk is in the middle. And when they proceed thereafter with the (meat) oblation, he thereby puts into him that vital air which is behind. The (remaining) offering and invitatory prayers should contain the word 'bright,' with the view of the obtainment of bright forms; and the word 'niyut' (team), for the obtainment of that form which has a team[1].

addressed to Pragâpati; and to him is also exceptionally offered the animal cake, which is here assigned the central position, and which, in the normal sacrificial order, would belong to the recipient of the animal sacrifice itself, or in the present case, to Vâyu Niyutvat. Sâyana, on the other hand, makes the above two verses, containing the word Ka, the invitatory and offering prayers of the cake-offering, as the MS. makes him say,—kadvatyau yâgyânuvâkye purodâsasya, 'âpo ha yad brihatîr' (Rik S. X, 121, 7), 'yaskid âpo' (X, 121, 8) ity etc. This, indeed, would also seem to be the opinion of Kâtyâyana, whose rules (XVI, 1, 39-43) are,—39. To Pragâpati belongs the animal cake at both (animal sacrifices); 40. The offering and invitatory formulas of the Prâgâpatya (animal sacrifice) contain the word 'Ka;' 41. Those of the Vâyavya contain the word 'bright;' 42. Optionally so, those of the omentum (but not at the meat portion, commentary); 43. The remainder is equal in all (three views).—Now it would indeed be the most natural, that the formulas of the cake-offering, here exceptionally assigned to Pragâpati, should be made to correspond to that deity: but the order in which the formulas are given in the Vâg. S. XXVII, 23-28 (cf. Âsval. III, 8, 1), as well as paragraph 13 above, seems to favour the first view; though the next paragraph shows that there were differences of opinion on this point. Cf. next note.

[1] The form of Pragâpati which has a team of horses is Vâyu, the god of wind; while his bright forms are represented by Agni, the fire (VI, 1, 3, 20, 'Agni is all bright things').—Vâg. S. XXVII, 29-34 gives six verses for use as invitatory and offering formulas

14. As to this they say, 'It is rather the two (prayers) of the Omentum that should contain (the word) "bright," for so far as the two (prayers) of the omentum containing (the word) "bright" extend, extends what is bright in the animal (sacrifice); and the two (prayers) of the (meat) oblation should contain (the word) "team," for the obtainment of that form of him (Pragâpati) which has a team.'

15. And, again, why he slaughters this animal;—in this animal doubtless the form of all (the five kinds of) animals is (contained): inasmuch as it is hornless and bearded, that is the form of man, for man is hornless and bearded; inasmuch as it is hornless and furnished with a mane, that is the form of the horse, for the horse is hornless and furnished with a mane; inasmuch as it is eight-hoofed, that is the bull's form, for the bull is eight-hoofed; inasmuch as its hoofs are like those of the sheep, that is the form of the

at the ish/akâpa*s*u to Vâyu. Five of these contain the word 'niyut,' team, but only the first two contain the word '*s*ukra' (bright): these two are presumably to be used on the present occasion; though I am at a loss to see what other two verses containing the word 'bright' are to be used; unless indeed '*s*uklavatya*h*' in the text means 'verses containing some word for bright,' in which case the ordinary verses used at an animal offering to Vâyu Niyutvat, viz. Vâg. S. XXVII, 23 and 24 (*Ri*k S. VII, 91, 3; 90, 3) which contain the word '*s*veta' (white, light), might be used. The MS. of Sâya*n*a's commentary is unfortunately very corrupt in this place; it alludes to the latter two verses, but whether to recommend them, or set them aside, for the present occasion, is not clear. He does, however, specially except the formulas of the animal cake from being included in the above specification. In the view put forth in paragraph 14, the above-mentioned two verses would apparently have to be used for the omentum-oblation, the two verses containing 'Ka' for the cake-oblation, and (any) two verses containing the word 'team' (either the ordinary ones, *Ri*k S. VII, 92, 5; VI, 49, 4; or some of the special ones) for the meat-oblation.

sheep; and inasmuch as it is a he-goat, that is that of the goat. Thus when he slaughters this one, thereby indeed all those (five) animals are slaughtered for him. Whichever of these may suit him—either those five animals, or that (he-goat) for Pragâpati, or that one for (Vâyu) Niyutvat [1]—

16. Let him slaughter it at full moon. 'Let him slaughter at new moon,' so say some, 'for Pragâpati is yonder moon: during that night (of new moon) he dwells here (on earth) [2], and it would be just as if he slaughtered him while staying near.'

17. But, indeed, this (takes place) at full moon, for the victim is yonder moon, and him the gods slaughter at full moon [3]: 'I will slaughter him at the time when the gods slaughter him,' thus he thinks, and therefore (he does so) at full moon. And, again, why at full moon;—the full moon no

---

[1] Sâya*n*a here supplies 'let him perform that,'—eshâm karma*n*â*m* madhye yat karmâsya sampadyeta tat kuryâd iti *s*esha*h*; but he then adds, that the pronoun 'it' (tam) at the beginning of the next paragraph is caused by proximity of the Niyutvatîya.

[2] See I, 6, 4, 5. 'Now this king Soma, the food of the gods, is no other than the moon. When he (the moon, masc.) is not seen that night either in the east or in the west, then he visits this world, and here he enters into the waters (f.) and plants (f.).' Thus Pragâpati is here identified with Soma, the moon, and food.

[3] Cp. I, 6, 4, 12-13. 'The full-moon oblation, assuredly, belongs to the V*r*itra-slayer, for by means of it Indra slew V*r*itra; and this new-moon oblation also represents the slaying of V*r*itra, since they prepared that invigorating draught for him who had slain V*r*itra. An offering in honour of the V*r*itra-slayer, then, is the full-moon sacrifice. V*r*itra, assuredly, is no other than the moon; and when during that night (of new moon) he is not seen either in the east or in the west, then he (Indra) finishes in destroying him by means of that (new-moon sacrifice), and leaves nothing remaining of him.'

doubt was the first to shine forth, hence also (the sacrifice takes place) at full moon.

18. And furthermore, at the Phâlguna (full moon), for that full moon of Phâlguna, that is, the second (Phâlguna)[1], is the first night of the year; and that first (Phâlguna) is the last (night of the year): he thus begins the year at the very mouth (beginning).

19. Now, as soon as he has performed the full-moon offering, let him slaughter the victim. For Indra, having driven away V*ri*tra, evil, by means of the full-moon offering, thus freed from evil entered upon this sacrificial performance; and in like manner the Sacrificer, having driven away V*ri*tra, evil, by means of the full-moon offering, thus freed from evil now enters on this (sacred) performance.

20. This is (performed) in a low voice, for by means of these victims Pragâpati sought to obtain this (sacred) work[2]; but that (work) was then, as it were, uncertain, indistinct: hence in a low voice.

21. And, again, why in a low voice;—this performance assuredly belongs to Pragâpati, for it is Pragâpati he enters upon by this performance; and Pragâpati is undefined.

22. And, again, why in a low voice;—there is seed here in the sacrifice, and seed is cast silently—the

[1] In the older division of the year the first or spring season (vasanta) begins with the month of Phâlguna, that is the month when the moon is in conjunction with the nakshatra of the Uttare Phalgunî, whence that full moon, in the Kaush. Br. 5, 1, is called the mouth, and that of the first Phalgunî the tail, of the year. See A. Weber, Nachrichten von den Naxatra, II, p. 329. In the above, somewhat bold figure, we are, Sâya*n*a reminds us, to understand the fifteenth or last day (of the dark fortnight) of the first Phalgunî, and the pratipad, or first day of the second Phalgunî.

[2] That is, the construction of the fire-altar.

omentum, the animal cake, and the chief oblation, for of that much consists the animal sacrifice.

23. On the eighth day (after full moon) he collects (the materials for) the fire-pan; for sacred to Pragâpati is that day, the eighth (after full moon), and sacred to Pragâpati is this (sacred) piece of work, the fire-pan: on a day sacred to Pragâpati he thus performs the work sacred to Pragâpati.

24. And as to why (it is performed) on the eighth day;—that eighth day no doubt is a joint of the year, and that fire-pan is a joint of Agni (the fire-altar): he thus makes joint upon joint.

25. And, again, why on the eighth day;—eightfold doubtless is the pan[1]—the bottom part, the two side-parts, the horizontal belt (or rim), that makes four; and four upright (bands), that makes eight: he thus makes the eightfold on the eightfold (or eighth).

26. He performs the initiation on the day of new moon; for from out of the new moon the sacrifice is spread: 'Whence the sacrifice is spread, thence will I generate the sacrifice,' so he thinks.

27. And, again, why he (does so) at new moon;—when he performs the initiation, he verily pours out his own self, as seed, into the fire-pan, the womb; and when he becomes initiated, he makes for it (his self) that world (or place) beforehand[2], and he is

[1] For the construction of the fire-pan, in which the sacred fire has to be kept up for a year, during which the initiation-ceremony is repeated day after day, see VI, 5, 2, 1 seq.

[2] There is kept up in these paragraphs a play on the word 'loka,' meaning both 'space' and 'world (or place of living),'—and applying both to the space occupied by a brick, in building up the altar; and to the place which the Sacrificer, by this performance, gains for himself in another world. The initiation period is here represented

born into the world made by him: hence they say, 'Man is born into the world made (by him)[1].'

28. Now, were he to be initiated during less than a year, he would build up bricks without space (for them)[2]: the bricks would exceed the spaces. And if, after making more spaces[3], he were not to fill up bricks in accordance therewith, the spaces would exceed the bricks. And when, after initiating himself at new moon, he buys (Soma) at new moon[4], he piles up as many bricks as he (during the interval) makes space for; and when his (Agni's second) wing is covered (with loose soil), the whole Agni is built up.

29. As to this they say, 'If at the time of the buying (of Soma) the days and nights (of the initiation-period) amount to just as many as there are bricks of that fire-altar, why then are not those

---

as the time during which the Sacrificer prepares both the requisite space for the altar (as it were, adding day by day so many brick-spaces, thus becoming available for the altar-pile at the time of construction), and an adequate place for himself in the celestial regions.

[1] That is, man receives, in a future existence, the reward or punishment for his deeds during this life.

[2] The author argues in support of the orthodox initiation-period of just one year, as just the amount of time required for preparing the exact amount of space (or brick-spaces) requisite for an altar of proper size. If the initiation were to last less than a year, he would not have had sufficient time to prepare the necessary amount of space, or rather, number of spaces required for the bricks; and, by implication, he would not acquire for himself an adequate place hereafter.

[3] That is to say, if he were to make the initiation-period last longer than a year, thus providing for more space than his supply of bricks would suffice to fill up.

[4] That is, after the expiration of the period of initiation, or just a year after the commencement of the latter.

spaces of his filled up (which are prepared) during the days there are after the buying (of Soma)[1]? Well, when he buys (Soma) at new moon, after becoming initiated at new moon (a year previously), then he piles up just as many bricks as (during that interval) he makes space for; and what days there then are after the buying (of Soma), during that interval the Adhvaryu builds up the fire-altar. But when should he build up, if there were not that interval? As many as there are days and nights in the year, so many are the bricks of that fire-altar. Thereto (comes) a thirteenth month, for there is that thirteenth month;—thus during the days there are after the buying (of Soma), those spaces of it (the altar) are filled up afterwards with those bricks of the thirteenth month: thus the spaces and the bricks become equal.

30. Thus, then, what first full moon there is (in the year) on that he slaughters the victim; and what first eighth-day there is, on that he prepares the fire-pan; and what first new moon there is, on that he becomes initiated: thus whatever first days there are in the year, of those he thereby takes possession for him (Agni, the altar), those he thereby gains. Now then as to the total amount (of the fire-altar)[2].

---

[1] That is, during the days from the commencement to the completion of the altar. These are the upasad-days (part ii, p. 104 seq.), the number of which varies from three days up to three years. During this period the Upasads have to be performed twice daily, and in the interval between the two performances the building of the altar takes place, a certain number of bricks being added each day.

[2] Or, rather, the correspondence, in toto, of the sacrificial performance with the object to be attained, viz. Agni, the fire-altar.

31. Here now they say, 'How does that sacrificial performance of his (the animal sacrifice) gain the year, Agni? how does it correspond[1] with the year, with Agni?' Well, for those five victims there are twenty-five kindling-verses, twelve Âprî-verses,—that makes thirty-six;—eleven after-offerings, eleven by-offerings[2],—that makes fifty-eight.

32. Now what forty-eight there are (in these fifty-eight), they are the *G*agati (metre) consisting of forty-eight syllables;—the *G*agati doubtless is this earth, for it is thereon that everything is that moves (*g*agat); and Agni also is this earth, for it is thereof that the whole Agni is built up: as great as Agni is, as great as is his measure, so great does this become[3].

33. And, again, why there are forty-eight;—of forty-eight syllables consists the *G*agatî; the *G*agati (comprises) all the metres; all the metres are Pragâpati (the sacrifice[4]); and Pragâpati is Agni: as great as Agni is, as great as is his measure, so great does this become.

34. And what (remaining) ten there are (in those fifty-eight), they are the Virâg, consisting of ten syllables; and the Virâg is Agni;—there are ten regions, and the regions are Agni; ten vital airs, and the vital airs are Agni: as great as Agni is,

[1] Or, come up to, tally with,—katha*m* sa*m*vatsare*n*a sampadyate sa*m*ga*kkh*ate vayavasâmyena, Sây.

[2] For these supplementary oblations at the animal sacrifice, see III, 8, 4, 10 seq.

[3] That is, the animal sacrifice that has been performed is thus made out to be equal to Agni, or to the object for which it was performed.

[4] That is, because all the metres are employed in the chants and recitations during the sacrifice.

as great as is his measure, so great does this become.

35. The omentum and the animal cake, that makes sixty;—sixty are the days and nights of a month: thus he gains the month; the month gained gains the season; and the season (gains) the year: he thus gains the year, Agni, and the wishes which are contained in the year, and what other food than that there is in the year, all that (he gains).

36. And for that (victim) of Pragâpati there are twenty-one kindling-verses, and twelve Âprî-verses, that makes thirty-three;—eleven after-offerings, eleven by-offerings, that makes fifty-five;—omentum, animal cake, and chief oblation, that makes fifty-eight: whatever wish is contained in the fifty-eight, that he gains even here[1];—two libations of ghee, that makes sixty: whatever wish is contained in the sixty, that he gains even here; and what other food than that there is in the year, all that (he gains).

37. And for that (victim) of (Vâyu) Niyutvat, there are seventeen kindling-verses, and twelve Âprî-verses, that makes twenty-nine;—eleven after-offerings, and eleven by-offerings, that makes fifty-one;—omentum, animal cake, and chief oblation, that makes fifty-four;—two libations of ghee, two (oblations to Agni) Svish*t*akr*i*t, that makes fifty-eight: whatever wish is contained in the fifty-eight, that he gains even here;—the wood-lord[2] (tree) and the oblation of gravy, that makes sixty: whatever wish is con-

[1] ?That is, also in this calculation, or in the parts of the sacrifice here enumerated.

[2] For the oblation to Vanaspati, see part ii, p. 208; for the vasâhoma, ib. 205.

tained in the sixty, that he gains even here, and what other food than that there is in the year, all that (he gains); and thus that sacrificial performance gains for him the year, Agni; thus it (the animal sacrifice) corresponds with the year, with Agni.

38. As to this they say, 'Of that animal he should offer no Samish*t*ayagus, nor should he go down with the heart-spit to the purificatory bath[1]; for that animal (sacrifice) is the commencement of Agni; the Samish*t*ayagus are the gracious dismissal of the deities[2]; and the purificatory bath is the completion;—lest he should at the very commencement dismiss the deities, and complete the sacrifice.' Let him nevertheless complete (the sacrifice): Pragâpati, having offered that animal, saw that he had not reached the end of him, Agni,—let him therefore complete (the sacrifice). And, again, why he completes it;—that animal sacrifice is his vital air, and if anything were to cut him off from that, it would cut him off from the vital air; and if anything were to cut him off from the vital air, he would thus die: let him therefore complete (the sacrifice). Now, then, as to the vows (rites of abstinence).

39. Here now they say, 'After he has performed that animal offering, he must not sleep upon (a couch), nor eat flesh, nor hold carnal intercourse; for that animal sacrifice is the first Dikshâ, and improper surely it would be, were the initiated to sleep upon (a couch), or were he to eat flesh, or hold carnal intercourse.' But in no way is this a Dikshâ, for there is neither a girdle, nor a black

[1] See III, 8, 5, 8 seq.

[2] See I, 9, 2, 26-27.

antelope skin[1]; but he makes this the first brick[2]: let him therefore, if he like, sleep upon (a couch); and whatever food animals here eat, all that is here obtained and taken possession of by him; and whatever kinds of food there are other than honey, of all those he may eat at pleasure, if he can get them. Carnal intercourse, however, he may not hold prior to the (offering of) clotted curds to Mitra and Varu*n*a[3]: the purport of this (will be explained) hereafter.

40. Here now they say, 'At this sacrifice he should give a Dakshi*n*â (sacrificial gift); thinking, "Lest my sacrifice should be without a dakshi*n*â!" let him give to the Brahman the prescribed dakshi*n*â, for the Brahman is the entire sacrifice: thus the entire sacrifice of his becomes healed.' Let him not do so; for he makes this a brick, and it would be just as if he were to give a present with each brick: only at that (proper) time[4] let him therefore give what it befits him (to give).

THIRD BRÂHMANA.

1. Now, the gods said, 'Meditate ye!'—whereby, no doubt, they meant to say, 'Seek ye a layer[5] (for the fire-altar)!' Whilst they were meditating,

[1] For the antelope skin used at the initiation-ceremony, see III, 2, 1, 1; for the girdle, ib. 10.

[2] See above, VI, 2, 1, 20.

[3] This is the concluding oblation of the Soma-sacrifice, performed at the close of the Agni*k*ayana; see IX, 5, 1, 54.

[4] Viz. at the proper time when the priests receive their fees, after the mid-day Soma-service, see part ii, p. 340.

[5] The author here connects the causal verb '*k*etay' (to reflect) with '*k*i,' to pile, to build; or rather with '*k*itim ish,' to desire building (an altar).

Pragâpati saw this earth, as a first naturally-perforated[1] layer: hence it is by means of Pragâpati that he lays on that (brick)[2].

2. Agni said to him (Pragâpati), 'I will step nigh!'—'Wherewith?'—'With cattle!'—'So be it!' He thereby doubtless meant to say, 'with the cattle-brick;' for that cattle-brick is the same as the dûrvâ-brick[3]: hence the dûrvâ-brick is laid so as not to be separated from the first naturally-perforated one; hence also not separated from this earth are the plants, the cattle, the fire,—for not separated (from the earth)[4] he (Agni) stepped nigh with this (brick).

3. They said, 'Meditate ye yet!' whereby no doubt they meant to say, 'Seek ye a layer! seek ye (to build) from hence upwards!' Whilst they were

[1] See p. 155, note 8.

[2] Or, that (layer), the three naturally-perforated bricks occupying the centre of the first, third, and fifth layers of the altar, these bricks are, as it were, the representatives of the respective layers. This first svayam-âtrinnâ brick is laid down with the formula, 'May Pragâpati settle thee!' See VII, 4, 2, 6.

[3] A stalk of Dûrvâ (Dûb) grass—Panicum (or Cynodon) dactylon, or Agrostis linearis—is laid upon the first naturally-perforated brick (which again lies on the man of gold) in such a way that the root lies upon it and the tops hanging down to the ground. 'Its flowers in the perfect state are among the loveliest objects in the vegetable world, and appear through a lens like minute rubies and emeralds in constant motion from the least breath of air. It is the sweetest and most nutritious pasture for cattle, and its usefulness, added to its beauty, induced the Hindus in the earliest ages to believe it was the mansion of a benevolent nymph.' Sir W. Jones, Works, vol. v, p. 78. Professor R. Wallace, in his 'India in 1887,' gives an excellent illustration of this famous grass. He remarks (p. 282) that 'it has a wonderful power of remaining green, being the grass of all Indian grasses which retains its succulence throughout the extreme heat of summer.'

[4] That is to say, immediately after (the earth-brick had been laid on).

meditating, Indra and Agni, and Vi*s*vakarman saw the air, as a second naturally-perforated layer: hence he lays on that (brick[1]) by means of Indra and Agni, and Vi*s*vakarman.

4. Vâyu said to them, 'I will step nigh!'—'Wherewith?'—'With the regions!'—'So be it!' He thereby doubtless meant to say, 'with the regional (bricks[2]):' hence on the second naturally-perforated one the regional ones are laid, without being separated from it[3]; and hence not separated from the air are the regions, the wind; for not separated therefrom he (Vâyu) stepped nigh with this (brick).

5. They said, 'Meditate ye yet!'—whereby no doubt they said, 'Seek ye a layer! seek ye (to build) from hence upwards!' Whilst they were meditating, Paramesh*th*in saw the sky, as a third naturally-perforated layer: whence it is by Paramesh*th*in (the most high) he lays on that (brick[4]).

---

[1] This second naturally-perforated brick, representing the air, forms the centre of the third layer of the altar. See VIII, 3, 1, 1 seq.

[2] That is, the bricks marking the regions, or quarters (di*s*yâ); five of these are laid down immediately after the self-perforated one, in the four directions from it, two of them being laid on the south. See VIII, 3, 1, 11.

[3] Viz. without being separated from the layer which the second svayam-âtri*nn*â represents. They would seem to lie about a foot away from the central brick; but as no other special brick lies between them, they may on that account be considered as not separated from it.

[4] The third svayam-âtri*nn*â, though considered as forming part of the fifth layer, is really laid on the top of it or rather on the 'punas*k*iti'—an additional pile of eight bricks laid over the central, gârhapatya-like, portion of the fifth layer (cf. VI, 6, 1, 14, with note). It is laid down with the formula 'May the Most High settle thee!'—and on it the fire is subsequently placed. See VIII, 7, 3, 13 seq.

6. Yonder Sun said to him, 'I will step nigh!'—'Wherewith?'—'With a space-filling (brick [1]).'—'So be it!'—Now he (the sun) indeed is the space-filler: 'by (mine own) self,' he thus means to say. Hence the third naturally-perforated one is laid on so as not to be separated from the space-filling one [2]; and hence yonder sun is not separated from the sky, for not separated therefrom did he step nigh with this (brick).

7. These six deities forsooth became all this (universe), whatsoever exists here. The gods and the *Ri*shis said, 'Those six deities forsooth have become all this (universe): bethink ye yourselves how we also may share therein!' They said, 'Meditate ye!' whereby doubtless they meant to say, 'Seek ye a layer! seek ye how we also may share in this [3]!' Whilst they were meditating, the gods saw a second, the *Ri*shis a fourth, layer [4].

8. They said, 'We will step nigh!'—'Wherewith?'—'With what is over and above these worlds!'—'So be it!' Now what there is above the earth on this side of the air, therewith the gods stepped nigh, that is this second layer; and what there

[1] See p. 153, note.

[2] The laying down of the last svayam-âtrinnâ (together with the likewise perforated 'vikarni') is immediately preceded by the filling up of the fifth layer with the 'space-filling' bricks, only one of which has the common formula pronounced over it. See VIII, 7, 2, 1 seq.

[3] Viz. in this universe, and, as a representation thereof, in this fire-altar.

[4] In the foregoing 1–5 paragraphs only those three layers, which have a 'naturally-perforated' brick in the centre, viz. the first, third, and fifth layers, were mentioned. The author now remarks on the two other layers, representing as it were the space between the three worlds.

is above the air on this side of the sky, therewith the *Ri*shis stepped nigh, that is this fourth layer.

9. Now when they said, 'Meditate ye (*k*etayadhvam)!' they doubtless meant to say, 'Seek ye a layer (*k*itim i*kk*hata)!' and inasmuch as meditating (*k*etay) they saw them, therefore they are 'layers' (*k*itaya*h*).

10. Pragâpati saw the first layer: Pragâpati assuredly is its (spiritual) ancestry. The gods saw the second layer: the gods assuredly are its ancestry. Indra and Agni, and Vi*s*vakarman saw the third layer: they assuredly are its ancestry. The *Ri*shis saw the fourth layer: the *Ri*shis assuredly are its ancestry. Paramesh*th*in saw the fifth layer: Paramesh*th*in assuredly is its ancestry. And, verily, whosoever so knows that (spiritual) ancestry of the structures (layers of the fire-altar), his structures are indeed possessed of an ancestry, possessed of relations (or, of mystic significance, bandhu).

THE SÂVITRA LIBATIONS.

THIRD ADHYÂYA. FIRST BRÂHMANA.

1. The gods then said, 'Meditate ye!' whereby doubtless they meant to say, 'Seek ye a layer!' Whilst they were meditating, Savit*ri* saw those Sâvitra (formulas); and inasmuch as Savit*ri* saw them, they are called Sâvitra. He offered that eightfold-taken libation; and when he had offered it, he saw this eightfold-appointed Ashâ*dh*â [1], which had been created aforetime.

[1] That is, the 'invincible' brick, being the first brick which is made, and that by the Sacrificer's chief wife (mahishî) herself. See VI, 5, 3, 1 seq.—Sâya*n*a remarks,—tâm âhuti*m* hutvâ imâm p*ri*thivîm âdhiyag*ñ*ikîm ash*t*adhâvihitâm m*ri*tsikatâbhi*h* p*ri*thivyavairiya*m* (? p*ri*thivyaṅgair imâm) ash*t*avihitâm ikâm ashâ*dh*âm ish*t*a-

2. Now when they said, 'Meditate ye!' they doubtless meant to say, 'Seek ye a layer!' and inasmuch as they saw it whilst meditating (*k*etay), therefore it is a layer (*k*iti). And the libation is a sacrifice; and inasmuch as he saw it after sacrificing (ish*t*vâ), it is a brick (ish*t*akâ).

3. Now that same (libation of ghee), while being a single one, he offers as an eightfold one[1] with eight formulas: whence this ('invincible' brick), while being a single one, is eightfold appointed.

4. He offers while raising upwards (the spoon);—he thereby raises this earth upwards by means of its forms[2]: whence this earth is raised (above the water) by its forms.

5. He offers it continuously;—for at that time the gods were afraid lest the Rakshas, the fiends, should come thither after them! They saw that continuous libation for preventing the Rakshas, the fiends, from coming after them: hence he offers it continuously.

6. And, again, why he offers that libation;—this Agni is Savit*ri*, and him he gratifies at the outset by this libation; and having sacrificed to, and gratified, him (Agni), he then puts him together. And inasmuch as by this (libation) he gratifies Savit*ri*, they (the formulas are called) Sâvitra: that is why he offers this libation.

---

kâm apa*s*yat; puraiva lokâpavarga kala (? kâle or kâlât) *sri*sh*t*â*m* satîm. Though in the cosmogonic account, VI, 1, 1, 13 seq., the earth is rather said to consist of nine different elements, the 'invincible' brick is commonly identified with the earth. See VI, 5, 3, 1. For the (eightfold) compositions of the clay used for the fire-pan and bricks, see VI, 5, 1, 1 seq.

[1] That is to say, the offering-spoon is filled by eight dippings with the dipping-spoon.

[2] That is, by means of its constituent elements;—p*ri*thivîm ûrdhvâ*m* rûpair m*ri*dâdibhir udgamayati, Sây.

7. And, again, why he offers this libation;—this Agni is Savitri, and him he pours out as seed at the outset by this libation; and whatlike seed is poured into the womb suchlike (offspring) is born. And inasmuch as by this (libation) he pours out Savitri as seed, they (the offering-formulas are called) Sâvitra: that is why he offers this libation.

8. Both an offering-spoon (sruk) and a dipping-spoon (sruva) are used thereat; for the offering-spoon is speech, and the dipping-spoon is breath; and with speech and breath the gods sought this sacred rite at the beginning: hence there are an offering-spoon and a dipping-spoon.

9. And, again, why there are an offering-spoon and a dipping-spoon,—what Pragâpati was, that indeed is this dipping-spoon, for the dipping-spoon is the breath, and the breath is Pragâpati. And what Vâk (speech) was, that is this offering-spoon; for Vâk is a female, and the offering-spoon (sruk, f.) is a female; and those waters which went forth from the world of Vâk (speech)[1], they are this (ghee) which he offers (in) this libation.

10. He offers it continuously, for those waters flowed continuously. And inasmuch as that Pragâpati entered the waters with the threefold science[2], that is these prayers (yagus) with which this (priest) now offers.

11. The first three which there are, are these (three) worlds; and what fourth prayer there is that

---

[1] See VI, 1, 1, 9.

[2] VI, 1, 1, 10.—The construction of the text is somewhat peculiar,—what the author means to say seems to be,—the threefold science (the Veda) with which Pragâpati entered the waters is the same as the prayers now offered up.

is the threefold science, that is the *G*agati,—the *G*agatî being all the metres, and all the metres (making up) the threefold science; and what last four (prayers) there are, they are the quarters: now Pragâpati indeed is those worlds and the quarters; and that (*g*agatî verse in the middle) is the threefold science.

12. He offers with (Vâg. S. XI, 1), 'Harnessing first the mind,'—Pragâpati, assuredly, is he that harnesses, he harnessed the mind for that holy work; and because he harnessed the mind for that holy work, therefore he is the harnessing one.

13. 'Savit*ri*, stretching out the thoughts,'—for Savit*ri* is the mind, and the thoughts are the vital airs;—'gazing reverently at Agni's light,'—that is, having seen Agni's light;—'bore up from the earth;' for upwards from the earth he indeed bears this (offering).

14. [Vâg. S. XI, 2] 'With harnessed mind we,'—he thereby harnesses the mind for this work, for with unharnessed mind one cannot now do anything;—'at the impulse of the god Savit*ri*,'—that is impelled (sped) by the god Savit*ri*,—'with power (we strive) for the heavenly;'—'that by this holy work he may go to the heavenly world,' he thereby means to say; 'with power,' he says, for by power (energy) one goes to the heavenly world.

15. [Vâg. S. XI, 3] 'Savit*ri*, having harnessed the gods,'—Savit*ri* is the mind, and the gods are the vital airs;—'going by thought to the light, to heaven,'—for as such as are going to the heavenly world by thought (devotion) he has harnessed them for this holy work;—'going to produce a mighty light,'—the mighty light assuredly is yonder sun, and

he is this Agni, and him they are indeed going to fit together (or, restore);—'may Savitri speed them!'—that is, 'may they perform this holy work, sped by Savitri.'

16. [Vâg. S. XI, 4] 'They harness the mind, and they harness the thoughts,'—for both the mind and the vital airs he harnesses for this holy work;—'the priests of the priest,'—the priest is Pragâpati, and the priests are the gods;—'of the great inspirer of devotion,'—the great inspirer of devotion[1] is Pragâpati;—'he hath assigned the priestly offices,'—now when he (Agni-Pragâpati) is built up, then he assigns the priestly offices, for the priestly offices are assigned over the built-up (fire-altar);—'the finder of rites,'—for he indeed found this rite;—'he alone,' for he alone found this whole holy rite;—'mighty is the praise of the god Savitri,'—that is, 'great is the praise of the god Savitri.'

17. [Vâg. S. XI, 5; *Ri*k S. X, 13, 1] 'By devotions I harness your old inspiration,'—the old inspiration (brahman) doubtless is the vital air, and devotion is food, and that food is this oblation: by means of this oblation, by means of this food, he harnesses the vital airs for this holy work,—'May the praise spread abroad on the lord's path,'—this he says in order that there may be for the Sacrificer the praise of fame among both gods and men;—'may all sons of the immortal hear!'—the immortal one doubtless is Pragâpati, and his sons are all the gods;—'who have resorted

[1] See III, 5, 3, 12, where 'b*ri*hat vipas*k*it' (in the same formula) is explained as referring to the sacrifice.

to the heavenly abodes;'—the heavenly abodes are these worlds: the gods that are in these worlds, with regard to them he says this.

18. [Vâg. S. XI, 6; *Rik* S. V, 81, 3] 'Whose course the others have followed,'—for Pragâpati first performed this rite, whereupon the gods performed it;—'the gods with vigour, the god's greatness,'—the greatness is the sacrifice, thus: 'the gods with vigour (followed) the god's sacrifice, his energy;'—'that dappled steed who hath measured the terrestrial (regions),'—whatsoever is on this earth that is terrestrial, all that he measures out; for with his rays he reaches down to it;—'the regions, he the god Savit*ri* by his greatness,'—the regions are these worlds, and the god Savit*ri* is yonder sun: he measures them by his greatness.

19. [Vâg. S. XI, 7] 'God Savit*ri*, speed the sacrifice, speed the lord of sacrifice unto his share!'—the god Savit*ri* is yonder sun, and his share is the sacrifice, that he means to say when he says 'speed the sacrifice, speed the lord of sacrifice!'—'May the heavenly, thought-cleansing Gandharva cleanse our thought!'—the heavenly Gandharva is yonder sun, and thought is (sacrificial) food; thus, 'May the food-cleanser cleanse our food!'—'May the lord of speech render agreeable our speech!'—this sacred rite is speech, and the lord of speech is the breath: thus, 'May the breath render agreeable this rite of ours!'

20. [Vâg. S. XI, 8] 'Further, O god Savit*ri*, this our sacrifice!'—the god Savit*ri* is yonder sun, and whatever sacrificial rite he furthers, that

reaches its end safely and auspiciously;—'as one pleasant to the gods,'—that is, as one which shall please the gods;—'friend-gaining, ever-winning, wealth-winning, heaven-winning,'—that is, one that may gain all this;—'Make the hymn-tune successful with the *rik* (verse), the Rathantara with the Gâyatra (metre), and the B*ri*hat, moving in Gâyatra measures!'—thus the sâmans (hymns);—'Hail!' thus the sacrificial formulas: this threefold science is first produced, even as it was there and then produced. And the Agni who was produced, he is this Agni (fire-altar) who is built up from hence upwards.

21. These then are the eight Sâvitra (formulas[1]);—the Gâyatrî has eight syllables, and Agni is Gâyatra: as great as Agni is, as great as is his measure, by just so much he pours him out as seed. There are nine of them, the call of 'Hail' (being) the ninth,—there are nine regions, and Agni is the regions; nine vital airs, and Agni is the vital airs: as great as Agni is, as great as is his measure, by so much he pours him out as seed. There are ten of them, the libation (being) the tenth,—the Virâ*g* has ten syllables, and Agni is Virâ*g* (the widely shining[2]); there are ten regions, and Agni is the regions; ten vital airs, and Agni is the vital airs: as great as Agni is, as great as is his measure, so great does this become.

22. This libation having been offered, Agni went away from the gods. The gods said, 'Agni is the

[1] Or, the single oblations, as distinguished from the whole continued libation.

[2] Dîptyâ virâ*g*amâna*h*, Sây.

cattle (or, an animal), let us search for him by means of the (different kinds of) cattle: he will become manifest unto his own form.' They searched for him by means of the cattle, and he became manifest to his own form: and hence even to this day the animal becomes manifest to its own form (kind)[1], cow to cow, horse to horse, and man to man.

23. They said, 'Surely, if we search with all of them, they will become used up and affording no livelihood; and if not with all, we shall get him (Agni) incomplete.' They saw one animal (as a substitute) for two animals[2], namely, the ass (as a substitute) for the cow and the sheep; and because they saw that one beast (would do) for two beasts, therefore that one (the he-ass), whilst being one, doubly impregnates[3].

24. The sham-man[4] (they saw to be a substitute) for man,—a sham-man doubtless is he who pleases neither the gods, nor the fathers, nor men. Thus they searched by means of all the beasts, and yet they (the beasts) did not come to be used up and affording no livelihood.

25. With three he searches,—Agni is threefold: as great as Agni is, as great as is his measure, with so much he thus searches for him. They are five

---

[1] That is to say, it shows itself openly, appears fearlessly before others of its kind;—Svâya rûpâyeti tâdarthye *k*aturthî; âvi*h* prakâ*s*o bhavati, tadanukâre*n*edânîm api pa*s*u*h* svâya rûpâya samânagâtîyâyâ prakâ*s*o bhavati, Sây.

[2] That is to say, they saw that one animal might do for two,—pa*ñk*amî pratinidhau, Sây. (Pâ*n*. II, 3, 11.)

[3] Viz. the she-ass and the mare.

[4] Anaddhâ-purusham alika-purusham purushât pratyapa*s*yan purushasthâne kalitavantas, Sây. Thus probably a counterfeit of a man, a doll or human effigy.

by way of (mystic) correspondence [1],—Agni (the fire-altar) has five layers; five seasons are a year, and the year is Agni: as great as Agni is, as great as is his measure, so great does this become.

26. They are fastened with halters of reed-grass to guard (Agni) against injury [2];—Agni went away from the gods; he entered into a reed, whence it is hollow, and whence inside it is, as it were, smoke-tinged: (thus) that, the reed, is Agni's womb, and Agni is these cattle; and the womb does not injure the child. For [3] it is from a womb that he who is born is born: 'from the womb he (Agni) shall be born when he is born,' thus he thinks.

27. They (the halters) are triple (strings), for Agni is threefold. They are made like a horse's halter, for the horse's halter lies all round the mouth, and the womb lies all round the child: thus it is made like the womb.

28. They (the animals) stand facing the east, first the horse, then the ass, then the he-goat; for this

[1] That is, in order that this item of the sacrificial performance should correspond with the nature of Agni. The number of five is obtained by the three beasts actually led forward,—a horse, an ass, and a he-goat—and the two beasts for which the ass was stated to be a substitute, viz. the cow (or bullock) and the sheep.—Sâyaṇa, whose comment is very corrupt in this place, remarks,—nânaddhâpurusho*tra gaṇyate.

[2] In the text the dative of purpose ('ahiṃsâyai') is as usual shifted right to the end of the train of reasoning explaining the *raison d'être* of this item of the performance.

[3] This final clause with 'vai' supplies the reason why Agni entered the womb, viz. because otherwise he could not be born;—just as the preceding clause with 'vai' (the womb does not injure the child) supplies the reason why reed grass is used; whilst the preceding clauses explain how the reed comes to be the womb whence Agni sprung.

is their proper order. For that horse (asva) is the tear (asru) which there (at the creation) formed itself; and that ass (râsabha) is that which, as it were, cried (ras); and that he-goat (aga, unborn) is the juice which adhered to the shell; and that clay which they are about to fetch is nothing else than the shell (of the egg): for it was from these forms that he was created at first[1], and from them he thus produces him.

29. They stand on the south side;—for the gods at that time were afraid, lest the Rakshas, the fiends, should smite their sacrifice from the south. They saw that thunderbolt, yonder sun; for this horse is indeed yonder sun; and by means of that thunderbolt they drove off the Rakshas, the fiends, from the south, and spread this sacrifice in a place free from danger and devilry. And in like manner does the Sacrificer now by this thunderbolt drive off the Rakshas, the fiends, from the south, and spread this sacrifice in a place free from danger and devilry.

30. On the right (south) side is the Âhavanîya fire, and on the left (north) lies that spade; for the Âhavanîya (m.) is a male, and the spade (abhri, f.) a female, and the male lies on the right side of the female[2]. [It lies] at a cubit's distance, for at a cubit's distance the male lies by the female.

31. It should be made of bamboo. Agni went away from the gods. He entered into a bamboo-stem; whence that is hollow. On both sides he made himself those fences, the knots, so as not

[1] See VI, 1, 1, 11.

[2] Dakshinato vai vrishâ yoshâm upasete;—compare: uttarato hi strî pumâmsam upasete, I, 1, 1, 20; II, 5, 2, 17.

to be found out; and wherever he burnt through, those spots came to be.

32. It (the spade) should be spotted, for such a one is of Agni's nature. If he cannot procure a spotted one, it may be unspotted, but hollow it must be, to guard (Agni) from injury[1];—(for) such a one alone is of Agni's nature; that, the bamboo, is Agni's womb; and this (lump of) clay is Agni; and the womb does not injure the child. For it is from a womb that he who is born is born: 'from the womb he (Agni) shall be born when he is born,' so he thinks.

33. It may be a span long, for the voice here speaks but as far as a span's distance[2]. It is, however, a cubit long, for the cubit is the arm, and strength is exerted by the arm: it thus becomes equal to his strength.

34. It may be sharp on one side only, for on one of the two sides is there a keen edge to this speech of ours[3]. But indeed it is one that is sharp on both sides, for on both sides is there a keen edge to this speech of ours, inasmuch as it speaks both what is divine and what is human[4], and both truth and untruth: therefore it is one that is sharp on both sides.

[1] For the construction, see p. 198, note 2.

[2] Prâdesamâtra*m* hîda*m* mukham abhi vâg vadati, mukham abhi var*n*âtmikâ vâg vadati vâktâstis (?) tasyâ*s* *k*a prâdesamâtratvam adhyâtmâvadhâritam ato*s*trâpi prâdesamâtrâ . . . yuktâ, Sây.

[3] According to Sâya*n*a the tip of the tongue is indicated (as VII, 2, 3, 3; 2, 4, 14, 'vâ*k*' means 'mouth'); but perhaps it is rather sharp, vituperative speech addressed to another person that is intended here.

[4] Sâya*n*a identifies the divine speech with Sa*m*skr*i*t, and the human speech with the Apabhra*m*sas, or low dialects (?mânusha*m* *k*âpâtro*s*am, MS.).

35. And, again, why it is sharp on both sides,—the strength of the spade doubtless is on that side on which there is its sharp edge: he thus lays strength into it on both sides.

36. And, again, why it is sharp on both sides,—when the gods had there discovered him (Agni), they dug him out from these worlds; and in like manner does he now, after discovering him, dig him out from these worlds.

37. When it digs thus (downwards), then it digs him out from this world; and when it moves upwards, then from yonder world; and when it moves about between the two, then from the air-world: it thus digs him out from all these worlds.

38. He takes it up, with (Vâg. S. XI, 9), 'At the impulse of the god Savitri, I take thee by the arms of the Asvins, by the hands of Pûshan, by the Gâyatri metre, Aṅgiras-like!' By means of those deities he thus takes it up, impelled by Savitri; by the Gâyatri metre: he thus imparts the Gâyatri metre to it. 'From the Earth's seat, Aṅgiras-like, bring thou Agni Purishya[1]!'—

[1] Mahîdhara says, Agni is called 'purîshya,' because loose soil (purîsha) is put in the fire-pan (ukhâ), on which the fire is then placed. It also doubtless refers to the loose soil which is spread over the different layers of the altar, thus serving as mortar to the bricks. In this epithet of Agni, 'purîsha' seems, however, to be taken in yet another, more subtle sense, the author apparently connecting with it its etymological meaning of 'that which fills, fillings, Germ. Füllung, Füllsel;' whilst the reference to cattle might also seem to point to the later ordinary meaning, 'faeces, manure.' Mahîdhara, on the force of the symbolical identification 'pasavo vai purîsham,' seems straightway to take 'purîsha' as a synonym of 'pasu,' when he says,—purîshebhyah pasubhyo hitah purîshyah. Sâyana's comment here is corrupt,—pasavo vai purîsham pûranâmûhi(?) kâryam pasavah pûrayanti.

now soil means cattle: thus, 'from the earth's lap bring thou Agni, favourable to cattle, as Agni (did)!'—'by the Trish/ubh metre, Aṅgiras-like!' he thereby takes it with the Trish/ubh metre and thus lays into it the Trish/ubh metre.

39. [Vâg. S. XI, 10] 'A spade thou art,'—for a spade it is: he thus takes it by means of the truth;—'A woman thou art!'—the spade is a thunderbolt, and the woman is a female, and a female injures no one: he thus appeases it so as not to do any injury. 'By thee may we be able to dig out Agni in the seat!' the seat no doubt is this (spot): thus, 'By thee may we be able to dig out Agni in this seat (place).'—'By the *G*agatî metre, Aṅgiras-like!' he thus takes it up by means of the *G*agatî metre, and lays the *G*agatî metre into it.

40. With three (formulas) he takes it up,—threefold is Agni: as great as Agni is, as great as is his measure, by so much he thus takes it. Having taken it up with three (formulas), he addresses it with a fourth; for the gods having thus taken it with three (formulas), then laid vigour into it by means of a fourth; and in like manner does he now, after taking it up with three (formulas), lay strength into it with the fourth.

41. [Vâg. S. XI, 11] 'Having taken into his hand, Savit*ri*,'—for it has indeed been taken into his (the Adhvaryu's) hand,—'bearing the spade,'—for he indeed bears it,—'the golden,'—for golden indeed is the one that consists of the metres (the Veda);—'beholding Agni's light,'—that is, seeing Agni's light,—'lifted it up from the earth,'—for he indeed lifts it up from the earth;—'by the Anush/ubh metre, Aṅgiras-like;'—he thus takes

it up by means of the Anush*t*ubh metre, and lays the Anush*t*ubh metre into it: for his undertaking that spade of bamboo is thus made to be those metres.

42. Some, indeed, make it of gold, saying, 'It is spoken of as golden.' Let him not do so: in that it is the metres, thereby that (spade) is gold, immortal gold, the immortal metres.

43. He takes it up with four (formulas), for all speech consists of four syllables: 'vâk' (speech) is one syllable, and 'aksharam' (syllable) consists of three syllables. Now that monosyllable 'vâk' is the same as this last one, the Anush*t*ubh; and that trisyllable 'aksharam' is the same as those former formulas: he thus digs up Agni by the whole speech, and equips it with the whole speech,—hence with four (formulas).

44. And, again, why with four (formulas);—there are four quarters: he thus lays speech into the four quarters, whence speech speaks in the four quarters. He takes it up both by metres and by formulas, that makes eight—there are four quarters, and four intermediate quarters: he thus lays speech into all the quarters, whence speech speaks in all the quarters.

THE SEARCH AND DIGGING FOR AGNI (THE LUMP OF CLAY).

SECOND BRÂHMA*N*A.

1. The spade is still in his hand, when he addresses the beasts. For when the gods at that time were about to search (for Agni) in these (animals) they placed their vigour in front; and in like manner does

this one, now that he is about to search in these (animals), place his vigour in front.

2. He addresses the horse, with (Vâg. S. XI, 12), 'Most speedily[1], O courser, run hither,'—what is swift, that is speedy, and what is swifter than swift, that is most speedy;—'along the widest range,'—the widest range doubtless is this (earth): thus, 'along this wide range;'—'in the sky is thy highest home, in the air thy navel, upon earth thy womb:' he thus makes it to be those deities, Agni, Vâyu, and Âditya (the sun), and thus lays vigour into the horse.

3. Then the ass, with (Vâg. S. XI, 13), 'Yoke ye two the ass,' he says this to the Adhvaryu and the Sacrificer;—'upon this course, ye showerers of wealth!'—that is, 'upon this performance, ye showerers of wealth;'—'him, bearing Agni, and helpful[2] unto us;'—that is, 'him, bearing Agni, and urged forward by us:' he thereby lays vigour into the ass.

4. Then the he-goat, with (Vâg. S. XI, 14), 'At every yoking, at every race, we call him, the most powerful,'—race[3] means food: thus, 'in every performance, in respect of every food we call him, the most powerful;'—'Indra to our help, we his friends!'—that is, 'him, the strong (indriyavat), to our help:' he thereby lays vigour into the he-goat.

5. With three (formulas) he addresses (the victims),—threefold is Agni: as great as Agni is, as

---

[1] Pratûrtam, 'sped forward, speeding forward.'

[2] Asmayu, 'tending towards us, favourable to us,' is explained differently by the author of the Brâhmana.

[3] The author here, as elsewhere, rather takes 'vâga' in the sense of 'strength, sustenance.'

great as is his measure, by so much he thus lays vigour into them.

6. He then makes them walk forward to the east: he thus searches for him (Agni) by means of these animals. He does not touch (them) lest he, Agni, should injure him; for Agni is the same as the animals[1].

7. He makes the horse walk on, with (Vâg. S. XI, 15), 'Forth-speeding, come treading down the curses!'—curse means evil: thus, 'running come, treading down the evil!'—'come, delighting, into Rudra's chieftainship!'—beasts belong to Rudra: thus, 'come thou, delighting, into the chieftainship of him who is thy deity!' he thus searches for him by means of the horse.

8. Then the ass with, 'Traverse the wide air, thou possessed of prosperous pastures and affording safety!'—as the text, so its meaning;—'with Pûshan as thy mate;'—Pûshan, doubtless, is this earth; thus, 'together with her as thy mate:' he thus searches for him by means of the ass.

9. Then the he-goat, with (Vâg. S. XI, 16), 'From the Earth's seat, Aṅgiras-like, bring thou Agni Purîshya!'—that is, 'from the Earth's lap bring thou Agni, favourable to cattle, as Agni (did)!' he thus searches for him (Agni) by means of the he-goat.

10. With three (animals) he searches,—threefold is Agni: as great as Agni is, as great as is his measure, with so much he thus searches for him.

---

[1] The text here has the ordinary Sanskrit construction, running literally thus:—he does not touch—Agni (being) the same as the animals—'lest he, Agni, should injure me!'

By three (formulas) he first addresses (the beasts); that makes six,—six seasons are a year, and the year is Agni: as great as Agni is, as great as is his measure, so great does this become.

Third Brâhmana.

1. Those fires have been kindled (afresh); and they (the priests and sacrificer) betake themselves to the lump of clay[1];—those fires doubtless are these worlds: when they are kindled, then they are these worlds. For formerly the gods were seeking this sacred rite outside of these worlds; and when he fetches the lump of clay after passing by those fires, he is seeking him (Agni) outside of these worlds.

2. They go eastwards; for the east is Agni's region: he thus seeks him in his own region, finds him in his own region.

3. They go forward, with, 'Aṅgiras-like, we go to Agni Purîshya;'—that is, 'like Agni, we are going to Agni, favourable to cattle.'

4. He then looks at the sham-man, with, 'Aṅgiras-like, we shall carry Agni Purîshya;'—that is, 'Like Agni, we shall carry Agni, favourable to cattle:' he thus searches for him by means of the sham-man.

5. Thereupon a hollow ant-hill is laid down midways (between the lump of clay and the Âhavanîya fire). He looks along it[2]; for the ant-hill is this

---

[1] The lump of clay which is to be used for the making of the fire-pan has been placed in a square hole east of the Âhavanîya fire.

[2] That is to say, he looks at the lump of clay through the hollow part of the ant-hill, whilst muttering the formula given in the next paragraph.

earth, and this earth is these worlds. For the gods searched for him (Agni) in these worlds part by part; and in like manner does this one now search for him in these worlds part by part.

6. [Vâg. S. XI, 17] 'Agni hath looked along the crest of the Dawns,'—thereby they sought him in the dawns;—'along the days, he, the first knower of beings,'—thereby they sought him in the days;—'and oftentimes along the rays of the sun,'—thereby they sought him in the rays of the sun;—'along the sky and the earth hast thou spread;'—therewith they sought him in the sky and the earth, and found him; and in like manner does this one thereby find him (Agni). When he sees him from afar, he throws down that (ant-hill); and they go up to the lump of clay.

7. He then addresses the horse; for the gods then said, 'Let us drive away his evil!' Now evil is weariness: thus, 'Let us drive away his weariness, the evil!' They drove away his weariness, the evil; and in like manner does this one now drive away his weariness, the evil.

8. [Vâg. S. XI, 18] 'The courser, having started on his way,'—for his way has indeed been started upon;—'shaketh off all assaults,'—assaults mean evils: thus, 'shakes off all evils;' and hence, indeed, the horse, whilst running, shakes itself;—'Agni he seeks to descry with his eye on the great seat;'—the great seat doubtless is this sacrificial (place): thus, 'Agni he wishes to see with his eye on this great seat.'

9. He then makes it (the horse) step on (the lump of clay with the left fore-foot); for having discovered him (Agni), it (the horse) then indicated

him to the gods, as if (it meant to say)[1], 'Just here he is!'

10. And, again, why he makes it step thereon;—the gods then were afraid, thinking, 'We hope the Rakshas, the fiends, will not slay here this our (Agni)!' They placed that thunderbolt upon him as a protector, to wit, yonder sun; for that horse is indeed yonder sun; and in like manner does this (Sacrificer, or priest) now place upon him that thunderbolt as a protector.

11. [Vâg. S. XI, 19] 'Having come upon the earth, O courser, seek thou Agni by thy light!'—the light is the eye: thus, 'Having come to the earth, thou, O courser, seek Agni with thy eye!'—'by pawing[2] the ground tell us where we may dig him out!'—that is, 'by pointing out that (spot) of the ground tell us where we may dig him out.'

12. He then pulls it up[3]; for the gods now endowed it with vigour (for) having indicated (Agni) to them; and in like manner does this one now endow it with vigour (for) having indicated (Agni) to him. He does so, with [Vâg. S. XI, 20], 'The sky is thy back, the earth thy resting-place, the air thy body, the sea thy womb;'—whereby he says, 'Such

[1] Or, as if one were to say,—yathâyam iha-sthâna âstha(?) iti kas*k*id brûyâd eva*m* proktavân, Sây.

[2] Or, by covering;—it is not easy to see what the author makes of 'v*ri*ttvâya,' for which the St. Petersburg dictionary suggests 'v*ri*tvâya.' Mahîdhara derives it from 'vart,' in the sense of 'to touch.' Perhaps, however, 'bhûmer' depends on 'yatas;' hence 'moving about, tell us from what spot of the ground we may dig him out.'

[3] That is, he pulls up its head (?); 'he rouses it, shakes it up,' St. Petersb. Dict.—Sâya*n*a, on the other hand, in accordance with Kâty. XVI, 2, 18, interprets 'unm*ri*s*ati' by 'he holds his hand over its back,'—p*ri*sh*th*asyopari pâ*n*im dhârayati.

thou art, such thou art;'—'Looking about with thine eye, tread down the assailers!'—that is, 'Looking about with thy eye, tread down all evil-doers!' He does not touch it, lest this thunderbolt should injure him, for the horse is a thunderbolt[1].

13. He then makes it step off (the lump of clay);—for the gods now said, 'What shall we cause it to obtain[2]?'—'Great beauty[3]!'—They caused it to obtain great beauty; and in like manner does this one now cause it to obtain great beauty,—with (Vâg. S. XI, 21), 'Go thou unto great beauty!'—that is, 'Go to thy great beauty!' and therefore, indeed, the horse is the most highly-favoured of animals;—'from this standing-place,'—that is, 'where thou now standest;'—'wealth-giver!'—for wealth it does give them;—'Courser!'—for this is a courser;—'May we be in the Earth's favour, whilst Agni we dig in her lap!'—that is, 'May we be in the favour of this earth, whilst digging (for) Agni in her lap!'

14. When it has stepped off he addresses it;—for as one would extol him who has given a gift, so the gods now praised and magnified it (for) having indicated (Agni); and in like manner does this one now praise and magnify it, with (Vâg. S. XI, 22), 'He hath come down,'—for it has indeed come down,—'the wealth-giver,'—for wealth, indeed, is given them;—'the racing courser,'—for it is indeed a racer and a courser;—'hath made good, well-made room on earth,'—that is, 'thou madest good, well-made room on earth;'—'thence let us

[1] For the construction, see on paragraph 6, p. 205, note.
[2] Literally, to step off to.
[3] Saubhaga, 'the state of being well-endowed, well-favoured.'

dig out the fair-looking Agni,'—'fair-looking,' he says, for Agni is indeed fair-looking on every side;—'ascending the heaven, unto the highest sky,'—the sky is the heavenly world: thus, 'mounting the heavenly world, unto the highest sky.' He makes it come up on the right side (of the lump) to where the two other beasts are: they stand on the right side, facing the east. The significance of the right-hand (southern) position here is the same as it was on that former occasion.

15. Sitting down he now offers upon the lump of clay;—for the gods then said, 'Meditate ye (*k*etay),' whereby, doubtless, they meant to say, 'Seek ye a layer (*k*iti)!' Whilst meditating they saw this libation, and offered it: after offering it, they saw the fire-pan (representing) these worlds.

16. They said, 'Meditate ye!' whereby, doubtless, they meant to say, 'Seek ye a layer!' Whilst meditating they saw this second libation, and offered it: after offering it, they saw the Visvagyotis (all-light bricks), that is, those deities Agni, Vâyu, and Âditya; for these deities are indeed all the light. And in like manner does the Sacrificer now, after offering those two libations, see the fire-pan, these worlds; and those all-light deities. He offers with two interlinked (verses)[1]: he thereby interlinks these worlds, and those deities.

17. And, again, why he offers these two libations;—he thereby gratifies both the clay and the water; and having offered to, and gratified, these two, he then brings them together. With two interlinked

[1] The two halves of the two verses (Vâg. S. XI, 23, 24) are uttered in the order 1 a, 2 b, 2 a, 1 b.

(verses) he offers: he thereby interlinks (combines thoroughly) the clay and the water.

18. He offers with ghee; for the ghee is a thunderbolt: he thus makes the thunderbolt its (or his, Agni's) protector. The ghee, moreover, is seed: he thus pours forth seed,—with the sruva-spoon; for the sruva (m.) is a male, and the male pours forth seed,—with 'Svâhâ (hail!),' for the Svâhâkâra (m.) is a male, and the male pours forth seed.

19. [Vâg. S. XI, 23[1]] 'Upon thee I sprinkle with thought, with ghee,'—that is, 'upon thee I offer with thought and ghee;'—'that dwellest near all beings,'—for he (Agni) indeed comes to dwell near every being;—'thee, large and great with side-spent force,'—for large he is, and directed sideways, and great with force, with smoke;—'most ample through food, and fierce to look at,'—that is, 'capacious with food, a consumer of food, and flaming.'

20. [Vâg. S. XI, 24] 'From all sides I sprinkle the hitherward looking,'—that is, 'from every side I offer upon the hitherward looking;'—'with spiteless mind let him relish this,'—that is, 'with unchafing mind may he relish this;'—'Agni, glorious as a wooer, and of pleasing colour,'—for Agni is indeed glorious as a wooer[2], and of pleasing colour;—'not to be touched, while raging with his body,'—for not to be touched is he, whilst flaming with his body.

21. With two (verses) he offers; for the Sacrificer

[1] *Rik* S. II, 10, 4, beginning, however, 'I sprinkle Agni with a ghee-oblation.'

[2] Mahîdhara and Sâyana (*Rik* S. II, 10, 5) take 'maryasrî' in the sense of 'resorted to, or worshipped, by men.'

is two-footed, and the Sacrificer is Agni: as great as Agni is, as great as is his measure, by so much he thus pours him forth as seed;—with two (verses) relating to Agni: it is Agni he thereby pours forth as seed. Inasmuch as they relate to Agni, they are Agni; and inasmuch as they are Trish*t*ubhs, they are Indra; and Agni (the fire) belongs to Indra and Agni: as great as Agni is, as great as is his measure, by so much he thus pours him forth as seed. Moreover, Indra and Agni are all the gods, and Agni (thus) contains all deities: as great as Agni is, as great as is his measure, by so much he thus pours him forth as seed.

22. He offers on the horse's footprint;—the horse is the same as that Agni, and so, indeed, these two libations come to be offered over Agni.

23. He draws lines around it (the lump, with the spade): he thereby puts a measure to it (or, to him, Agni), as if saying, 'So great thou art!'

24. And, again, why he draws a line around it;—the gods now were afraid, thinking, 'We hope the Rakshas, the fiends, will not smite here this (Agni) of ours!' They drew that rampart round it; and in like manner does this one now draw that rampart round it,—with the spade, for the spade is the thunderbolt, and he thus makes the thunderbolt its (or his, Agni's) protector. He draws it all round: on every side he thus makes that thunderbolt to be its (or his) protector[1]. Three times he draws a line: that threefold thunderbolt he thus makes to be a protector for him.

25. [Vâg. S. XI, 25–27] 'Around the wise lord

[1] Or, he makes that protecting thunderbolt for it (or him).

of strength—[1],' 'Around (us) we (place) thee, O Agni, as a rampart—[2],' 'With the days, thou Agni—[3],' in thus praising Agni he makes a fence for him by means of (verses) containing the word 'pari' (around), for all round, as it were, (run) the ramparts;—(he does so by verses) relating to Agni: a stronghold of fire he thus makes for him, and this stronghold of fire keeps blazing;—(he does so) by three (verses): a threefold stronghold he thus makes for him; and hence that threefold stronghold is the highest form of strongholds. Each following (circular) line he makes wider, and with a larger metre: hence each following line of strongholds is wider, for strongholds (ramparts) are lines.

26. He then digs for him (Agni)[4] in this earth. For the gods then were afraid, thinking, 'We hope the Rakshas, the fiends, will not smite him here[1]!' For the sake of protection they made this earth to be a self (body, âtman) for him, thinking, 'His own self will protect his own self.' It (the lump of clay) should be as large as the hole: thus this earth (or clay) becomes his (Agni's) self. And as to its (being) as large as the hole,—this earth is the womb, and this (clay) is seed; and whatever part of the seed

[1] Vâg. S. XI, 25; *Ri*k S. IV, 15, 3, 'Around the offering, Agni, the wise lord of strength, hath come, bestowing precious gifts upon the worshipper.'

[2] Vâg. S. XI, 26; *Ri*k S. X, 87, 22, 'Around we place thee, the priest, as a rampart, O mighty Agni, the bold-raced slayer of the wily day by day.'

[3] Vâg. S. XI, 27; *Ri*k S. II, 1, 1, 'With the days, O Agni, thou, longing to shine hither, art born forth from the waters, out of the shore, from the woods, from the herbs, thou the bright, O man-lord of men.'

[4] Or he digs out that (lump of clay).

exceeds the womb, becomes useless; and what is deficient, is unsuccessful; but that part of the seed which is within the hole is successful. Four-cornered is this hole, for there are four quarters: from all the (four) quarters he thus digs him.

Fourth Adhyâya. First Brâhmana.

1. He now digs it (the lump of clay)[1] up from that (hole);—for the gods, having found him (Agni), then dug him up; and in like manner this one, after finding him, now digs him up,—with (Vâg. S. XI, 28), 'At the impulse of the god Savitri, by the arms of the Asvins, by the hands of Pûshan, I dig thee, the Agni Purîshya, from the lap of the earth, Angiras-like;'—impelled by Savitri, he thus, by means of those deities, digs him up, the Agni favourable to cattle, as Agni (did).

2. 'Thee, O Agni, the bright, the fair-faced,'—for this Agni is indeed bright and fair-faced;—'glowing with perpetual sheen,'—that is, 'shining with perpetual light;'—'thee, kind to creatures, and never harming, the Agni Purîshya we dig up from the lap of the earth, Angiras-like;'—that is, 'thee, kind to creatures, and never harming, the cattle-loving Agni we dig up from the lap of the earth, as Agni (did).'

3. With two (formulas) he digs,—two-footed is the Sacrificer, and the Sacrificer is Agni: as great as Agni is, as great as is his measure, with so much he thus digs him up. And twofold also is that form of his, (consisting as it does of) clay and water.

4. He digs, with, 'I dig,'—'we dig;' for with, 'I

[1] Or him, Agni; the identity of the two being kept up throughout.

dig,' Pragâpati dug for him (Agni); and with, 'we dig,' the gods dug for him, therefore (he digs), with, 'I dig,'—'we dig.'

5. Now while digging with the spade, he says with speech 'I dig,' 'we dig,' for the spade is speech. It is for his undertaking that this bamboo (spade) is made; and with speech for a spade, the gods dug him up; and in like manner does this one now dig him up with speech for a spade (or, with the speech-spade).

6. He then deposits it upon the black antelope skin, for the black antelope skin is the sacrifice[1]: in the sacrifice he thus deposits it (or him, Agni);—on the hair (side); for the hair is the metres: he thus deposits him on the metres. That (skin) he spreads silently; for the black antelope skin is the sacrifice; and the sacrifice is Pragâpati, and undefined is Pragâpati. North (of the hole he spreads it),—the meaning of this (will be explained) hereafter;—on (the skin spread) with the neck-part in front, for thus (it is turned) towards the gods.

7. And he deposits it on a lotus-leaf (placed on the skin); for the lotus-leaf is the womb, and into the womb he pours that seed; and the seed which is poured into the womb, becomes generative. He spreads that (leaf) with a formula; for the formula is speech, and the lotus-leaf is speech[2].

8. [Vâg. S. XI, 29] 'Thou art the waters'

[1] Regarding the skin of the black antelope, considered as a symbol of Brâhmanical worship and civilisation, see part i, p. 23, note 2. As to the white and black hair of it representing the hymn-verses (*rik*) and tunes (sâman), and those of undecided colour the Yagus-formulas, see I, 1, 4, 2.

[2] Viz. because from speech the waters were produced (VI, 1, 1, 9), and from them the lotus-leaf has sprung. Sây.

back, Agni's womb,' for this is indeed the back of the waters, and the womb of Agni;—'around the swelling sea,'—for the sea indeed swells around it;—'thou, growing mighty upon the lotus,'—that is, 'growing, prosper thou on the lotus.'—'With the measure of the sky, extend thou in width!'—with this he strokes along it (so as to lie even on the skin); for that Agni is yonder sun; and him assuredly none other than the width of the sky can contain: 'having become the sky, contain him!' this is what he thereby says.

9. He spreads it over the black antelope skin; for the black antelope skin is the sacrifice; and the black antelope skin is this earth, and the sacrifice is this earth, for on this earth the sacrifice is spread. And the lotus-leaf is the sky; for the sky is the waters, and the lotus-leaf is the waters; and yonder sky is above this earth.

10. He touches both of them—he thereby brings about concord between them—with (Vâg. S. XI, 30), 'A shelter ye are, a shield ye are!'—for both a shelter and a shield these two indeed are;—'uninjured both, and ample,'—for uninjured and ample both these indeed are;—'capacious, guard ye,'—that is, 'spacious, guard ye!'—'bear ye Agni Purîshya!'—that is, 'bear ye Agni, favourable to cattle[1]!'

11. [Vâg. S. XI, 31] 'Guard ye, light-finders, uniting with each other, with the breast, with the self,'—that is, 'guard him, ye light-finders, uniting with each other, both with your breast and your self;'—'bearing within the brilliant, the

[1] See p. 201, note 1.

everlasting;'—this Agni indeed is yonder sun, and he is the brilliant, the everlasting one; and him these two bear between (them): hence he says, 'the brilliant, the everlasting.'

12. He touches them with two (verses);—two-footed is the Sacrificer, and the Sacrificer is Agni: as great as Agni is, as great as is his measure, by so much he thus brings about concord between these two. And, again, (he does so) because that form of theirs is twofold, (there being) a black antelope skin and a lotus-leaf.

Second Brâhmana.

1. He then touches the lump of clay, with (Vâg. S. XI, 32), 'Thou art the Purîshya[1],'—that is, 'Thou art favourable to cattle;'—'all-supporting,'—for he (Agni) indeed supports everything here;—'Atharvan was the first that kindled thee, O Agni!'—Atharvan doubtless is the breath, and the breath indeed churned him out (produced him) at first: 'Thou art that Agni who was produced at first,' this he means to say; and that same (Agni) he thus makes it (the lump) to be.

2. He then takes hold of it with the (right) hand and spade on the right side; and with the (left) hand on the left side, with, 'From the lotus Atharvan churned thee forth,'—the lotus doubtless means the waters, and Atharvan is the breath; and the breath indeed churned him (Agni, the fire) out of the waters at first;—'from the head of every offerer[2],'—that is, 'from the head of this All (universe).'

[1] See p. 201, note 1.

[2] ? Or, of every priest (visvasya vâghatah). There is nothing to

3. [Vâg. S. XI, 33; *Ri*k S. VI, 16, 14] 'Also the sage Dadhya*ñk*, the son of Atharvan, kindled thee;'—Dadhya*ñk*, the Âtharvana, doubtless is speech; and he did kindle him therefrom;—'as the V*ri*tra-slayer, the breaker of strongholds,'—V*ri*tra is evil, thus: 'as the slayer of evil, the breaker of strongholds.'

4. [Vâg. S. XI, 34; *Ri*k S. VI, 16, 15] 'Also Pâthya, the bull, kindled thee, as the greatest slayer of enemies,'—Pâthya, the bull, doubtless is the Mind, and he did kindle him therefrom;—'as a winner of wealth in every battle,'—as the text, so its meaning.

5. With Gâyatrî verses (he performs),—the Gâyatrî is the vital air: he thus lays vital air into him. With three (verses);—there are three vital airs, the out-breathing, the in-breathing, and the through-breathing: these he thus lays into him. These (verses) consist of nine feet, for there are nine vital airs, seven in the head, and two downward ones: these he thus lays into him.

6. And these two following ones are Trish*t*ubhs,—(Vâg. S. XI, 35, 36; *Ri*k S. III, 29, 8; II, 9, 1). Now, the Trish*t*ubh is the body (self): it is his (Agni's) body he makes up by means of these two

show how the author of this part of the Brâhma*n*a interprets 'vâghat.' Cf. VI, 4, 3, 10.—Professor Ludwig (*Ri*k S. VI, 16, 13) translates, 'from the head of the priest Visva.' Mahîdhara offers several interpretations, according to which 'vâghata*h*' may either be taken as nom. plur., the verb being again supplied in the plural,—'the priests churned thee out from the head of the universe,' or 'the priests of the universe (or all priests) churned thee out,'—or 'vâghata*h*' may be ablative sing., like 'mûrdhna*h*,' qualifying 'pushkarât,'—from the lotus, the head, the leader (or, starter, vâhakât) of the universe.

(verses). 'Seat thee, O Hotri, in thine own place, thou, the mindful,'—the Hotri, doubtless, is Agni; and this, the black antelope skin, is indeed his own place; 'the mindful,' that is, 'the wise one;'—'establish the sacrifice in the seat of the good work!'—the seat of the good work doubtless is the black antelope skin;—'god-gladdening, thou shalt worship the gods with offering!'—that is, 'being a god, gratifying the gods, thou shalt worship (them) with offering;'—'Bestow, O Agni, great vigour upon the Sacrificer!'—thereby he implores a blessing upon the Sacrificer.

7. 'The Hotri, in the Hotri's seat, the knowing,'—the Hotri, doubtless, is Agni; the Hotri's seat is the black antelope skin; and the knowing[1] means the wise one;—'the impetuous and glowing one, of great power, hath sat down,'—that is, the impetuous and shining one, of great power, has sat down;—'the guardian of undisturbed rites, the most wealthy,'—for he indeed is the guardian of undisturbed rites, and the most wealthy;—'the bearer of thousands, the brilliant-tongued Agni,'—a thousand means all, thus, 'the all-bearer, the brilliant-tongued Agni.' With two Trishtubh (verses) relating to Agni (he performs): the meaning of this has been told.

8. Then there is this last Brihatî verse, for this (fire-altar) when completely built up becomes like the Brihatî (the great) metre: whatlike seed is infused into the womb, suchlike is (the child) born; and because he now makes this verse a Brihatî,

---

[1] Thus the author evidently interprets 'vidânah,' instead of 'being found,' 'se trouvant,' as is its real meaning.

therefore this (altar) when completely built up becomes like the B*ri*hatî.

9. [Vâ*g*. S. XI, 37; *Ri*k S. I, 36, 9] 'Seat thee, thou art great,'—he now causes the infused seed to establish itself, whence the seed infused into the womb establishes itself;—'burn thou, best gladdener of the gods!'—that is, 'shine thou, best gladdener of the gods;'—'send forth, O Agni, worthy partaker of the offering, thy showy, ruddy smoke!' for when he (Agni) is kindled, he sends forth his ruddy smoke,—the showy, for it, as it were, shows itself.

10. These (verses) amount to six,—six seasons are a year, and Agni is the year: as great as Agni is, as great as is his measure, so great does this become. And what comes to be like the year, comes to be like the B*ri*hatî; for the year is the B*ri*hatî,—twelve full moons, twelve eighth days[1] (of the fortnight of waning moon), twelve new moons, that makes thirty-six, and the B*ri*hatî consists of thirty-six syllables. He takes it (the lump of clay) from the right (south) to the left (north) side (of the hole), for from the right side seed is infused into the womb; and this (hole) now is his (Agni's) womb. He takes it thither without stopping, so as not to stop the seed.

THIRD BRÂHMA*N*A.

1. He then pours water into it (the hole), for whatever is injured or torn in this earth that is healed by water: by means of the water he thus joins together and heals what is injured and torn in her.

---

[1] See VI, 2, 2, 23.

2. [Vâ*g*. S. XI, 38] 'Let flow the divine waters, the honey-sweet, for health, for progeny!'—honey means sap (essence): thus, 'the sapful, for health, for progeny;'—'from their seed let plants spring forth, full-berried!' for full-berried plants indeed spring forth from the seat of the waters.

3. He then heals her with air[1]; for whatever is injured and torn in this earth that is healed by the air: by means of air he thus joins together and heals what is injured and torn in her.

4. [Vâ*g*. S. XI, 39] 'May Vâyu Mâtari*s*van heal,'—Vâyu Mâtari*s*van, doubtless, is he (the wind) that blows yonder;—'the broken heart of thee stretched out with upward look!' for this (hole) is the broken heart of this earth stretched out with upward look;—'thou who goest along by the breath of the gods,'—for he (the wind) indeed goes along by means of the breath of all the gods;—'to thee, Ka, be vasha*t* (success), O god!'—Ka ('Who?') doubtless is Pra*g*âpati, for him he makes this earth to be the Vasha*t*, for there is so far no other oblation than that.

5. He then heals her by means of the quarters, for whatever is injured and torn in this earth, that is healed by the quarters: by means of the quarters he thus draws and joins together what is injured and torn in her. He joins together this and this quarter[2], whence these two quarters are joined

[1] Viz. by fanning air into the hole with the hand.

[2] With his 'nameless' (or little) finger, he pushes some of the loose soil into the hole, first from the front (east) and back (west) sides, and then from the right (south) and left (north) sides. Thus, according to Kâty. XVI, 3, 4, the sunwise movement is

together; then this one and this one, whence these two also are joined together: first thus, then thus; then thus, then thus. This is moving (from left) to right, for so (it goes) to the gods: with this and this one a means of healing is prepared; with this and this one he heals.

6. He then takes up together the black antelope skin and the lotus-leaf; for the lotus-leaf is the womb, and with the womb he takes up that infused seed: whence the infused seed is taken up by the womb. [He does so, with, Vâ*g*. S. XI, 40] 'Well-born with splendour, the refuge and shelter, hath he settled down in the light;' for well-born he is, and he settles down in the refuge, and shelter, and light.

7. He then ties it (the lump) up: he thereby keeps the seed within the womb; whence the seed kept within the womb does not escape. With a string (he ties it), for with the string they yoke the draught beast;—with a triple one of reed grass: the significance of this has been told [1].

8. He lays it round (the skin), with, 'Invest thyself, O lustrous Agni, in the many-coloured garment!' In the sacrifice the cord is Varu*n*ic; having thereby made it non-Varu*n*ic, he makes him put on (the skin) as one would make a garment be put on.

9. He then takes it and rises;—that Agni being yonder sun, he thus causes yonder sun to rise;—with (Vâ*g*. S. XI, 41) [2], 'Rise, thou of good rites,'—the sacrifice doubtless is a rite: thus, 'rise thou, well

obtained by the hand moving from east (along the south) to west, and then from south (along the west) to north.

[1] See VI, 3, 1, 27.

[2] See *Ri*k S. VIII, 23, 5, differing considerably.

worthy of sacrifice;'—'Guard us with godly wisdom!'—that is, 'whatever divine wisdom is thine, therewith guard us!'—'Most brilliant to see with great light,'—that is, 'in order to be seen most brilliant with great light;'—'hither, O Agni, come thou with praises!'—the praises[1] are the steeds: thus, 'hither, O Agni, come with the steeds.'

10. He then lifts it upwards from there towards the east; for this Agni is yonder sun: he thus places yonder sun upwards from here in the east, and hence yonder sun is placed upwards from here in the east. [He does so, with, Vâg. S. XI, 42; *Rik* S. I, 36, 13] 'Upright for our protection, stand thou like the god Savit*ri*!'—as the text, so its meaning;—'upright, as a bestower[2] of strength,'—for standing upright he (the sun) indeed bestows[2] strength, food;—'when we utter our call with the shining offerers'—the shining offerers[3], doubtless, are his (the sun's) rays: it is these he means. He lifts it up beyond the reach of his arms, for beyond the reach of his arms is that (sun) from here. He then lowers it; and having lowered it, he holds it above the navel: the meaning of this (will be explained) hereafter[4].

[1] The author might seem to connect '*s*asti' (in su*s*asti) with '*s*âs,' to rule, control, instead of with '*s*ams,' to praise; Sâya*n*a, however, takes 'su*s*asti' as a bahuvrîhi, 'with the praiseworthy,' i. e. with the steeds deserving praise, because they draw well (*s*obhanâ *s*astir eshâm . . . sâdhu vahanty a*s*vâ*h*). It is indeed not improbable that this was the author's intention.

[2] Or, a winner—wins.

[3] Añgayo vâghata*h*. See p. 217, note 2.

[4] See VI, 7, 1, 8 seq.

FOURTH BRÂHMANA.

1. That (lump of clay representing Agni) is still in his hand when he addresses the animals; for the gods, being about to equip[1] (Agni), now first laid vigour into them; and in like manner does this (Sacrificer, or priest) now, being about to equip (Agni), first lay vigour into these (cattle).

2. He addresses the horse, with (Vâg. S. XI, 43; *Ri*k S. X, 1, 2), 'Thus born, art thou the child of the two worlds;'—the two worlds, doubtless, are these two, heaven and earth; and he (Agni) thus born, is the child of these two;—'O Agni, the lovely (child), distributed among the plants,'—for he, the lovely one, is indeed distributed among all the plants[2];—'a brilliant child, through gloom and night,'—for as a brilliant child, he (Agni) indeed shines beyond gloom and night;—'crying aloud thou didst go forth from the mothers;'—his mothers, doubtless, are the plants, and from them he comes forth crying aloud. He thereby lays vigour into the horse.

3. Then (he addresses) the ass, with (Vâg. S. XI, 44), 'Steadfast be thou, firm-limbed, and a swift racer be thou, O steed!'—that is, 'be thou steadfast, and firm-limbed, and swift, and a racer, O steed!'—'Ample be thou, and well to sit upon, thou, the bearer of Agni's supply!'—that is, 'be

[1] For the ceremony of 'equipping' Agni, see part i, p. 276, note 1.

[2] Viz. inasmuch as fire may be elicited from dry wood. See also I, 6, 4, 5, where Soma, frequently identified with Agni (see VI, 5, 1, 1), is said at new moon to come down to the earth, and enter the waters and plants in order to be born anew from them.

thou ample (broad), well to rest upon, thou, Agni's provender-bearer[1]!' He thereby lays vigour into the ass.

4. Then the he-goat, with (Vâg. S. XI, 45), 'Be thou propitious unto human creatures, O Aṅgiras!'—for Agni is Aṅgiras, and the he-goat is sacred to Agni: he thus appeases him with a view to his doing no injury;—'Scorch not heaven and earth, nor the air, nor the trees!'—that is, 'do not injure anything!' He thereby lays vigour into the he-goat.

5. With three (verses) he addresses (the animals), for threefold is Agni: as great as Agni is, as great as is his measure, with so much he thus lays vigour into them.

6. He then holds it (Agni, the lump of clay) over these animals, whereby he equips him (Agni) with these cattle. He does not touch them, lest he should injure that seed by the thunderbolt, for cattle are a thunderbolt, and this (clay) is seed; or lest that Agni should injure those cattle, for that (lump of clay) is Agni, and these (animals) are cattle.

7. In the first place he holds it over the horse, with (Vâg. S. XI, 46), 'Let the racer start forth neighing lustily,'—that is, 'Let the racer start forth neighing repeatedly;'—'the running ass, crying aloud!' He thus mentions the ass in the formula of the horse, and thereby imbues the ass with sorrow[2];—'bearing Agni Purishya, may he

[1] Literally, Agni's bearer of what is suitable for the cattle, or perhaps, be thou, for Agni, the bearer of (himself) favourable to cattle;—'pasavya' being here as elsewhere used (see p. 201, note) to explain 'purîsha,' that which fills, the mould or soil used as mortar for the layers of bricks, in building up the fire-altar.

[2] On account of his being compared with the horse, Sây. The author probably alludes to the dejected, spiritless look of the ass, as

not perish before his full measure of time!'—that is, 'bearing Agni favourable to cattle, may he (the horse) not perish before (the completion of) this sacred work.' He thereby equips him (Agni) with the horse.

8. Then (over) the ass, with, 'The male carrying Agni, the male,'—for Agni is a male, and the he-ass is a male: that male carries the male;—'the sea-born child of the waters,'—for he (Agni) is the sea-born child of the waters. He thereby equips him with the ass.

9. He then takes it off, with, 'O Agni, come hither to the feast!'—that is, 'in order to rejoice.' By means of the brahman, the ya*g*us (formula), he thus removes him (Agni) from the *S*ûdra caste.

10. Then (he holds it over) the he-goat, with (Vâ*g*. S. XI, 47), 'The law—the truth, the law—the truth!'—the (divine) law doubtless is this Agni; and the truth is yonder sun; or, rather, the law is yonder (sun), and the truth is this (Agni); but, indeed, this Agni is both the one and the other: hence he says, 'the law—the truth, the law—the truth.' He thereby equips him with the he-goat.

11. With three (beasts) he equips (Agni),—threefold is Agni: as great as Agni is, as great as is his measure, with so much he thus equips him. With three (verses) he previously addresses (the beasts),—that makes six: the significance of this (number) has been explained.

12. They then make the beasts return (to the Âhavanîya): the he-goat goes first of them, then the ass, then the horse. Now, in going away from this

---

compared with that of the horse. The word '*suk*' might, however, perhaps also be taken in the sense of 'fervour, fire.'

(Âhavanîya[1]), the horse goes first, then the ass, then the he-goat,—for the horse corresponds to the Kshatra (nobility), the ass to the Vaisya and Sûdra, the he-goat to the Brâhmana.

13. And inasmuch as, in going from here, the horse goes first, therefore the Kshatriya, going first, is followed by the three other castes; and inasmuch as, in returning from there, the he-goat goes first, therefore the Brâhmana, going first, is followed by the three other castes. And inasmuch as the ass does not go first, either in going from here, or in coming back from there, therefore the Brâhmana and Kshatriya never go behind the Vaisya and Sûdra: hence they walk thus in order to avoid a confusion between good and bad. And, moreover, he thus encloses those two castes (the Vaisya and Sûdra) on both sides by the priesthood and the nobility, and makes them submissive.

14. He then looks at the sham-man, with, 'Agni Purishya we bear, Aṅgiras-like;'—that is, 'Agni, favourable to cattle, we bear, like Agni.' He thereby equips him with the sham-man.

15. He (the Adhvaryu) arrives (near the fire) while holding (the lump of clay) over the he-goat; for the he-goat is sacred to Agni: he thus equips him (Agni) with his own self, with his own godhead. And, moreover, the he-goat is the Brahman (priesthood): with the Brahman he thus equips him.

16. He then takes it down, with, 'O plants, welcome ye with joy this propitious Agni coming hitherwards!' for the plants are afraid lest he (Agni) should injure them: it is for them that he

[1] See VI, 3, 2, 6 seq.

now appeases him, saying, 'Welcome ye him with joy, propitious he comes to you; he will not injure you!'—'Removing all infirmities, afflictions; settling down, drive off from us evil intention!' that is, 'removing all infirmities and afflictions, settling down, drive off from us all evil!'

17. [Vâg. S. XI, 48] 'O plants, receive him joyfully, ye blossoming, full-berried ones!' for that is their perfect form when they are blossoming and full-berried: thus, 'Being perfect, receive ye him joyfully!'—'this timely child of yours hath settled down in his old seat;' that is, 'this seasonable child of yours has settled down in his eternal seat.'

18. With two (verses) he takes it down,—two-footed is the Sacrificer, and the Sacrificer is Agni: as great as Agni is, as great as is his measure, with so much he thus takes it down. He takes it down from the right (south) to the left (north) side: the significance of this has been explained. Raised and sprinkled is (the place) where he takes it down, for on a (mound), raised and sprinkled, the (sacrificial) fire is laid down. Gravel is strewed thereon: the significance of this (will be explained) hereafter[1].

19. It is enclosed on all sides[2]; for at that time the gods were afraid, thinking, 'We hope the Rakshas, the fiends, will not smite here this (Agni) of ours!' They enclosed him with this stronghold; and in like manner does this one now enclose him with this stronghold. And, again, this is a womb;

---

[1] See VII, 1, 1, 9.

[2] The lump of clay is deposited on a raised mound (or perhaps rather on a cut-out piece of ground, uddhata), in an enclosed shed, (with a door on the east side) north of the Âhavanîya.

and this (clay) is seed; and in secret, as it were, the seed is infused into the womb: it is thus made of the form of the womb; and hence it is only in secret that one would have intercourse even with his own wife.

20. He then unties it (the lump of clay): whatever part of his (body) pains him (Agni) when tied up, that pain he now puts outside of him; and, moreover, he causes him to be born from that womb (the antelope skin).

21. [He unties it, with Vâg. S. XI, 49; *Ri*k S. III, 15, 1] 'Blazing forth with wide glare,'—that is, 'Shining brightly with wide glare;'—'chase away the terrors of the hating demons!'—that is, 'chase away all evils!'—'May I be in the protection of the great, the good protector, in the guidance of Agni, ready to our call!' thereby he invokes a blessing.

22. He then cuts off some goat's hair, and lets loose the animals towards the north-east; for this, the north-east, is the region of both gods and men: he thus bestows cattle on that region, and hence both gods and men subsist on cattle.

THE MAKING OF THE FIRE-PAN (UKHÂ).

FIFTH ADHYÂYA. FIRST BRÂHMANA.

1. That water (used for working the clay) has been boiled by means of resin of the palâsa tree (butea frondosa), just for the sake of firmness. And as to why (it is done) by palâsa resin;—the palâsa tree doubtless is Soma[1], and Soma is the moon, and that (moon) indeed is one of Agni's

[1] See part i, p. 183.

forms: it is for the obtainment of that form of Agni (that palâ*s*a resin is used).

2. He pours it on (the clay), with (Vâ*g*. S. XI, 50–52; *Ri*k S. X, 9, 1–3), 'Refreshing ye are, O waters[1]!' To whatever deity a *Ri*k-verse, and to whatever deity a Ya*g*us formula applies, that *Ri*k-verse is that very deity, and that Ya*g*us formula is that very deity: hence this triplet (XI, 50–52) is these waters, and they are those very waters which appeared as one form[2]: that form he now makes it.

3. He then produces foam and puts it thereto: the second form which was created (in the shape of) foam[3], that form he thus makes it. And the clay he now mixes is that very clay which was created as the third form. It was from these forms that he (Agni) was created at the beginning, and from them he now produces him.

4. He then mixes it with the goat's hair, just for the sake of firmness. And as to why with goat's hair,—the gods then collected him (Agni) from out of the cattle, and in like manner does this one now collect him from out of the cattle. And as to why with goat's hair, it is because in the he-goat (is contained) the form of all cattle; and as to its being hair, form is hair[4].

5. [Vâ*g*. S. XI, 53] 'Mitra having mixed the earth and ground with light,'—Mitra doubtless

---

[1] The whole triplet runs thus: 'Refreshing ye are, O waters; lead us to strength, to see great joy!—whatever is your most benign sap, therein let us share, like loving mothers!—For you we will readily go to him, to whose abode ye urge us, O waters, and quicken us.'

[2] See VI, 1, 1, 12.

[3] VI, 1, 1, 13.

[4] That is, the hair of cattle is the most obvious characteristic of their outward appearance.

is the breath, and the breath first did this sacred work;—'I mix (fashion) thee, the well-born knower of beings, for health to creatures,'—as the text, so its meaning.

6. Then there are these three kinds of powder (dust) —(sand of) gravel, stone, and iron-rust—therewith he mixes (the clay), just for firmness. And as to why (it is mixed) therewith, it is because thereof this (earth) consisted when it was created in the beginning: thus whatlike this (earth) was created in the beginning, such he now makes it (the earth, or fire-pan).

7. [Vâg. S. XI, 54] 'The Rudras, having mixed the earth, kindled the great light;'—for this Agni is yonder sun: thus it is that great light which the Rudras, having mixed the earth, did kindle;—'yea, never-failing and brilliant, their light shineth among the gods;'—for that never-failing and brilliant light of theirs does indeed shine among the gods.

8. With two (verses) he mixes (the clay),—two-footed is the Sacrificer, and the Sacrificer is Agni: as great as Agni is, as great as is his measure, so great he thus mixes (fashions) him.

9. He then kneads it, with (Vâg. S. XI, 55), 'Mixed by the Vasus, the Rudras,'—for this (clay) has indeed been mixed both by the Vasus and the Rudras: by the Vasus, because by Mitra; and by the Rudras, because by the Rudras;—'by the wise, the clay suitable for the work;'—for wise those (gods) are, and suitable for the (sacred) work is this clay;—'making it soft with her hands, may Sinîvalî fashion it!'—Sinîvalî doubtless is speech: thus, 'May she, having made it soft with her hands, fashion it!'

10. [Vâg. S. XI, 56] 'Sinivalî, the fair-knotted, fair-braided, fair-locked,'—for Sinivalî is a woman, and that is indeed the perfect form of woman, to wit, the fair-knotted, fair-braided, fair-locked: he thus makes her perfect;—'may she place the fire-pan into thy hands, O great Aditi!'—the great Aditi doubtless is this earth: it is to this earth that he says this.

11. [Vâg. S. XI, 57] 'Let Aditi fashion the fire-pan, by her skill, her arms, her wisdom!'—for by her skill, by her arms, and by her wisdom she does indeed fashion it;—'may she bear Agni in her womb, even as a mother (bears) her son in her lap!'—that is, 'as a mother would bear her son in her lap, so may she (Aditi) bear Agni in her womb!'

12. With three (formulas) he kneads (the clay),—threefold is Agni: as great as Agni is, as great as is his measure, with so much he thus kneads him. With two (verses) he mixes,—that makes five;—of five layers consists the fire-altar (Agni); five seasons are a year, and the year is Agni: as great as Agni is, as great as is his measure, so great does this become. With three (formulas) he pours water thereto,—that makes eight;—of eight syllables the Gâyatrî metre consists, and Agni is Gâyatra: as great as Agni is, as great as is his measure, so great does this become. And, moreover, as one of eight syllables[1] this (earth) was created in the beginning: thus as great as this (earth) was created in the beginning, so great he thus makes this (fire-pan representing the earth).

[1] See VI, 1, 2, 6-7.

SECOND BRÂHMANA.

1. He then takes a lump of clay, as much as he thinks sufficient for the bottom part, with, 'Makha's head thou art!'—Makha, doubtless, is the sacrifice, and this is its head; for the Âhavanîya fire is the head of the sacrifice, and that Âhavanîya (fire-altar) he is now about to build: hence he says, 'Makha's head thou art!'

2. And, again, as to why he says, 'Makha's head thou art!'—when he (Agni) is built up, then he is born, and it is by the head (issuing first), by the top, that he who is born is born: 'when he is born, may he be born by the head, by the top!' so he thinks.

3. He spreads it out, with (Vâg. S. XI, 58), 'May the Vasus, Aṅgiras-like, fashion thee by the Gâyatrî metre!'—for the bottom part is this (terrestrial) world, and this the Vasus fashioned by means of the Gâyatrî metre; and in like manner does this one now fashion it by means of the Gâyatrî metre;—'Aṅgiras-like,' he says, for Aṅgiras is the breath. 'Thou art steadfast!'—that is, 'thou art firm,' or, 'thou art fixed;'—'Thou art the earth!'—for this bottom part is indeed the earth;—'Establish in me offspring, increase of wealth, lordship of cattle, manhood, clansmen for the Sacrificer!' For the Vasus, having fashioned this (terrestrial) world, invoked this blessing thereon; and in like manner does the Sacrificer, having fashioned this world, now invoke this blessing thereon. Having made it of the measure of a span (in each direction), he then turns up its edge on each side.

4. He then lays thereon the first (lower) side-part,

with, 'May the Rudras, Aṅgiras-like, fashion thee by the Trish*t*ubh metre!'—for this side-part is the air, and this the Rudras fashioned by means of the Trish*t*ubh metre; and in like manner does this one now fashion it by means of the Trish*t*ubh metre;—'Aṅgiras-like,' he says, for Aṅgiras is the breath;—'Thou art steadfast!'—that is, 'thou art firm,' or 'thou art fixed;'—'Thou art the air!' for this side-part is indeed the air;—'Establish in me offspring, increase of wealth, lordship of cattle, manhood, clansmen for the Sacrificer!' For the Rudras, having fashioned the air, invoked this blessing thereon; and in like manner does this Sacrificer, having fashioned the air, now invoke this blessing thereon. Having stroked and smoothed it all over—

5. He lays on the upper side-part, with, 'May the Âdityas, Aṅgiras-like, fashion thee by the *G*agatî metre!' for this side-part is yonder sky, and this the Âdityas fashioned by means of the *G*agatî metre; and in like manner does this one now fashion it by means of the *G*agatî metre;—'Aṅgiras-like,' he says, for Aṅgiras is the breath;—'Thou art steadfast!'—that is, 'thou art firm,' or 'thou art fixed;'—'Thou art the sky!' for that side-part is indeed the sky;—'Establish in me offspring, increase of wealth, lordship of cattle, manhood, clansmen for the Sacrificer!' For the Âdityas, having fashioned the sky, invoked this blessing thereon; and in like manner the Sacrificer, having fashioned the sky, now invokes this blessing thereon.

6. He then makes it (complete), with this fourth prayer, 'May the All-gods, the friends of all

men, fashion thee, Aṅgiras-like, by the Anush*t*ubh metre!'—this prayer, doubtless, is the (four) quarters, and the All-gods, the friends of all men, did then, by means of this prayer, put the quarters into these worlds, (that is) into the fire-pan; and in like manner does the Sacrificer, by means of this prayer, now put the quarters into these worlds, into the fire-pan;—'Aṅgiras-like,' he says, because Aṅgiras is the breath;—'Thou art steadfast!'—that is, 'thou art firm,' or 'thou art fixed;'—'Thou art the quarters!' for this prayer indeed is the quarters;—'Establish in me offspring, increase of wealth, lordship of cattle, manhood, clansmen for the Sacrificer!' For the All-gods, the friends of all men, having fashioned the quarters, invoked this blessing on them; and in like manner the Sacrificer, having fashioned the quarters, now invokes this blessing on them.

7. With that same formula he fashions it both inside and outside, whence the quarters are both inside and outside these worlds. He therewith fashions it without restriction (to any part of the pan), for unrestricted are the quarters.

8. He makes it just a span high, and a span sideways; for Vish*n*u, when an embryo, was a span long, and this (fire-pan) is the womb: he thus makes the womb of equal size with the embryo[1].

9. Were it larger than a span, he would make it smaller by that prayer; and were it smaller, (he would make it) larger thereby[2].

---

[1] Vish*n*u is identical with Agni, inasmuch as both are the sacrifice.

[2] That is to say, if the pan, thus fashioned, is not quite of the exact measure, the formula is supposed to set this right.

10. If there be one victim, let him make it (the pan) one span wide; and if there be five victims, let him make it five spans wide, or an arrow's width; for the arrow means strength: he thus makes it to be composed of strength. But, indeed, an arrow formerly used to be five spans long[1].

11. He then lays round the horizontal belt (or rim);—that is the quarters; for the gods, having made these worlds, the fire-pan, strengthened and encircled them by the quarters; and in like manner the Sacrificer, having made these worlds, the fire-pan, thus strengthens and encircles them by the quarters.

12. He lays this (rim) on the upper third (of the side), for it is there the ends of these worlds meet, and he thus makes them firm thereby.

13. [He does so, with Vâ*g*. S. XI, 59] 'Thou art Aditi's girdle!'—in the sacrifice the string relates to Varu*n*a: he thus lays this belt round after (expressly) making it one not relating to Varu*n*a.

14. He then silently makes four upright (bands), for these are the quarters;—for the gods, having made these worlds, the fire-pan, made them firm on all sides by means of the quarters[2]; and in like manner the Sacrificer, having made these worlds, the fire-pan, now makes them firm on all sides by means of the quarters.

15. These (vertical bands) run up to (the rim of) it, for they did then support it, and so do they now support it: thus that upper part of it becomes firm

[1] Yasmin kâle dhanurvedânusâre*n*a dharmata*h* kshatriyâ yudhyante tasmin kâle pa*ñk*aprâde*s*eshur âsît, adhunâ tv iyam aniyataparimâ*n*â vartante, Sây.

[2] Viz. by means of the mountains, according to Sâya*n*a.

by means of the horizontal belt, and that lower part of it by means of these (vertical bands).

16. At their tops they form nipples; for the gods, having made these worlds, the fire-pan, drew forth for themselves from these nipples all (objects of) their desires; and in like manner the Sacrificer, having made these worlds, the fire-pan, draws forth from these nipples all his desires.

17. This (fire-pan) indeed is a cow, for the fire-pan is these worlds, and these worlds are a cow: that horizontal belt is its udder; it is in the (upper) third of it, for the udder is in one-third of the cow.

18. He forms nipples to it, whereby he forms the nipples of the udder: it has four nipples, for the cow has four nipples.

19. Some, indeed, make it with two nipples, or also with eight nipples; but let him not do so, for those cattle which have fewer nipples than a cow, and those which have more nipples, are less fit to yield him a livelihood: hence they make this (fire-pan) less fit to yield a livelihood; and, indeed, they do not make it (like) a cow, but (like) a bitch, or a ewe, or a mare; hence let him not do so.

20. He then takes hold of its bowl, with, 'May Aditi seize thy bowl!' Aditi, doubtless, is Speech; and the gods, having then fashioned it, perfected it by means of Aditi, speech; and in like manner this one, having fashioned it, now perfects it by means of Aditi, speech.

21. Having grasped it with both hands, he sets it down, with, 'She, having fashioned the great (mahîm) fire-pan,'—that is, 'she, having fashioned the great (mahatim) fire-pan;'—'the earthen womb for Agni;'—for this is indeed Agni's

earthen womb;—'Aditi offered it unto her sons, thinking, They shall bake it!'—for Aditi, indeed, having fashioned it, offered it to the gods, her sons, to bake it; and in like manner does this one now, after fashioning it, offer it to the gods to bake it.

22. Now some make three (fire-pans), saying, 'Three (in number) are these worlds, and the fire-pans are these worlds;' and also for mutual expiation, thinking, 'If the one will break, we shall carry (Agni) in the other, and if the other (breaks), then in the other (or third).' Let him not do so; for that first bottom part is this world; and that first (lower) side-part is the air; and the upper one is the sky; and that fourth, the prayer, doubtless is the quarters; and just as much as these worlds and the quarters are, so much is this whole (universe). But were he to add anything thereto, he would make it to be redundant, and whatever redundant (act) is done in the sacrifice is left over for the Sacrificer's spiteful rival. And as to the expiation in case of the (fire-pan being) broken, that (will be told) in a subsequent chapter[1].

Third Brâhmana.

1. Of that same (clay) she (the queen) forms the first, the 'invincible' (brick); for the invincible one (Ashâ*dh*â) is this earth, and this earth was created first of these worlds. She forms it of that same clay, for this earth is (one) of these worlds. The (Sacrificer's) consecrated consort (mahishî) forms it; for this earth is a 'mahishî' (female buffalo, a cow). She who is first taken to wife is the consecrated consort.

[1] VI, 6, 4, 8.

2. It measures a foot (in length and breadth), for the foot is a foundation, and this earth also is a foundation. It is marked with three lines, for this earth is threefold[1].

3. Now he (the Sacrificer) makes the fire-pan: he thereby makes these worlds. He then makes the (three) 'all-light' (bricks), that is these deities, Agni, Vâyu, Âditya, for those deities indeed are all the light. He makes them from that same clay (as the fire-pan): he thus produces these gods from these worlds. The Sacrificer makes them. They are marked with three lines, for threefold are these gods[2]. Thus as regards the deities.

4. Now as regards the self (or body): the fire-pan, indeed, is the self (of Agni). The 'invincible' (brick) is speech: that she (the wife) makes first, for this speech is foremost in the body. She makes it from that same clay, for this speech is of the body. The (Sacrificer's) consecrated consort makes it, for speech is a 'mahishi.' It is marked with three lines, for speech is divided into three kinds, *Ri*k-verses, Yagus-formulas, and Sâman-tunes; and because of this threefold form of speech, low-voiced, half-loud, and loud.

5. He makes the fire-pan: thereby he makes (Agni's) self. He then makes the 'all-light' (bricks), —the 'all-light' (brick) is offspring, for offspring indeed is all the light: he thus causes generation to take place. He makes them of the same clay (as the fire-pan): he thus produces offspring from the self. The Sacrificer makes them: the Sacrificer thus

[1] See VI, 1, 1, 14.

[2] Viz. those of the sky, the air, and the earth. See VI, 1, 2, 10.

produces offspring from his own self. He makes them without interruption: he thus produces uninterrupted offspring from his own self. He makes them subsequently (to the fire-pan): he thus produces the offspring subsequently to his own self. They are marked with three lines, for generation is threefold, father, mother, and son; or, the embryo, and the inner and outer membrane.

6. He makes these from (clay) prepared with prayer, the others from (clay) prepared without prayer; for these are defined, the others undefined; these are limited (in number), the others unlimited.

7. That Agni is Pragâpati; but Pragâpati is both of this, defined and undefined, limited and unlimited: thus when he makes (bricks) from (clay) prepared with prayer, he thereby makes up that form of his (Pragâpati's) which is defined and limited; and when he makes them from (clay) prepared without prayer, he thereby makes up that form of his which is undefined and unlimited. Verily, then, whosoever knowing this does it on this wise, makes up the whole and complete Agni. From the (clay) lying ready prepared, he leaves over a lump for expiations[1].

8. He (the Adhvaryu) now fumigates it (the fire-pan)—just for the sake of strength, or to (mark) the progress of the work. And, again, as to why he fumigates,—that fire-pan is the head of the sacrifice, and the smoke its breath: he thus puts breath into the head.

9. He fumigates it with horse-dung, to insure it against injury; for the horse is sacred to Pragâpati,

[1] That is, in case the fire-pan were to break. See VI, 6, 4, 8 seq.

and Pragâpati is Agni, and one does not injure one's own self. And with dung (he does it) because that is what was eaten (by the horse) and is useless; and thus he does not injure the horse itself, nor the other cattle.

10. [Vâg. S. XI, 60] 'May the Vasus make thee fragrant by the Gâyatrî measure, Aṅgiras-like!—May the Rudras make thee fragrant by the Trish*t*ubh metre, Aṅgiras-like!—May the Âdityas make thee fragrant by the *G*agatî metre, Aṅgiras-like!—May the All-gods, the friends of all men, make thee fragrant by the Anush*t*ubh metre, Aṅgiras-like!—May Indra make thee fragrant!—May Varu*n*a make thee fragrant!—May Vish*n*u make thee fragrant!'—he thus fumigates it by means of the deities.

11. Seven balls of horse-dung are (used), and seven formulas: those deities are sevenfold[1], and seven vital airs there are in the head. But also what is many times, seven times seven, is (expressed by) seven[2]: he thus puts the seven vital airs into the head.

Fourth Brâhmana.

1. He now digs that (hole)[3] in the earth; for the gods now were afraid, thinking, 'We hope the Rakshas, the fiends, will not smite here this (Agni) of

[1] ? Or, divided into groups of seven each, as, for instance, the Maruts, see II, 5, 1, 13.

[2] Comp. the Germ. 'seine sieben Sachen (or, Siebensachen) packen,' to pack one's traps.

[3] One might take 'athainam asyâ*m* khanati' to mean, 'he now digs for him (Agni) in the earth,' or 'digs him into the earth.' Cf. VI, 4, 1, 1, 'athainam ata*h* khanati.' Sâya*n*a, however (in accordance with the formula in paragraph 3), supplies 'ava*t*am,' 'a hole.'

ours!' They made this (earth) to be his self (body), for protection, thinking, 'The self will protect itself.'

2. He digs him out with (the help of) Aditi, in order to guard him from injury; for Aditi is this earth, and one does not injure one's own self; but were he to dig with (the help of) another deity, he surely would injure him (Agni).

3. [Vâg. S. XI, 61] 'May the divine Aditi, dear to all the gods, dig thee, Aṅgiras-like, O hole, in the lap of the earth!'—for this hole (is dug) among the gods. That bamboo spade now disappears. This hole is four-cornered, for there are four quarters: he thus digs it from all the quarters[1]. Having then laid down fuel in it, he silently puts the 'invincible' (brick) thereon, for that is made first.

4. He then sets down the fire-pan (with the bottom part upwards), with, 'May the divine wives of the gods, dear to all the gods, place thee, Aṅgiras-like, O fire-pan, in the lap of the earth!' for of old the divine wives of the gods, dear to all the gods, indeed, like Aṅgiras, placed that (fire-pan) into the lap of the earth, and by (the help of) them he now places it. But, surely, these are the plants,—the wives of the gods are indeed the plants; for by the plants everything here is supported: by means of the plants he thus supports this (fire-pan). He then lays down silently the 'all-light' (bricks). Having then placed fuel thereon he kindles it.

5. 'May the divine Dhishaṇâs, dear to all the gods, kindle thee, Aṅgiras-like, O fire-pan, in the lap of the earth!' for of old the divine

[1] Sarvâbhyo digbhya enam avaṭaṁ khanati taṁ ka sarvâsu dikshu nâshṭrâ na hiṁsanti, Sây.

Dhishanâs, dear to all the gods, indeed kindled it, like Aṅgiras, in the lap of the earth, and with their help he now kindles it. But, surely, this is Vâk (speech),—the Dhishanâs are indeed speech[1], for by speech everything is kindled here: by means of speech he thus kindles this (fire-pan). Whilst looking at it, he then mutters these three formulas:

6. 'May the divine protectresses, dear to all the gods, heat thee, O fire-pan, Aṅgiras-like, in the lap of the earth!' for of old the divine protectresses, dear to all the gods, indeed, like Aṅgiras, heated it in the lap of the earth; and by them he now heats it. But, surely, these are the days and nights,—the protectresses are indeed the days and nights; for by days and nights everything is covered here: by means of the days and nights he thus heats it.

7. 'May the divine ladies, dear to all the gods, bake thee, Aṅgiras-like, O fire-pan, in the lap of the earth!' for of old the divine ladies, dear to all the gods, did, like Aṅgiras, bake it in the lap of the earth, and with their help he now bakes it. But, surely, these are the metres,—the ladies (gnâ) are indeed the metres (scripture texts), for by means of these men go (gam) to the celestial world: by means of the metres he thus bakes it.

8. 'May the divine women, with unclipped wings, dear to all the gods, bake thee, Aṅgiras-like, O fire-pan, in the lap of the earth!' for

[1] Whether 'Dhishanâ' (the name of certain female divinities who have the power of bestowing prosperity and granting wishes) is here connected with 'dhishnya,' fire-hearth; or whether it is taken by the author in some such primary sense as 'intelligence' or 'inspiration,' it were difficult to decide. Sâyana connects it with 'dhî,'—vâg vai dhishanâ, sâ hi dhiyam karma gñâvâsani (?) sambhagate.

of old the divine women, with unclipped wings, dear to all the gods, did bake it, like Aṅgiras, in the lap of the earth; and with their help he now bakes it. But, surely, these are the stars,—the women (*g*ani) are indeed the stars, for these are the lights of those righteous men (*g*ana) who go to the celestial world: it is by means of the stars that he thus bakes it.

9. Now he digs with one (formula), he sets down (the fire-pan) with one, he kindles with one, he heats with one, he bakes (pa*k*) with two, whence twice in the year food is ripened (pa*k*); these amount to six, —six seasons are a year, and Agni is the year: as great as Agni is, as great as is his measure, so great does this become.

10. And as often as he attends to (the fire by adding fresh fuel)[1] he attends to it with the prayer relating to Mitra, '[The protection] of Mitra, the preserver of men[2] . . .;' for a friend (mitra) does not injure any one, nor does any one injure his friend; and in like manner does this one not injure that (fire-pan), nor does it (injure) him. By day he should put (fuel) on it, by day he should clear it (of the ashes).

11. He clears it (of the ashes) with a prayer relating to Savit*ri*,—for Savit*ri* is the impeller: impelled

[1] The St. Petersburg dictionary seems to take 'yâvat kiya*k* *k*opanyâ*k*arati' in the sense of 'as much (or, as deep) as he enters (into the pan).' But see III, 2, 2, 19, where 'yâvat kiya*kk*a . . . upasp*ri*set' has likewise the meaning 'as often as he touches.' Cf. also Kâty. *S*r. XVI, 4, 15, He keeps up (the fire by adding fuel), with 'Mitrasya . . .;' 16, [He repeats the formula] as often (or long) as he keeps it up (or, adds fuel).

[2] Vâ*g*. S. XI, 62; *Ri*k S. III, 59, 6, 'The gainful protection of the God Mitra, the preserver of men, is glorious and of most wonderful renown.'

by Savit*ri*, he thus clears it—[Vâg. S. XI, 63] 'May the divine Savit*ri*, the well-handed, well-fingered, and well-armed, clear thee by his might!'—for Savit*ri* is all that.

12. He then turns it (the fire-pan) round, with, 'Not tottering upon the earth, fill the regions, the quarters!'—that is, 'not tottering, fill thou with sap the regions and quarters on earth!'

13. He then takes it up, with [Vâg. S. XI, 64], 'Having risen, do thou become great,'—for these worlds, having risen, are great;—'and stand up steadfast!' that is, 'stand thou up firm and fixed!'

14. Having taken it in both hands, he sets it down, with, 'O Mitra, unto thee I consign this fire-pan for safety: may it not break!' for Mitra is that wind which blows yonder: it is to him he thus consigns it for protection; for these worlds are protected by Mitra (or by a friend), whence nothing whatever is harmed in these worlds.

15. He then pours (milk) into it,—just for strength, or to (mark) the progress of the work. And, again, why he pours (milk) into it,—that fire-pan is the head of the sacrifice, and milk is breath: he thus lays breath into the head. Moreover, the fire-pan (ukhâ, f.) is a female: he thus lays milk into the female, whence there is milk in the female.

16. He pours goat's milk into it to avoid injury[1]; for the goat sprang from Pragâpati's head, and Pragâpati is Agni; and one does not injure one's own self. And as to why it is goat's (milk),—the goat eats all (kinds of) herbs: he thus pours into it (the pan) the sap of all (kinds of) herbs.

[1] The construction of this, and similar previous passages, is the same as that referred to in part ii, p. 15, note 3.

17. [Vâg. S. XI, 65] 'May the Vasus fill thee with the Gâyatrî metre, Aṅgiras-like!—May the Rudras fill thee with the Trishtubh metre, Aṅgiras-like!—May the Âdityas fill thee with the Gagatî metre, Aṅgiras-like!—May the All-gods, dear to all men, fill thee with the Anushtubh metre, Aṅgiras-like!'—by these deities he thus moistens it: by whatever deities he fashions it, by them he fumigates it, and by them he moistens it. For he who performs a work, knows the practice of it: hence by whatever deities he fashions it, by them he fumigates and moistens it.

THE DÎKSHÂ, OR INITIATION.

SIXTH ADHYÂYA. FIRST BRÂHMANA.

1. Many[1] are the oblations, in the building of the fire-altar, as well as at any other (special ceremony) than the building of the fire-altar. For there are supernumerary rites,—supernumerary are those which are (performed) over and above another rite: of these[2] are the building of the altar (Agnikityâ), the Râgasûya, the Vâgapeya, and the Asvamedha; and because they are over and above the other (normal) rites, therefore they are supernumerary.

[1] Or rather, too many, more (than are required at one of the normal Soma-sacrifices),—âdhvarikebhyo bahutarâni, Sây.

[2] That is, as would seem from Sâyana, of such ceremonies as have supernumerary, or additional, oblations to the normal ones connected with them. This discussion seems to be introduced here on account of the additional oblation (that to Vaisvânara) offered at the initiation ceremony. As an 'additional' or special, oblation at the Vâgapeya, Sâyana refers to the pap of wild rice (V, 1, 4, 12); whilst at the Râgasûya the one to Anumati (V, 2, 3, 4) is said to belong to the same category.

2. A cake[1] on eleven potsherds to Agni and Vishnu,—that is the initiation (offering) of the (Soma) sacrifice;—one on twelve potsherds to Vaisvânara, and a pap to the Âdityas,—these two belong to Agni.

3. Now were he to prepare only the one for Agni and Vishnu, and not the other two oblations, then only the initiation (offering) of the (Soma) sacrifice would be performed, and not those of Agni (the fire-altar); and were he to prepare only the other two oblations, and not the one to Agni and Vishnu, only the initiation (offering) of Agni would be performed, and not that of the sacrifice.

4. He prepares both that of the sacrifice, and those of Agni, for this rite is both a rite of sacrifice, and a rite of fire: first (comes) that of the sacrifice, and then that of the fire, for the rite of the fire is an accessory rite.

5. Now as regards that (cake) for Agni and Vishnu, its mystic import is the same as what is (implied) in a preparatory ceremony. And the (cake) on twelve potsherds for Vaisvânara is for

[1] These and the subsequent offerings form part of the Dikshâ, or initiation ceremony, for the Soma-sacrifice to be performed after the completion of the fire-altar. This initiation ceremony commences on the day of new moon, a week after the preparation of the ukhâ, or fire-pan. An integral part of (the first day of) this ceremony is the kindling of a fire in the ukhâ—the 'Ukhya Agni'—which ultimately serves to supply the fires for the brick altars built on the completion of the period of initiation. The Dikshâ is, as a rule, to be performed daily for a year, during which time the fire has to be kept up in the ukhâ, and carried about by the Sacrificer for a time each day. While the cake to Agni-Vishnu here mentioned is the ordinary cake-offering prescribed for the Dikshâ of the normal Soma-sacrifice (see III, 1, 3, 1), the Vaisvânara cake is peculiar to the Agnikayana.

the obtainment of all the fires, Vaisvânara being all the fires;—it is one of twelve potsherds, for twelve months are a year, and Vaisvânara is the year.

6. And, again, as to why he prepares one for Vaisvânara,—it is because he is about to produce Agni as Vaisvânara (belonging, or dear to, all men): in the initiation offering he first pours him forth as seed, and whatlike the seed is that is poured into the womb, suchlike is (the child) born therefrom; and inasmuch as he now pours forth that (Agni) Vaisvânara as seed, therefore he is born hereafter as Vaisvânara.

7. And why he prepares those two (other) oblations,—Vaisvânara is the ruling power, and that Âditya pap is the people: he thus makes both the ruling power and the people. The Vaisvânara (cake) he prepares first, and having thereby made the ruling power, he makes the people.

8. That (Vaisvânara cake) is one single (oblation), having one single deity: he thus makes the ruling power to be concentrated in one (person), and excellence to be concentrated in one. The other, the pap, has many deities, for the pap is a multiplicity of rice-grains, and those Âdityas are a multiplicity of gods: he thus bestows multiplicity on the people. Thus much as to the deities.

9. Now as regards the self (or body of Agni). The Vaisvânara (cake) is the head, and that Âditya pap is the body: he thus makes both the head and the body. The Vaisvânara (cake) he prepares first; and having thereby made the head, he then makes the body.

10. That (Vaisvânara cake) is one single (oblation), for the head is, as it were, one only; and the

other, the pap, has many deities, for that pap is a multiplicity of rice-grains, and this body is a multiplicity of limbs: he thus bestows on the body a multiplicity of limbs.

11. That (pap) is (prepared) on ghee, for the Âdityas are consumers of ghee: he thus gratifies them, each by his own share, by his own liquor. These offerings are (made) silently, for here in the sacrifice there is seed, and silently seed is infused.

12. He then offers the Audgrabhana (libations)[1], for by the Audgrabhanas (elevatory libations) the gods raised themselves from this world to the heavenly world: and inasmuch as (thereby) they raised themselves (ud-grabh), they are called 'audgrabhana;'—and in like manner does the Sacrificer, by means of the Audgrabhanas, now raise himself from this world to the heavenly world.

13. There are many of these, in the building of the fire-altar as well as at any other (special ceremony): the significance of this has been told. They are of both kinds: (the significance) of this has been told;—first those of the sacrifice, and then those of the fire: (the significance) of this also has been told.

14. He offers five of the sacrifice[2],—the sacrifice is fivefold: as great as the sacrifice is, as great as is its measure, by so much he thus pours it forth as seed. Seven (libations) of the fire,—the fire(-altar) consists of seven layers[3]; seven seasons are a year, and

[1] See III, 1, 4, 1.

[2] Viz. the five Audgrabhana libations of the ordinary Soma-sacrifice offered in the manner there described. See part ii, p. 20, note.

[3] Though Agni, or the fire-altar, is commonly called the five-layered one (pañkakitika), consisting as it does of five complete

Agni is the year: as great as Agni is, as great as is his measure, by so much he thus pours him forth as seed. Those two kinds (of libations) amount to twelve,—twelve months are a year, and Agni is the year: as great as Agni is, as great as is his measure, so great does this become.

15. He offers[1], with (Vâ*g*. S. XI, 66-67), 'The Purpose, Agni, the Impulse, hail!'—from purpose, indeed, this sacred rite originated at first, and he now impels (yokes, uses) it for this rite.

16. 'Mind, Wisdom, Agni, the Impulse, hail!'—from the mind indeed this sacred rite originated at first, and he now impels it for this rite.

17. 'Thought, knowledge, Agni, the Impulse, hail!'—from thought, indeed, this sacred rite originated at first, and he now impels it for this rite.

18. 'The distinction of Speech, Agni, the Impulse, hail!'—from speech, indeed, this sacred rite originated at first, and he now impels it for this rite.

19. 'To Pra*g*âpati, to Manu, hail!'—Manu, forsooth, is Pra*g*âpati, for he thought out (man) all this (universe); and Pra*g*âpati, indeed, of old performed this rite, and he now makes use of him for this rite.

20. 'To Agni Vai*s*vânara, hail!'—Agni Vai*s*vânara, doubtless, is the year; and the year, indeed,

layers of bricks, on the top of these there is a small additional pile of two layers, the lower one (punas*k*iti) in the form of the Gârhapatya hearth (VII, 1, 1, 1 seq.), and the upper one, consisting of two bricks, on which the fire is ultimately laid down. See p. 188, note 4. Hence Agni is also called 'sapta*k*itika.'

[1] Viz. the seven special Audgrabha*n*a libations of the Agni*k*ayana.

of old performed this rite; and he now makes use thereof for this rite.

21. He then offers the one to Savitri, for Savitri, indeed, of old performed this rite, and he now makes use of him for this rite,—(Vâg. S. XI, 67; Rik S. V, 50, 1), 'Every mortal would choose the friendship of the divine Guide; every one craves riches, and would have glory for him to prosper, hail!' He who chooses the friendship of the god Savitri, chooses both glory and prosperity; and he who performs this rite, indeed chooses his friendship.

22. Now some offer these Audgrabhana libations into the fire-pan itself, saying, 'These, surely, are offered for (special) objects of desire, and that fire-pan is the Sacrificer's self: we thus secure for the Sacrificer's self all his objects of desire.' Let him not do so; for the fire which is kindled (in the fire-pan) is the essence of the completed sacrifice and of those libations, and when he puts the fire-pan on the fire, after the sacrifice has been completed and the Audgrabhanas offered, then the sacrifice mounts it (the pan), and it bears the sacrifice: let him, therefore, put the fire-pan on the fire only after the sacrifice is complete, and the Audgrabhanas have been offered.

23. It is covered with a layer of Muñga grass, just for the purpose that it may blaze up. And as to why it is with a layer of Muñga grass, (it is done) to avoid injury, for that Muñga grass is a womb, and the womb does not injure the child; for he who is born, is born from a womb: 'May he (Agni), when he is born, be born from the womb,' thus he thinks.

24. Inside[1] there is a layer of hemp, just for the purpose that it may blaze up. And as to its being a layer of hemp,—the inner membrane (amnion) of the womb from which Pragâpati was born consists of flax, and the outer membrane (chorion) of hemp: hence the latter is foul-smelling, for it is the outer membrane of the embryo. [It is so used] to avoid injury, for the outer membrane does not injure the embryo; and it is from the outer membrane of the embryo that he who is born is born: 'May he (Agni), when he is born, be born from the outer membrane of the embryo!' thus he thinks.

SECOND BRÂHMANA.

1. Standing he puts it (the pan) on the fire, for the fire-pan is these worlds, and these worlds stand, as it were. And, moreover, whilst standing one is strongest.

2. Standing (with his face) towards north-east, for standing towards north-east Pragâpati created creatures.

3. And, again, why (he does so) standing towards north-east;—that (quarter), the north-east, is the quarter of both gods and men.

4. And, again, why standing towards north-east,—in that quarter is the gate of the world of heaven, hence it is standing with his face towards north-east that one offers libations, and standing towards north-east that one leads up the dakshinâs: it is by the gate that he thus makes him enter into the world of heaven.

[1] That is, underneath the layer of muñga. Both the reed-grass and the hemp are to be crushed and reduced to the condition of powder previously to their being strewed into the fire-pan.

5. [Vâg. S. XI, 68] 'Break not! Suffer not injury!'—as the text, so its meaning;—'O mother, bear up bravely!'—for the fire-pan (ukhâ, f.) is a woman; and 'O mother' is a term for addressing a woman: 'bear up well, indeed!'—'(Thou) and Agni will do this (work)!'—for (the fire-pan) and Agni will indeed be doing this (sacred work).

6. [Vâg. S. XI, 69] 'Stand firm, divine Earth, for our well-being!' as the text, so its meaning;—'A divine (âsura) contrivance thou art made in the wonted manner;'—the vital spirit (asu) is the breath, and this (fire-pan) has indeed been made its contrivance in the wonted manner;—'May this offering be agreeable to the gods!' he thereby means those libations which he intends to offer in that fire; and moreover, that (fire-pan) itself is an offering;—'unharmed rise thou in this sacrifice!' this he says with the view that it may rise unharmed, uninjured, in this sacrifice.

7. With two (verses) he heats it on the fire,—the Sacrificer is two-footed, and the Sacrificer is Agni: as great as Agni is, as great as is his measure, by so much he thus heats it (the pan). [He does so] with a gâyatrî and a trish*t*ubh verse,—the Gâyatrî is the vital air, and the Trish*t*ubh the body; and the animal is as much as the vital air and the body: thus by as much as the animal (consists of) he puts that (pan) on the fire. And, again, the Gâyatrî is Agni, and the Trish*t*ubh is Indra; and the fire relates to Indra and Agni: as great as the fire is, as great as is its measure, by so much he thus heats it. These two (verses) have seven feet (viz. three and four respectively),—the fire-altar consists of seven

layers[1]; seven seasons are a year, and Agni is the year: as great as Agni is, as great as is his measure, so great does this become.

8. When the fire heats it, then the flame mounts up to it; for the fire-pan is a female, and the fire is a male: hence when the male heats the female, he infuses seed into her.

9. Now, if the flame is too long in mounting up, some throw coals on (the pan), thinking, 'There is fire now on both sides.' But let him not do so; for the animal is indeed born with bones[2]; but it is not forced in with bones, as it were, at first; but it is introduced only as seed. Now that flame is boneless seed: hence the flame alone should mount up to it.

10. When the flame mounts up to it, he places a kindling-stick thereon: thereby the seed enters it (the fire-pan), and that fire imparts growth to that seed (in the shape of) this (kindling-stick).

11. It should be one of k*ri*muka wood. Now, the gods and the Asuras, both of them sprung from Pragâpati, strove together. The gods, having placed Agni in front, went up to the Asuras. The Asuras cut off the point of that flame held forward. It settled down on this earth, and became that k*ri*muka tree: hence it is sweet, for there is vital essence (in it). Hence also it is red, for it is a flame, that k*ri*-

---

[1] See p. 249, note 3.

[2] The fire ultimately to be placed on the new Gârhapatya hearth (VII, 1, 1, 1 seq.)—whence the Âhavanîya on the great fire-altar has to be kindled—is to be produced in the ukhâ, or pan, as it were in its womb; but the material (grass and hemp) which has already been put in the pan, is only to be kindled by the blaze of the fire on which the pan has been placed, without any burning coals being applied to the fuel within the pan.

muka tree being the same as this Agni: it is (in the shape of) fire that he imparts growth to it.

12. It (the kindling-stick) is a span long, for Vishnu, as an embryo, was a span long: he thus imparts to it growth equal to his body.

13. It is soaked in ghee;—the inner membrane of the womb from which Agni was produced consisted of ghee: hence he now blazes up towards it, for it (the stick) is his self (body); and hence it (the krimuka) has no ashes: (Agni) himself now enters into his own self,—to avoid injury[1], for the inner membrane does not injure the embryo; and it is from the inner membrane that he who is born is born: 'When he (Agni) is born, may he be born from the inner membrane!' thus he thinks.

14. He puts it (the kindling-stick) on, with (Vâg. S. XI, 60; *Ri*k S. II, 7, 6), 'The wood-eating, ghee-drinking,'—that is, he who has wood for his food, and ghee for his drink,—'the primeval, desirable Hot*ri*,'—that is, 'the old, desirable Hot*ri*;'—'the wonderful son of power,'—power is strength: thus, 'the wonderful son of strength.' Standing he puts it on with the 'Svâhâ:' the meaning of this (will be explained) hereafter[2].

15. Now the fire-pan is the body, the reed-grass (fuel) the womb, the hemp the inner membrane[3],

[1] The dative 'ahi*m*sâyai' again doubtless belongs to the first sentence of the paragraph ('it is soaked in ghee'), the intervening clauses being inserted for explanation. For a similar construction, see above, p. 198, note 2.

[2] See VI, 7, 2, 1.

[3] The inverted order of the words '*san*â *g*arâyu' is peculiar. It seems to have been resorted to with the view of keeping together the two pairs of subjects, 'mu*ñg*â*h*-*san*â*h*' and '*g*arâyu-ulbam.'

the ghee the outer membrane, and the kindling-stick the embryo.

16. The pan is outside, and the reed-grass (fuel) is inside; for the body is outside, and the womb inside. The reed-grass is outside, and the hemp inside; for the womb is outside, and the outer membrane is inside. The hemp is outside, and the ghee is inside; for the outer membrane is outside, and the inner membrane is inside. The ghee is outside, and the kindling-stick is inside; for the inner membrane is outside, and the embryo is inside. It is from these that he who is born is born, and from them he thus causes him (Agni) to be born.

Third Brâhma*n*a.

1. He then puts on a vikaṅkata (flacourtia sapida) one. When Pra*g*âpati performed the first offering, a vikaṅkata tree sprang forth from that place where, after offering, he cleansed (his hands). That vikaṅkata, then, is that first offering; it is that he now offers on this (fire), and he therewith gratifies him (Agni). [Vâ*g*. S. XI, 71; *Ri*k S. VIII, 75, 15] 'From the far region come thou over to the near one: do thou protect that wherein I am!' as the text, so its meaning.

2. He then puts on an udumbara (ficus glomerata) one. The gods and the Asuras, both of them sprung from Pra*g*âpati, strove together. Now all the trees sided with the Asuras, but the udumbara tree alone did not forsake the gods. The gods, having conquered the Asuras, took possession of their trees.

3. They said, 'Come, let us lay into the udumbara tree whatever pith, whatever vital sap there is in these trees: were they then to desert us, they would

desert us worn out, like a milked-out cow, or like an ox that has been (tired out by) drawing (the cart).' Accordingly they laid into the udumbara tree what pith and essence there was in those trees; and on account of that pith it matures (fruit) equal to all the (other) trees[1]: hence that (tree) is always moist, always full of milky sap,—that udumbara tree, indeed, (being) all the trees, is all food: he thus gratifies him (Agni) by every kind of food, and kindles him by all trees (kinds of wood).

4. [Vâg. S. XI, 72] 'From the farthest distance,'—that is, '(from) what farthest distance there is;'—'O red-steeded, come hither!' for red, indeed, is Agni's horse;—'Purîshya, much-loved,'—that is, 'favourable to cattle, dear to many;'—'O Agni, overcome thou the scorners!' that is, 'O Agni, overcome all evil-doers!'

5. He then puts on one not cut by an axe,—that (Agni) is born when he is built up: it is for all (kinds of) food that he is born. Now that (wood) not cut by an axe is one kind of food (for the fire): it is thereby that he now gratifies him. [Vâg. S. XI, 73; *Ri*k S. VIII, 102, 20] 'Whatsoever wood we lay upon thee, O Agni, let all that be ghee unto thee, do thou relish that, O youngest!' as the text, so its meaning: whatever (wood there is) not cut by the axe, that he makes palatable to him; and having made it food for him, he sets it before him.

6. He then puts on one that has lain on the ground,—he (Agni) is born when he is built up: it is for all (kinds of) food that he is born. Now that

[1] According to Ait. Br. V, 24, its fruits ripen three times a year.

(wood) which has lain on the ground is one kind of food (for the fire): it is thereby he now gratifies him. [Vâg. S. XI, 74; *Ri*k S. VIII, 102, 21] 'What the red ant eats, what the white ant crawls over,'—for either the red ant eats it, or the white ant crawls over it;—'let all that be ghee for thee, do thou relish that, O youngest!' as the text, so its meaning: whatever (wood) has lain on the ground, that he makes palatable for him; and having made it food for him, he sets it before him.

7. The remaining (kindling-sticks) are of palâ*s*a wood (butea frondosa);—the Palâ*s*a tree is the Brahman, it is by the Brahman he thus kindles him (Agni). And, again, why they are palâ*s*a ones;—the Palâ*s*a tree is Soma, and he, Soma, doubtless is the supreme offering: it is that he now offers on this (fire), and by that he gratifies him (Agni).

8. [He puts them on, with Vâg. S. XI, 75-82] 'Day by day bearing unremittingly,'—that is, 'Day by day bringing not unmindful;'—'food to him like unto a standing horse,'—that is, 'food as to a standing (resting) horse;'—'we, rejoicing in wealth-thrift and sap,'—that is, 'rejoicing in wealth, and thrift, and sap;'—'O Agni, let not us, thy associates, suffer injury!' this he says with a view that his (Agni's) associate (the Sacrificer) may not suffer injury.

9. 'While Agni is kindling on the earth's navel,'—that (place) where he is now being kindled is indeed the navel of the earth;—'we call for great wealth-thrift,'—that is, 'we call for wealth and great thrift;'—'Unto him, the draught-delighted,'—for he is indeed delighted (or, in-

ebriated) by the draught,—'of high praise,'—for he is indeed highly praised;—'the adorable'—that is, 'worthy of adoration;'—'Agni, the conqueror, overpowering in battles;'—for Agni is indeed a conqueror, and overpowering in battles.

10. 'Whatever aggressive armies there are, onrushing with drawn-up lines; whatever thieves and robbers, those I cast into thy mouth, O Agni.'—'Devour thou in a lump the waylayers with thy two tusks, the thieves with thy teeth, and the robbers with thy jaws, O holy one!'—'What waylayers there are among men, what thieves and robbers in the wood, what miscreants in the lurking-places, I throw them into thy jaws.'—'Whatever man may plot against us, and whosoever may hate us, or abuse and seek to hurt us, every one of them burn thou to ashes!'

11. For the gods then made food of whosoever hated them, and of whomsoever they hated, and gave them up to him (Agni), and thereby gratified him; and this, then, became his food, and he burnt up the evil of the gods: and in like manner does the Sacrificer now make food of whosoever hates him, and of whomsoever he hates, and give them up to him (Agni), and thereby gratify him; and this, then, becomes his food, and he burns up the Sacrificer's evil.

12. These eleven (kindling-sticks) he puts on for one who is not either a noble, or a domestic chaplain (purohita); for incomplete are those eleven, and incomplete is he who is not either a noble, or a domestic priest.

13. Twelve (he puts on) for a noble or a domestic

chaplain; for those twelve are a complete whole (or everything), and he who is either a noble or a domestic chaplain is everything.

14. In the case of a Purohita, he puts it on, with (Vâg. S. XI, 81), 'Perfected is my sanctity (brahman), perfected the vigour, the strength, perfected the victorious power (kshatra) whose Purohita I am!'—he thus perfects both his sanctity and power[1].

15. And in the case of a nobleman, with (Vâg. S. XI, 82), 'I have raised their arms, their lustre and strength: by the spiritual power I destroy the enemies, and elevate mine own (relatives)!' this he says with the view that he may destroy his enemies, and elevate his own relatives. Let him put on both these (kindling-sticks); for both the Brahman and the Kshatra are this Agni; and it is this Agni he thus kindles by those two, by the Brahman and the Kshatra.

16. These (kindling-sticks) amount to thirteen;—thirteen months are a year, and Agni is the year: as great as Agni is, as great as is his measure, by so much food he thus gratifies him.

17. They are a span long, for Vishnu, as an embryo, was a span long; and this is (Agni's or Vishnu's) food: he thus gratifies him with food proportionate to his own body. But the food which is proportionate to one's body satisfies, and does no injury; but what is too much that does injury, and what is too little that does not satisfy. Standing he puts them on—the significance of this (will be ex-

[1] Or, his spiritual and political power, his priesthood and nobility.

plained) further on;—and with the Svâhâ ('hail!'); for seed is infused here (in the sacrifice,—to wit,) this Agni; and were he to put on the logs unconsecrated by Svâhâ, he would injure him (Agni). Now inasmuch as they are kindling-sticks, they are not oblations; but inasmuch as (they are put on) with the Svâhâ, they are food, for the Svâhâ is food; and thus he does not injure him (Agni).

Fourth Brâhmana.

1. Having then stridden the Vish*n*u strides, and reverentially stood by (the fire) with the Vâtsapra[1] (hymn), after the sun has set, he in the first place throws out the ashes (from the fire-pan). For at that (former) time he regales him (Agni) with that food, those kindling-sticks; and the foul part of that eaten food sinks to the bottom as ashes. He now clears him thereof, and infuses speech into him[2], thus freed from foulness. Having infused speech, he puts on a kindling-stick,—and thereby regales him with food for the night,—with, 'Night for night bearing unremittingly[3]'—the meaning of this has been told: he prays for that same security and well-being for the night; and whatsoever he puts on thereafter by night, that he puts on as a libation offered to him[4].

2. And in the morning, when the sun has risen, he in the first place throws out the ashes. For at that (former) time he regales him with that food, that kindling-stick; and the foul part of that eaten food which he puts on during the night sinks to the

[1] See VI, 7, 4, 1 seq.

[2] Or, sets free the speech in him.

[3] See above, VI, 6, 3, 8.

[4] Lit. 'made into a libation for him.'

bottom as ashes. He now clears him thereof, and infuses speech into him thus freed from foulness. Having infused speech, he puts on a kindling-stick,—and thereby regales him with food for the day—with, 'Day by day bearing unremittingly;'—the meaning of this has been told: he prays for that same security and well-being for the day; and whatsoever he puts on thereafter by day, that he puts on as a libation offered to him.

3. Verily, day and night passing on come up to a year, and the year is everything here: he prays for that security and well-being for a succession of days.

4. And when they give him (the Sacrificer) the fast-milk, he puts on a kindling-stick, after dipping it into the fast-milk. Some, however, say, 'Let him not dip it into the fast-milk: he would be offering a libation, and it would be improper were one who is initiated to offer a libation.'

5. Let him nevertheless dip it in, for that (Âhavanîya fire) is his (the Sacrificer's) divine body, and this (real body of his) is his human one. Now were he not to dip it in, he would not be satisfying that divine body of his; but when he dips it in, he does so satisfy that divine body. And in that it is a kindling-stick, it is not a libation; and in that it is dipped into the fast-milk, it is food, for the fast-milk is food.

6. And having put on the kindling-stick, he drinks the fast-milk; for that (fire) is his divine body, and this (body of his) is the human one; and the gods (come) first, and then men: hence he drinks the fast-milk after putting the kindling-stick on (the fire).

7. [He puts it on, with Vâg. S. XI, 83] 'O

Lord of food, give us of thy food!'—that is, 'O Lord of viands, give us of thy viands!'—'of the pain-allaying, strengthening'—that is, 'of the hunger-allaying, strengthening (food),'—'Onward, onward lead thou the giver!'—the giver, doubtless, is the Sacrificer: thus, 'Onward lead thou the Sacrificer!'—'Give us sustenance for the two-footed and the four-footed!'—he thereby asks a blessing. Now as to the expiation in case of (the fire-pan being) broken which, he said, would be explained 'in a subsequent chapter[1].'

8. If the fire-pan were to break, let him pour that (fire in the pan) into any such unbroken, new pot with a wide mouth as there may be; for the pan which is broken indeed suffers injury, but uninjured is this deity (Agni): 'Uninjured I will bear him in the uninjured!' so he thinks. Into that (pot) he first throws a potsherd of the (broken) pan, and thus he (Agni) is not deprived of that womb of his.

9. He then takes the (remaining[2]) clay, and having pounded both the (broken) pan and that remainder, and mixed it, he makes a (new) pan in the very same way, without using any formula, quite silently. Having baked it, he pours (the fire) over. The expiation in this case is one of performance only. Having again thrown that potsherd into the (new) pan, and pounded both the (temporary) pan and the remaining clay, and mixed it, he lays it aside for expiation.

10. And if the fire in the pan (Ukhya Agni) were to go out, it is doubtless to the Gârhapatya that it goes, for from the Gârhapatya it has been taken. Having then taken it out of the Gârhapatya eastwards (to the place of the Âhavanîya), and put fuel on it, let him

[1] See VI, 5, 2, 22. [2] See VI, 5, 3, 7.

put the fire-pan on it in the same way (as before), without using any formula, quite silently. When the fire rises up to it,—

11. He performs two expiations. For it is for (the obtainment of) all his wishes that he makes up that (fire); and whatever part of his wishes is here cut off when the fire goes out, that he thereby joins together and heals. He performs both expiations, that of the (Soma) sacrifice and that of the fire-altar,—first that of the sacrifice, then that of the fire-altar: the significance of this has been explained[1].

12. Having cut out with a kindling-stick some of the butter, he offers sitting a libation, with (Vâg. S. XII, 43), 'To Visvakarman, hail!' Then stepping near he puts the kindling-stick on the fire, with (Vâg. S. XII, 44), 'Again the Âdityas, the Rudras, the Vasus may kindle thee, again the Brâhmans with sacrifices, O bringer of good things!'—that is, 'May those deities again kindle thee!'—'With ghee make thou grow thy body, let the wishes of the Sacrificer be true!'—that is, 'With ghee indeed make thou grow thy body, and for whatever wishes the Sacrificer makes up a fire, may they all come true!'

13. And if the Gârhapatya fire were to go out, it is doubtless to the churning-sticks that it goes, for from the churning-sticks it has been taken. Having churned it out with the churning-sticks, and put fuel on it, he performs two expiations.

14. And if the Âhavanîya fire were to go out whilst the pressing (of Soma) proceeds, it is doubtless to the Gârhapatya that it goes, for from the Gârhapatya it has been taken. Having taken it straight-

[1] See VI, 6, 1, 3 seq.

way eastward from the Gârhapatya, and put fuel on it, he performs two expiations: whatever (kind of Soma) sacrifice may be (performed) at the time, the expiation of that sacrifice he should perform; and of like kind is the expiation of the fire-altar.

15. And if the Âgnîdhriya fire were to go out, it is doubtless to the Gârhapatya that it goes, for from the Gârhapatya it has been taken. Having taken it from the Gârhapatya eastward along the north of the Sadas, and put fuel on it, he performs two expiations. And if the Gârhapatya were to go out, the meaning (procedure) of that has been explained.

SEVENTH ADHYÂYA. FIRST BRÂHMANA.

1. He hangs a gold plate (round his neck), and wears it; for that gold plate is the truth, and the truth is able to sustain that (fire[1]): by means of the truth the gods carried it, and by means of the truth does he now carry it.

2. Now that truth is the same as yonder sun. It is a gold (plate), for gold is light, and he (the sun) is the light; gold is immortality, and he is immortality. It (the plate) is round, for he (the sun) is round. It has twenty-one knobs, for he is the twenty-first[2]. He wears it with the knobs outside, for the knobs are his (the sun's) rays, and his rays are outside.

[1] That is, the Ukhya Agni, or fire in the pan, which the Sacrificer will have to carry about during his time of initiation; and which, moreover, is here taken to be the Sacrificer's divine body (VI, 6, 4, 5).

[2] See I, 3, 5, 12,—twelve months of the year, five seasons, and three worlds: this makes twenty; and he that burns yonder is the twenty-first. See also Ait. Br. IV, 18, where the sun is identified with the Ekavimsa or Vishuvat day, the central day of the year, by which the gods raised the sun up to the heavens.

3. And as to why he puts on and wears the gold plate;—that plate is yonder sun, and man, in his human form, is unable to sustain that fire: it is only in this (solar or divine) form that he bears that (divine) form.

4. And, again, why he puts on and wears the gold plate;—this fire is seed poured out here; and the gold plate means vital energy (or brilliance) and vigour: he thus lays vital energy and vigour into that seed.

5. And, again, why he puts on and wears the gold plate;—the gods now were afraid lest the Rakshas, the fiends, should destroy here that (Agni) of theirs. They made that (plate), yonder sun, to be his (Agni's) protector (standing) by his side, for the gold plate is yonder sun: and in like manner does this (Sacrificer) now make that (plate) to be his (Agni's) protector by his side.

6. It is sown up in a black antelope's skin; for the black antelope skin is the sacrifice, and the sacrifice is able to sustain that (Agni): by means of the sacrifice the gods carried him, and by means of the sacrifice he now carries him;—with the hair (inside), for the hair are the metres, and the metres are indeed able to sustain him: by the metres the gods carried him, and by the metres he now carries him.

7. It is sown into the white and black hair, for these two are forms of the *rik* (hymn-verse) and the sâman (hymn-tune), and the *rik* and sâman are indeed able to sustain him (Agni): by the *rik* and sâman the gods carried him, and by the *rik* and sâman he now carries him. The hempen sling of the gold plate is a triple (cord): the significance of this has been explained.

8. He wears it over the navel; for that gold plate is yonder sun, and he (stands) over the navel (of the earth or sky).

9. And, again, why over the navel,—below the navel is the seed, the power of procreation, and the gold plate represents vital energy and vigour: (he does so, thinking,) 'Lest the gold plate burn up my seed, my power of procreation, my vital energy and vigour.'

10. And, again, why over the navel;—sacrificially purer is that part of the animal (victim) which is above the navel, and more in contact with ordure is that which is below the navel: he thus carries it (the plate) by means of that part of the animal which is sacrificially purer.

11. And, again, why over the navel,—that part of the vital air which is immortal is above the navel, and streams out by upward breathings; but that which is mortal passes by and away from the navel: he thus makes him (the Sacrificer) obtain the part of the vital air which is immortal, and by that he then carries it (the fire).

12. Now, he carries that (fire in the pan) on a seat;—the seat (âsandi) doubtless is this earth, for on her everything here is settled (âsanna); and she indeed is able to sustain him (Agni): it was thereby that the gods carried him, and thereby he now carries him.

13. It is made of udumbara wood (ficus glomerata), for the Udumbara tree is sustenance (sustaining strength), life-sap: by means of sustenance, life-sap, he thus carries him. Moreover, that Udumbara represents all the trees here (on earth), and all the trees (together) are capable of sustaining that (fire):

by means of all the trees the gods bore (or, maintained) it, and by means of all the trees does he now bear it.

14. It (the seat) is a span high; for Vishnu, as an embryo, was a span high: he thus makes the womb equal in size to the embryo. It is a cubit across; for the cubit is (the length of) the (fore-) arm, and strength is exerted by the arm. It thus is made equal to strength, and strength is indeed capable of sustaining him (Agni): by means of strength the gods did bear him, and by means of strength does he now bear him.

15. The feet and boards[1] are four-cornered; for there are four regions, and the regions are able to sustain him: by means of the regions the gods bore him, and by the regions does he now bear him. It is interwoven with cords of reed-grass, triple ones,—the significance of this has been explained;—and smeared over with clay,—(the significance) of this also has been explained; but it also serves to keep them from taking fire[2].

16. Now he carries him (Agni, the fire) by means of a netting[3],—he, Agni, is these worlds, and the netting is the regions, for by means of the regions these worlds are able to stand; and inasmuch as they are so able (*s*ak), it is called a netting (*s*ikya): he thus carries him by means of the regions. It is furnished with six strings,—for there are six

[1] That is, the boards forming the seat itself, and being a cubit long.

[2] Lit. 'from (the fire in the pan) burning over (or through the clay);' or 'from (their) being burnt over.'

[3] Apparently a round netted mat, on which the fire-pan is to be placed, and which is fastened to a cord by means of six strings, thus somewhat resembling the scale of a balance.

regions;—made of reed-grass, triply wound—the significance of this has been explained;—and smeared with clay—(the significance) of this also has been explained; but it also serves to keep them from taking fire.

17. The waters are his (Agni's) foundation, for on the waters these worlds are founded. The sun is the connecting link [1], for to the sun these worlds are linked by means of the quarters: whosoever thus knows this, carries suchlike a one by suchlike a one [2].

18. And, again, why he carries him by means of a netting,—he, Agni, is the year, and the netting is the seasons; for by means of the seasons the year is able to exist, and inasmuch as it is so able (*s*ak), therefore (the netting is called) '*s*ikya:' he thus carries him by the seasons. It is furnished with six strings, for there are six seasons.

19. Day and night are his foundation, for on day and night this year is founded. The moon is the connecting link, for to the moon this year is linked by means of the seasons: whosoever thus knows this, carries suchlike a one by suchlike a one. And verily by him who so knows this, he (Agni) is carried for a year; and by him who does not so know it, he is attended to for a year [3]. Thus as to the deities,—

---

[1] Or, the central point, the hinge or hook, to which the worlds are attached.

[2] Lit. carries that form by that form,—that is to say, he sustains, by means of the sun, the whole world in the form of Agni.

[3] That is to say, he who desires to derive the full benefit from the initiation ceremony, and the Agni*k*ayana generally, must not only keep up the Ukhya Agni (or pan-fire) during the year of the initiation, but must also carry him at least for a time every day during that period.

20. Now as to the self (or body of Agni). Agni doubtless is the self, and the netting is the vital airs, for by means of the vital airs that self is able to exist; and inasmuch as it is so able (sak) therefore (the netting is called) 'sikya:' he thus carries (sustains) him by means of the vital airs; and it is furnished with six strings, because there are six vital airs.

21. The mind is his foundation, for on the mind this body is founded,—and food is the connecting link, for to food this body is linked by means of the vital airs: whosoever thus knows this, carries suchlike (Agni) by suchlike means.

22. Now he carries him by means of the fire-pan; for the pan is these worlds, and these worlds are indeed able to hold him: by means of these worlds the gods carried him, and by means of them he (the Sacrificer) now carries him.

23. And as to why it is called 'Ukhâ;'—by means of this sacred performance and this process the gods at that time dug out these worlds; and inasmuch as they so dug out (ut-khan), it (the pan representing the worlds) is called 'utkhâ,'—'utkhâ' being what they mysteriously (esoterically) call 'ukhâ,' for the gods love the mysterious.

24. Now 'ukhâ' (consists of) two syllables,—the Sacrificer is two-footed, and the Sacrificer is Agni: as great as Agni is, as great as is his measure, by so much he thus carries him. And that same (pan) is a pot (kumbhî), it is a cauldron (sthâlî)[1]; this

[1] These words, according to Sâyana, are merely intended as synonymous (paryâya) for 'ukhâ,' or fire-pan, not as different vessels (such as the pot used temporarily when the pan is broken) as one might suppose.

makes six (syllables),—six seasons are a year, and the year is Agni: as great as Agni is, as great as is his measure, so great does this become.

25. He now takes hold of him (Agni[1]) by means of two (straw) pads[2]; for he, Agni, is yonder sun, and the two pads are day and night: he thus takes hold of yonder sun by means of the day and the night, and hence that (sun)[3] is encompassed by day and night.

26. And, again, why he takes hold of him by means of two pads,—he, Agni, is yonder sun, and the two pads are these two worlds: he thus encompasses yonder sun by these two worlds, and hence he is encompassed by these two worlds. They are round, for these two worlds are round; of reed-grass, triply wound,—the significance of this has been told;—and smeared with clay,—(the significance) of this also has been told, but it also serves to keep them from taking fire.

27. Now then the (mystic) correspondence (of the number of objects to the nature of Agni),—the seat, the fire-pan, the sling of the gold plate, the fire, and the gold plate,—these amount to six;—six seasons are a year, and the year is Agni: as great as Agni is, as great as is his measure, so great does this become. Two pads, that makes eight,—the Gâyatrî has eight syllables, and Agni is Gâyatra: as great as Agni is, as great as is his measure, so great does this become.

[1] That is, of the pan containing the fire.

[2] Sâyana (on VII, 2, 1, 15) explains them as two balls of straw. The comparison in 26 rather points to their being round mats.

[3] Thus Sâyana. If, on the other hand, Agni be intended here, this might be taken as an illusion to the regular worship of the fire at the morning and evening twilights (cf. VI, 7, 2, 3).

28. Now the total correspondence,—four feet and four boards (of the seat), the netting, and the sling of the gold plate, or any other corded netting; after that the pan and fire, and the gold plate,—that makes thirteen;—thirteen months are a year, and the year is Agni: as great as Agni is, as great as is his measure, so great does this become.

Second Brâhmana.

1. Standing he puts on that (gold plate)[1],—for that gold plate is yonder sun, and yonder sun stands, as it were; and moreover, while standing one is stronger. [He does so] standing with his face towards north-east: the significance of this has been explained.

2. [Vâg. S. XII, 1; *Ri*k S. X, 45, 8] 'Looking like[2] a golden disk he hath shone far and wide,'—for that gold plate, being seen, indeed shines far and wide;—'flashing forth unquenchable[3] life for glory,'—for not easily dying is his (Agni's) life (vital power); and for glory he does shine;—'Agni became immortal by his powers, when Dyaus bore him—,' for Dyaus (the sky) did bear him;—'she that hath good seed—,' for good seed indeed she has whose seed he (Agni) is.

3. He then takes hold of him by means of the two pads, with (Vâg. S. XII, 2[4]), 'Night and Dawn,

[1] The author now proceeds to give further particulars regarding the ceremonial details treated of in the preceding chapter (VI, 7, 1, 1 seq.).

[2] Literally, 'seen' or 'appearing (like).'

[3] Rather 'irresistible, difficult to bear (against);' but the author connects 'durmarsha' with 'mar,' to die.

[4] *Ri*k S. I, 96, 5, slightly different.

of one mind, unlike in form,'—night and dawn, doubtless, are day and night, (and they are) of one mind[1], and unlike in form;—'nourish one child, combining together,'—whatever belongs to the day and the night, therewith they, combining together, indeed nourish him (Agni);—'a golden disk, he shineth between heaven and earth,'—whilst taking it (the fire), he mutters this prayer; for heaven and earth are those two, the sky and the earth; and moving between these two he shines: that is why, in taking it, he mutters this prayer;—'the wealth-giving gods kept Agni;'—therewith, having taken hold of it in both hands, he sets it down; for the wealth-giving gods are the vital airs, and they indeed kept up Agni at first: by means of them he now keeps him up.

4. He then puts round his (neck) the sling of the netting, with (Vâg. S. XII, 3; *Ri*k S. V, 81, 2), 'The wise putteth on all forms,'—the wise one, doubtless, is yonder sun, and the netting is all forms;—'he hath brought forth what is good for the two-footed and four-footed,'—for in rising he does bring forth what is good for the two-footed and four-footed;—'the adorable Savit*ri* hath glanced over the firmament,'—the firmament, doubtless, is the heaven, and even in rising he looks along it;—'he flasheth forth after the starting[2] of the Dawn,'—for the Dawn shines forth first, and after her shining forth he (the sun) follows, flashing forth.

5. By means of the fashioning (formula) he then fashions him out of that (matter): he thereby

[1] That is to say, they are allied.

[2] Or, perhaps, after the precedence (example) of the Dawn.

fashions that infused seed, whence the seed infused into the womb is fashioned.

6. [Vâg. S. XII, 4] 'A well-winged bird thou art!'—the well-winged bird means vigour: he thus forms him so as to be (endowed with) vigour;—'the Trivr*i*t is thy head,'—he thus makes the Trivr*i*t stoma (nine-versed hymn) his head;—'the Gâyatra thine eye,'—he thus makes the Gâyatrî metre his eye;—'the Br*i*hat and Rathantara thy wings,'—he thus makes the Br*i*hat and Rathantara (hymn-tunes) his wings;—'the hymn is the self,'—the Pañ*k*avi*m*sa stoma (twenty-five-versed hymn) he makes the self (soul, or body);—'the metres the limbs,'—for the metres are indeed his (Agni's) limbs;—'the prayers his name,'—the prayers (yagus) are his name 'Agni' by which they call him,—'the Vâmadevya sâman is thy body,'—the body, doubtless, is the self: thus 'the Vâmadevya (hymn-tune) is thy body, thy self;'—'the Yag*ñ*âyag*ñ*iya thy tail,'—he thus makes the Yag*ñ*âyag*ñ*iya [1] his tail;—'the hearths thy hoofs,'—by means of the hearths he (Agni) is indeed established in this world;—'thou art a well-winged bird: go to the heaven! fly to the light!'—thus having made him a well-winged bird [2], he says, 'Go to the gods! fly to the heavenly world!'

7. He fashions him here (in the pan or womb) into (a bird) with wings and tail; for whatlike the seed is fashioned in the womb, suchlike it is born; and because he here fashions him as (a bird) with

[1] The ordinary hymn-tune of the Agnish*t*oma-sâman, the last and characteristic stotra of the simplest, or Agnish*t*oma Soma-sacrifice.

[2] Or, the bird (or eagle, supar*n*a) Garutmat.

wings and tail, therefore he is hereafter born with wings and tail.

8. Now some, after addressing him by that fashioning (formula), build a different altar (than of an eagle's shape), either one constructed in the form of a trough[1], or like a chariot-wheel, or like a kite, or like the front part of a thill, or like a thill on both sides, or one consisting of a heap of loose soil[2]. Let him not do so, (but) in such wise as one might carve a young one with wings and tail: let him therefore build it (the fire-altar) in the form of an eagle.

9. With that fashioning (formula) he holds him high up from thence towards east[3]; for he, Agni, is yonder sun: he thus places yonder sun high up from here in the east; and hence yonder sun is placed high up from here in the east. He holds him up so as to be beyond the reach of the arms, for he (the sun) is beyond the reach of the arms from here. He then lowers him, and, having lowered him, he holds him above the navel: the significance of this has been explained[4].

10. He then strides the Vishnu-strides[5]. For the gods, in the form of Vishnu (the sun), then strode through these worlds; and inasmuch as, in the form of Vishnu, they thus strode, they are called the Vishnu-strides: in like manner does the Sacrificer,

[1] Sâyana seems to make this a round vessel,—dronah parimandalânâma-(? lamâna)rûpam dronam iva kiyate dronakit.

[2] Samuhya samuhya purisham tenaiva kevalena kiyata iti samuhyapurishah, Sây.

[3] As in the case of the lump of clay, VI, 4, 3, 10.

[4] VI, 7, 1, 8 seq.

[5] Or the Vishnu-steps, as the term, for a special reason, was translated at V, 4, 2, 6.

in the form of Vishnu, now stride through these worlds.

11. Now he who is Vishnu is this sacrifice; and he who is this sacrifice is that same Agni in the ukhâ (fire-pan): into that same (Agni) the gods changed themselves, and strode through these worlds; and in like manner the Sacrificer, having changed himself into that same (Agni), strides through these worlds.

12. Standing with his face towards north-east (he strides); for standing towards north-east Pragâpati created offspring by means of the Vishnu-strides: in like manner does the Sacrificer now, standing towards north-east, create offspring by means of the Vishnu-strides.

13. [Vâg. S. XII, 5] 'Thou art Vishnu's stride,'—for in the form of Vishnu he strides;—'the slayer of foes;'—for he now slays his foes;—'mount thou the Gâyatrî metre,'—the Gâyatrî metre he does mount,—'stride along the earth!'—along the earth he indeed strides. He stretches forward his (right) foot and strides: he raises the fire upwards, for upwards he ascends.

14. 'Thou art Vishnu's stride,'—for in the form of Vishnu he strides;—'the slayer of plotters,'—for he now does slay the plotters;—'mount thou the Trishtubh metre!'—the Trishtubh metre he does mount;—'stride along the air!'—along the air he indeed strides. He stretches forward his foot and strides: he raises the fire (yet further) upwards, for upwards he ascends.

15. 'Thou art Vishnu's stride,'—for in the form of Vishnu he strides;—'the slayer of the evil-minded,'—for he now does slay the evil-

minded;—'Mount the *G*agati metre!'—for the *G*agatî metre he does mount;—'stride along the sky!'—along the sky he indeed strides. He stretches his foot forward and strides: he raises the fire (yet further) upwards, for upwards he ascends.

16. 'Thou art Vish*n*u's stride,'—for in the form of Vish*n*u he strides;—'the slayer of the hostile,'—for he now does slay the hostile;—'mount thou the Anush*t*ubh metre!'—the Anush*t*ubh metre he does mount;—'stride along the quarters!'—he looks along the (four) quarters; he does not stretch forward his foot, thinking, 'Lest I lose these worlds!'—He raises the fire right up, for he ascends completely (to the top).

THIRD BRÂHMANA.

1. He then holds it (the fire in the pan) up thus (towards north-east). Now the gods at that time were desiring, 'May we be like Parganya (the rain-god)!' By that body (of his [1]) they became like Parganya, and in like manner does the Sacrificer by that body (of his) become like Parganya.

2. [Vâg. S. XII, 6; *Ri*k S. X, 45, 4] 'Agni roared like the thundering sky,'—for he (Agni) indeed roars like the thundering Parganya;—'again and again licking the ground, stroking [2] the plants,'—for Parganya, whilst licking again and

[1] Viz. by the Agni who is now being held up, and of whom Parganya is said to be another form, at VI, 1, 3, 15. It is probably the smoke rising from the fire-pan that suggests the idea of the Jupiter pluvius sending forth his flashes of light from the dark cloud.

[2] Literally, anointing (? either furbishing, or impregnating).

again the ground, does stroke the plants;—'scarce born, the kindled shone forth,'—for scarce born he indeed lights up everything here;—'with his light he shineth between the two worlds,'—the two worlds, doubtless, are the heaven and the earth, and these two he indeed illumes by his light. He holds it (the fire in the pan) up so as to be beyond the reach of his arms, for Parganya is beyond the reach of (our) arms.

3. He then lowers it; for whatever sap, whatever sustenance there is in this world, that rises upwards with it through these worlds, for Agni is the sap, Agni is the substance in this world: thus were that always to be so[1], then there would be no sap, no sustenance in this world; but when he lowers (the fire), he bestows sap and sustenance on this world.

4. And, again, why he lowers it,—he then indeed rises upwards from here through these worlds: that is, as it were, a rising away from here. But this earth is the resting-place; and were that always to be so, the Sacrificer would be removed from this world. But when he lowers (the fire), he thereby comes back to this resting-place, and stands firmly on this resting-place.

5. And, again, why he lowers it,—there, indeed, in rising upwards, he conquers these worlds from here: that is, as it were, a conquering in a forward direction. Now the conquest of him who conquers only in a forward direction is completed by others; but for him who conquers both ways there is free scope: thus, when he lowers (the fire) he conquers

[1] Literally, were that to be so much only (i.e. were the fire always to be held up there).

these worlds both from here upwards and from thence backwards.

6. [Vâ*g*. S. XII, 7–10] 'Ever returning Agni, turn thou back unto me, with life, with vigour, with offspring, with riches; with gain, with wisdom, with wealth, with prosperity!—O Agni, Aṅgiras! may thine be a hundred courses, and a thousand returns: with increase of increase bring back what was lost by us, and bring us again riches!—Return again with sustenance, again, O Agni, with food and life, guard us again from trouble!—With wealth return, O Agni, overflow with the all-feeding stream on every side!'—that is, 'with all this return thou to me!' Four times he lowers (the fire further and further), for four times it rises upwards: thus as often as it rises upwards, so often he lowers it; and having lowered it (completely), he holds it above his navel: the significance of this has been explained[1].

7. He then addresses him (Agni); for Agni is vital power: he thus lays vital power into his self: [Vâ*g*. S. XII, 11] 'Hither have I brought thee,'—for they do indeed bring him hither;—'thou hast entered,'—he then lays vital power into his self;—'stand thou firm, never staggering!'—he thus lays the vital power firmly into his self;—'may all the people long for thee!'—the people are food: thus, 'may all food long for thee!'—'may thy rule not fall away from thee!'—rule means glory: thus, 'may thy glory not fall away from thee!'

8. He then unties the sling of the netting, and the sling of the gold plate; for the sling belongs to

[1] VI, 7, 1, 8 seq.

Varu*n*a: he thus frees himself from Varu*n*a's noose. He does so with a verse to Varu*n*a: he thus frees himself from Varu*n*a's noose by its own self, by its own deity. [Vâg. S. XII, 12; *Ri*k S. I, 24, 15] 'Take off from us, O Varu*n*a, the uppermost cord, down (take) the lowest, away the middle one!'—as the text, so the meaning;—'and so, O Âditya, may we be sinless in thy service for safety (Aditi)!'—Aditi is this earth: thus, 'Sinless may we belong to thee and to her (the earth)!'

9. He then holds him (Agni) up thus (towards south-east); for on that former occasion he raises him upwards from here towards the east with the fashioning formula[1]; and he then holds him up thus (towards north-east[2]). Now were that alone to take place, he (the sun), surely, would stop even there (in the north); but inasmuch as he now holds him up thus (towards south-east), he (the sun) having gone thus (in a northerly direction), then comes back again thus (in a southerly direction).

10. [Vâg. S. XII, 13; *Ri*k S. X, 1, 1] 'The great hath stood up erect before the Dawns,'—for before the dawn the great one (Agni) indeed stands up erect;—'emerged from the gloom he hath come with light,'—for emerged from the gloom, the night, he indeed comes with light, with the day;—'well-shapen with white light,'—for he, Agni, is indeed well-shapen with white light;—'when born, he hath filled all homesteads;'—all homesteads, doubtless, means these worlds, and these he indeed fills, when born. He holds him up so as to be beyond the reach of the arms, for he (the

---

[1] VI, 7, 2, 9. [2] VI, 7, 3, 1.

sun) is beyond the reach of arms from here. He then lowers him: he thereby comes back to this resting-place, and stands firmly on this resting-place. [He does so] with a gagatî verse[1], for the Gagatî gains these worlds from above hitherwards.

11. [Vâg. S. XII, 14; *Ri*k S. IV, 40, 5] 'The swan dwelling in the light,'—the swan dwelling in the light, doubtless, is yonder sun;—'the Vasu dwelling in the air,'—the Vasu dwelling in the air, doubtless, is the wind;—'the priest seated on the altar,'—the priest seated on the altar, doubtless, is Agni;—'the guest,'—for he (Agni) is indeed the guest of all beings;—'dwelling in the retreat[2],'—that is, 'dwelling in rugged places;'—'the man-dwelling,'—the man-dwelling, doubtless, is the vital air; and men are human beings: he thus means that vital air, that fire, which (burns) in human beings;—'the space-dwelling,'—for he (Agni) indeed is seated in all spaces;—'the law-seated,'—that is, 'the truth-seated;'—'the sphere-dwelling,'—for he is indeed seated in all spheres;—'the water-born, cow-born'—for he is indeed both water-born and cow-born;—'law-born,'—that is, 'truth-born;'—'rock-born,'—for he is born from the rock;—'the law,'—that is, 'the truth.' With 'the Great!' he deposits it (the fire): for he (Agni) is indeed the great (truth): he thus deposits him (on the seat) after making him what he is.

12. [He does so] with two syllables ('b*ri*hat'),—the Sacrificer is two-footed, and the Sacrificer is

[1] It is rather a trish*t*ubh verse.

[2] Rather, (the guest) dwelling in the house (duro*n*a-sad), but the author evidently derives 'duro*n*a' from 'dus' (bad), making it a synonym of 'durga.'

Agni: as great as Agni is, as great as is his measure, with so much he thus deposits him.

13. He then stands worshipping by him; for he makes, as it were, light of him, when he strides with him through these worlds both thus (upwards), and thus (downwards): he now makes amends to him, so that he (Agni) may not hurt him.

14. And, again, why he stands by him;—the gods at that time were afraid, lest he should injure these worlds of theirs from anigh: they thereby appeased him towards these worlds; and in like manner does he (the Sacrificer) now appease him towards these worlds.

15. [Vâg. S. XII, 15–17] 'Seat thee in this thy mother's lap, thou, O Agni, knowing all ordinances! burn her not with thy heat, thy flame! shine in her with a brilliant light!—Glowing with light and heat within thine own seat, be thou gracious unto this Ukhâ, O knower of beings!—Being gracious unto me, O Agni, now seat thee graciously! seat thee here in thine own seat, having made happy all the regions!'—by saying 'Gracious—Gracious,' he appeases him, so that he may not injure any one, and thus he, being appeased, does not injure these worlds.

16. With three (verses) he stands by worshipping;—three in number are these worlds, and threefold is Agni: as great as Agni is, as great as is his measure, with so much he thereby makes amends to him, and with so much does he thereby appease him towards these worlds.

FOURTH BRÂHMANA.

1. He then stands by him worshipping with the Vâtsapra rite[1]. For Pragâpati, having by means of the Vishnu-strides produced creatures, created vital power for them by means of the Vâtsapra rite; and in like manner the Sacrificer, having, by means of the Vishnu-strides, produced creatures (or, subjects), creates vital power for them by means of the Vâtsapra rite.

2. Now the Vâtsapra rite, doubtless, is he, the golden-handed[2] (Agni);—hence whomsoever that is born one may wish to obtain the full (measure of) life, let him touch that one with the Vâtsapra rite, and he thereby creates vital power for that new-born one; and accordingly that one obtains the full (measure of) life. And whomsoever one may wish to be vigorous, let him first address that one with the Vikriti (fashioning) formula[3], and that one accordingly becomes vigorous.

3. [Vâg. S. XII, 18-20] 'From the sky Agni was first born;'—the sky, doubtless, is the breath, and from the breath he (Agni) was indeed first born,—'from us the second time, the knower of beings,'—inasmuch as he, man-like, on that occasion generated him a second time[4];—'the

[1] That is, the recitation of Vâg. S. XII, 18-28 or 29 (Rik S. X, 45), ascribed to the poet Vatsapri Bhâlandana. The Brâhmana, however, comments only on the first three verses, and perhaps these alone were used for the purpose at the time when the Brâhmana was composed.

[2] This is a somewhat doubtful meaning of 'dâkshâyana-hasta.' The synonyms (if correct), hiranyapâni and hiranyahasta, always refer to Savitri, the sun.

[3] See VI, 7, 2, 5-6.

[4] ? Or, as a second; see above, VI, 1, 1, 11.

third time in the waters,'—inasmuch as he there did generate him a third time from the waters;—'he, the manly-minded, (kindling him) the imperishable,'—the manly-minded, doubtless, is Pragâpati; and the imperishable, Agni[1];—'kindling him the mindful praises (gar) him,'—for he who kindles him generates him, mindful.

4. 'We know, O Agni, thy threefold three,'—Agni, Vâyu (wind), Âditya (sun), these are his three in three forms;—'We know thy manifold scattered sites,'—inasmuch as he (Agni) is here distributed manyways;—'we know thy highest name which is in secret,'—'the youngest,' that indeed is his highest name in secret;—'we know that source whence thou art come;'—the source, doubtless, is the (heavenly) waters, for from the waters he first came.

5. 'In the sea the manly-minded (kindled) thee, in the waters,'—the manly-minded is Pragâpati: thus, 'In the waters Pragâpati (kindled) thee;'—'the man-watcher hath kindled thee, O Agni, in the udder of the sky,'—the man-watcher, doubtless, is Pragâpati, and the udder of the sky is the waters;—'thee, whilst standing in the third region,'—the third region, doubtless, is the sky;—'the buffaloes made (thee) grow in the lap of the waters;'—the buffaloes, doubtless, are

[1] The construction of the text here favoured by the author is very doubtful. It has probably to be construed,—'the third time (he, Agni, was born) in the waters, he, the manly-minded (or, friendly to men). Kindling him, the imperishable (Agni), the heedful (? or pious) one praises him,'—or perhaps, 'While kindling him, the considerate one praises him unceasingly.' A point which favours the author's construction is that, in verse 3, 'nrimanaas' certainly refers not to Agni, but to him who generated him.

the vital airs: thus, 'the vital airs made thee grow in the sky.'

6. These (three verses[1]) have one and the same explanation regarding him (Agni): they are Trish*t*ubh verses relating to Agni. Inasmuch as they relate to Agni, they are Agni; and inasmuch as they are Trish*t*ubhs, and eleven (syllables), they are Indra;—but Agni consists of Indra and Agni: as great as Agni is, as great as is his measure, with so much he thus stands worshipping by him. And Indra and Agni are all the gods, and Agni includes (or belongs to) all the deities: as great as Agni is, as

[1] The remaining verses (XII, 21-29) are as follows:—

1. Agni roared like the thundering sky, &c. (see VI, 7, 3, 2).

2. The upraiser of glories, the upholder of riches, the inspirer of thoughts, the guardian of Soma; the excellent son of power, shines forth as king in the waters, kindled before the dawns.

3. A beacon unto all that is, the child of the world filled the two spheres even when born; even the hard rock he broke going thither when the five peoples worshipped Agni.

4. An eager cleanser, a wise messenger, the immortal Agni has been set up among the mortals; flickering (?) he sends forth the red smoke, striving with his bright flame to reach the sky.

5. Looking like a golden disk, &c. (see VI, 7, 2).

6. Whoso maketh for thee this day a ghee-baked cake, O divine Agni of auspicious flame, lead him onwards to bliss, unto god-allotted glory, O youngest!

7. Make him share in the songs of triumph, make him share in every hymn that is sung! Dear be he unto Sûrya, dear unto Agni; let him prevail with the living one and with them that are to be born!

8. They that worship thee day by day, O Agni, win all desirable boons; ardently wishing for wealth, they have opened with thee the stable filled with cows!

9. Agni Vaisvânara has been celebrated by the *R*ishis, the guardian of Soma, most gracious unto men: let us invoke heaven and earth who are free from hatred! grant us wealth, ye gods, with abundance of men!

great as is his measure, with so much he thus stands worshipping by him.

7. And, again, why the Vishnu-strides and the Vâtsapra rite are (performed);—by the Vishnu-strides Pragâpati created this world, and by the Vâtsapra the fire (Agni); by the Vishnu-strides Pragâpati created the air, and by the Vâtsapra the wind (Vâyu); by the Vishnu-strides Pragâpati created the sky, and by the Vâtsapra the sun (Âditya); by the Vishnu-strides Pragâpati created the regions, and by the Vâtsapra the moon; by the Vishnu-strides Pragâpati created that which has been, and by the Vâtsapra that which shall be; by the Vishnu-strides Pragâpati created possession (wealth), and by the Vâtsapra hope; by the Vishnu-strides Pragâpati created the day, and by the Vâtsapra the night; by the Vishnu-strides Pragâpati created the former (bright) fortnights, and by the Vâtsapra the latter (dark) fortnights; by the Vishnu-strides Pragâpati created the half-months, and by the Vâtsapra the months; by the Vishnu-strides Pragâpati created the seasons, and by the Vâtsapra the year: thus the reason why the Vishnu-strides and Vâtsapra are (performed) is that he thereby even now creates everything.

8. And, again, why the Vishnu-strides and the Vâtsapra rite are (performed). By the Vishnu-strides Pragâpati drove up to heaven. He saw that unyoking-place, the Vâtsapra, and unyoked thereat to prevent chafing; for when the yoked (beast) is not unloosed, it is chafed. In like manner the Sacrificer drives up to heaven by the Vishnu-strides; and unyokes by means of the Vâtsapra.

9. Having stridden the Vishnu-strides, he then

forthwith stands by the fire worshipping it with the Vâtsapra, just as one who has journeyed would forthwith unyoke. Men (proceed) after the manner of the gods: hence even now, when a troop of men have journeyed they forthwith unyoke.

10. Now, the Vishnu-strides indeed are the day and the night, and the Vâtsapra is the day and the night: he thus journeys for a day and a night, and takes rest for a day and a night: and hence even now when a troop of men have journeyed for a day and a night they take rest for a day and a night.

11. Only for one half of the year he strides the Vishnu-strides, and for one half he worships the fire with the Vâtsapra; for the world of heaven is in the midst of the year: thus were he to stride for less than half (a year), he would not reach that world of heaven; and were he to do so for more than half (a year), he would pass beyond that world of heaven and lose it; but when he strides for one half, and worships the fire for one half, he unyokes forthwith after reaching the world of heaven.

12. He proceeds with these two alternately[1], even as one would accomplish a long way by (repeatedly) unyoking. Both before and after (the Dikshâ), he combines both, the Vishnu-strides and the Vâtsapra; for the Vishnu-strides are the day, and the Vâtsapra the night; and Pragâpati, both when he was about to generate and when he had generated this universe, enclosed it on both sides by day and night: in like

[1] That is, whilst on the first day of the Dikshâ, as well as on the day after its completion, both the Vishnu-strides and the Vâtsapra are performed, during the intermediate period of one year they are performed on alternate days,—the Vishnu-strides on even, and the Vâtsapra on uneven days.

manner the Sacrificer now, both when he is about to generate and when he has generated this universe, encloses it on both sides by day and night.

13. As to this they say, 'If the Vish*n*u-strides are the day, and the Vâtsapra the night, and both of them are (performed) during the day, not during the night, how then are they both performed for (or by) him also during the night?' Well, on that (first) occasion, when he is being initiated, he, at the outset, combines both (performances) in the afternoon; for the afternoon is the same thing as the night. Then throwing them thus together, he at the end combines them both in the forenoon; for the forenoon is the same thing as the day; and in this way they are both performed during the day, and both during the night.

14. Now early on the day on which he may intend to combine them, when the sun has risen, he first throws out the ashes (from the pan); having thrown out the ashes, he releases his speech; having released his speech, he puts on a kindling-stick; having put on a kindling-stick, he takes the ashes down to (and throws them into) the water. In the same way as he takes them down he returns after taking some of the ashes; and having thrown it into the pan he stands reverentially by the fire. He then performs two expiations.

15. And if the day should be one for the Vish*n*u-strides, let him, after striding the Vish*n*u-strides, worship the fire with the Vâtsapra; and if it be one for the Vâtsapra, let him, after worshipping with the Vâtsapra, and striding the Vish*n*u-strides, finally perform the Vâtsapra. Let him not conclude by performing the Vish*n*u-strides, for that would be as if

after going for a drive he were not to unyoke; but when he concludes by performing the Vâtsapra—the Vâtsapra being a halting-place—(it is) as if he made a halt and unloosed (the team): let him therefore conclude by performing the Vâtsapra.

EIGHTH ADHYÂYA. FIRST BRÂHMANA.

1. 'Let him drive Agni about while keeping him up,' so they say. The gods and the Asuras, both of them sprung from Prâgâpati, were contending. The gods drove about on wheels (cars), and the Asuras stayed at home. The gods, while driving about on wheels, saw[1] this rite (sacrificial performance), for it was indeed in driving about on wheels that they saw this rite: hence it is to the cart that the formulas relate at the (performance with) sacrificial cakes[2], and to the cart in the building of the fire-altar[3].

2. Now he who drives Agni about goes to the gods by the sacred performance, for divine is the rite performed by him; but he who does not drive him about goes to the Asuras by the sacred performance, for demoniac is the rite performed by him.

3. Here now some say, 'It is by himself that he (Agni) is driven about; for by the Vishnu-strides he drives forward, and by the Vâtsapra he unyokes.' Let him not think this to be so; for divine (to the gods) is that progress of his, to wit, the Vishnu-strides; and divine the unyoking, to wit, the Vâtsapra. But human would be that progress of his, which he makes in this manner, and human the unyoking he makes.

[1] Sâyana says, 'vîrasiddheh,' 'by the heroes' success.'

[2] See I, 1, 2, 5.

[3] Sâyana refers to Vâg. S. XII, 31, 'upwards may the All-gods bear thee . . .' (paragraph 9 below), as a passage in point.

4. This Agni is Pragâpati; and Pragâpati is both the gods and men. Now when the Vishnu-strides and the Vâtsapra are (performed), he thereby makes up that form of his which is divine; and when he drives him about he thereby makes up that form of his which is human. Verily, then, he who, knowing this, drives him about, makes up that whole and entire Pragâpati: let him therefore by all means drive him (Agni) about.

5. Now on any day on which he may intend to drive, he gets the chariot placed north of the fire (with the pole) to the east; and puts a kindling-stick on it (the fire); for at that time the gods first regaled him (Agni) with food, with that kindling-stick, when he was about to start: and in like manner does this one now first regale him with food, with that kindling-stick, when he is about to start.

6. [Vâg. S. XII, 30; *Ri*k S. VIII, 44, 1] 'With fuel serve ye Agni!'—that is, 'with fuel worship ye Agni!'—'with draughts of ghee awake ye the guest, offer ye libations unto him!'—that is, 'with (draughts of) ghee do ye awake the guest, and offer libations unto him!'—with a (verse) containing (the verb) 'awake' he awakens him for the starting.

7. He then lifts him (the fire) up, with (Vâg. S. XII, 31), 'Upwards may the All-gods bear thee, O Agni, by their thoughts!'—at the beginning all the gods did indeed bear him upwards by their thoughts, for that (or, he) was then their thought: in like manner does this (Sacrificer) now bear him upwards by his thoughts, for this now is his thought;—'be thou gracious unto us, of fair look, and rich splendour!'—as the text, so its meaning. From the south he places him (Agni) northwards

on (the chariot)—the significance of this has been explained. Having put the Gârhapatya into a pot, he places it on (the chariot) behind (the Âhavanîya, or Ukhya Agni). If he choose, he himself may mount up beside him (Agni), or he may walk by the side (of the chariot).

8. He then yokes two oxen, first the right one, then the left one: so (it is done) with the gods, otherwise in human (practice). And in whatever direction he may intend to drive, let him first drive east, for the east is Agni's region: he (Agni) thus proceeds towards his own region.

9. [Whilst driving thither, he mutters, Vâg. S. XII, 32] 'Go forth, O Agni, brilliant thou with propitious flames!'—that is, 'Brilliant, O Agni, go thou forth with propitious, shining flames!'—'Beaming with great beams injure not my people with thy body!'—that is, 'With great shining flames do not injure my people by thyself!'

10. Whenever the axle creaks, let him mutter that prayer (Vâg. S. XII, 33); for demoniacal is that voice which is in the axle: he thereby appeases that (voice) and makes it as of the gods.

11. And, again, why he mutters that prayer;—with whomsoever, mounted (on a chariot), the axle creaks, this is his own voice: hence when the axle creaks while Agni is mounted, this is the voice of Agni himself. It was Agni indeed whom the gods thereby praised and magnified; and in like manner does this (Sacrificer) thereby praise and magnify him: 'Agni roared like the thundering sky,'—the meaning of this has been explained[1].

---

[1] See above, VI, 7, 3, 2.

12. If he unyokes before (reaching) his dwelling, let the fire remain on the chariot itself; but when he unyokes for (staying at) his dwelling, he stops the chariot (with the pole) to the east; and north of it he raises and sprinkles (a place) where he takes it (the fire) down. He takes it down from south to north: the meaning of this has been explained.

13. He then puts a kindling-stick thereon; for on that occasion the gods regaled him (Agni) with food, with that kindling-stick, after he had travelled: in like manner does this (Sacrificer) now regale him, after he has travelled, with food, with that kindling-stick.

14. [He puts it on, with Vâg. S. XII, 34; *Ri*k S. VII, 8, 4] 'Far, far famed is this Agni of the Bharata (tribe),'—the Bharata[1], doubtless, is Pragâpati, for he sustains (bhar) this entire (universe);—'that his great light shineth brightly, as the sun,'—that is, 'that, like the sun, his great light shines brightly;'—'he who overthrew Pûru in battles,'—Pûru, by name, was an Asura-Rakshas: him Agni overthrew (abhi-sthâ) in battles;—'blazed up hath the divine guest, gracious unto us;'—that is, 'being kindled, the divine guest is gracious to us.' With a (verse) containing (the verb) 'sthâ' (he performs), for he thereby makes him stop (sthâ) for (staying at) his home.

15. Now, then, the (symbolic) correspondence,—with the first (formula) he puts on a kindling-stick, with one he lifts him up, with one he starts, with one he addresses the axle, with the fifth he puts on a

[1] Mahîdhara, in accordance with Nigh. III, 18 (priest), explains 'bharata' as the one who brings (bhar) offerings; and, with Sâya*n*a, identifies the Bharata with the Sacrificer.

kindling-stick, that makes five,—of five layers consists the fire-altar, five seasons are a year, and the year is Agni: as great as Agni is, as great as is his measure, so great does this become.

SECOND BRÂHMA*N*A.

1. Now, then, as to the taking down of the ashes (to the water [1]). Now, the gods at that time threw out the ashes (from the pan). They said, 'If we make this, such as it is, part of our own self, we shall become mortal carcases, not freed from sin; and if we cast it away, we shall put outside of Agni what therein is of Agni's nature: find ye out in what manner we shall do this!'—They said, 'Meditate ye (*k*it)!' whereby, indeed, they said, 'Seek ye a layer (or altar, *k*iti). Seek ye in what manner we shall do this!'

2. While meditating, they saw this,—'Let us take it down to the water; for the water is the foundation of this universe: having settled it on that wherein is the foundation of this universe, we shall reproduce from out of the water what there is of Agni's nature in this (heap of ashes).' They then took it down to (and threw it into) the water; and in like manner does this (Sacrificer) now take it down to the water.

3. [Vâ*g*. S. XII, 35] 'O divine waters, receive ye these ashes, and put them in a soft and fragrant place!'—that, being consumed (matter), has run its course (is useless): regarding that he says, 'Put it in the most fragrant place!'—'May

[1] The ashes removed from the 'ukhâ' or fire-pan are put in a bag made of leaves of some sacred tree, and are then thrown into the water in two portions. As they are floating on the water, a small portion is taken from them again with the little finger and put in the pan.

the wives, wedded to a good lord, bow down to him,'—the wives, doubtless, are the waters, for from the waters this universe is produced; and in Agni the waters have indeed a good lord;—'bear it on the waters, even as a mother (bears) her son!' —that is, 'as a mother would bear her son on her lap, so bear ye this!'

4. [Vâg. S. XII, 36; *Ri*k S. VIII, 43, 9] 'In the waters, O Agni, is thy seat,'—that is, 'in the waters, O Agni, is thy womb;'—'as such thou clingest to the plants,'—for he does indeed cling to (love) the plants,—'being in (their) womb thou art born again,'—when he is in the womb he is indeed born again.—[Vâg. S. XII, 37] 'Thou art the child of the herbs, the child of the trees, the child of all that is, O Agni, thou art the child of the waters;'—he thus makes him (Agni) the child of this entire (universe).

5. With three (verses) he throws (the ashes into the water),—threefold is Agni: as great as Agni is, as great as is his measure, by so much he thus throws them down. First with one (prayer), and then with two; or first with two, and then with one,—but at two separate times he throws them down: he thus throws them down by means of the two-footed animals.

6. He then takes some (of the ashes) therefrom: he thereby reproduces from the waters what there is of Agni's nature in that (heap of ashes). [He takes it] with that (nameless or little finger), for with that (finger) medicine is prepared: it is with that one he thus puts him (Agni) together. [Vâg. S. XII, 38-41] 'Having settled[1] in the womb, as

[1] 'Pra-sad' (=pra-âp, Mahîdhara) seems here really to have the

ashes, in the waters, and the earth, O Agni,'—by his ashes he is, indeed, settled in the womb, that is, both in the waters and in the earth;—'having united with the mothers, thou hast again, brightly shining, seated thee;'—that is, 'Having joined thy mothers, thou, the shining one, hast again seated thyself (in thy home).'—'Having again seated thee in thy seat, the waters and the earth, O Agni, thou liest in her (the earth, or pan) most happy, as in a mother's lap.'—'Return again with sustenance, again, O Agni, with food and life; guard us again from trouble!—With wealth return, O Agni, overflow with the all-feeding stream on every side!'—that is, 'With all this return thou to me!'

7. With four (verses) he takes (some of the ashes);—he thereby supplies him (Agni) with four-footed animals; and animals being food, it is with food he thus supplies him. With three (verses) he takes (the ashes) down (to the water),—that makes seven, for of seven layers consists the fire-altar[1], seven seasons are a year, and the year is Agni: as great as Agni is, as great as is his measure, so great does this become.

8. Having taken some of the ashes, and returned, he throws it into the fire-pan, and stands by (the fire) worshipping it; for when he throws Agni into the water he does what is improper; he now makes amends to him so that he may not injure him. With two (verses) relating to Agni (he worships),—for it is to Agni that he makes amends,—and with such

meaning of 'abhiprasad' or 'anuprasad,' as the accusative can scarcely be taken along with 'âsada*h*.'

[1] See p. 249, note 3.

as contain (the verb) 'budh' (to attend to, awake), in order that Agni may attend to this speech of his.

9. [Vâg. S. XII, 42-3; *Ri*k S. I, 147, 2; II, 6, 4] 'Attend thou to this word of mine, O youngest!'—that is, 'attend to this word of mine, O youngest!'—'put forth most plentifully, O faithful one!'—that is, 'put forth most abundantly, O faithful one!'—'this one revileth thee, and that one singeth thy praises,'—that is, 'one (man) reviles thee, and another sings thy praises;'—'reverently I revere thy body, O Agni!'—that is, 'I, thy reverer, revere thy body, O Agni!'—'Be thou a munificent patron of offerings, O lord of wealth, the bestower of wealth, keep off from us the haters!' this he says in order that he may keep off haters from him. With two (verses) he worships the fire, a Gâyatrî and a Trish*t*ubh verse: the significance of this has been explained.

10. These make nine (verses),—there are nine regions [1], and Agni is the regions; nine vital airs, and Agni is the vital airs: as great as Agni is, as great as is his measure, so great does this become.

11. He then performs two expiations; for it is for (the obtainment of) all his desires that he sets up that (fire);—thus whatever part of his desires is here cut off when the fire is thrown into the water, that he thereby joins together and restores. He performs both expiations which (are performed) when the fire has gone out [2]: the significance of this has been explained.

[1] Viz. the four cardinal points, and the four intermediate points, of the compass, and the upper region. To these paragraph 12 adds, as a tenth, the lower region.

[2] VI, 6, 4, 10 seq.

12. This makes ten (performances),—the Virâg consists of ten syllables, and Agni is the Virâg[1]; there are ten regions, and Agni is the regions; ten vital airs, and Agni is the vital airs: as great as Agni is, as great as is his measure, so great does this become.

[1] That is, the wide-shining, or wide-ruling one.

SEVENTH KÂNDA.

THE GÂRHAPATYA HEARTH.

First Adhyâya. First Brâhmana.

1. Being about to build the Gârhapatya (fire-place), he sweeps (its site) with a Palâsa (butea frondosa) branch. For when he builds the Gârhapatya[1] he settles on that place; and whatsoever builders of fire-altars (there have been), they are indeed settled on this earth; and when he sweeps (that place) he thereby sweeps away those settled (there before him), thinking, 'Lest I should settle on those already settled (here).'

2. [He sweeps, with Vâg. S. XII, 45] 'Off with you! away with you! crawl away from here[2]!'—that is, 'Go off, go away, and crawl away from here!' he says this to those that crawl on their belly;—'Ye that are here of old and of late!' that is, 'both ye who were here of yore, and ye of the present day.'

3. 'Yama hath given the settlement on earth (to this Sacrificer);'—for Yama indeed rules over the settling on this earth, and it is he who grants to this (Sacrificer) a settlement on this earth.

[1] That is, 'the householder's fire,' which represents the Sacrificer's domestic hearth.

[2] This first pâda is taken from Rik S. X, 14, 9. The four pâdas of the verse are muttered by the Adhvaryu while sweeping the four sides of the site respectively, beginning in the east and ending in the north. On this place when swept the circular site of the Gârhapatya is then marked off by saline soil being scattered over it (cf. Taitt. S. V, 2, 3, 2–3).

4. 'The Fathers have prepared this place for him!' for Yama is the Kshatra (nobility, or ruling power), and the Fathers (deceased ancestors) are the clansmen; and to whomsoever the chief (kshatriya), with the approval of the clan, grants a settlement, that (settlement) is properly given: and in like manner does Yama, the ruling power, with the consent of the Fathers, the clan, now grant to this (Sacrificer) a settlement on this earth.

5. With a palâsa branch he sweeps; for the Palâsa tree is the Brahman[1]: it is by the Brahman he thus sweeps away those already settled;—with a prayer (he does so), for the prayer is the Brahman: it is by the Brahman he thus sweeps away those already settled. He throws it (the branch) out towards the north[2].

6. He then scatters saline soil (over the hearth-site); for the Gârhapatya is this world, and salt means cattle: he thus bestows cattle on this world,—hence those cattle here in this world.

7. And again why he scatters saline soil. Pragâpati created creatures; he created them with different kinds of amnions: they did not agree together. He desired, 'May they agree together!' He made them to be of the same (kind of) amnion: hence even to this day, being of equal amnions, they agree together. And he who offers, offers thinking, 'May I be (born) with the same (kind of) amnion as the gods!' and when he scatters saline salt (in the hearth-site) he thereby becomes of equal amnion with the gods.

[1] For the identification of the Palâsa with the Brahman (sacred writ, or the holy spirit embodied therein), see part i, p. 90, note 1.

[2] 'He throws it upwards,' Delbrück, Synt. F. V, 79.

8. [He does so, with Vâg. S. XII, 46] 'Concord thou art!' for thereby they agreed together[1];—'fulfilment of desire;' for salt is cattle, and fulfilment of desire means cattle;—'In me may there be the fulfilment of thy desire!' that is, 'May there be on me cattle for thee!'—He covers with it the whole (circular) Gârhapatya; for the Gârhapatya altar is the womb, and the saline soil is the amnion: he thus covers the whole womb with the amnion.

9. He then scatters sand to keep (the saline soil, or amnion) from being scorched[2];—for sand is nothing else than the ashes of Agni Vaisvânara, and him, Agni Vaisvânara, he is indeed about to build up; and Agni does not scorch his own self.

10. And again why he scatters sand,—sand is nothing else than the seed of Agni Vaisvânara[3], and him, Agni Vaisvânara, he is about to build up; but nothing is fashioned from out of the seedless: 'May he (Agni) be fashioned from out of this seed!' so he thinks.

11. [He scatters it, with Vâg. S. XII, 46] 'Agni's ashes thou art! Agni's soil thou art!' for Agni's ashes are useless, and the sand is not useless: he thus makes it (the Gârhapatya hearth) to be useful. He covers with it the whole Gârhapatya; for the

---

[1] Sâyana, on Taitt. S. IV, 2, 4, takes 'samgñânam' in the sense of 'knowledge, recognition;' explaining it from the fact that cattle by their smell recognise the places of saline soil and lick them.

[2] Or, to keep (the fire) from burning over (or through the sand, and injuring the saline soil or amnion). For the construction, see p. 198, note 2.

[3] This notion is apparently based on the supposed etymological connection of 'sikatâ,' sand, with the root 'sik.'

Gârhapatya altar is the womb, and the sand is seed: he thus fills the whole womb with seed.

12. He then encloses it with enclosing-stones; for the enclosing-stones are the womb: he thus encloses the seed here cast in the womb; and hence the seed which is cast is enclosed in the womb.

13. And, again, why he encloses it with enclosing-stones;—the Gârhapatya hearth is this (terrestrial) world, and the enclosing-stones are the waters: he thus surrounds this world with water,—it is with the ocean that he thus surrounds it on all sides, and hence the ocean flows round this world on all sides. (He puts up the stones) by turning to the right (or south)[1], whence the ocean flows round this world (from the east) southwards;—by means of a dug out (hole, or moat)[2], whence the ocean flows round this world in a moat.

14. [Vâg. S. XII, 46] 'Ranging ye are!' for he does range them;—'ranging around ye are!' for he does range them all round;—'upwards ranging get ye fixed!' thus he says, placing them upright: hence the ocean surges upwards; but were he to place them sideways, the ocean surely would all at once overflow all this (earth). He does not settle them, for unsettled are the waters; nor does he pronounce the Sûdadohas (verse) on them[3].

---

[1] That is, from east to south, &c., following the course of the sun.

[2] ? That is, by digging in each stone, the circle consisting of altogether twenty-one stones.

[3] The two ceremonies here referred to, viz. the 'sâdana' (settling, setting, steadying, viz. by means of the formula, XII, 53, 'with the help of that deity lie thou steady, like Aṅgiras,' see VII, 1, 1, 30) and the muttering of the Sûdadohas verse (Vâg. S. XII, 55, for which

15. For the enclosing-stones are the bones, and the Sûdadohas is the breath; and there is no breath in the bones. With one and the same formula he lays down many bricks[1], for of one and the same form are the waters; and as to there being many enclosing-stones, it is because there are many waters.

16. The enclosing-stones, then, are the womb; the saline earth is the amnion, and the sand is the seed. The enclosing-stones are outside, and the saline earth is inside; for the womb is outside, and the amnion inside. The saline earth is outside, and the sand inside; for the amnion is outside, and the seed inside. He who is born is born from these: it is from them that he thus causes him (Agni) to be born.

17. Thereon he now builds it (the hearth): he

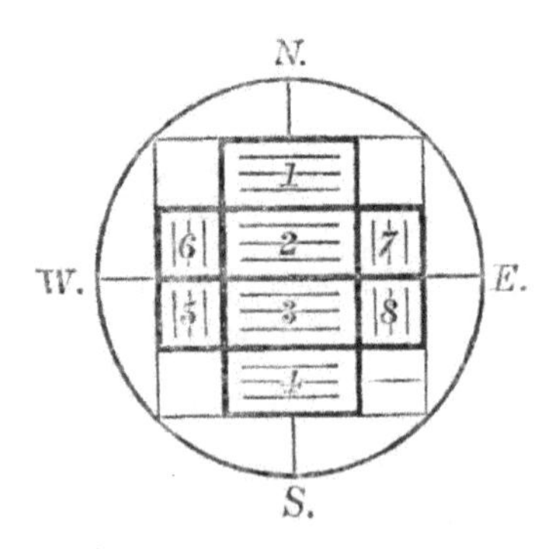

Gârhapatya Hearth.

thereby fashions that infused seed; and hence the infused seed is fashioned in the womb.

---

see note to paragraph 31), are the so-called 'necessary' rites, because they have as a rule to be performed on each (special) brick, when it has been laid down in building up the fire-altar.

[1] Viz. the so-called 'lokamprinâ' (or space-filling bricks), for which see p. 153, note.

18. He puts on (the circular site) four (bricks) running eastwards[1]; two behind running crosswise (from south to north), and two (such) in front. Now the four which he puts on running eastwards are the body; and as to there being four of these, it is because this body (of ours) consists of four parts[2]. The two at the back then are the thighs; and the two in front the arms; and where the body is that (includes) the head.

19. Now he here fashions him (Agni) with wings and tail; for whatlike the seed is fashioned in the womb suchlike (offspring) is born: thus inasmuch as he now fashions him with wings and tail, he is born hereafter[3] with wings and tail.

20. While being indeed furnished with wings and tail, people do not see him as one having wings and tail[4]: hence one does not see the child in the womb in its proper shape; but hereafter they (will) see him as one having wings and tail, and hence one sees the child after it is born in its proper shape.

21. Four (bricks) he puts on first, for of him that

---

[1] That is, with the lines by which they are marked running from west to east. Whilst these four bricks are oblong ones, measuring two feet by one, the four placed at the back and in front of them measure each a foot square, as do also those placed in the corners of the square pile, except the south-east corner, where two bricks are to be placed measuring one foot by half a foot each.

[2] See VI, 1, 1, 3-6.

[3] Or 'yonder,' that is, as the great fire-altar, soon to be built, which is ultimately to receive the Âhavanîya fire, taken from the Gârhapatya.

[4] While in the form of the Gârhapatya the wings and tail are not represented at all, these appendages form an important part of the great altar of the Âhavanîya fire. In the Gârhapatya hearth, Agni would seem represented rather as a man lying on his back with the head towards the east.

is being produced it is the body (trunk) that is produced first. Sitting south (of the hearth-site) with his face to the north he puts on first one (brick) of the upper (north) part[1] (of the trunk); and in this manner that Agni of his comes to be built up towards (or for the Sacrificer) himself.

22. [He puts it on, with Vâg. S. XII, 47; *Ri*k S. III, 22, 1, &c.] 'This is the Agni wherein Indra taketh the Soma-juice,' for the Gârhapatya hearth is this (terrestrial) world, and the Soma-juice is the waters: Indra thus took up the waters in this world;—'into his belly, craving it,'—for the belly is the centre;—'thousandfold strength, like a swift racer,'—the thousandfold strength, doubtless, is the waters,—'thou, having gained, art exalted, O knower of beings!' that is, 'thou, being built, art built[2], O knower of beings!'

23. [The second brick, with Vâg. S. XII, 48] 'O Agni, what splendour is thine in the heaven,'—his splendour in the heaven doubtless is the sun;—'on earth,' that on earth is this fire;—'and that which is in the plants, in the waters, O holy one!' he thereby means the fire that is both in the plants, and in the waters;—'wherewith thou hast overspread the wide air,'—that is, the wind;—'brilliant is that light, surging, man-viewing;' that is, 'great is that light, surging, man-viewing.'

24. [The third, with Vâg. S. XII, 49] 'O Agni,

[1] In laying down the bricks he again follows the course of the sun, that is, he lays down the four large or central ones from north to south, then the two back ones from south to north, and finally the two front ones from north to south.

[2] ?That is, Thou, being built (as the Gârhapatya), art built (once more as the Âhavanîya).

thou goest up to the flood of the heaven;' the flood of that heaven doubtless is the waters (of the atmosphere): to them he goes by his smoke; —'hither callest thou the divine inspirers,'— the divine inspirers doubtless are the vital airs, for these inspire all thoughts;—'the waters approach (thee), they that are beyond the luminous sphere of the sun, and they that are below here;'—the luminous sphere doubtless is that world yonder where that (sun) is burning: he thereby means both the waters which are beyond, and those which are below that (sun).

25. [The fourth one, with Vâg. S. XII, 50] 'The Agnis Purîshyas,'—that is, the Agnis favourable to cattle;—'together with those of the streams (prâvana);' this is a form of starting[1] (prâyana), for the Gârhapatya is indeed a starting of the fire;— 'may they, benevolent, accept the sacrifice, the copious, salutary draughts!' that is, 'may they benevolently accept the sacrifice, the copious, innocuous draughts!'

26. He puts them down separately: what different desires there are, those he thereby lays into the self. He 'settles' them once: he thereby makes the self one. He pronounces the Sûdadohas[2] verse on them; for the Sûdadohas is the vital air: by means of the vital air he thus makes him (Agni) continuous, joins him together.

27. Thereupon going round behind, he sits down on the north side with his face to the south, and puts on first the southern one of the two behind,

[1] Viz. inasmuch as 'prâvana' begins with the preposition 'pra,' forward, Sây.

[2] See p. 307, note 2.

with (Vâg. S. XII, 51), 'Potent nourishment, O Agni, the possession of kine,'—nourishment means cattle: he thus invokes for him the blessing of cattle;—'Grant thou perpetually unto him that calleth!'—he that calls doubtless is the Sacrificer;—'May there be to us a son, the perpetuator of the race,'—a son means offspring;—'let that, O Agni, be thy good-will unto us!' he therewith invokes a blessing.

28. Then the northern one, with (Vâg. S. XII, 52; *Ri*k S. III, 29, 10), 'This is thy natural womb, whence born thou shonest forth,'—that is, 'this (householder's hearth) is thy primeval, perennial womb (birth-place), whence born thou wert enkindled;'—'knowing it, ascend, O Agni, and increase our substance!' as the text, so its meaning.

29. These two are his (Agni's) thighs,—separately he puts them on, separately he 'settles' them, separately he pronounces the Sûdadohas verse upon them, for separate are these two thighs. There are two of them, for there are two thighs. Behind he puts them on, for behind are those thighs. At their upper ends they are joined (to the central ones [1]), for so are these thighs joined (to the body) at their upper ends.

30. Thereupon, going round again by the same way, he sits down on the south side, with his face to the north, and puts on first the northern one of the two (bricks) in front, with (Vâg. S. XII, 53),

[1] They are joined to each other, according to Sâya*n*a, but this can hardly be the meaning intended, as the stones lie close to each other also at the lower (western) end.

'Ranging thou art: by that deity, Aṅgiras-like, lie thou steady[1]!' Then the southern one, with, 'Ranging round thou art: by that deity, Aṅgiras-like, lie thou steady[1]!'

31. These two are his (Agni's) arms,—separately he puts them on, separately he 'settles' them, separately he pronounces the Sûdadohas[2] verse on them; for separate are these two arms. There are two of them, for there are two arms. He puts them on in the forepart, for these arms are here in front. At their upper ends they are joined (to the central ones), for so are these two arms joined (to the body) at the upper ends. Those two (arms) he puts on thus (from north to south), and those two (thighs) thus (from south to north): that is (from east to) southward[3], for thus it is with the gods[4].

32. Eight bricks he puts on (the hearth-site),—the Gâyatrî consists of eight syllables, and Agni is Gâyatra[5]: as great as Agni is, as great as is his measure, so great he thus builds him. Five times he 'settles' (the bricks)—the fire-altar consists of five layers; five seasons are a year, and Agni is the year: as great as Agni is, as great as is his measure,

[1] This common portion of the two formulas forms the so-called 'settling' (or 'setting') formula (sâdana); Kâty. Sr. XVI, 7, 14; cf. VI, 1, 2, 28, and p. 301, note 3. 'Aṅgiras-like' apparently means, 'as (thou didst) in the case of, or with, Aṅgiras.'

[2] Vâg. S. XII, 55; *Ri*k S. VIII. 69, 3. 'At his birth the well-like milking, speckled ones mix the Soma (draught), the clans of the gods in the three spheres of the heavens.' This difficult verse has been differently translated by different translators. The Brâhma*n*a itself also gives a very different, doubtless quite fanciful, interpretation of it at VIII, 7, 3, 21.

[3] That is, in accordance with the course of the sun.

[4] Or, 'thus (it goes,—or, Agni, as a bird, flies) to the gods.'

[5] See VI, 1, 1, 15.

so great he thus builds him. Eight bricks he 'settles' five times, that makes thirteen,—thirteen months are a year, and there are thirteen layers of earth in the fire-altar: as great as Agni is, as great as is his measure, so great does this become.

33. He then puts on a space-filling one: the significance of that one (will be explained) further on [1]. Three there are in front [2],—threefold is Agni: as great as Agni is, as great as is his measure, so great he thus builds him;—and ten those that follow [3],—the significance of these (will be explained) further on. Or first two, then ten, and then one, for in this way they build up the pile,—these amount to thirteen: the significance of this has been told.

34. Both these kinds (of bricks) amount to twenty-one;—there are twelve months, five seasons, these three worlds, and yonder sun as the twenty-first: that sun he thus establishes in this fire-altar.

35. Moreover, there are twenty-one enclosing-stones,—twelve months, five seasons, these three worlds, and that Agni from yonder (sun) [4] as the twenty-first: this Agni he thus establishes in yonder sun. And inasmuch as he puts on those (bricks) in this way, he thereby establishes those two (the sun and the fire) in each other, and (accordingly) those two are established in each other; for both of them he now makes out to be the twenty-first, and both

[1] VIII, 7, 2, 1 seq.

[2] Viz. one in the north-east, and two (of half the size) in the south-east corner.

[3] Viz. one in the south-west, and one in the north-west corner; and further, eight more filling up the four segments of the circle. See the outline of the Gârhapatya altar at p. 302.

[4] Or, perhaps that Agni on yonder sky (or fire-altar?). In any case it is the sun that is referred to.

of them are then here[1], as the Âhavanîya and the Gârhapatya.

36. He then throws thereon a layer of earth,—the significance of this (will be told) further on[2]. He takes it from the edge of the pit (*K*âtvâla); for the *K*âtvâla is the same as Agni[3], and in this way does that which is of Agni's nature become his. It (the Gârhapatya altar) should be even with the mouth (of the fire-pan): the significance of this has been told[4].

37. It (the Gârhapatya hearth) measures a fathom (in diameter[5]), for man is a fathom high, and man is Pragâpati (the lord of generation), and Pragâpati is Agni: he thus makes the womb of equal size to his (Agni's) body. It is circular, for the womb is circular; and moreover the Gârhapatya is this (terrestrial) world, and this world doubtless is circular.

---

[1] That is to say, they will be here after the completion of the two altars,—the Gârhapatya fire being the Agni proper, and the Âhavanîya fire the sun.

[2] For this, and the formula (Vâg. S. XII, 56) used therewith, see VIII, 7, 3, 1 seq.

[3] See part ii, p. 116, note 3. 'The earth taken from the pit being used for constructing the high altar, both are of the same size or cubic extent.'

[4] See VI, 3, 3, 26.

[5] Or rather, it is a circle corresponding in area to a square of one fathom; which gives a diameter somewhat exceeding in length a fathom (that is, the space between the tips of the middle fingers when the arms are extended). The measurement is (at least theoretically) a relative one, being adapted to the Sacrificer's size; but practically the fathom (vyâma, or purusha, man) may be taken to be of about 6 feet, the vyâma being equal to 4 aratnis (cubits) of 2 prâdesas (spans of some 18 inches each). This allows for a central square of 4 feet, and about 1 foot (in reality somewhat less) for each of the two bisectors of the segments.

38. He then pours those two (fires) together[1],—he thereby establishes concord between them—with (Vâg. S. XII, 57–60), 'Unite ye two, and get ye on together, loving, radiant, well-disposed, dwelling together for food and drink!—Together have I brought your minds, together your rites, together your thoughts: O Agni Purishya[2], be thou the overlord, and bestow thou food and drink upon our Sacrificer!—O Agni, thou art the Purishya, wealthy, prosperous: having made happy all the regions, seat thee here in thine own seat!—Be ye two unto us of one mind, of one thought, without guile! Injure ye not the sacrifice, nor the lord of the sacrifice, and be ye propitious unto us this day, ye knowers of beings!' He therewith pacifies them for (mutual) safety, so that they shall do no injury to one another.

39. With four (verses) he pours them together,—he thereby establishes concord between them by whatever four-footed cattle there are; and cattle being food, it is by means of food that he establishes concord between them.

40. Let him not look at that (pan) while empty: 'I must not look at the empty one!' so he thinks. Were he to look at the empty (pan), it would certainly devour him.

41. He then pours sand into it[3], for sand (sikatâ) is

---

[1] That is, he pours the fire of the pan (ukhyâgni) on the Gârhapatya (hearth).

[2] 'Purîshya' seems here to have the sense of 'rich, plentiful.' See p. 201, note.

[3] 'Ukhâ,' the pan, is feminine, and represents the womb from which Agni is born.

the seed of Agni Vaisvânara: he thus pours (sic) Agni Vaisvânara as seed into it. It should be even with the brim: the significance of this has been explained.

42. He then unlooses it, to keep it from chafing; for if that which is yoked is not unloosed it is chafed. Now when yoked there, it (the fire-pan) bore this Agni within it as seed, and him it has now brought forth. It now conceives a second time; for the 'Ukhâ' is a female, and hence when a female has brought forth the seed the first time, it conceives a second time.

43. [He unlooses it from the netting, with Vâg. S. XII, 61] 'Even as a mother her son, so hath the Earth borne Agni Purîshya,'—that is, Agni, favourable to cattle;—'she, the Ukhâ, in her own womb;' that is, the Ukhâ has borne Agni in her own womb;—'May Pragâpati, the all-former, release her, in concert with the All-gods, the seasons!' the All-gods doubtless are the seasons: thus Pragâpati, the all-former, releases it, in concert with the All-gods, the seasons. He deposits it north of the fire, at a cubit's distance: the significance of this has been explained [1].

44. He then pours milk into it,—it first receives seed, and now it receives milk; for the fire-pan is a female: hence when a female receives seed, then it receives milk. The sand is below, and the milk above, for the seed is below, and the milk above. He pours it into the middle, so that thereon he may place the human head [2].

---

[1] VI, 3, 1, 30.

[2] See VII, 5, 2, 14.

Second Brâhmana.

1. Pragâpati produced creatures. Having produced creatures, and run the whole race, he became relaxed[1]. From him, when relaxed, the vital air went out from within: then his vigour went out of him. That having gone out, he fell down. From him, thus fallen, food flowed forth: it was from that eye on which he lay that his food flowed. And, verily, there was then no firm foundation whatever here.

2. The gods spake, 'Verily, there is no other foundation than this: let us restore even him, our father Pragâpati; he shall be our foundation.'

3. They said unto Agni, 'Verily, there is no foundation other than this: in thee we will restore this our father Pragâpati; he shall be our foundation.'—'What will then be my reward?' said he.

4. They spake, 'This Pragâpati is food: with thee for our mouth we will eat that food, and he (Pragâpati) shall be the food of us, having thee for our mouth.' He said, 'So be it!' Therefore the gods eat food with Agni as their mouth; for to whatsoever deity men offer, it is into Agni that they offer, since it is with Agni for their mouth that the gods thus took in the food.

5. Now the vital air which went out from within him is no other than the wind that blows yonder; and the vigour which went out of him is yonder sun; and the food which flowed from him is all the food which there is within the year.

6. The gods heated him in the fire; and when the

[1] Literally, fallen asunder, i.e. broken to pieces, or disjointed ('opened,' Delbrück, Synt. F. V, p. 385).

fire rose over him thus heated, that same vital air which had gone out from within him came back to him, and they put it into him; and the vigour which had gone out of him they put into him; and the food which had flowed from him they put into him. Having made him up entire and complete, they raised him (so as to stand) upright; and inasmuch as they thus raised him upright he is these worlds.

7. This (terrestrial) world truly is his foundation; and what fire there is in this world that is his (Pragâpati's) downward vital air. And the air is his body, and what wind there is in the air, that is that vital air of his in the body. And the sky is his head; the sun and the moon are his eyes. The eye on which he lay is the moon: whence that one is much closed up, for the food flowed therefrom.

8. Now that same foundation which the gods thus restored is the foundation here even to this day, and will be so even hereafter.

9. And the Pragâpati who became relaxed is this same Agni who is now being built up. And when that fire-pan lies there empty before being heated, it is just like Pragâpati, as he lay there with the vital air and the vigour gone out of him, and the food having flowed out.

10. He heats it on the fire, even as the gods then heated him (Pragâpati). And when the fire rises over it thus heated, then that same vital air which went out from within him comes back to him, and he puts it into him. And when, putting on the gold plate, he wears it, he puts into him that very vigour which had gone out of him. And when he puts on kindling-sticks, he puts into him that very food which had flowed from him.

11. He puts them on in the evening and morning, for the food both of the day and the night was flowing out. These same (ceremonies) should be (performed) during a whole year, for that Pragâpati whence those (substances) went out is the year: into that whole (Pragâpati) he thus puts all that (which belongs to him). And in whatever part of this (year) he should therefore[1] not do so, into that part of him (Pragâpati) he would not put that (which belongs therein). 'One must not even be a looker-on at the (building up of a fire) not carried about for a year,' Vâmakakshâyana was wont to say, 'lest he should see this our father Pragâpati being torn to pieces[2].' He restores him so as to be whole and complete, and raises him to stand upright, even as the gods then raised him.

12. This (terrestrial) world in truth is his (Pragâpati's) Gârhapatya (hearth); and what fire there is in this world that to him is the fire on the Gârhapatya. And what space there is between the Âhavanîya and the Gârhapatya, that is the air[3]; and that wind in

[1] Or, in whatever part of this (year) from henceforward he should not do so.

[2] It is very doubtful whether this second clause of the oratio directa is really meant to belong to Vâmakakshâyana's argument, or whether it is the author's own, in which case it has to be taken with what follows. 'Lest he should . . . pieces, he (first) restores him,' &c. That is, he is not to place him (Pragâpati) in an upright position, until he has been completely restored. The particular form of the participle qualifying Pragâpati (vikhidyamâna) might seem to favour the former alternative; see, however, paragraph 23, antayoh samskriyamânayor, 'after the two ends have been perfected.'

[3] In this and the following paragraphs the ordinary position of subject and predicate seems often reversed: in the present case one would expect—that air is to him the space between the two fires.

the air is for him the fire on the Âgnîdhrîya. The sky is his Âhavanîya (hearth), and those two, the sun and the moon, are the fire on the Âhavanîya. This then is indeed his own self[1].

13. The Âhavanîya truly is his head; and the fire which is on the Âhavanîya is that vital air of his in the head. And as to why it (the Âhavanîya) has wings and tail, it is because that vital air in the head has wings and tail[2];—the eye is its head, the right ear its right wing, the left ear its left wing, the vital air its central body[3], and the voice is the tail (and) the foundation (the feet): inasmuch as the vital airs subsist by eating food with speech (voice)[4], the voice is the tail, the foundation.

14. And what space there is between the Âhavanîya and Gârhapatya, that is the body (trunk); and the fire on the Âgnîdhriya is to him that vital air inside the body. The Gârhapatya is his foundation; and the fire on the Gârhapatya is his downward vital air.

15. Now some build it (the Gârhapatya) in three layers, saying, 'There are here three downward vital airs.' Let him not do so: they who do so do what is excessive,—one amounting to twenty-one, one amounting to the Anush*t*ubh, and one amounting to the B*ri*hatî; for this (altar) is of one single form—a

[1] Viz. the sacrificial ground thus becomes identical with the universe, i.e. with Pragâpati.

[2] That is, it is (like) a bird. The word 'prâ*n*a' might almost be rendered here by 'the living being.'

[3] In the text this is reversed, the head is the eye, the right wing the right ear, the left wing the left ear, the central body the vital air, which can scarcely be the construction intended by the author.

[4] Or, with the mouth. In VIII, 5, 4, 1; X, 5, 2, 15, 'vâ*k*' is identified with the tongue.

womb. And as to those downward vital airs, they are indeed a bringing forth, for even the urine and faeces he voids are 'brought forth.'

16. Now then the (mystic) correspondence,—twenty-one bricks, nine formulas [1], that makes thirty;—and the 'settling' and Sûdadohas verse, that makes thirty-two,—the anush/ubh verse consists of thirty-two syllables: this is an anush/ubh [2].

17. And, again, there are twenty-one enclosing-stones; the formula the twenty-second; the formula for the sweeping, the saline earth and its formula, the sand and its formula, the 'filling' (soil) and its formula; with four (formulas) he pours (the two fires) together; with a fifth he unties (the pan); then this (Nirriti) with three [3],—the anush/ubh verse consists of thirty-two syllables: this then is an anush/ubh.

18. Then there are these two formulas [4], and they are indeed an anush/ubh—the Anush/ubh is speech: thus what twofold form of speech there is, the divine and the human, loud and low, that is those two.

19. The Gârhapatya pile thus is those three

[1] Viz. XII, 47-54 (XII, 53, consisting of two formulas).

[2] That is to say, these thirty-two items form, as it were, an Anush/ubh verse consisting of thirty-two syllables.

[3] See VII, 2, 1, 1 seq.

[4] I do not see what other formulas can be intended here except those addressed to the enclosing stones, concluding with the 'sâdana,' or 'settling' formula, viz. Vâg. S. XII, 53; see above, VII, 1, 1, 30; though these do not exactly yield thirty-two syllables, but thirty-four (see, however, paragraph 22). Our available MSS. of the commentary are unfortunately defective at this place.—On the artificial manipulation of making up imaginary metres by the mere number of syllables, irrespective of their real prosodic value, see Professor Weber, Ind. Stud., VIII, p. 23 seq.

anush/ubh verses. And as to why they make up three anush/ubhs in this (Gârhapatya), it is because all these (three) worlds then come to be (contained) therein. From it they take one of the two (first) anush/ubhs of thirty-two syllables (to be) the Âhavanîya,—that Âhavanîya is that sky, that head (of Pragâpati). Then one of the two (anush/ubhs) is left here (to be) this Gârhapatya, this foundation, this very (terrestrial) world.

20. And as to those two formulas, they are that space between the Âhavanîya and the Gârhapatya, that air (-world), that body (of Pragâpati). And because there are two of them (making up one anush/ubh), therefore that space (and hearth) between the Âhavanîya and the Gârhapatya (viz. the Âgnîdhriya hearth [1]) is smaller; and therefore the air-world is the smallest of these worlds.

21. That same Anush/ubh, speech, is threefold. That fire, taking the form of the vital air, goes along with it (speech),—the fire which is on the Âhavanîya (altar) is the out-breathing, and yonder sun; and the fire which is on the Âgnîdhriya is the through-breathing, and the wind which blows yonder; and the fire which is on the Gârhapatya is the in-breathing, and what fire there is here in this (earth-) world. And verily he who knows this makes up for himself the whole Vâk (speech), the whole vital air, the whole body (of Pragâpati).

[1] Or, the Dhishnya hearths (see paragraph 23), which are more properly situated between the Gârhapatya and the Âhavanîya fire-places. See the plan of the sacrificial ground in part ii; where, however, the Âhavanîya of the Prâkînavamsa (hall), or the so-called sâlâdvârya (hall-door fire), would represent the Gârhapatya for the Âhavanîya of the Mahâvedi.

22. Then that Brihatî (metre),—the two (verses) of thirty-two syllables: that makes thirty-two; then those two formulas: that makes thirty-four; Agni the thirty-fifth;—a metre does not vanish by a syllable (too much or too little), neither by one nor by two[1];—moreover, that (Agni) consists of two syllables: that makes thirty-six. The Brihatî consists of thirty-six syllables,—it is the Brihatî that that (Âhavanîya) pile thus amounts to; for whatlike the seed which is infused into the womb, suchlike (offspring) is born therefrom: thus in that he makes up that Brihatî (metre) in this (Gârhapatya hearth), thereby that (Âhavanîya) fire-altar amounts to the Brihatî.

23. As to this they say, 'As the Gârhapatya is this (terrestrial) world, the Dhishnya hearths the air, and the Âhavanîya the sky, and the air-world is not separated from this (earth-) world, why then, after building the Gârhapatya, does he build the Âhavanîya, and (only) then the Dhishnyas?' Well, at first these two worlds (heaven and earth) were together; and when they parted asunder, the space which was between (antar) them became that air (antariksha); for 'îksha[2]' indeed it was theretofore, and 'Now this "îksha" has come between (antarâ),' they said, whence 'antariksha' (air). And as to why, after building the Gârhapatya, he builds the Âhavanîya, it is because these two worlds were created first. Then, going back, he throws up the Dhishnya hearths, just to prevent discontinuity of

[1] The same latitude in the computation of the number of syllables constituting a metre is conceded, Ait. Br. I, 6.

[2] ? That is, 'visible,' or, 'capable of being seen through.'

the sacred work; and thus indeed the middle is completed, after the two ends have been completed.

THE ALTAR OF NIRRITI.

Second Adhyâya. First Brâhmana.

1. They now take the Nirriti (bricks) from there. For, having built the Gârhapatya, the gods then ascended it,—the Gârhapatya being this (earth-) world, it is this world they ascended after completing it. They saw nothing but darkness not to be seen through.

2. They said, 'Think ye upon this, how we may dispel that darkness, evil!' They said, 'Meditate ye (ketay)!'—whereby indeed they said, 'Seek ye to build an altar (kitim)!'—'Seek ye so that we may dispel that darkness, evil!'

3. Whilst meditating, they saw those Nirriti bricks; they piled them up, and by them dispelled that darkness, evil; for Nirriti (corruption, or destruction) is evil; and inasmuch as by them they dispelled Nirriti, evil, these are Nirriti's (bricks).

4. Now that same thing which the gods did, is done here: even now that darkness, that evil, has indeed been dispelled by the gods themselves; but when he now does this, it is because he thinks, 'I must do what the gods did.' And, besides, he removes, by means of these (bricks), whatever evil, whatever corruption there is; and because he removes by them evil, corruption (nirriti), therefore these are Nirriti's (bricks).

5. And, again, why they take these (bricks) of Nirriti;—when the gods restored the relaxed Pragâpati, they cast him as seed into the fire-pan, the

womb; the fire-pan being indeed a womb. In the course of a year they prepared for him this foundation, even this (terrestrial) world: the Gárhapatya (hearth) being this world: therein they generated him. And whatever evil there was in him, whatever mucus, whatever inner and outer membrane, that they removed from him by means of these (bricks); and inasmuch as thereby they removed his evil, his corruption, these are Nirriti's (bricks).

6. In like manner the Sacrificer now casts his own self[1], as seed, into the fire-pan, the womb; the fire-pan being indeed a womb. In the course of a year he prepares for that (self of his) this foundation, even this (terrestrial) world; the Gârhapatya being this world: therein he generates it. And whatever evil there is of it, whatever mucus, whatever inner and outer membrane, that he removes therefrom by these (bricks); and inasmuch as he thereby removes its evil, its corruption, these are Nirriti's (bricks).

7. They measure a foot (square): he thus treads evil, corruption, under foot. They are unmarked; for whatever is not, that is unmarked (by characteristics): he thus makes evil, corruption to be non-existent. They get baked by (rice) husks, for husks belong to Nirriti: by Nirriti's own (objects) he thus performs Nirriti's rite. They are black, for black was that darkness; and black in truth is Nirriti (corruption).

8. With them they proceed towards that (southwestern) quarter, for that is Nirriti's quarter: he thus places Nirriti (corruption) in Nirriti's quarter.

[1] Or (Pragâpati's), Agni's self, or body.

And anywhere where there is a self-produced hollow[1] or cleft in the ground, he lays down those (bricks); for on whatever part of this (earth) there is a cleaving, or in whatever part of it plants are not produced, verily that part of it Nirriti seizes upon: he thus places corruption in a (part) of the earth set aside for Nirriti. Having put them in their places in a direction away from himself[2], he lays them down[3].

9. [He lays them down, with Vâg. S. XII, 62-64] 'Seek thou him that offereth not Soma, nor other offering!' him who neither presses Soma nor makes offering Nirriti indeed visits;—'Of the thief do thou follow the way, of the robber!' that is, 'follow the way both of the thief and the robber, and even as a thief or a robber remains concealed, so do thou remain concealed!'—'Seek thou some one other than us: this is thy way;' that is, 'seek him who is ignorant of this (sacred work);'—'Homage be to thee, O divine Nirriti!' he thus turns Nirriti aside by rendering homage to her.

10. 'Homage be unto thee full well, O sharp-edged Nirriti!' for Nirriti is indeed sharp-edged: to her he thereby renders homage;—'loose thou

[1] Or probably, a barren spot, see p. 43, note 2.

[2] That is, whilst himself remaining north of the place, and facing the south, he puts them down in the direction from north to south.

[3] That is, he performs the formal ceremony of 'laying down (upadhâna)' whilst muttering the respective verses. In the present case the 'laying down' of the bricks is to be performed by him whilst muttering the formulas, but without touching the bricks themselves. The direction that the bricks are to be deposited in a direction 'away from him' perhaps refers to the 'laying down' instead of to the actual placing them.

this iron bond!' for it is indeed with an iron bond that Nirriti binds him whom she binds;—'being of one mind with Yama and Yamî,'—Yama doubtless is Agni, and Yamî is this (earth), and by these two everything here is kept in check: thus, 'being of one mind with those two,'—'raise him unto the highest firmament!' the firmament is the heavenly world: thus, 'raise the Sacrificer up to the heavenly world!'

11. 'Thee, O awful (goddess), into whose mouth I offer—' Nirriti is indeed awful, and into her mouth he now offers when he performs this divine rite;—'for the unloosing of these bonds;' that is, of those bonds with which he has been bound;—'Thee whom people rejoice in calling Earth,'—the Earth is this (world), and he who exists, exists thereon,—'but I know thee to be Nirriti everywhere!' that is, in every respect I know that thou art Nirriti. Now Nirriti is this earth, and this earth makes him decay who becomes corrupted: in speaking thus, it is as if he were to say, 'Thou art So and So, the son of So and So, I know thee, do not injure me!' for in no wise does he who is known injure one when spoken to.

12. He does not touch (the bricks),—Nirriti being evil,—lest he put himself in contact with evil. He does not 'settle' them,—settlement being a firm footing—lest he give a firm footing to evil. He does not pronounce the Sûdadohas verse upon them,—the Sûdadohas being the vital air,—lest he should join Nirriti (corruption) together, and restore her.

13. Now some lay (the bricks) down from the farther end towards themselves,—Nirriti (corruption) being evil,—lest they themselves should go the way

to corruption. Let him not do so, but let him lay them down in the direction away from him: he thus drives evil, corruption, away from him.

14. Three bricks he lays down,—threefold is Agni: as great as Agni is, as great as is his measure, by so much he thus repels evil, corruption.

15. The seat, the netting, the sling of the gold plate, and the two pads he throws down on the farther side (of the bricks),—the sling[1] is sacred to Nirriti: from Nirriti's sling he is thus freed. [He throws them down, with Vâg. S. XII, 65] 'The indissoluble bond which the divine Nirriti hath fastened upon thy neck,'—indissoluble indeed for him who does not know this;—'that (bond) of thine I unloose, as from the middle of Âyus,'—Âyus[2] doubtless is Agni, and his middle (body) is that Gârhapatya which has been built;—not yet built is the Âhavanîya: hence whether a youth builds the altar, or an old man, he says 'as from the middle of Âyus;'—'now, being urged forward, eat thou this nourishment!' nourishment means food: thus, 'now, set free, eat thou this food.' With Trishtubh verses (he performs this rite), for the Trishtubh is a thunderbolt: it is thus with a thunderbolt that he repels evil, corruption.

16. There are three bricks, the seat, the netting, the sling of the gold plate, and the two pads; that makes eight;—the Gâyatrî consists of eight syllables,

[1] According to Sâyana the sling of the gold plate is here singled out, because the other objects have necessarily been damaged by the hot fire-pan and are consequently thrown away as a matter of course.

[2] See III, 4, 1, 22. In the formula 'âyus' may rather have to be taken in the sense of 'life,' or 'vital power.' Mahidhara takes 'na' in the sense of 'now (samprati),' instead of 'as.'

and Agni is Gâyatra: as great as Agni is, as great as is his measure, by so much he thus repels evil, corruption.

17. On the space between (the Sacrificer and the bricks) he pours out a jarful of water,—water is a thunderbolt: with a thunderbolt he thus separates from himself evil, corruption. With 'Homage to (the goddess of) Prosperity who hath done this!' they rise, for it was with a view to prosperity that the gods at first performed this rite, and to that (goddess) they then rendered homage; and for prosperity indeed this (Sacrificer) now performs this rite, and to that (goddess) he now renders homage. They go back (to the sacrificial ground) without looking back: they thus abandon evil, corruption, even without looking back to it.

18. Having returned, he stands worshipping by the fire; for when he goes into that (south-western) direction whilst Agni is only half built up, he does what is improper: he now makes amends to him to prevent his doing any harm.

19. And again, why he stands by (the fire). The Gârhapatya (hearth) is this (terrestrial) world; for the Gârhapatya is a foundation, and the foundation doubtless is this (earth). Now when he goes into that direction, he goes where there is no path; and when he stands by (the fire), he thereby returns to this (earth), the foundation, and establishes himself upon this foundation.

20. [He worships, with Vâg. S. XII, 66] 'The harbourer and gatherer of riches,' for a harbourer this world indeed is, a gatherer of riches;—'all form he watches over with his favours,'—that is, 'all forms (of being) he watches over with

his favours;'—'like the god Savitri, like Indra, he of true covenant stood at the meeting of ways[1];' as the text, so its meaning.

PREPARATION OF THE SITE OF THE GREAT (ÂHAVANÎYA) ALTAR.

SECOND BRÂHMANA.

1. He then prepares the Prâyanîya[2] (opening sacrifice). With the Havishkrit of that (oblation) he releases (the Sacrificer's) speech[3]. Having released his speech, he throws away the grass-bush (stambayagus[4]). Having thrown away the grass-bush, and drawn the first line of enclosure[5], and the lines (across the mahâ-vedi), he says, 'Throw thrice!' and the Âgnîdhra throws thrice (the wooden sword)[6].'

2. Having returned (to the offering, or hall-door

[1] Mahîdhara takes 'samare pathînâm' in the sense of 'in the battle of (i.e. with) the waylayers (paripanthibhih saha).'

[2] See part ii, p. 47 seq.

[3] Viz. by calling out three times 'Havishkrit, come hither,' whereby the Adhvaryu summons one of the priests, or maid-servants, to assist in preparing the material for offering. See part i, p. 27 seq.

[4] Part i, p. 55 seq.

[5] Part i, p. 59 seq.

[6] See part i, p. 55. It must, however, be borne in mind that the passage here referred to relates to the construction of the Vedi of an ordinary ishti, whilst in the present instance we have to do with a Mahâvedi, as prescribed for Soma-sacrifices (cf. part ii, p. 111 seq., where, however, only a few distinctive points are adverted to). The plan of the Mahâvedi, given at the end of part ii, shows at the eastern end a square mound, the so-called uttara-vedi, or higher, upper altar, on which the Âhavanîya, or offering, fire is maintained. On a similar earth mound, but raised in the centre of the square site (see VII, 3, 1, 27), the Agnikayana requires the erection of the large brick fire-altar, the preparation of the site of which is explained from the next paragraph.

fire) he proceeds with the opening sacrifice. Having performed the opening sacrifice, he yokes a plough. For the gods at that time, being about to heal him (Agni-Pragâpati), first supplied him with food, and in like manner does this (Sacrificer) now that he is about to heal him, first supply him with food. It (the food) is the plough (sîra), for 'sîra' is the same as 'sera[1]:' he thus puts food into him.

3. It is made of udumbara (ficus glomerata) wood,—the Udumbara tree being sustenance, life-sap: he thus supplies him with sustenance, with life-sap. The cordage of the plough consists of *muñga* grass, triply twisted: the significance of this has been explained.

4. Standing behind the right (southern) hip of Agni (the site of the fire-altar) he (the Prati-prasthâtri) addresses it (the plough) while being yoked (by the Adhvaryu) in front of the left (northern) shoulder, with (Vâg. S. XII, 67, 68; *Rik* S. X, 101, 4, 3), 'The skilful yoke[2] the ploughs, and stretch across the yokes,'—the skilful are those who know, and they do yoke the plough and stretch the yokes across;—'the wise, with mind devoted to the gods,'—devotion means sacrifice: thus, 'the wise, performing sacrifice to the gods.'

5. 'Yoke ye the ploughs, and stretch across the yokes!'—they indeed yoke the plough, and stretch the yokes across;—'into the ready womb here cast ye the seed!' it is for the seed that that womb, the furrow, is made; and if one casts

[1] That is 'sa + irâ,' with draught or food.

[2] Or rather, put (the oxen) to the ploughs. Professor Ludwig takes 'sîrâ' in the sense of 'straps, traces,'—the skilful fasten the traces.

(seed) into unploughed (ground), it is just as if one were to shed seed elsewhere than into the womb. 'And plentiful yield[1] be there through our song!'—the song is speech, and yield means food;—'and let the ripe crop go anigh the sickle!' for when food gets ripe, people approach it with the sickle. With two (verses) he yokes, a Gâyatrî and a Trish*t*ubh one: the significance of this has been explained.

6. He yokes the right (ox) first, then the left one: thus it is (done) with the gods, differently in human (practice). It is a team of six oxen, or one of twelve oxen, or one of twenty-four oxen: it is the year (he obtains) as the consummation.

7. He then ploughs through it,—ploughing means food; and the gods at that time when they were about to heal him (Agni-Pra*g*âpati) first put food into him; and in like manner does this (Sacrificer) now when he is about to heal him, first put food into him.

8. Only the body (of the altar-site) he ploughs through, not the wings and tail: he thus puts food into the body. And, indeed, the food which is put into the body benefits the body as well as the wings and tail; but that which (is put) into the wings and tail does not benefit either the body or the wings and tail.

9. On the right (south) side of the fire-altar, he ploughs first a furrow eastwards[2] inside the enclosing-stones, with (Vâ*g*. S. XII, 69; *Ri*k S. IV, 57, 8), 'Right luckily may the plough-shares plough up the ground, luckily the tillers ply with their

[1] Or, concession (Erhörung).

[2] That is, from the right thigh to the right shoulder (south-west to south-east).

oxen!'—'luckily—luckily,' he says, 'for what is successful that is lucky:' he thus makes it (the furrow) successful.

10. Then on the hindpart (he ploughs a furrow) northwards[1], with (Vâg. S. XII, 70), 'With sweet ghee let the furrow be saturated,'—as the text so its meaning;—'approved of by the All-gods, by the Maruts!' for both the All-gods and the Maruts have power over the rain;—'sapful, and teeming with milk,'—milk means life-sap: thus, 'teeming with life-sap and food;'—'with milk, O furrow, turn thou unto us!' that is, 'with life-sap, O furrow, turn thou unto us!'

11. Then on the left (north) side (he ploughs a furrow) eastwards[2], with (Vâg. S. XII, 71), 'The share-shod[3] plough,'—that is, 'the plough abounding in wealth,'—'propitious, offering prospect for the Soma-cup[4]'—for Soma is food;—'it throweth up the cow, the sheep, the lusty wife, the swift-

[1] That is, from the right thigh to the left thigh (south-west to north-west). Whilst the first furrow was ploughed from the south-west to the south-east corner, the present and two following furrows are ploughed 'sunwise' from south-west to north-west, north-west to north-east, and north-east to south-east respectively. We are not told in what manner the plough is to be got back from the south-east to the south-west corner after the ploughing of the first furrow, whether it is to be carried there, or to be pulled back outside the enclosed square.

[2] That is, from the left thigh to the left shoulder (north-west to north-east).

[3] Or, the metal-shod. The author's reason for interpreting 'pavîravat' by 'rayimat' is not clear.

[4] According to the St. Petersburg dictionary, 'somapitsaru' is probably a corrupt form, like the various readings 'somasatsaru' (Ath. S. III, 17, 3) and 'sumatitsaru' (Taitt. S. IV, 2, 5, 6 = 'moving up and down,' Sâyana). Cf. Vâsishtha Dharmasâstra (Bühler's translation, Sacred Books of the East, vol. xiv, p. 13), where 'soma-

wheeled waggon,' for all this the furrow throws up (yields).

12. Then on the forepart (he ploughs a furrow) southwards[1], with (Vâg. S. XII, 72), 'Milk out, O cow of plenty, their desire to Mitra, and to Varu*n*a, to Indra, to the Asvins, to Pûshan, to creatures and plants!' husbandry is (beneficial) to all deities: thus, 'Milk out for these deities all their desires!'—He first ploughs thus (south-west to south-east), then thus (south-west to north-west), then thus (north-west to north-east), then thus (north-east to south-east): that is (sunwise), for thus it is with the gods[2].

13. Four furrows he ploughs with prayer: he thereby puts into him (Pragâpati-Agni) what food there is in the four quarters; and that with prayer,—true is the prayer, and true (manifest) are those quarters.

---

pitsaru' is explained in the text as meaning 'provided with a handle (tsaru) for the Soma-drinker' (somapi). Also Indische Studien, XVII, p. 259, where Professor Weber proposes to divide the word 'somasatsaru' into 'soma(n),' with thongs, and 'sa-tsaru,' with handle. If 'somapi-tsaru' really represent the constituent elements, 'tsaru,' handle, may indeed be intended as having special reference to the handle of the Soma-cup (*k*amasa); though 'somapi' could only be taken in the sense of 'Soma-drinker,' and not in that of 'Soma-cup,' optionally suggested by Mahîdhara.

[1] That is, from the left to the right shoulder (north-east to south-east).

[2] Or, perhaps, thus it goes to the gods; this tends godward. Whilst the last three furrows are indeed ploughed 'sunwise' (east to south, &c.), the first furrow was ploughed in the opposite direction (south-west to south-east). The reason for this is that the whole performance is to take place in an easterly direction, so as to tend towards the gods. Were he to start at the south-east corner, and then plough right round, he would be moving away from the gods, who are supposed to reside in the east.

14. He then ploughs (again) through the body: he thereby puts into him what food there is in the year. Silently (he does so), for what is silent is undetermined, and the undetermined is everything: by means of everything he thus puts food into him. He first ploughs thus (through the middle from south to north), then thus (south-west to north-east), then thus (east to west), then thus (north-west to south-east),—that is sunwise[1], for thus it is with the gods.

15. Three furrows he ploughs each time,—threefold is Agni: as great as Agni is, as great as is his measure, with so much he thus puts food into him.

16. Twelve furrows he ploughs silently,—the year (consists of) twelve months, and the year is Agni: as great as Agni is, as great as is his measure, by so much he thus puts food into him.

17. Both kinds (of furrows) amount to sixteen,—of sixteen parts Pragâpati consists, and Pragâpati is Agni: he thus puts into him food proportionate to his body. And, indeed, the food which is proportionate to the body, satisfies, and does no harm; but that which is too much, does harm, and that which is too little, does not satisfy.

[1] Here, again, the sunwise motion of the plough only applies to the three last furrows (or sets of furrows), which always move from left to right,—south-west to north-east, east to west, north-west to south-east. The first set of furrows—drawn from south to north, or along the 'cross-spine' (as distinguished from the real, or easterly spine running from west to east)—are apparently drawn in this way, in order to avoid the southerly direction, as that would imply speedy death to the Sacrificer,—his going to the Fathers, or deceased ancestors, who are supposed to reside in the south. In drawing the furrows in the way they do, the priests not only avoid that region, but at the very outset move away from it, and thereby assure long life to the Sacrificer.

18. And, again, why he ploughs through him,—the gods being about to put him (Pragâpati) together, thereby in the first place put the vital airs into him; and in like manner does this (Sacrificer), being about to put him together, thereby in the first place put the vital airs into him. They (the furrows) are lines, for these vital airs (move) in lines (channels).

19. Four furrows he ploughs with prayer: he thereby puts into him those four well-defined vital airs which are in the head; and this (he does) with prayer,—true is the prayer, and true (manifest, real) are these vital airs in the head.

20. And as to why he ploughs through the body: he thereby puts into him those vital airs which are inside the body. Silently (he does so), for who knows how many vital airs there are inside the body?

21. Having gained the object for which he yokes those (oxen), he now unyokes them, with (Vâg. S. XII, 73), 'Be ye unyoked, ye inviolable (oxen)!' for inviolable[1] they indeed are with the gods;—'Ye godward-striding!' for with them he performs the divine work;—'We have come to the end of this gloom;'—gloom doubtless means famine: thus, 'we have come to the end of this famine;'—'we have attained the light!' for he who attains the gods, the sacrifice, indeed attains the light. He then lets them loose towards north-east—the significance of this has been explained[2]. He gives them to the Adhvaryu, for it is he that does the work with them: let him assign them (to him) at the time of (the presentation of) the Dakshinâs.

[1] See part ii, p. 216, note 2, where 'aghnyâ' was used of cows.

[2] See VI, 4, 4, 22. The plough is put aside on the utkara (heap of rubbish).

THIRD BRÂHMANA.

1. He then places a bunch of darbha (kusa) grass (poa cynosuroides) on (the middle of the altar-site); for the gods then placed plants thereon, and in like manner does the Sacrificer now place plants thereon.

2. And, again, why he places a bunch of grass thereon;—when he (Agni) is built up, he is born, and he is born here for all (kinds of) food; but these darbha plants (contain) both kinds of food, for they are both water and plants. Now the waters which, loathing V*ri*tra, rose up on the dry land forming bushes, became those grasses[1],—inasmuch as they rose forming bushes (d*ri*bh), they are (called) darbha-grasses. These darbha-grasses, then, are the water (which remained) pure, and meet for sacrifice, when V*ri*tra flowed towards it; and inasmuch as they are darbha-grasses, they are plants: by both kinds of food he thus gratifies him (Agni).

3. [He places it] at the meeting of the furrows, for the meeting of furrows is speech (the mouth)[2], and the furrows (channels) are the vital airs; and this is their place of meeting; and in the mouth food is put for the vital airs. In the middle (he places the bunch), whereby he puts it into the very

[1] The author here alludes to the legend given at I, 1, 3, 4-5,—V*ri*tra lay enveloping all that space which extends between heaven and earth, and because he lay enveloping (v*ri*) all that, he is called V*ri*tra. Him Indra slew. Being slain, he flowed stinking in all directions towards the water; for in every direction lies the ocean. Now some of the water loathed him, it rose higher and higher and flowed over: hence (sprang) these kusa grasses,—they are indeed the water which was not putrified; but with the other water some (matter) has indeed become mixed when the putrid V*ri*tra flowed into it.

[2] See p. 200, note 3.

middle of him; silently (he does so), for what is silent is undefined, and the undefined is everything: with everything he thus puts food into him.

4. He then offers thereon,—when he (Agni) is built, he is born, and he is born here for all (kinds of) food; but that ghee is the life-sap (essence) of this universe, for it is the life-sap of both the waters and plants: he thus gratifies him by the life-sap of this universe. And as far as the life-sap extends, so far extends the body: he thus gratifies him by this universe. With (ghee) taken in five (ladlings, he offers),—the fire-altar consists of five layers, five seasons are a year, and the year is Agni: as great as Agni is, as great as is his measure, with so much food he thus gratifies him.

5. And, again, why he offers thereon;—when in the beginning the *Ri*shis, the vital airs[1], put together this Agni, they gained for themselves that fore-share[2] in him: hence they are the fore-sharers. Thus when he offers on (the grass-bush) he thereby gratifies those *Ri*shis, the vital airs, who gained for themselves the fore-share in him (Agni). With fivefold-taken ghee (he offers): the significance of this has been explained.

6. And, again, why he offers thereon;—whatever forms, whatever modes of chanting, whatever p*ri*sh*th*a (stotras), whatever metres he is now going to bestow on Agni, for them he prepares this fore-share, and it is them he thereby gratifies. With

---

[1] See VI, 1, 1, 1.

[2] Literally, a share in front, in the first place, i.e. a preferential share, or fore-taste. Being accented separately, 'purastât' here, however, forms no compound with 'bhâga;' though it does in 'purastâdbhâga,' fore-sharer. Cf. Taitt. S. V, 6, 4, 2.

fivefold-taken ghee (he offers): the significance of this has been explained.

7. And, again, why he offers thereon;—at that time the gods were afraid, thinking, 'Long indeed is this performance: we hope the Rakshas, the fiends, will not smite here this (Agni) of ours!' They saw this preliminary conclusion[1] of this performance, and brought that whole (Agni) to completion even at that (point), and built him up then; and in like manner this (Sacrificer) brings that whole (Agni) to completion even at this (point), and builds him now.

8. [Vâg. S. XII, 74] 'The year,' this is a layer (of bricks);—'together with the dark half-months,' this is a layer of earth;—'the Dawn,' this is a layer (of bricks);—'together with the ruddy (cows),' this is a layer of earth;—'the two Asvins,' this is a layer (of bricks); 'together with their wonderful deeds,' this is a layer of earth;—'the Sun,' this is a layer (of bricks);—'together with the dappled horse,' this is a layer of earth;—'(Agni) Vaisvânara,' this is a layer (of bricks);—'together with Idâ,' this is a layer of earth;—'with ghee,' this is a layer (of bricks);—'Svâ-,' this is a layer of earth;—'hâ!' this is a layer (of bricks).

9. There are thirteen utterings,—thirteen months are a year; thirteen in number are the layers of bricks and earth of the fire-altar: as great as Agni is, as great as is his measure, so great he thus builds him up. With butter he sacrifices,—butter is the

[1] Literally, a conclusion previously, or at the beginning of the performance.

same as Agni: it is Agni he thus builds up. With fivefold-taken (butter he offers),—the altar consists of five layers,—five seasons are a year, and the year is Agni: as great as Agni is, as great as is his measure, so great he thus builds him up. He offers raising (the spoon) upwards: he thus builds Agni upwards by means of the layers (of the altar).

Fourth Brâhma*n*a.

1. He then pours out jarfuls of water,—for the gods then said, 'Meditate ye (*k*etay)!' whereby they doubtless meant to say, 'Seek ye a layer (*k*itim)!' Whilst meditating they saw the rain to be a (suitable) layer, and put it on that (altar-site); and in like manner does this (Sacrificer) now put it thereon.

2. Jarfuls of water are (poured out); for rain is water: it is rain he thereby bestows on it. With an udumbara jar (he pours them on): the significance of this has been told;—with a four-cornered one;—four quarters there are: from all quarters he thus bestows rain thereon.

3. Three jarfuls he pours out each time [1],—threefold is Agni: as great as Agni is, as great as is his measure, with so much he thus bestows rain thereon.

4. Twelve jarfuls of water he pours on the ploughed ground,—twelve months are a year, and the year is Agni: as great as Agni is, as great as is his measure, by so much he thus bestows rain thereon.

---

[1] On every four of the sixteen furrows, in the order in which they have been ploughed, he is to empty three jarfuls of water, making altogether twelve jars of water.

5. On the ploughed ground he pours (water), whence it rains for (the benefit of) the ploughed land. Now were he only to pour it on the ploughed ground, and not on the unploughed, it would only rain for the ploughed land, not for the unploughed. And were he only to pour it on the unploughed ground, and not on the ploughed, it would only rain for the unploughed land, and not for the ploughed. He pours it both on the ploughed, and the unploughed, ground; whence it rains both for the ploughed, and the unploughed, ground.

6. Three (jarfuls)[1] he pours both on the ploughed, and on the unploughed, ground;—threefold is Agni: as great as Agni is, as great as is his measure, with so much he thus bestows rain thereon.

7. And, again, why he pours out jarfuls of water;—at that time the gods, being about to put him (Agni-Pragâpati) together, in the first place put water into him; and in like manner does this one now, being about to put him together, in the first place put water into him.

8. Three jarfuls he pours out each time,—threefold is Agni: as large as Agni is, as large as is his measure, by so much he thus puts water into him.

9. Twelve jarfuls he pours on the ploughed ground,—twelve months are a year, and the year is Agni: as great as Agni is, as great as is his measure, by so much he thus puts water into him.

10. On the ploughed ground he pours it: he thereby puts water into the vital airs. But were he to pour (water) only on the ploughed ground, and

[1] These are additional three jarfuls poured over the whole Agnikshetra, or site of the altar.

not on the unploughed, there would be water only in (the channels of) the vital airs, and not in the other (parts of the) body. And were he to pour (water) only on the unploughed ground, and not on the ploughed, there would be water only in (the other parts of) the body, and not in the vital airs. He pours it both on the ploughed, and the unploughed, ground, whence there is water here both in (the channels of) the vital airs and in the body.

11. Three (jarfuls) he pours both on the ploughed, and on the unploughed, ground;—threefold is Agni: as great as Agni is, as great as is his measure, with so much he thus puts water into him.

12. Fifteen jarfuls of water he pours out,—fifteenfold is the thunderbolt: by that fifteenfold thunderbolt of his he thus drives away all evil.

13. He then sows all (kinds of) herb (-seed);—for the gods then said, 'Meditate ye!' whereby doubtless they meant to say, 'Seek ye a layer!' whilst meditating, they saw food to be a (suitable) layer, and put that on (or, into) him (Agni); and in like manner does this one now put it into him.

14. It is (seed) of all herbs,—all herbs means all food; he thus puts all (kinds of) food into him. Let him omit one of those kinds of food, and not eat thereof as long as he lives. By means of the udumbara jar (he sows the seed): the significance of this has been explained;—with a four-cornered one,—there are four quarters: from all quarters he thus puts food into him (Agni). He sows it with anush/ubh (verses),—the Anush/ubh (metre) is speech, and by means of speech (the mouth [1]) food is eaten.

[1] See p. 200, note 3.

15. With three verses he sows each time[1],—threefold is Agni: as great as Agni is, as great as is his measure, with so much he thus puts food into him.

16. With twelve verses he sows on the ploughed ground,—twelve months are a year, and the year is Agni: as great as Agni is, as great as is his measure, with so much he thus puts food into him.

17. On the ploughed ground he sows, whence food ripens on ploughed ground. Were he to sow only on the ploughed ground, and not on the unploughed, food would only ripen on ploughed ground, not on unploughed; and were he to sow only on unploughed ground, and not on ploughed ground, food would only ripen on unploughed ground, and not on ploughed ground. He sows on both the ploughed, and the unploughed, ground: hence food ripens both on ploughed, and on unploughed, ground.

18. With three (verses) he sows both on the ploughed, and on the unploughed, ground,—threefold is Agni: as great as Agni is, as great as is his measure, by so much he thus puts food into him.

19. And, again, why he sows all (kinds of) herb (-seed),—the gods at that time, being about to put him (Agni-Pragâpati) together, in the first place healed him by healing medicine; and in like manner does this one now, being about to put him together, first heal him with healing medicine.

20. It is (seed) of all herbs;—all herbs is the

[1] The sowing of the seed is done after the manner of the watering of the site, viz. so as to finish the sowing of every four furrows with the completion of the muttering of three verses (Vâg. S. XII, 75–86); whereupon the remaining seed is scattered over the whole site with additional three verses (87–89).

same as all (kinds of) medicine: by all (kinds of) healing medicine he thus heals him.

21. With three verses he sows each time,—threefold is Agni: as great as Agni is, as great as is his measure, with so much he thus heals him.

22. With twelve verses he sows on the ploughed ground,—twelve months are a year, and the year is Agni: as great as Agni is, as great as is his measure, with so much he thus heals him.

23. On the ploughed ground he sows: he thereby heals the vital airs. And were he to sow only on the ploughed ground, and not on the unploughed, he would only heal the vital airs, and not the other (parts of the) body; and were he to sow only on the unploughed, and not on the ploughed, ground, he would only heal the body, and not the vital airs: he sows both on the ploughed, and on the unploughed, ground; and thus he heals both the vital airs and the body.

24. With three (verses) he sows both on the ploughed, and on the unploughed, ground,—threefold is Agni: as great as Agni is, as great as is his measure, with so much he thus heals him.

25. Fifteen jarfuls of water he pours out, and with fifteen verses he sows,—that makes thirty,—the Virâg (metre) consists of thirty syllables, and the Virâg (the far-shining, or far-ruling) is the whole food: the whole food he thus puts into him.

26. [He sows, with Vâg. S. XII, 75 seq.; *Ri*k S. X, 97] 'The herbs first grown three ages before the gods[1],'—the gods doubtless are the seasons,

[1] Thus the St. Petersburg dictionary; while Professor Ludwig construes 'triyugam purâ' together,—'the herbs first come from

and from them those (herbs) used to grow thrice, in spring, in the rainy season, and in the autumn;—'of the brown ones will I ponder,'—the brown one, doubtless, is Soma, and the herbs are related to Soma, and the Purusha (Pragâpati) is related to herbs[1];—'the hundred powers,'—inasmuch as he here lives a hundred (years), and has a hundred merits, and a hundred energies, there are in him those hundred powers;—'and seven,'—he thereby speaks of those seven vital airs in the head.

27. 'Yours, O Mother, are a hundred powers, and yours a thousand growths,'—inasmuch as (the plants) here are shooting out a hundredfold, and a thousandfold;—'Ye of a hundred virtues, render ye free from sickness this one of mine!' that is, him whom I am now healing.

28. These (verses)[2] have one and the same ex-

---

the gods before the three ages;'—but is there any other example of 'purâ' with the accusative? The author of the Brâhma*n*a, on the other hand, takes 'triyugam purâ' as adverbs independent of each other,—'formerly at three periods.'

[1] Or, consists of herbs.

[2] That is, the two verses just explained, as well as the remaining thirteen verses (Vâ*g*. S. XII, 77 seq.; *Ri*k S. X, 97, 3 seq.), viz.:—

3. Rejoice ye at the plants, the full-budded, abounding in shoots: like victorious mares, the herbs are eager to win (or, to save).

4. As plants, O divine mothers, I call upon you: horse, and cow, and raiment would I win, and thine own self, O Purusha!

5. On the Asvattha tree is your abode, on the Par*n*a dwelling is made for you: possessed of cattle shall ye be, when ye save the Purusha.

6. Wherein the herbs have met together, even as the nobles in the assembly, that priest is called physician, demon-killer, pain-remover.

7. The (herb) rich in horses, the one rich in Soma, the

planation with regard to this (Agni-Pragâpati),—how he may heal him, and preserve him. They are anush/ubh verses,—the Anush/ubh is speech, and speech is all healing medicine: by means of all healing medicine he thus heals him.

29. Now, then, regarding the defined and the undefined (ceremonies):—with prayer he yokes two oxen, silently the others; with prayer he ploughs four furrows, silently the others; silently he puts on the grass-bush, with prayer he makes a libation thereon; silently he pours out the jarfuls of water, with prayer he sows.

30. This Agni is Pragâpati, and Pragâpati is both the defined and the undefined, the limited and the

strengthening, most powerful,—all herbs have I found for healthfulness to him (the Purusha).

8. Forth rush the energies of the plants, like kine from the stable, eager to win wealth, eager to win wealth, O Purusha!

9. Strength-giving (ishkr/ti) is the name of your mother, hence ye are healing powers (nishkr/ti): winged furrows ye are; what ye make sick, ye heal.

10. All obstacles have they overcome, even as the thief the cow-pen; the herbs have expelled whatever defect of the body there was.

11. When, to give strength, I take these herbs in my hand, the self of Yakshman (consumption) perishes, as from the clutches of the living (? i.e. from death, Ludw.).

12. Whose every limb, whose every joint ye, O herbs, flow through, from him ye chase away (the demon) Yakshman,—mighty (he is) and, as it were, abiding in the core.

13. Fly forth, O Yakshman; together with the garrulous jay; vanish with the gliding of the wind, with the whirlwind (?)!

14. May one of you help the other, may ye lend help to one another! Of one mind, help ye forward this word of mine!

15. Those bearing fruit, and those without fruit, the flowerless and the flowering, urged forward by Br/haspati, may they preserve us from trouble!

The Vâg. S. also gives the remaining verses of the hymn, which are not, however, required on the present occasion.

unlimited. Now whatever he does with prayer thereby he restores that form of his which is defined, limited; and whatever he does silently, thereby he restores that form of his which is undefined, unlimited,—verily, whosoever, knowing this, performs thus, restores this whole and complete Pragâpati. The outer forms are defined, and the inner ones are undefined; and Agni is the same as an animal: hence the outer forms of the animal are defined, and the inner ones undefined.

Third Adhyâya. First Brâhmana.

1. Built is the Gârhapatya, unbuilt the Âhavanîya; he then buys the king (Soma): the Gârhapatya being this (terrestrial) world, the Âhavanîya the sky, and Soma he that blows yonder, he thus places him (Vâyu, the wind) between these two worlds; and hence he blows between these two worlds.

2. And as to why he buys the king when the Gârhapatya is built, and the Âhavanîya unbuilt,—Agni is the body, and Soma the vital air: he thus places the vital air in the middle of the body, and hence that vital air is in the middle of the body.

3. And, again, why he buys the king when the Gârhapatya is built, and the Âhavanîya unbuilt,—Agni is the body, and Soma is the life-sap: he thus supplies the body with life-sap, and hence this body (of ours) is supplied with life-sap from end to end.

4. Having bought the king, and driven him about, he then takes out the material for the guest-meal. With the Havishkrit of that (ceremony) he releases speech. And in this way[1] he interlinks the per-

[1] That is, in performing the various rites of the Soma-sacrifice,

formance of the (Soma) sacrifice and the performance of the fire (altar) for the purpose of unity of performance, thinking, 'Uniform shall be this performance!'

5. And, again, why he interlinks them,—Agni (the fire-altar) is the body, and the (Soma) sacrifice is the vital air: he thus places the vital air in the midst of the body, and hence that vital air is in the middle of the body.

6. And, again, why he interlinks them,—Agni is the body, and the (Soma) sacrifice is the vital sap: he thus supplies the body with vital sap, and hence this body is supplied with vital sap from end to end. He then returns to the site of the Âhavanîya.

7. Now some sweep with the palâsa branch on both occasions[1], saying, 'Surely, on both occasions he builds (an altar).' Let him, however, not do so; for by (building) the Gârhapatya he settles, and by the Âhavanîya he rises upwards: therefore let him not do so.

8. And only on the Gârhapatya (site) he throws saline soil, not on the Âhavanîya; for the Gârhapatya is this (terrestrial) world, and saline soil means cattle: he thus bestows cattle on this world, whence there are cattle in this world.

9. And only on the Âhavanîya (site) he places a lotus leaf, not on the Gârhapatya; for the lotus leaf means water, and the Âhavanîya the sky: he thus places the waters (vapours) in the sky. On both he

and at the same time doing all that is necessary for the building of the fire-altar, on which the Soma-offering itself is ultimately to be performed.

[1] Viz. in consecrating the site of the Âhavanîya, as well as that of the Gârhapatya altar (see VII, 1, 1, 1).

scatters sand; for sand means seed, and in both (fire-altars) fashioning (of Agni) takes place: 'May he be fashioned from out of that seed!' thus he thinks.

10. He scatters it with two different formulas; for the Gârhapatya is the world of men, and the Âhavanîya is the world of the gods, and different indeed are the divine and the human. With the longer formula he scatters it on the Âhavanîya, and with the shorter one on the Gârhapatya, for longer is the life of the gods, and shorter the life of men. On the Gârhapatya he scatters the sand before (the setting up of) the enclosing-stones; for sand is seed: 'May these be fashioned from out of that seed!' thus he thinks.

11. As to this they say, 'If the enclosing-stones are the womb, and the sand is seed, and the sand is strown on the Gârhapatya before (the setting up of) the enclosing-stones, how, then, is that seed of his not shed aside, (but) is received (by the womb)?' Well, the saline soil is the amnion, and inasmuch as he strews first the saline soil, that seed of his is not shed aside, but is received by that amnion. He now addresses the enclosing-stones on the Âhavanîya: the meaning of this has been explained [1]. He then scatters sand: sand being seed, that seed of his is not shed aside, but is received also by that womb.

12. And only on the Âhavanîya he strokes it (even) with two (verses) containing (the verb) 'to grow [2],' not on the Gârhapatya; for the Gârhapatya is this (terrestrial) world, and the Âhavanîya is the heavenly world; and this Sacrificer, being indeed

[1] VII, 1, 1, 14.

[2] See paragraphs 45, 46.

born in this world, is really intended to be born in the heavenly world: when he strokes (the sand) even on the Âhavaniya with two (verses) containing (the verb) 'to grow,' and not on the Gârhapatya, he causes him to be born in the heavenly world.

13. He now puts clod-bricks thereon[1],—that fire-altar is these worlds, and the clod-bricks are the regions: he thus places the regions into these worlds; whence there are those regions in these worlds.

14. He takes them from outside the (site of the) fire-altar; for those regions which are in these worlds are already possessed by him (Agni); and he now bestows on him those regions which are beyond these worlds.

15. From outside the Vedi (he takes them);—the Vedi being this (earth), and those regions which are on this (earth) being already possessed by him, he now bestows on him those regions which are beyond this (earth).

16. And, again, why he puts clod-bricks thereon,—when Pragâpati was disjointed, his vital sap flowed over all the regions (or, in all directions); and when the gods restored him[2] they, by means of these clod-bricks, put into him that vital sap; and in like manner does this one now put that vital sap into him.

17. He takes them from outside (the site of) the fire-altar; for the vital sap which is in these worlds is already possessed by him (Agni), and he now puts

[1] He places a clod of earth on each end of the two 'spines,' that is to say, in the middle of each of the four sides of the square constituting the 'body' of the altar-site.

[2] Or, when they put him together (by building the fire-altar).

into him that vital sap which flowed away beyond these worlds[1].

18. From outside the Vedi (he takes them),—the Vedi being this (earth), and that vital sap which is in this (terrestrial) world being already possessed by him, he now puts into him the vital sap which flowed beyond this (earth).

19. He takes them with the sacrificial (wooden) sword,—the sword is a thunderbolt, and the thunderbolt means force, and this (earth) means wealth: by force he thus obtains wealth.

20. From the front side he brings one, with (Vâg. S. XII, 102), 'May he not injure me who is the begetter of the Earth!'—the begetter of the Earth doubtless is Pragâpati (the lord of creatures and generation): thus, 'May Pragâpati not injure me!'—'Or he of true ordinances who hath pervaded the sky,' that is, 'Or he of true ordinances who has created the sky;'—'Or he who first begat the shining waters,'—the shining waters doubtless are the men: thus, 'he who first created men;'—'To the god Ka (who?) let us do homage by offering!' Ka doubtless is Pragâpati, thus, 'To him let us do homage by offering!' Having brought it he puts it on the body (of the altar-site) inside the enclosing-stones: he thereby puts into him (Agni) what vital sap had flowed away from him in the eastern direction, and also the eastern region itself he bestows upon him.

21. Then (he fetches a clod) from the south, with (Vâg. S. XII, 103), 'Turn hither, O Earth, with

[1] Viz. when these worlds were plunged into the water, see VI, 1, 1, 12.

sacrifice, with milk!' as the text, so the meaning;—'Agni, sent forth, hath mounted thy skin;' whatsoever is on this (earth) that is her skin; and that (skin) Agni mounts, when sent forth, when blazing forth. Having brought it he puts it on the body (of the altar) inside the junction of the (right) wing (and the body): he thereby puts into him (Agni) what vital sap had flowed from him in the southern direction, and also the southern region itself he bestows upon him.

22. Then from behind (he fetches one, with Vâg. S. XII, 104), 'O Agni, what in thee is pure, what brilliant, what clean, what meet for sacrifice,'—Agni doubtless is this (earth): of her he says this;—'that do we bring to the gods,' that is, 'that we bring for this divine work.' Having brought it he puts it on the body (of the altar) inside the junction of the tail (and the body): he thereby puts into him what vital sap had flowed away from him in the western direction, and also the western region itself he bestows upon him. Let him not take it exactly from the back (west) lest he should take the vital sap from the path of the sacrifice: he takes it from about there[1].

23. Then from the north, with (Vâg. S. XII, 105), 'Sap and strength have I taken from here[2],'—that is, 'Sap and strength I take from here;'—'the womb of sacred law,' the sacred law doubtless is the truth: thus, 'the womb of the truth;'—'the stream of the mighty,' the mighty (buffalo, or

[1] Viz. from some place towards north-west from the middle of the western side of the body of the altar.

[2] Mahîdhara takes 'âdam' here as the regular imperfect of 'ad,' I ate.

mahisha) doubtless is Agni, for he, being born here great (mahat), animated everything;—'May it accrue to me in the cows, in the bodies,'—the body is the self: thus, 'May it accrue to me both in the cows and in (my own) self;'—'I leave behind decline, weakness, sickness!' therewith he spreads the sand (by stroking): he thereby consigns to that (northern) region whatever decline, weakness, and sickness there is; whence hungry people (live) in that region. Having brought that (clod), he puts it on the body (of the altar) on the middle of the junction of the (left) wing (and the body): he thereby puts into him (Agni) what vital sap flowed away in the northerly direction; and also the northern region itself he bestows upon him.

24. These same (clods) are the regions; he places them on all sides: he thus places the regions on all sides; whence the regions are on every side. [He places the clods so] as to face each other from every side: he thereby places the regions to face each other from every side, and hence the regions face each other from every side. He places them separately, 'settles[1]' them separately, and separately pronounces the Sûdadohas upon them; for separate from each other are the regions. Standing he places them, for the regions, as it were, stand; and stronger, indeed, one is whilst standing.

25. These same (clods) are bricks having special prayers (yagushmati[2]): on the body (of the altar) he places them, not on the wings and tail; for bricks having special prayers are placed on the body, not on the wings or tail.

[1] See p. 301, note 3. [2] See p. 153, note 1.

26. As to this they say, 'How do these (clod-bricks) come to be put on as baked, as heated (burnt) ones?' Well, these (clods) are vital sap, and the vital sap (blood) is naturally-heated; and, moreover, whatever comes in contact with Agni Vaisvânara, even thereby comes to be put on as baked, as heated.

27. He then throws up the Uttara-vedi[1] (high-altar),—the Vedi is this (earth), the Uttara-vedi the sky, and the clod-bricks are the regions: thus when he puts on the clod-bricks between (the preparation of) the Vedi and (that of) the Uttara-vedi, he thereby places the regions between these two worlds; whence the regions are between these two worlds. He makes it either a yoke long on each side, or forty feet,—whichever way he pleases. He then throws sand thereon: the meaning of this has been explained.

28. He throws it on the Uttara-vedi;—the Uttara-vedi is the womb: he thus infuses seed into the womb; and the seed which is infused into the womb becomes generative. He covers the whole body (of the altar) with that (sand): he thus puts seed into the whole body[2]; whence the seed is produced from the whole body.

29. [He throws it on the high-altar, with Vâg. S. XII, 106–111; *Ri*k S. X, 140] 'Thine, O Agni, is glory and vigour,'—his glory (*s*ravas) and vigour doubtless is the smoke, for that announces (*s*râvaya) him in yonder world,—'mighty shine forth the

[1] See p. 325, note 6.

[2] That is to say, he first throws down sand on the Uttara-vedi, and then covers with it the whole of the body of the altar, so as to make it even with the Uttara-vedi.

flames, O rich-beamed one!' that is, 'the flames of (thee), the mighty one, shine forth, O thou, abounding in wealth!'—'With might, O wide-rayed one (thou bestowest) strength, worthy of song,' might is power: thus, 'By (thy) power, O wide-rayed one, (thou givest) food worthy of song;'—'bestowest thou upon the worship, O sage!' worship doubtless is the Sacrificer: thus, 'Upon the worship thou bestowest, O sage!'

30. 'Pure-flamed, bright-flamed,' for pure-flamed and bright-flamed he (Agni) is; 'full-flamed, didst thou burst forth with light,' that is, 'full-flamed shonest thou forth with light;'—'running about as their son thou helpest the two mothers,' for as their son he does help the two mothers;—'thou fillest both spheres,' the two spheres doubtless are these two, heaven and earth, and these two he indeed fills,—with smoke yonder (sky), with rain this (earth).

31. 'Child of strength, knower of beings, in benedictions,' that is, 'child of strength, knower of beings, in praises,'—'delight thou, kindly in thoughts,' that is, 'shine thou, kindly in thoughts;'—'in thee have they brought together multiform nourishments,' that is, 'in thee have they brought together many-formed nourishments;'—'of wondrous help are the fair-born,' as the text, so the meaning.

32. 'Ruling, O Agni, spread thou by beings'—the beings are men: thus, 'Shining, O Agni, spread thyself by men!'—'riches amongst us, O immortal!' that is, 'bestowing wealth upon us, O immortal!'—'Of beautiful form, shinest thou'—for he indeed shines, of beautiful form;—'thou

fillest (us with) profitable[1] wisdom;' that is, 'thou fillest (us with) perennial wisdom.'

33. 'Him, the wise arranger of the cult,'—the cult is the sacrifice: thus, 'him, the wise preparer of the sacrifice;'—'ruling over great wealth,' that is, 'ruling in great wealth;'—'the bestowal of good things,—prosperous, mighty (mah) nourishment,'—that is, 'the bestowal of good things; prosperous, ample (mahat) nourishment,'—'givest thou, and profitable substance,' that is, 'givest thou, and perennial substance.'

34. '[Thee,] the righteous,' that is, 'the truthful;'—'the mighty,' the mighty (or buffalo) doubtless is Agni;—'the all-remarkable,' for he (Agni) is indeed remarkable to all;—'(thee), Agni, men have placed foremost for happiness,' happiness doubtless is the sacrifice, and for the sacrifice they indeed place him foremost;—'thee, the hearer, the far-ruling, divine one, with song the human tribes;' that is, 'thee who hearest, thee, the far-ruling god, we men invoke.'

35. Now this hymn of six verses is that same Agni Vais*v*ânara; and it is in order to make a beginning (in the building of the altar) that that sand is scattered,—he thereby pours into it Agni Vais*v*ânara as seed;—(he does so) with a six-versed hymn: six seasons are a year and the year is Vais*v*ânara (belonging to all men).

36. As to this they say, 'If the seed is said to be seed what is its seed characteristic?'—Let him say, 'white;' for seed is white;—or 'speckled,' for seed is, as it were, speckled.

[1] The author connects 'sânasi' with 'sanâtana' (old, perpetual).

37. As to this they say, 'As seed is moist, and he scatters dry sand, how does it become moist for him, after the manner of seed?' Well, the metres are vital sap, and vital sap is moist; and inasmuch as he scatters that (sand) with metres, it is thus that it becomes moist for him, after the manner of seed.

38. As to this they say, 'How does it come to be put on for him by means of the day and the night?' Well, day and night are two, and there are two (kinds of) seed, the white and the black: as black and white it is thus put on for him by means of the day and the night.

39. As to this they say, 'How does that (sand), put on by the days and nights, become complete (or perfect) for him, neither deficient, nor superabundant?' Well, endless are the days and nights, and endless is the sand: it is thus that, put on by the days and nights, it becomes complete for him, neither deficient, nor superabundant. 'And wherefrom (is obtained) the oceanic (Samudriya [1]) metre?' The ocean is endless, and the sand is endless: that is the oceanic metre.

40. As to this they say, 'How is that (sand) of his put on separately with different prayers?' Well, prayer is thought; this thought, prayer, comes to be equal to the whole sand [2]: and thus that (sand) of his comes to be put on separately with different prayers.

41. As to this they say, 'How does that (sand) of his come to be put on by all the metres?'—Inasmuch as he scatters it with that hymn of six verses; for as many syllables as there are in the

[1] The exact purport of this term is not clear.

[2] Sikatâh, sand, is plural, consisting as it does of a multiplicity of sand-grains.

seven metres, so many syllables there are in that hymn of six verses[1]: thus that (sand) of his comes to be put on by all the metres.

42. And as to why he scatters sand,—that Agni (fire-altar) is Pragâpati, and Pragâpati is the whole Brahman. Now that sand is (put) in (the place of) the lost part of the Brahman; and that part of it which has not been lost is this fire-altar which is now being built: thus when he scatters sand he restores to him that lost part of the Brahman. That (sand which) he scatters is unnumbered, unlimited; for who knows how great is that lost part of the Brahman? And verily he who, knowing this, scatters sand, restores the whole, complete Pragâpati.

43. As to this they say, 'What is the number of these unnumbered sand grains?' Let him say, 'Two;' for there are two kinds of sand, the white and the black: or let him say, 'Seven hundred and twenty,' for so many days and nights there are in the year; or 'Two hundred and fifty-two,' for so many syllables there are in that hymn of six verses; or 'Twenty-five,' for seed is twenty-fivefold[2].

44. This same (sand represents) bricks with special prayers; he places it on the body (of the altar), not

[1] This is a somewhat loose calculation. As a matter of fact, the seven principal metres, viz. Gâyatrî (24), Ushnih (28), Anushtubh (32), Brihatî (36), Paṅkti (40), Trishtubh (44), Gagatî (48), contain together 252 syllables. The hymn recited in scattering the sand, on the other hand, consists of one Vishtârapaṅkti (40), three Satobrihatîs (3 × 40), the Uparishtâggyotis (? 40), and one Trishtubh (44), or together of 244 syllables. On similar cases of looseness in computing the syllables of metres, see p. 318, note 1.

[2] Viz. inasmuch as it emanates from the body (paragraph 28), and the body consists of twenty-five parts—the trunk, the four limbs, and twenty fingers and toes. Cf. VI, 2, 1, 23, where, however, the trunk is not taken into account.

on the wings and tail; for bricks with special prayers are placed on the body, not on the wings and tail. He does not 'settle' it, lest he should stop the seed, and generation.

45. He then strokes it (the sand) even by means of two verses containing the verb 'to grow:' he thereby causes that infused seed to grow, whence the seed infused into the womb grows;—with two (verses) relating to Soma (he strokes the sand); for Soma is breath: he thus puts breath into the seed; whence the infused seed becomes possessed of breath. But, indeed, were it to come forth without breath it would become putrid; and this indeed is the Sûdadohas[1] in this case; for Soma is breath, and the Sûdadohas is breath.

46. [Vâ*g*. S. XII, 112, 113; *Ri*k S. I, 91, 16, 18] 'Grow thou! let manly power gather in thee from all sides, O Soma!' manly power doubtless is seed: thus, 'Grow thou! let seed gather in thee from every side, O Soma!'—'Be thou in the gathering of strength!' in food doubtless is strength: thus, 'be thou in the gathering of food!'—'Let the drinks, let the forces gather in thee!'—drink doubtless means vital sap, and in food are forces: thus, 'let vital sap, let food gather itself in thee!'—'and manly powers in thee, the overcomer of enemies;' that is, 'and seed in thee, the overcomer of evil;'—'growing, O Soma, for the sake of immortality,' he thereby lays immortality into the generative power, whence generative power is immortal;—'gain thou the highest glory in the heavens!' his highest glory

[1] See p. 301, note 3.

in the heavens doubtless is the moon, for that one causes him to be celebrated in yonder world[1]. With two (verses) he makes him grow, a gâyatrî and a trishtubh one,—the significance of this has been explained.

47. Now then the (mystic) correspondence,—four clod-bricks he puts on; with a six-versed (hymn) he scatters (the sand); with two (verses) he makes (the seed) grow; that makes twelve,—twelve months are a year, and the year is Agni: as great as Agni is, as great as is his measure, so great does this become.

Second Brâhmana.

1. Having smoothed (the sand) down with the two verses containing (the verb) 'to grow,' and returned (to the hall) he proceeds with the guest offering. Having performed the guest offering, he proceeds with the Pravargya and the Upasad[2]. Having performed the Pravargya and the Upasad, they appease that (first) layer on the (red ox-)skin. And as to why on a skin: for the obtainment of the forms, the skin being outward form;—on the hairy side: for the obtainment of the forms, hair being outward form;—on a ruddy (skin): for the obtainment of all forms, all forms (colours being contained) in the ruddy;—on (the skin) of an ox: for the obtainment of Agni's forms, the ox being the same as Agni;—on (the skin spread) with the neck towards the east, for that (tends) godward.

[1] Sâyana remarks,—The high glory, in the heaven, of Soma growing in the form of a creeper is said to be the moon: in yonder heavenly world that moon indeed, when being drunk (by the gods) in the form (?) of ambrosia, causes him, Soma, to be celebrated.

[2] See part ii, p. 104.

2. He spreads it in front of the Gârhapatya, on the Vedi, with the hairy side upwards, and the neck towards the east: thereon they appease that layer. Now he sprinkles (the bricks);—when he sprinkles, he thereby makes it pure, sacrificially clean;—with clarified butter (he sprinkles), for that is pure, sacrificially clean; and also with the view of its being unsurpassed[1], for no other sacrificial food is sprinkled with ghee;—silently (he sprinkles), for what is (done) silently is undefined, and the undefined is everything: by means of everything he thus makes it pure, and sacrificially clean; and also with the view of its being unsurpassed, for no other sacrificial food is sprinkled silently.

3. And, again, why he sprinkles,—this (layer of bricks) is sacrificial food, and as such he bastes it[2]; for whatever sacrificial food is buttered, and basted, that is palatable and sacrificially clean. With ghee (he bastes it), for sacrificial food is basted with ghee; silently (he does so), for silently sacrificial food is basted;—by means of stalks of Kusa grass, for these are pure, and sacrificially clean;—by means of the tops, for the top is sacred to the gods.

4. As to this they say, 'When he sprinkles only the first layer, how does that whole fire-altar of his come to be sprinkled, how does it come to be led forward on the skin, and how led forward by the horse[3]?' Inasmuch as in this (layer) he (symbolically)[4] sprinkles the bricks of all the layers; and

[1] Literally, for not surmounting.

[2] See part i, p. 192, note 1.

[3] On the leading forward of the fire, and laying it down on the foot-print of a horse, see II, 1, 4, 23 seq.

[4] According to Kâty. XVII, 3, 18-19 some ritualists would seem to put the (yagushmatî) bricks of all the layers on the skin. But

thus indeed that whole fire-altar of his comes to be sprinkled, and led forward on the skin, and led forward by the horse. They lift up this (first) layer[1].

5. He (the Adhvaryu) then says (to the Hot*ri*), 'Recite to the fires being led forward!' For at that time when the gods were setting out to spread the sacrifice, the Rakshas, the fiends, sought to smite them, saying, 'Ye shall not sacrifice! ye shall not spread the sacrifice!' Having made those fires, those bricks, to be sharp-edged thunderbolts, they hurled these at them, and laid them low thereby; and having laid them low, they spread that sacrifice in a place free from danger and devilry.

6. Now, what the gods did is done here,—even now those Rakshas are indeed smitten by the gods themselves; and when he nevertheless does this, it is because he thinks, 'I must do what the gods did.' And so, having made those fires, those bricks, to be sharp-edged thunderbolts, he hurls them at whatever Rakshas, whatever evildoers there may be, and lays them low thereby; and having laid them low, he spreads the sacrifice in a place free from danger and devilry.

7. And as to why (he recites) to the fires,—it is because there are here many fires, to wit, those layers; and as to (his reciting) to them being led forward (pra-har), it is because he hurls (pra-har) them forward (as thunderbolts).

---

perhaps this is merely a wrong interpretation of this passage of the Brâhma*n*a; though the three 'naturally-perforated' bricks are probably placed together.

[1] The Adhvaryu's attendants take up the ox-skin with the bricks for the first layer lying on it.

8. Now some recite (Vâg. S. XII, 50), 'The Agnis Purîshyas, together with those of the streams,'—a form of starting[1]. Let him not do so; let him recite gâyatrî verses addressed to Agni, and relating to (objects of) desire: (Vâg. S. XII, 115; *Ri*k S. VIII, 11, 7), 'Hither may Vatsa lead thy mind even from the highest seat, O Agni, with the song desirous of thee!'—(Vâg. S. XII, 116; *Ri*k S. VIII, 43, 18), 'To thee, O Agni, best of Aṅgiras, all good homesteads have laid themselves out for (the obtainment of) their desire.'—(Vâg. S. XII, 117), 'Agni, the one all-ruler, shineth in the beloved homes, the (object of) desire of all that is and shall be.'

9. Verses addressed to Agni he recites for the obtainment of Agni's forms;—and such as relate to desire, for the obtainment of his desires;—Gâyatrî ones,—Agni is Gâyatra: as great as Agni is, as great as is his measure, with so much he thus pours him forth as seed;—with three (verses),—Agni is threefold: as great as Agni is, as great as is his measure, with so much he thus pours him forth as seed. These (three), with the (first and last verses) recited thrice, amount to seven,—of seven layers consists the fire-altar[2], seven seasons are a year, and the year is Agni: as great as Agni is, as great as is his measure, so great does this become. He recites in a low voice, for here in the sacrifice seed is (cast), and seed is cast silently. He (the Hot*ri*) marches reciting behind (the bricks carried by the attendants); he thus marches, defending the sacrifice by the metres from behind.

[1] See VII, 1, 1, 25.

[2] See p. 249, note 3.

10. And in front they lead a white horse. For at that time the gods were afraid lest the Rakshas, the fiends, should smite them here. They saw that thunderbolt, even yonder sun; for that horse is yonder sun: having driven off the Rakshas, the fiends, in front, by that thunderbolt, they obtained well-being in a place free from danger and devilry. They arrive at the (site of) the fire-altar; south of the tail (of the altar) they set down the layer (of bricks); from the north they make the horse step (on the site of the altar).

11. They lead it eastward on the left (north) side of the altar, inside the enclosing-stones, whereby they ward off evil from the eastern region; then southward, whereby they ward off evil from the south; then westward, whereby they ward off evil from the western region; then northward, whereby they ward off evil from the northern region. Having thus warded off the Rakshas, the fiends, from all the regions, he sets it (the horse) free towards northeast: the significance of this has been explained.

12. Whilst it goes westward he makes it smell (kiss) that layer (of bricks);—that horse is yonder sun, and those bricks are the same as all these creatures (on earth): thus even as he makes (the horse) smell, so yon sun kisses these creatures [1]. And hence, by Pragâpati's power, every one now thinks, 'I am!' And as to why he makes it smell while going westward, it is because, whilst going (from east) to west, that (sun) kisses all these creatures.

[1] According to Sâyana, it is by his rays (identified with the vital airs of living beings) that the sun kisses (or puts himself in contact with) the creatures (and animates them); so that every one feels that he is 'labdhâtmaka,' or has obtained 'a self,' or life and being.

13. And, again, why he makes it smell;—that horse is yonder sun, and those naturally-perforated (bricks) are these worlds; and even as he makes it smell, so yonder sun strings these worlds to himself on a thread[1]. And as to that thread, the significance of that (will be explained) further on.

14. And, again, why he makes it smell;—Agni went away from the gods; he entered the water. The gods said to Pragâpati, 'Go thou in search of him: to thee, his own father, he will reveal himself.' He became a white horse, and went in search of him. He found him on a lotus leaf, having crept forth from the water. He eyed him, and he (Agni) scorched him: hence the white horse has, as it were, a scorched mouth[2], and indeed is apt to become weak-eyed. He (Agni) thought he had hit and hurt him, and said to him, 'I grant thee a boon!'

15. He (Pragâpati) said, 'Whoever shall seek thee in that form (of a white horse), shall find thee!' And, accordingly, he who seeks him (Agni) in that form, finds him; and having found him, he then builds him up.

16. It should be a white (horse), for that is a form of him (the sun) who burns yonder. If he cannot obtain a white one, one that is not white might do; but a horse it should be. If he cannot obtain a horse, even an ox might do, for the ox is of Agni's nature, and Agni is the repeller of all evils.

---

[1] That is, he passes a thread through them (as through pearls), fastened to himself. Regarding this Thread, or spiritual bond, holding together all sentient existences of the universe, see XIV, 6, 7, 2 seq.

[2] That is, according to Sâyana, a reddish mouth.

17. Now, then, as to the mounting[1] (of the altar). Now some mount it from the front (east) towards the back, or from the back towards the front: let him not do so; for that Agni (the fire-altar) is an animal; and if one mounts an animal (ox) from the front towards the back, it strikes him with its horns; and if he mounts it from the back towards the front, it does so with its feet. Let him mount it only by the middle body[2]; for the animal which people mount by the (middle) body, carries them forward, and does not hurt them. From the left (north) side (he should mount it), for any animal which people mount they mount from the left side. By mounting the (body of the) altar from the left side, and performing the work connected with the Uttara-vedi, he takes hold of Agni in the (middle) body (or, into himself); and having taken Agni into his own self, he sings the 'true hymn.' He puts a lotus-leaf on (the altar): thereof further on.

18. Now that horse they lead about when evening is closing in; for at that time the gods were afraid lest the Rakshas, the fiends, should there smite that (Agni, or altar) of theirs. They made that thunderbolt, to wit, yonder sun, his protector, for that horse is yonder sun; and in like manner does this one now make that thunderbolt his (Agni's) protector.

19. He leads it about towards the setting of the sun; for he (the sun) is manifestly his protector by day; and the Rakshas are the associates of the

[1] That is, as to the way in which the priests and sacrificer are to step on the body of the altar-site, when coming from outside.

[2] That is to say, from sideways as in getting on the saddle of a horse.

night: for the night he thus makes that thunderbolt his protector. He leads it about on every side: on every side he thus makes that thunderbolt his protector. Thrice he leads it about: he thus makes that thunderbolt his (Agni's) threefold protector. He then lets it loose towards north-west: the purport of this has been explained. It afterwards returns (to the sacrificial ground): the purport of this (will be explained) further on.

THE BUILDING OF THE ALTAR.

THE FIRST LAYER.

FOURTH ADHYÂYA. FIRST BRÂHMAYA.

1. Being about to build Agni (the fire-altar), he takes him up into his own self; for from out of his own self he causes him to be born, and wherefrom one is born, suchlike he becomes. Now were he to build up Agni without taking him up into his own self, he would beget man from man, mortal from mortal, one not freed from sin from one not freed from sin; but when he builds up Agni after taking him up into his own self, he causes Agni to be born from Agni, the immortal from the immortal, the sinless from the sinless.

2. He takes him in (by muttering, Vâg. S. XIII, 1), 'Within me I first take Agni,' he thereby first takes Agni into his own self;—'for increase of wealth, for healthy progeny, for vigorous manhood!' and hereby he takes all blessings to himself;—'and may the deities stand by me!' and hereby he takes all the gods to himself; and thus he takes into his own self all that he is about to generate from his own self. Having taken Agni

into his own self whilst standing, he builds him up sitting;—Agni is an animal: hence the animal, having received the fœtus standing, gives birth after lying down.

3. He now sings the Satya Sâman[1] (true hymn). For the gods then said, 'Let us make the truth (satya) his mouth (or beginning): thus we shall become the truth, truth will turn unto us, and true will become that wish of ours for which we are about to perform this rite!'

4. They sang that 'true hymn' at the outset, and thus made the truth his (Agni's) mouth; and they became the truth; the truth turned unto them, and true became that wish of theirs for which they performed this rite.

5. And in like manner when the Sacrificer now, at the outset, sings the 'true hymn,' he thereby makes the truth his (Agni's) mouth; and he (himself) becomes the truth; and truth turns unto him; and true becomes that wish of his for which he performs this rite.

6. Now that truth is the same as the waters, for the waters are the truth. Hence they say, 'Whereby[2] the waters flow, that is a form of the truth.' It is the waters indeed that were made first of this universe: hence when the waters (rains) flow, then everything whatsoever exists is produced here.

7. He then puts down a lotus-leaf (in the centre of

[1] Probably Sâma-v. S. I, 99 (*Rik* S. I, 69, 4), 'O Agni, lord of bovine food, child of strength, grant unto us, O knower of beings, great glory!' See Weber, Ind. Stud. XII, p. 148, note 2.

[2] ?Or, in that (or because, yena) the waters flow,—that is to say, the flowing of the waters (rain, &c.) is a manifestation of eternal truth.

the altar-site);—the lotus-leaf is a womb: he hereby puts a womb to it (for Agni to be born from).

8. And, again, why he puts down a lotus-leaf;—the lotus means the waters, and this earth is a leaf thereof: even as the lotus-leaf here lies spread on the water, so this earth lies spread on the waters. Now this same earth is Agni's womb, for Agni (the fire-altar) is this earth, since thereof the whole Agni is built up: it is this earth he thus lays down. He lays it down so as not to be separated from the truth: he thereby establishes this earth on the truth;—hence this earth is established on the truth; and hence the truth is this earth, for this earth is the most certain of these worlds.

9. [He lays it down, with Vâg. S. XIII, 2] 'The waters' back thou art, the womb of Agni,' for this earth is indeed the back of the waters, and the womb of Agni;—'around the swelling ocean,' for the ocean indeed swells around this earth;—'growing great on the lotus,' that is, 'growing, flourish thou on the lotus;'—'spread out with the extent, with the breadth, of the sky!' with this he strokes along (the leaf),—for this Agni is yonder sun, and no other extent but that of the sky is able to contain him: he thus says (to the leaf), 'Having become the sky, contain him!' He lays it down with a Svarâg verse, for self-rule (svârâgya) belongs to the waters. Having 'settled' it, he pronounces the Sûdadohas[1] upon it: the significance of this has been explained.

10. He then puts the gold plate[2] thereon. Now

[1] See p. 301, note 3.

[2] Viz. the one the Sacrificer wore round his neck during the initiation period. See VI, 7, 1, 1 seq.

this gold plate is yonder sun, for he shines over all the creatures here on earth; and 'rokas' (shine) they mystically call 'rukma' (gold plate), for the gods love the mystic: he thus lays down yonder sun (on the altar). It is golden, and round, with one and twenty knobs,—the significance of this has been explained. He puts it down with the knobs pointing downward; for the knobs are his (the sun's) rays, and his rays (shine) downwards.

11. He puts it down on the lotus-leaf;—the lotus-leaf is a womb: in the womb he thus places him (Agni).

12. And, again, why he puts it on the lotus-leaf;—the lotus-leaf is a foundation, for the lotus-leaf is this earth, and this earth is the foundation: he who is not settled on this earth, is unsettled even as one who is far away. Now by means of his rays that (sun) is settled on this earth: he thus settles him (Agni) on this earth, as his foundation.

13. And, again, why he puts it on the lotus-leaf. When Indra had smitten V*ri*tra, he, thinking that he had not laid him low, entered the waters. He said to them, 'I am afraid: make ye a stronghold for me!' Now what essence of the waters there was that they gathered upwards (on the surface), and made it a stronghold for him; and because they made (kar) a stronghold (pû*h*) for him, therefore it is 'pûshkara;' 'pûshkara' being what is mystically called 'pushkara' (lotus-leaf), for the gods love the mystic. Now when he puts it (the gold plate) on the lotus-leaf, he then establishes him (Agni) in that essence which the waters gathered together for him (Indra), and in that stronghold which they made for him.

14. [He puts it down, with Vâg. S. XIII, 3]

'The Brahman first born in front;' the Brahman doubtless is yonder sun, and he is born day by day in front (in the east);—'from the summit[1] he, the longing, overspread the shining,' the summit doubtless is the middle, the shining ones are these worlds, and the longing one is yonder sun,—he is the longing one inasmuch as he longed to be born; and in rising he overspreads[2] these (worlds) from the summit, from the middle;—'he (overspread) the nighest extents of the deep,' his nighest extents of the deep doubtless are the regions, for he (the sun) does extend nigh to them;—'the womb of the existent and of the non-existent did he overspread!' the womb of the existent and of the non-existent doubtless are these worlds; for both what exists and what does not exist is born from these worlds. He puts it on with a trish/ubh verse, for yonder (sun) is related to the Trish/ubh[3]. Having 'settled' it, he pronounces the Sûdadohas[4] verse upon it: the significance of this has been explained.

15. He then lays the (gold) man thereon,—he is Pragâpati, he is Agni, he is the Sacrificer. He is made of gold, for gold is light, and fire is light; gold is immortality, and fire is immortality. It is a man (purusha), for Pragâpati is the Man.

---

[1] 'Sîmata/*h*' would rather seem to mean 'from the boundary line,' but the author here takes 'sîman' in the sense of (sîmanta) 'hair-line, parting of the hair, crown of the head (Scheitel).'

[2] In the Sanskrit participial (or gerundial) construction, the relation between the primary and secondary notions is usually the reverse of ours,—thus 'he rises in overspreading.'

[3] It is usually with Indra that the Trish/ubh metre is connected—see part i, introduction, p. xviii; Sat. Br. IX, 4, 3, 7 (cf. VIII, 5, 1, 10)—the Trish/ubh being also the emblem of the nobility (III, 4, 1, 10).

[4] See p. 301, note 3.

16. And, again, why he lays down the man. When Pragâpati was relaxed, his pleasing form went out from within; when it had gone out of him, the gods left him. When the gods restored him, they put that pleasing form into him, and the gods were pleased with that (form) of his; and inasmuch as the gods were pleased (ram) with that pleasing (ramya) form of his, it is called 'hiramya:' 'hiramya' being what is mystically called 'hiranya' (gold), for the gods love the mystic. And in like manner does this (Sacrificer) now put that pleasing form into him (Agni), and the gods are pleased with that (form) of his. But that pleasing form of his is the vital air: it is that vital air he thus puts into him.

17. He lays him on the gold plate, for the gold plate is yonder sun: that same man who is in that (sun's) disk, it is him he now lays down (on the altar).

18. He lays him down on his back[1];—for the gods at that time said, 'If we lay down these two[2] both looking hitherwards, they will burn up everything here; and if (we lay) both so as to be turned away from here, they will give warmth only in the opposite direction; and if facing each other, then there will be light only between those two, and they will injure each other.' They laid down the one so as to look hitherwards, and the other so as to look away from here: that one (the sun), the gold disk, looking downwards, gives warmth by his rays, and

[1] Professor Weber, Ind. Stud. XIII, p. 249, takes 'uttânam' in the sense of 'standing erect,' with his face towards the east; but this surely must be a mistake.

[2] Viz. both the gold plate (the sun), which was laid down with the embossed or front side downwards, and the gold man.

that man (tends) upward by his vital airs[1]. He lays him down (with the head) towards the east, for (with the head) towards the east this Agni (the fire-altar) is built up.

19. [He lays him down, with Vâg. S. XIII, 4; *Ri*k S. X, 121, 1] 'Hira*n*yagarbha came first into existence,' for that golden child did come first into existence;—'born he was the one lord of being;' for he indeed was born as the one lord of all this being;—'he upholdeth this earth and the sky,' for he (the sun) does uphold both the sky and the earth;—'to the god Ka let us do homage by offering!' Ka (Who?) is Pragâpati: thus, 'let us do homage to Him by offering!'

20. [Vâg. S. XIII, 5; *Ri*k S. X, 17, 11] 'The drop leaped along the earth and sky;' the drop is yonder sun, and he leaps both to the sky and to the earth—thus (in rising) to that (sky), and thus (in setting) to this (earth);—'along this seat, and that which was afore;' that is, to this world, and to that one; or this (Âhavanîya altar) which is now being built, and that (Gârhapatya altar) which yonder was built before;—'(the drop) moving along the common seat;' for he (the sun) moves along that common seat;—'the drop I offer along the seven hotrâs;' the drop is yonder sun; and the seven hotrâs are the regions: he thus establishes yonder sun in the regions.

21. With two (verses) he lays him down;—two-footed is the Sacrificer, and the Sacrificer is Agni: as great as Agni is, as great as is his measure, with so much he thus lays him down;—with two trish*t*ubh

[1] Cf. VI, 7, 1, 11, where it is said that the immortal part of the vital air of man streams out by upward breathings. Cf. p. 359, n. 1.

verses, for he (the sun) is related to the Trish/ubh. Having 'settled' him, he pronounces the Sûdadohas on him: the significance of this has been explained.

22. He then sings a Sâman. For the gods, having laid down that man, then saw him (looking) even suchlike as yonder dry plank.

23. They said, 'Think ye upon this, how we may put vigour into this man!' They said, 'Meditate ye (/*k*etay)!' whereby, doubtless, they meant to say, 'Seek ye to build up (/*k*itim ish)! seek ye how we shall put vigour into this man!'

24. Whilst meditating, they saw this Sâman, and sang it, and thereby put vigour into him; and in like manner does this (Sacrificer) thereby put it into him: he sings on the man, he puts vigour into the man;—he sings on the bright one [1], for Agni is all bright things. After he has laid him down, let him not walk round him in front, lest that Agni should injure him.

25. He (the Sacrificer) then stands by (the gold man) worshipping him with the Sarpanâma (serpent-named) formulas. The serpents doubtless are these worlds, for these glide along (sarp) with everything here whatsoever there is; and Agni is no other than the self (body) of all the gods. They, the gods, having laid down (on the altar) that self of theirs, were afraid lest these worlds should glide away with that self of theirs.

26. They saw those Sarpanâma and worshipped with them; by these (verses) they stopped these worlds for him, and caused them to bend themselves; and because they caused them to bend (nam) them-

[1] That is, he sings the *K*itra-sâman, Sâma-v. I, 169 (Vâg. S. XXVII, 39). 'With what favour will the bright one, the ever-growing friend, be with us; with what mightiest host?'

selves, therefore (the formulas are called) Sarpanâma. And in like manner does the Sacrificer, when he stands by worshipping with the Sarpanâma formulas, stop these worlds for him, and cause these worlds to bend themselves; and so they do not glide away with that self of his.

27. And, again, why he stands by worshipping with the Sarpanâma formulas;—the serpents are these worlds, for whatever creeps (sarp), creeps in these worlds. Now when he worships with the Sarpanâma formulas—whatever fiend there is in these worlds, whatever devourer, whatever ogress,—all that he thereby appeases.

28. [Vâg. S. XIII, 6–8] 'Homage be to the serpents, whichever are on earth, and they that are in the air, and they that are in the sky, to those serpents be homage!' whatever serpents there are in these three worlds to them he thereby does homage.

29. 'They that are the darts of demons,' for some (of the serpents), sent by demons, bite;—'and those on the trees, and those which lie in holes, to those serpents be homage!' he thereby does homage to the serpents that lie both in trees, and in holes.

30. 'Or those that are in the luminous sphere of the sky; or those in the rays of the sun; those by which abode is made in the waters, to those serpents be homage!' he hereby does homage to them wheresoever they are. He does so by 'homage, homage,' for homage is sacrifice (worship): by sacrifice, by homage, he thus worships them. Let him therefore not say 'homage be to thee,' to one not worthy of sacrifice, for it

would be just as if he said 'sacrifice (or, worship) be to thee!'

31. With three (formulas) he worships,—three are these worlds, and threefold, also, is Agni: as great as Agni is, as great as is his measure, by so much he thus stops these worlds (from moving); and by so much does he appease everything here. Standing he worships, for these worlds stand, as it were; and besides, while standing one is stronger.

32. Thereupon, having sat down he offers on (the gold man) with fivefold-taken ghee,—the significance of this has been explained. On each side (of the fire he offers), moving round: he thus gratifies him (Agni) with food from all quarters.

33. And, again, why he offers thereon. The gods, having laid down that body of theirs, now were afraid lest the Rakshas, the fiends, should smite that (body) of theirs. They saw those Rakshas-killing counter-charms[1],—(Vâg. S. XIII, 9-13; *Ri*k S. IV,

[1] See p. 53, note 2. In the present instance, the sacrificial formulas themselves constitute these charms. The five verses, only the first pâda of the first of which is given in the text, are as follows:—

1. Put forth thy power as (if it were) a broad host (or, net); go forth, like a mighty king with his following, following up the swift host! An archer thou art: pierce the Rakshas with thy fieriest (darts).

2. Swiftly fly thy whirling (darts): fiercely burning attack thou boldly! Unfettered, O Agni, with thy tongue pour forth on all sides winged flames and firebrands.

3. Thou, the most rapid, send forth thy spies: be thou an undaunted protector to this people (from him) who planneth evil against us from afar or from near by; O Agni, let none dare to attack us without thy cognizance.

4. Rise, O Agni, spread thyself out, and burn down the foes, O sharp-darted: whosoever hath done us injury, burn him down, O flaming one, like dry brushwood.

4, 1–5), 'Put forth thy power, like a broad army!' slayers of Rakshas are the counter-charms: having, by means of these counter-charms, repelled the Rakshas, the fiends, in every quarter, they (the gods) restored that body in a place free from danger and devilry; and in like manner this Sacrificer, having, by means of these counter-charms, repelled the Rakshas, the fiends, in every quarter, now restores that body (of Agni) in a place free from danger and devilry.

34. He offers with ghee; for the ghee is a thunderbolt: by the thunderbolt he thus repels the Rakshas, the fiends;—with fivefold-taken (ghee),—of five layers consists the fire-altar; five seasons are a year, and the year is Agni: as great as Agni is, as great as is his measure, with so much he thus repels the Rakshas, the fiends;—with (five) verses addressed to Agni, for the Rakshas-killing light is Agni: by Agni he thus repels the Rakshas, the fiends;—with trish/ubh verses,—the Trish/ubh is a thunderbolt: by the thunderbolt he thus repels the Rakshas, the fiends. On each side (he offers) moving round: in every quarter he thus repels the Rakshas, the fiends.

35. Behind the altar (he offers) while seated with his face towards the east; then on the left (north) side (looking) to the south; then in front (looking) to the west; then going round behind, (he offers) on the right (south) side while sitting with his face towards the north. Thus (he moves) to the right, for

5. Stand up, O Agni; strike out for our sake, and manifest thy divine powers! unstring the strong (arrows, or bows) of the goblins; crush the enemies, be they kindred or strangers!

that (leads) to the gods. Thereupon, going back, (he offers) while sitting behind, with his face towards the east; and in this way that performance of his takes place towards the east[1].

36. He then lays down two offering-spoons,—the offering-spoons are arms[2]: it is his arms he thus restores to him (Agni). And as to why offering-spoons (are laid down), it is because the arms are offering-spoons,—that bowl and the handle are two, for there are two of these arms. He lays them down at the (left and right) sides, for these arms (of ours) are at the sides.

37. On the right (south) side he lays down one of kârshmarya (gmelina arborea) wood. For at that time the gods were afraid lest the Rakshas, the fiends, should destroy their sacrifice from the south. They saw that Rakshas-killing tree, the Kârshmarya: having by that tree repelled the Rakshas, the fiends, on the south, they spread that sacrifice in a place free from danger and devilry. And in like manner the Sacrificer, having by that tree repelled the Rakshas, the fiends, on the south, now spreads that sacrifice in a place free from danger and devilry. It (the spoon) is filled with ghee;—the ghee is a thunderbolt: it is by the thunderbolt he thus repels the Rakshas, the fiends, on the south.

38. On the left (north) side he then lays down one of udumbara (ficus glomerata) wood; for the Udumbara means strength, life-sap: strength, life-sap he thus puts into him. It is filled with sour

[1] The order in which he offers would thus be,—west, north, east, (then going back along the north and west sides) south, west.

[2] They are indeed of an arm's length, with bowls of the shape and size of the hand, see part i, p. 67, note 2.

curds,—sour curds are life-sap: it is life-sap he thus puts into him.

39. And, again, why he lays down two offering-spoons. When Pragâpati was relaxed, Agni took his (Pragâpati's) fiery spirit, and carried it off to the south, and there stopped; and because after carrying (karsh) it off he stopped (ud-ram), therefore the Kârshmarya (sprang up). And Indra took his (Pragâpati's) vigour and went away to the north: it became the Udumbara tree.

40. He (Pragâpati) said to those two, 'Come ye to me, and put back into me that (substance) of mine wherewith ye have gone off!'—'Well then, bestow thou all food here on us two!' they said.—'Well then, join me, becoming these two arms of mine!'—'So be it!' He bestowed all food on them, and they joined him, becoming those two arms of his: hence it is by the arms that food is made, and by means of the arms that it is eaten, for he (Pragâpati) bestowed all food on the two arms.

41. The kârshmarya one he lays down on the right side, with (Vâg. S. XIII, 13), 'By Agni's fiery spirit I settle thee!'—that fiery spirit of his (Pragâpati's) which Agni then took and carried off to the south, he now puts back into him.—'Agni, the head, the summit of the sky, he, the lord of the earth, animates the seeds of the waters,' for Agni indeed is this (spoon). With a Gâyatrî verse (he performs),—Agni is Gâyatra: as great as Agni is, as great as is his measure, with so much he thus lays down that (spoon). It is filled with ghee, for ghee belongs to Agni: with his own share, with his own life-sap he thus gratifies him.

42. He then lays down the udumbara one on the

left (north) side, with (Vâg. S. XIII, 14), 'By Indra's vigour I settle thee!' that vigour of his (Pragâpati's) which Indra then took and went away to the north, he now puts back into him.—(Vâg. S. XIII, 15; *Ri*k S. X, 8, 6), 'Thou hast become the leader of the sacrifice, and of the sphere to which thou tendest with propitious teams; the light-giving head hast thou lifted to the sky; thy tongue, O Agni, hast thou made the bearer of the offering;'—Indra indeed is this (spoon). And as to its being a verse addressed to Agni, it is because it is the performance of Agni (the fire-altar);—and a trish*t*ubh one, because Indra is connected with the Trish*t*ubh; and Agni includes Indra and Agni: as great as Agni is, as great as is his measure, with so much he thus lays it down. Moreover, all the gods are Indra and Agni, and Agni belongs to all the deities: as great as Agni is, as great as is his measure, with so much he thus lays it down. It is filled with sour curds, for sour curds belong to Indra: with his own share, with his own life-sap he thus gratifies him.

43. Indra and Agni indeed are those two arms of his (Pragâpati's): they join him with fiery spirit and vigour. Where he (the Sacrificer) touches (the ground with his arms), whilst viewing intently the gold man with his breast close to him[1], there he

[1] There seems to be considerable difference of opinion between Kâtyâyana and Sâya*n*a regarding this point of the ceremonial. The gold man lies stretched out on his back with his head towards the east. According to Kâtyâyana, XVII, 4, 10, he (the Sacrificer) is to lie down so as to cover the gold man, but without actually touching him with his breast, and at the extreme end of where the arms touch (the ground) he is to make two marks, where the spoons are then to be laid down with the bowl towards the east. Sâya*n*a,

(the Adhvaryu) makes a mark and lays down those (spoons); for that is the place of those two (arms).

44. Now some lay them down sideways (from south to north), saying, 'Sideways run these two arms (of ours).' Let him not do so, but let him lay them with the bowl towards the front (east), for this Agni (altar) is built with the head towards the front; and, besides, in this way the arms are stronger. Separately he lays them down, separately he 'settles' them, and separately he pronounces the Sûdadohas verse on them; for separate are these two arms.

45. As to this they say, 'Let him make no arms to this (gold) man[1], lest he should cause him to be redundant; for these two spoons are (in lieu of) his arms.' Let him nevertheless make (him with arms), for those two spoons are (merely) after the manner of the two arms. Moreover, those two (arms of Agni) are wings; and whatever forms, whatever stomas, whatever p*ri*sh*th*as, whatever metres he will be applying to that fire-altar, that will be the perfection, that will be the growth of those two: let him therefore make arms to that (gold) man.

on the other hand, explains—'Let the Adhvaryu lay down the two spoons close to the breast of the laid-down gold man. Having beheld (i.e. recognised)—or, whilst beholding (?)—that man, wherever the laid-down pair of spoons reaches his breast there, having made a mark, let him lay down the two spoons: that part of the breast doubtless is the place of those two (spoons, or gods?) extolled as the arms.' Perhaps the text of this comment is somewhat corrupt. The ceremony is apparently intended to symbolise the identification of the Sacrificer with the sacrificial man, or the sacrifice itself. The Sacrificer lies down so as to rest on his fore-arms; the spoons being afterwards laid down on the marks left by the fore-arms (and naturally running in an easterly direction).—For Professor Weber's view, see p. 367, note 1.

[1] That is to say, Let it be a gold statuette without arms.

SECOND BRÂHMANA.

1. He puts a Svayam-âtrinnâ (naturally-perforated brick) on (the gold man);—the (first) naturally-perforated one being this earth, he thus puts this earth thereon. He puts it on so as not to be separate from the man; for the naturally-perforated one means food, and the naturally-perforated one means this earth, and this earth is food, since it is on her that all food ripens: he thus places food close to him (the man, Agni). Upon (the man he puts it): he thus places the food upon him [1].

2. And, again, why he puts on a naturally-perforated one;—the naturally-perforated (brick) is the breath (or vital air), for the breath thus bores itself (svayam âtrintte) through the body: it is breath he thus bestows on it. He puts it so as not to be separate from the man; for the naturally-perforated one is the breath, and the naturally-perforated one is this earth, and this earth is the breath, since this earth bears everything that breathes: he thus puts the breath so as not to be separate from him. Upon (the man he places the brick): he thus puts the breath upon him [1].

3. And, again, why he puts thereon the naturally-perforated one. The deities, taking up the disjointed Pragâpati, separated; and, having obtained a resting-place in them, thus separated, he settled down.

4. Now that Pragâpati who became disjointed is this very Agni (fire-altar) that is now being built up; and that resting-place (or, foundation) is this first

[1] Viz. inasmuch as the food is introduced into the body from above. It might also mean, he makes the food superior to the body, inasmuch as the body cannot exist without it. Similarly as regards the breath in the next paragraph.

naturally-perforated (brick) ;—thus when he now puts it on, he thereby puts upon this (altar-site) that (foundation[1]) which there was for his body: that is why he now puts it on.

5. He puts it on by means of Pra*g*âpati, for Pra*g*âpati thereby took back to himself (that foundation) of his body. [Vâ*g*. S. XIII, 16] 'Steady thou art,' that is, 'Firm thou art, or established thou art;'—'supporting,' for that which supports is a foundation;—'laid down by Vi*s*vakarman;' Vi*s*vakarman is Pra*g*âpati, thus, 'laid down by that one;'—'May the ocean, may the bird not injure thee!' the ocean doubtless is the gold plate, and the bird is the man: thus, 'May those two not injure thee!'—'Not shaking, steady thou the earth!' as the text, so the meaning.

6. [Vâ*g*. S. XIII, 17] 'May Pra*g*âpati settle thee'—for Pra*g*âpati saw this first layer[2];—'on the back of the waters, on the way of the ocean,' the back of the waters doubtless is this earth, and the way of the ocean is this earth;—'thee, the wide, the broad one!' for this earth is both wide and broad;—'broaden thou: thou art the broad one!' that is, 'broaden thou, and thou art the broad (earth, p*ri*thivî).'

7. [Vâ*g*. S. XIII, 18] 'Thou art the earth (bhû),' for this is the earth;—'thou art the ground (bhûmi),' for this is the ground;—'Thou art Aditi,'—Aditi is this earth, for this earth gives (dad)

[1] The 'pratish*th*â' (basis) of the bird-shaped Agni includes the parts on which the bird stands or sits, viz. the feet, and the hind-part of the body. Sâya*n*a, on the other hand, takes it to mean the 'pu*m*liṅga,' which seems very improbable.

[2] See VI, 2, 3, 1.

everything here;—'the all-containing,' for on this earth everything is contained;—'supporter of all the world,' that is, supporter of the whole world;—'sustain the earth, steady the earth, injure not the earth!' that is, sustain thyself, steady thyself, injure not thyself!

8. [Vâ*g*. S. XIII, 19] 'For all breathing, out-breathing, through-breathing, and up-breathing;' for the naturally-perforated (brick) is the breath, and the breath serves for all that;—'for a resting-place, for a moving-place;' the naturally-perforated (bricks) are these worlds [1], and these worlds are the resting-place, the moving-place;—'May Agni guard thee'—that is, may Agni protect thee!—'with mighty well-being!' that is, with great well-being;—'with the safest roof,' that is, with whatever roof (abode) is the safest. Having 'settled' it [2], he pronounces the Sûdadohas [3] on it: the meaning of this has been explained. He then sings a Sâman: the meaning of this (will be explained) further on.

9. Here now they say, 'How is it that that (gold) man is not held (weighed) down by the naturally-perforated (brick) [4]?' Well, the naturally-perforated (brick) is food and breath; and man is not held down either by food or by his breath.

10. He then lays the Dûrvâ-brick [5] thereon;—the Dûrvâ-brick being cattle; it is with cattle he

[1] See p. 155, note 8.

[2] That is, by adding the formula, 'By that deity, Aṅgiras-like, lie thou steady!'

[3] See p. 301, note 3.

[4] That is to say, How will he (the Sacrificer) be able to rise upwards to heaven, when that brick is lying on him?

[5] See p. 187, note 3.

thus endows it: these are the same cattle together with which Agni on that former occasion approached[1]; it is them he now puts thereon. He lays it down immediately on the naturally-perforated (brick); the naturally-perforated (brick) being this earth, he thus places the cattle immediately on this earth. Upon (the brick he places it): upon this earth he thereby places cattle.

11. And, again, why he lays down the Dûrvâ-brick. The hair of Pragâpati which were lying on the ground when he was disjointed became these herbs. The vital air then went out from within him, and, that having gone out, he fell down.

12. He said, 'Verily, this (vital air) has undone me!' and because he said, 'it has undone (dhûrv) me,' hence (the name) 'dhûrvâ;' 'dhûrvâ' doubtless being what is mystically called 'dûrvâ,' for the gods love the mystic. That (dûrvâ grass) is the ruling power (Kshatra), for it is this vital sap, the breath; and the other plants are the hair: in laying down that (dûrvâ plant) he lays down all (kinds of) plants.

13. When the gods restored him, they put that life-sap, the breath, inside him; and in like manner does this (Sacrificer) now put it into him. He lays it down immediately on the naturally-perforated (brick); the naturally-perforated one being this earth, he thus places the plants immediately on this earth. Upon (the brick he lays it): upon this earth he thus places the plants. It should be with root and top, for completeness' sake. Let him lay it on in such manner that while lying on the naturally-perforated (brick) it touches the ground (with its

[1] See VI, 2, 3, 2.

tops)[1], for on this earth those (plants) spring up, and along her they grow.

14. He lays it on, with (Vâg. S. XIII, 20-21), 'Growing up joint by joint, knot by knot;' for joint by joint, and knot by knot that (grass) does grow up;—'so do thou prolong us, O Dûrvâ (plant), by a thousand, and a hundred (descendants)!' as the text, so its meaning.

15. 'Thou that spreadest by a hundred, and branchest out by a thousand (shoots);' for by a hundred (shoots) it spreads, and by a thousand it branches out;—'to thee, O divine brick, we will do homage by offering;' as the text, so the meaning. With two (verses) he puts it on: the meaning of this has been explained. Having 'settled' it, he pronounces the Sûdadohas upon it: the meaning of this has been explained.

16. He then puts down a Dviyagus[2] (brick). Indra and Agni desired, 'May we go to the heavenly world!' They saw that dviyagus brick, even this earth, and laid it down; and having laid it down, they went to the heavenly world from that foundation. In like manner when this Sacrificer lays down a dviyagus (brick), (he does so) thinking, 'I want to go to the heavenly world by the same means (rûpa), by performing the same rite by which Indra and Agni went to the heavenly world!' And as to its being called 'dviyagus,' it is because two deities saw it. And as to why he lays down a dviyagus one: the dviyagus doubtless is the Sacrificer.

[1] The root is to lie on the brick from which (as representing the earth) it is supposed to have sprung; the tops then spreading along the ground.

[2] This brick is placed close beside the svayamâtrinnâ (naturally-perforated one) in front (east) of it, on the 'anûka' or spine.

17. Here now they say, 'If (the dviyagus) is that same Sacrificer who is that gold man, which then is that (real) form of his?' Well, that (gold man) is his divine body, and this (brick) is his human one. As to that gold man, that is his immortal form, his divine form; gold being immortal. And as to this (brick) being made of clay, it is because this is his human form.

18. Now were he only to lay down that (golden man), and not to let this dviyagus (brick) remain [1], the Sacrificer surely would quickly pass away from this world; but now that he allows this (brick) to remain, he thereby leaves to him this human form of his; and so he attains with this body the full (measure of) life.

19. And were he not to put it on after (the gold man), he assuredly would not afterwards find out that divine body [2]; but now that he puts it on thereafter, he does so afterwards find out that divine body. He lays it down close to the dûrvâ-brick: the dûrvâ-brick being cattle, he thus establishes the Sacrificer in (the possession of) cattle.

20. Here now they say, 'How do those two bodies of his come to be connected together by the breath, and not severed?' Well, the naturally-perforated (brick) is the breath, and the dûrvâ-brick is the breath, and the dviyagus (-brick) is the Sacri-

[1] The verb 'apa-sish' is taken similarly by Sâyana (avaseshayet); whilst the St. Petersburg dictionary assigns to it the meaning 'to omit, leave out' (weglassen), which can hardly be correct (? misprint for übriglassen). It might, however, possibly be taken in the sense of 'vi-sish,' to specify, to single out.

[2] That is to say,—he would not, after quitting his mortal body, know or find out that divine body with which he wishes to invest himself.

ficer: and inasmuch as he lays down the dûrvá-brick close to the naturally-perforated one, he thereby connects and joins breath with breath; and inasmuch as he lays down the dviyagus one close to the dûrvâ-brick—the dûrvâ-brick being the breath, and the dviyagus the Sacrificer—those two bodies of his (the human one and the divine one) thus become connected together by the breath, and not severed.

21. [He lays down the dviyagus brick, with Vâg. S. XIII, 22, 23] 'O Agni, what lights of thine in the sun overspread the sky by their beams, with all those help us to light and to people!—O ye gods, what lights of yours are in the sun, and what lights are in kine and horses, O Indra and Agni, with all those bestow light upon us, O B*ri*haspati!' for 'light' he prays each time: light being immortality, it is immortality he thus bestows on him (Agni, and the Sacrificer). With two (verses) he lays it down: the significance of this has been explained. And, moreover, it is because that material form (of the brick) is a twofold one, (consisting as it does of) clay and water. Having 'settled' it, he pronounces the Sûdadohas upon it: the significance of this has been explained.

22. He then lays down two Reta*h*si*k* (seed-shedding bricks);—the seed-shedders doubtless are these two worlds, for these two worlds do shed seed;—this (terrestrial world) sheds seed upwards from here (in the form of) smoke; it becomes rain in yonder world, and that rain yonder world (sheds) from above: hence (creatures) are born within these two worlds, and therefore these two worlds are seed-shedders.

23. [He lays them down, with Vâg. S. XIII, 24]

'The wide-ruling one contained the light;' the wide-ruling one[1] doubtless is this (terrestrial) world: it contains this fire, the light.—'The self-ruling one contained the light,' the self-ruling[1] one doubtless is yonder world: it contains yonder sun, the light. And the wide-ruling one and the self-ruling one being these two worlds, he lays them down separately, for separate are these two worlds. He 'settles' them once: he thereby makes them one and the same (or, joined together), whence the ends of these two worlds meet.

24. And, again, why he lays down two seed-shedders; the seed-shedders are the testicles, for only he who has testicles sheds seed. 'The wide-ruling one contained the light;—the self-ruling one contained the light,' he says; for the wide-ruling and the self-ruling ones are the testicles: they contain that light, the seed, Pra*g*âpati. He lays them down separately, for separate are these testicles. He 'settles' them once: he thereby makes them one and the same, whence they have a common connecting-part. He lays them down close to the dviya*g*us (brick)[2]: the dviya*g*us being the Sacrificer, he thus puts the testicles together with the Sacrificer.

25. He then lays down a Vi*s*va*g*yotis (all-light brick)[3];—the first 'all-light' (brick)[4] is Agni, for Agni

[1] Or, the wide-shining . . . the self-shining one.

[2] The two Reta*h*si*k* bricks are laid down immediately in front (east) of the Dviya*g*us one, one on each side of the 'spine,' which thus coincides with their line of separation.

[3] See VI, 5, 3, 3.

[4] As in the case of the Svayamât*ri*n*n*âs (naturally-perforated bricks, see pp. 155, note 8; 187, note 2), so there are three Vi*s*va-*g*yotis or 'all-light' bricks, placed in the first, third, and fifth layers

is all the light in this (terrestrial) world: it is Agni he thus lays down. He lays it down close to the seed-shedding ones,—the seed-shedding ones being these two worlds, he thus places Agni together with these two worlds. He lays it down between (the two Reta*h*si*k*[1]), for Agni (the fire) is within these two worlds.

26. And, again, why he lays down an 'all-light' (brick);—the 'all-light' (brick) is progeny, for progeny is all the light: he thus lays generative power (into Agni). He lays it down so as not to be separated from the seed-shedding (bricks),—the seed-shedders being the testicles, he thus makes the generative power inseparable from the testicles. He lays it down between (those two), for within the testicles progeny is produced.

27. [He lays it down, with Vâg. S. XIII, 24] 'May Pragâpati settle thee'—for Pragâpati saw this first layer[2];—'on the back of the earth, thee the brilliant one!' for on the back of the earth this brilliant Agni indeed is.

28. 'For all breathing, out-breathing, through-breathing,'—the all-light (brick) is breath, and breath is (necessary) for this entire universe;—'give all the light!' that is, 'give the whole light;'—'Agni is thine over-lord,' he thus makes Agni the over-lord of this earth. Having 'settled' it[3], he

of the altar, and representing the light (or ruling deity) of the respective world represented by the svayamâtr*inn*â of the same layer.

[1] In reality the Visvagyotis brick is not placed between the two Reta*h*si*k*, but in front of the line separating them from each other.

[2] He 'saw' the first naturally-perforated brick, which, as the central brick of the first layer, represents the latter, as well as the lowest of the three worlds, the earth. See VI, 2, 3, 1.

[3] Viz. by adding, 'by that deity, Angiras-like, lie thou steady!'

pronounces the Sûdadohas upon it: the significance of this has been explained.

29. He then lays down two *Ri*tavya (seasonal bricks);—the two seasonal (bricks) being the same as the seasons, it is the seasons he thus lays down. [Vâg. S. XIII, 25] 'Madhu and Mâdhava, the two spring seasons,'—these are the names of those two: it is thus by their names that he lays them down. There are two (such) bricks, for two months are a season. He 'settles' them once[1]: he thereby makes (the two months) one season.

30. And as to why he now lays down these two;—this Agni (fire-altar) is the year, and the year is these worlds; the first layer is this (terrestrial) world thereof, and the spring season also is this world thereof; and when he now lays down those two (bricks), he thereby puts back into him (Agni-Pragâpati) what those two (the first layer and the spring) are to that body of his[2]: this is why he now lays down those two (bricks).

31. And, again, why he now lays down these two;—this Agni is Pragâpati, and Pragâpati is the year; the first layer is his foundation, and the spring season also is his foundation;—thus when he now lays down these two (bricks), he thereby puts back into him what those two are to that body of his: this is why he now lays down those two (bricks). He lays them down close to the 'all-light' brick: the 'all-light' brick being progeny, he thus lays progeny close together with the seasons; whence progeny is produced in accordance with the seasons, for by seasons people compute (the age of man)

[1] That is, he pronounces the sâdana-formula once only.

[2] Viz. its foundation.

whilst in the state of embryo, and by seasons when he is born.

32. He then lays down the Ashâdhâ (invincible brick)[1],—the 'invincible one' being this earth, it is this earth he thus lays down. He puts it on the fore-part (of the altar-site), for this earth was created first.

33. And as to its being called Ashâdhâ. The gods and the Asuras, both of them sprung from Pragâpati, strove together. The gods saw this invincible brick, even this earth; they put it on (the altar); and having put it on, they conquered (and drove) the Asuras, the enemies, the rivals, from this universe; and inasmuch as (thereby) they conquered (asahanta), it is called Ashâdhâ. In like manner the Sacrificer, after putting on that (brick), conquers (and drives) his spiteful rival from this universe (or, from everything here).

34. And, again, why he lays down the Ashâdhâ. The Ashâdhâ is speech, and by speech[2] the gods then indeed conquered (and drove) the Asuras, the enemies, the rivals, from this universe; and in like manner the Sacrificer, by means of speech, conquers (and drives) his spiteful rival from this universe: it was speech the gods then laid down (or bestowed on Agni), and in like manner the Sacrificer now lays down speech.

35. This earth is the bearer of what is desirable; for—the desirable being the vital airs—this earth bears everything that breathes, and for that reason this earth is the bearer of what is desirable. But

[1] See VI, 5, 3, 1–2.

[2] Viz. by threats, vituperation, &c., Sây.

speech (the mouth) also indeed is the bearer of what is desirable; for the desirable is the vital airs, and for the (channels of) the vital airs food is put into the mouth: therefore speech is the bearer of what is desirable.

36. Now the Ashâ*dh*â is the same as those vital airs; he lays it down in the fore-part (of the altar): he thus bestows (on Agni the organs of) the vital airs in front; whence there are here (organs of) the vital airs in front (of the body). Let him not in this layer enclose this (Ashâ*dh*â) in front by any other brick which has a special prayer of its own, lest he close up (the organs of) the vital airs.

37. And as to why he lays down in front five Apasyâs[1],—water (ap) is food, and by food (the organs of) the vital airs are not closed up. He lays down (the Ashâ*dh*â) close to the two seasonal ones: he thereby establishes speech in the seasons, and hence speech (the mouth) speaks here, firmly established in the seasons.

38. Here now they say, 'If the Vi*s*va*g*yotis (brick) is progeny, and the Ashâ*dh*â speech, why does he put the two seasonal ones between them?' Well, the seasonal ones being the year, he thus separates speech from progeny by the year, and hence children utter speech at the time (or age) of a year.

39. [He lays down the Ashâ*dh*â, with Vâ*g*. S. XIII, 26] 'Thou art Ashâ*dh*â, the conquering,' for the gods thereby conquered the Asuras,—'conquer the enemies! conquer the hostile!' as the text, so the meaning;—'thou hast a thousand energies: do thou speed me!' a thousand means

[1] See VII, 5, 2, 40 seq.

all: thus, 'thou hast all energies, do thou speed me!' When he has 'settled' it, he pronounces the Sûdadohas on it: the significance of this has been explained.

40. Here now they say, 'Why are those other bricks placed in front of the naturally-perforated one?' Let him say, There are two wombs (birth-places)—the one being the womb of the gods, the other the womb of men: the gods have their birth-place in the east, and men in the west; and when he lays down those (bricks) in front, he thereby causes the Sacrificer to be born from the womb of the gods.

FIFTH ADHYÂYA. FIRST BRÂHMANA.

1. He then puts down a (living) tortoise;—the tortoise means life-sap: it is life-sap (blood) he thus bestows on (Agni). This tortoise is that life-sap of these worlds which flowed away from them when plunged into the waters[1]: that (life-sap) he now bestows on (Agni). As far as the life-sap extends, so far the body extends: that (tortoise) thus is these worlds.

2. That lower shell of it is this (terrestrial) world; it is, as it were, fixed; for fixed, as it were, is this (earth-)world. And that upper shell of it is yonder sky; it has its ends, as it were, bent down; for yonder sky has its ends, as it were, bent down. And what is between (the shells) is the air;—that (tortoise) thus is these worlds: it is these worlds he thus lays down (to form part of the altar).

3. He anoints it with sour curds, honey, and ghee,—sour curds doubtless are a form of this (earth-)

[1] See VI, 1, 1, 12.

world, ghee of the air, and honey of yonder sky: he thus supplies it (the tortoise) with its own form. Or, sour curds are the life-sap of this (earth-)world, ghee that of the air, and honey that of yonder sky: he thus supplies it with its own life-sap.

4. [He anoints it, with Vâg. S. XIII, 27-29; *Ri*k S. I, 90, 6-8] 'Honey the winds pour forth for the righteous, honey the rivers; full of honey may the plants be for us!—Honey by night and morn, rich in honey may the region of the earth be for us, honey the father Heaven!—rich in honey may the tree be for us, rich in honey the sun, full of honey the kine!' To whatever deity a *Ri*k-verse, and to whatever (deity) a Yagus formula applies, that very deity the verse is, and that very deity the sacrificial formula is[1]. This triplet then is honey (madhu); and honey being life-sap, it is life-sap he thus puts into him (Agni). With three Gâyatrî verses (he performs): the significance of this has been explained.

5. And as to its being called 'kûrma' (tortoise);—Pragâpati, having assumed that form, created living beings. Now what he created, he made; and inasmuch as he made (kar), he is (called) 'kûrma;' and 'kûrma' being (the same as) 'kasyapa' (a tortoise), therefore all creatures are said to be descended from Kasyapa.

6. Now this tortoise is the same as yonder sun: it is yonder sun he thus lays down (on the altar). He lays it down in front with the head towards the back (west): he thus places yonder sun in the east

[1] That is to say, each Vedic text is identical with the deity to which it is addressed. Cf. VI, 5, 1, 2.

looking thitherwards (or moving westward); and hence yonder sun is placed in the east looking thitherwards. On the right (south) of the Ashâ*dh*â (he places it), for the tortoise (kûrma, masc.) is a male, and the Ashâ*dh*â a female, and the male lies on the right side of the female;—at a cubit's distance[1], for at a cubit's distance the male lies by the female. That Ashâ*dh*â is the consecrated queen (mahishî) of all the bricks, hence being on the right (south) side of her, it (the tortoise) is on the right side of all the bricks.

7. And, again, why he puts down a tortoise;—the tortoise (kûrma) is the breath, for the breath makes (kar) all these creatures: it is breath he thus puts into him (Agni). He puts it down in front looking towards the back: he thus puts in the breath in front tending towards the back; whence the breath is taken in from the front backwards. [He puts it down so as to be] turned towards the (gold) man: he thus puts breath into the Sacrificer. South of the Ashâ*dh*â (he puts it), for the tortoise is breath, and the Ashâ*dh*â speech; and the breath (prâ*n*a, masc.) is the male, the mate, of speech (vâ*k*, fem.).

8. [He sets it down, with Vâg. S. XIII, 30-32] 'Seat thee in the depth of the waters!' for that indeed is the deepest (place) of the (heavenly) waters where yonder (sun) burns;—'lest the sun, lest Agni Vai*s*vânara should scorch thee!' that is, lest the Sun, lest Agni Vaisvânara injure thee;—'Overlook the creatures with unbroken wings,' that is, overlook all these uninjured, unharmed creatures, that is, these bricks;—'may

[1] While the bricks generally measure a pâda or foot square, the cubit measures about two feet.

heaven's rain favour thee!' this he says in order that the rain of heaven may favour him.

9. He then makes it move[1], with, 'Over the heaven-reaching three oceans he crept,' the three heaven-reaching oceans doubtless are these worlds, and over them he crept in the shape of a tortoise;—'the lord of waters, the bull of the bricks,' for he (the tortoise) indeed is the lord of waters, and the bull of the bricks;—'induing the covering of him, the well-made, in the world,' the covering (purîsha) means the cattle: thus, entering the (form of the) cattle of the well-made (Agni) in the world;—'go thither whither the former have passed away!' that is, go thither whither by this performance former (tortoises) went.

10. 'The mighty sky and the earth,' that is, the great sky and the earth;—'shall mix (prepare) this our sacrifice!' that is, shall favour this sacrifice;—'they shall fill us with nourishments!' that is, they shall nourish us with nourishments! With the last (verse) relating to heaven and earth he puts it down, for the tortoise represents heaven and earth.

11. With three (formulas) he puts it on (the altar);—three are these worlds, and threefold is Agni: as great as Agni is, as great as is his measure, by so much he thus puts it on. With three (formulas) he anoints it; that makes six: the significance of this (number) has been explained. There are avakâ-plants[2] below and avakâ-plants above (the

[1] He sets the tortoise down with three verses; and in muttering the second verse he makes it move while he still holds it in his hand.

[2] Blyxa octandra, a grassy plant growing in marshy land ('lotus-flower,' Weber, Ind. Stud. XIII, p. 250).

tortoise),—the avakâ-plant means water: he thus places it in the midst of water. Having 'settled' it, he pronounces the Sûdadohas upon it: the significance of this has been explained.

12. He then puts down a mortar and pestle. Vishnu desired, 'May I be an eater of food!' He saw these two bricks, the mortar and pestle. He placed them on (the altar); and by placing them thereon, he became an eater of food. In like manner, when the Sacrificer now places a mortar and pestle thereon, (he does so) thinking, 'I want to be an eater of food by the same means (rûpa), by performing the same rite by which Vishnu became an eater of food.' Now the mortar and pestle mean all (kinds of) food; for by the mortar and pestle food is prepared, and by means of them it is eaten.

13. He puts them down at the distance of the two retahsik[1],—the retahsik being the ribs, and the ribs being the middle: he thus puts food into the middle of him (Agni);—on the north (upper) side (of the central brick): he thus puts the food upon him;—at the distance of a cubit, for from a cubit's distance food is (taken by the hand and) eaten.

14. They measure a span, for Vishnu, when an embryo, was a span long; and these (mortar and pestle) being food, he thus puts food into him (Agni-Vishnu) proportionate to his body. And indeed the food which is proportionate to the body satisfies,

[1] The mortar and pestle are to be placed as far north of the central (naturally-perforated) brick, as the two retahsik lie in front (towards the east) of it. This distance is ascertained by means of a cord stretched across the bricks hitherto laid down (from the Svayamâtrinnâ to the Ashâdhâ), and knots made in the cord over the centre of the respective bricks.

and does no harm; but that which is excessive does harm; and that which is too little does not satisfy.

15. They are made of Udumbara wood;—the Udumbara (ficus glomerata) being strength, life-sap, he thus puts strength, life-sap into him. And, again, the Udumbara being all the trees, by putting on those two, he puts all trees on (the altar). At the distance of the two retahsik (bricks, he places the mortar and pestle),—the 'seed-shedders' being these two (worlds[1]), he thus puts the trees in these two (worlds), and hence there are trees in these two (worlds). It (the mortar) is four-cornered,—there being four quarters, he thus places trees in all the quarters; whence there are trees in all the quarters. It is contracted in the middle, to give it the form of a (real) mortar.

16. And, again, why he places a mortar and pestle thereon. From Pragâpati, when relaxed, the breath wanted to go out from within. He kept it back by means of food: hence the breath is kept back by food, for he who eats food, breathes.

17. The breath being kept back, the food wanted to go out of him. He kept it back by means of the breath: hence food is kept back by the breath, for he who breathes, eats food.

18. Those two being kept back, strength wanted to go out of him. He kept it back by those two: hence strength is kept back by those two; for he who eats food, breathes; and to him it gives strength.

19. Strength being kept back, those two wanted

[1] I do not see what else could here be referred to than the heaven and the earth (cf. VII, 4, 2, 22), though in that case one might rather expect 'imau (lokau)' instead of 'ime.' Possibly, however, the earth and atmosphere may be intended.

to go out of him. He kept them back by means of strength: hence those two are kept back by strength; for he to whom one gives strength, breathes and eats food.

20. Those (energies) thus were kept back by one another. Having kept them back by one another, he (Pragâpati) caused them to enter his own self; and that food having entered, all the gods entered along with it; for everything here lives on food.

21. It is thereto that this verse applies,—'Then, indeed, he became that breath,'—for that breath he then indeed became;—'having become the great Pragâpati,'—for great he indeed then became, when those gods entered him;—'having obtained the benefits, the beneficial,'—the benefits doubtless are the vital airs (breaths), and the beneficial are the food: thus, having obtained all that;—'when he breathed the breaths in the stronghold;'—the stronghold doubtless is the self (body), and inasmuch as he breathed the breaths, the gods are the breaths; and inasmuch as Pragâpati breathed, the breath also is Pragâpati; and verily he who is that breath, he is that Gâyatri;—and as to that food, that is Vishnu, the deity; and as to that strength, that is the Udumbara (tree).

22. He said, 'Verily this one has lifted me from out of all evil;' and because he said 'he has lifted me out (udabhârshît),' hence (the name) 'udumbhara;'—'udumbhara' doubtless being what is mystically called Udumbara, for the gods love the mystic. 'Wide space (uru) shall it make (karat) for me!' he said, hence 'urukara;' 'urukara' doubtless being what is mystically called 'ulûkhala' (the mortar); for the gods love the mystic. Now that mortar is

the birth-place of all breaths; and the birth-place of the breaths being the head—

23. It (the mortar) is of the measure of a span, for the head is, as it were, of the measure of a span;—four-cornered, for the head is, as it were, four-cornered;—contracted in the middle, for the head is, as it were, contracted in the middle.

24. Now when the gods restored him (Pragâpati-Agni), they put all that inside him—breath, food, strength; and in like manner this (Sacrificer) now puts that into him. At the distance of the two reta*h*si*k* (he places it),—the reta*h*si*k* being the ribs, and the ribs the middle, it is thus in the middle of (or, inside) him that he puts all that.

25. [He sets them down[1], with Vâg. S. XIII, 33; *Ri*k S. I, 22, 19] 'See ye the deeds of Vish*n*u'—deed doubtless means power: thus, see ye the powers of Vish*n*u;—'whereby he beheld the sacred ordinances,'—ordinance means food: thus, whereby he did behold the food;—'Indra's allied friend,' for he is indeed Indra's allied friend. With a (verse) relating to two deities he sets them down, for the mortar and pestle are two. Once he 'settles' them: he thereby makes them one and the same; for one and the same is that food. Having 'settled' it, he pronounces the Sûdadohas on it: the significance of this has been explained.

26. He then places the fire-pan thereon,—the fire-pan is a womb: a womb (birth-place) he thus gives to him (Agni). He places it on the mortar,—the mortar is the air, and everything that is above this

[1] The mortar, according to the commentaries to Kâty., is partly dug into the ground, with the open part upwards; the pestle being then placed to the right (south) of it.

earth is air; and the air is the middle: he thus places the womb in the middle; whence the womb of all beings, even of trees [1], is in the middle.

27. And, again, why he places the fire-pan thereon;—that same Pragâpati who became disjointed doubtless is this same fire-pan, for the fire-pan is these worlds, and Pragâpati is these worlds. He places it on the mortar: he thereby establishes him (Pragâpati) in all that—breath, food, strength; and thus he places him so as not to be separated from all that.

28. Thereupon, having pounded the remainder (of the clay), and having put the fire-pan in its place, he throws (the pounded clay) in front of the fire-pan; for this is the place of that (remainder [2]), and thus that (remainder) is not separated therefrom [3].

---

[1] Viz., according to Sâyana, because they spring from the germ in the centre of the fruit.

[2] ?Or, of it (the fire-pan). There is some uncertainty regarding this item of the ceremonial. Kâtyâyana's rule (XVII, 5, 4)—'Having placed the Ukhâ (pan) on the mortar, pounded the remainder of clay, and thrown it down in front, with the text "Dhruvâ asi," (of) the Ukhâ'—is evidently intentionally vague. Mahîdhara (on Vâg. S. XIII, 34) gives the following interpretation of it,—'Having first silently placed the Ukhâ on the mortar, then pounded the remaining clay, and thrown it down on the ground in front of the Ukhâ, let him place the Ukhâ thereon with two formulas.' According to this, the Ukhâ would only temporarily be placed on the mortar, its proper and permanent place (loka) being on the powdered clay in front (to the east) of the mortar. The text of the Brâhmana, as it stands, however, cannot possibly be construed so as to accord with Mahîdhara's interpretation. This would require some such reading as,—athoparayâm pishtvâ, purastâd ukhâyâ upanivapya lokabhâgam ukhâm karoti. See, however, paragraph 38 below, which evidently applies to the permanent position of the pan.

[3] For the genitive 'asya' (viz. lokasya) with 'antarita'—instead

29. Here now they say, 'How does that (remainder) of his come to be put on as cooked, as baked?'—In that it is prepared with a sacrificial formula; and, moreover, whatever comes in contact with Agni Vaisvânara even thereby comes to be put on as something cooked, as baked.

30. [He sets the fire-pan down, with Vâg. S. XIII, 34-35] 'Steady thou art, supporting,' the meaning of this has been explained[1];—'from here he was at first born, from these wombs, the knower of beings;' for from these wombs the knower of beings (Agni) was indeed born at first;—'by the Gâyatrî, the Trish*t*ubh, and the Anush*t*ubh, may he, the knowing, bear the offering to the gods!'—by means of these metres he, the knowing, indeed bears the offering to the gods.

31. 'For sap, for wealth, do thou rest, for might in glory, for strength, for offspring!' that is, for all that do thou rest!—'all-ruling thou art, self-ruling thou art!' for both all-ruling and self-ruling he (Agni) indeed is;—'may the two Sârasvata wells cheer thee!' Sarasvat (m.) is the Mind, and Sarasvatî (f.) Speech,—these two are the Sârasvata wells: thus, may these two cheer thee! With two (formulas) he sets it down: the significance of this has been explained; and, moreover, twofold is that form, (consisting as it does of) clay and water. Having 'settled' it, he pronounces the Sûdadohas on it: the significance of this has been explained.

32. He then offers upon it;—now seed was poured into it before, (in the shape of) sand[2]; that he now

of the more usual ablative—see VI, 2, 2, 38, 'prâ*n*asya tad antariyât.'

[1] VII, 4, 2, 5.

[2] See VII, 1, 1, 41.

fashions[1], whence the seed injected into the womb is fashioned. He offers with the dipping-spoon, with 'Hail!' with two Gâyatri verses relating to Agni: the significance of this has been explained.

33. [Vag. S. XIII, 36-37; *Rik* S. VI, 16, 43; VIII, 75, 1] 'O Agni, harness those good steeds of thine: they draw equal to thy mettle!—Like a chariot-fighter, harness thou the steeds, the best callers of the gods, O Agni! take thy seat as the old Hot*ri*!' with two (verses) containing the (verb) 'yug' (to harness, fasten),—he thus settles that seed injected into the womb, whence the seed settled in the womb does not escape.

34. If (the fire in the pan) has been carried about for a year[2], in that case he should now offer; for (the fire) which has been carried about for a year is everything, and that also whereon he offers is everything. But if it has not been carried about for a year, let him only stand by (worshipping) it; for (the fire) which has not been carried about for a year is not everything; and that by which he stands (worshipping) is not everything. Let him nevertheless offer thereon.

35. Now that Agni is an animal, and even now he is (being) made up whole and complete: the naturally-perforated (brick) is his lower vital air, the

[1] The verb 'abhi-k*ri*' is here taken in the sense of 'vi-k*ri*' (he gives form to it); and in that sense I would now take it at II, 3, 1, 4, 'he fashions (gives human shape to) that embryo,' instead of 'he benefits that embryo.' The St. Petersburg dictionary proposes the meaning, 'to do something with reference to (or, for the benefit of).' The proper German meaning would rather seem to be 'bearbeiten.' The preposition 'abhi' is probably used here with reference to the 'abhi-guhoti.'

[2] See p. 269, note 3.

dviyagus the hip, the two retahsik the ribs, the visvagyotis the breast-bone, the two seasonal ones the back, the ashâdhâ the neck, the tortoise the head, and the vital airs in the tortoise are those vital airs in the head.

36. Now that (Agni) he builds upwards from here (as flying) towards the east, and that Agni being yonder sun, he thereby places yonder sun upwards from here in the east; whence yonder sun is placed upwards from here in the east.

37. He then turns him towards the right[1],—he thereby turns yonder sun towards the right, whence yonder sun moves round these worlds (from left) to right.

38. The fire-pan is the belly, the mortar the womb;—the fire-pan is above, and the mortar below; for the belly is above, and the womb below. The pestle is the *sisna*; it is round-like, for the *sisna* is round-like. He places it to the right (south of the mortar), for the male lies on the right side of the female. And what food there is for the consecrated animal, that is the dûrvâ-brick. The left (north) side of that (Agni or altar) is more raised,—that Agni is an animal, and hence the left side of the belly of a well-filled beast is more raised (than the right side).

SECOND BRÂHMANA.

1. He puts the heads of the victims in (the fire-pan),—the heads of the victims being animals (or cattle), it is animals he thus puts thereon. He puts them in the fire-pan;—the pan being these worlds, and the heads of the victims being beasts, he thus

[1] ? Viz. by filling up the vacant spaces of the altar from left to right.

puts animals in these worlds; whence there are animals in these worlds.

2. And as to why (he puts the heads) in the fire-pan;—the fire-pan being a womb, and the heads of the victims being animals, he thus establishes the animals in the womb: hence animals, though being eaten and cooked, do not diminish, for he establishes them in the womb.

3. And, again, why he puts the heads of the victims therein;—what (animal) perfections (*s*ri)[1] there were, they are these victims' heads; and what rumps there were, they are those five layers (of the altar). Now those five layers are these worlds, and these worlds are this very fire-pan: thus, when he puts the heads of the victims in the fire-pan, he thereby unites those rumps with those heads.

4. He puts them in the fore-part, so as to look towards the back (west). For when, on that (former) occasion, Pra*g*âpati wanted to slaughter these animals, they, being about to be slaughtered, wanted to run away. He seized them by (the organs of) the vital airs[2]; and having seized them by the vital airs, he took them into himself from the front (mouth) towards the back (inside).

5. Now the same thing which the gods did is done here. The animals do not, indeed, want to run away from him; but when he does this, it is because he wants to do what the gods did: having thus seized them by (the outlets of) the vital airs, he takes them into himself from the front towards the back.

[1] See VI, 1, 1, 4; 2, 1, 7.

[2] That is, by the head, according to Sâya*n*a.

6. And, again, why he puts the heads of the victims thereon. Pragâpati alone was here at first[1]. He desired, 'May I create food, may I be reproduced!' He fashioned animals from his vital airs, a man from his soul (mind), a horse from his eye, a cow from his breath, a sheep from his ear, and a goat from his voice; and inasmuch as he created them from the vital airs, people say that 'Animals are vital airs.' The soul is the first of the vital airs; and inasmuch as he fashioned man from his soul, they say that 'Man is the first, and strongest of animals.' The soul is all the vital airs, for in the soul all the vital airs are established. And inasmuch as he fashioned man from his soul, they say that 'Man is all animals,' for they all belong to man.

7. Having created that food, he took it into himself from the front towards the back; and hence whosoever prepares for himself food, takes it into himself from the front towards the back (inside). That (animal food being put) in the fire-pan, and the fire-pan being the belly, he thus puts the food into the belly.

8. He now (in the first place[2]) thrusts gold chips into each of them,—gold is vital air, and the vital airs go out of these animals when slaughtered: thus, when he thrusts gold chips into each of them, he puts the vital airs into them.

9. Seven (chips) he thrusts into each,—seven vital airs there are in the head: these he thereby puts into it. And if there are five victims, let him thrust in five times seven (chips); for those five victims he puts on (the fire-pan), and there are seven vital

[1] See J. Muir, Original Sanskrit Texts, V, p. 391.
[2] That is, before putting the heads in the fire-pan.

airs in each victim: he thus puts the vital airs into all of them.

10. Now, even if there is only one victim[1], some people thrust five times seven (into that one head), thinking, 'Those five victims he puts down (symbolically), and there are seven vital airs in each victim: thus we put the vital airs into all of them.' Let him not do so, for in this animal the form of all animals is contained[2]; and when he thrusts (seven chips) into this one, he thereby puts the vital airs into all of them.

11. The first (chip) he thrusts into the mouth, with (Vâg. S. XIII, 38; *Ri*k S. IV, 58, 6, 5), 'Fitly flow the draughts of milk like rivers,'—draughts of milk are food, and that indeed flows fitly into this mouth;—'purified within by the heart, by the mind,'—for the food is indeed purified by the heart and mind within him who is righteous;—'the streams of ghee I behold,' he thereby means the libations he is about to offer on that fire;—'the golden reed (is) in the middle of Agni,' he thereby means that gold man.

12. With (Vâg. S. XIII, 39), 'For praise thee!' (he thrusts one in) here (into the right nostril); praise (or splendour) means breath, for with breath one praises;—with, 'For sheen thee!' here (into the left nostril); sheen means breath, for by breath one shines; and also because everything here shines for breath;—with, 'For brightness thee!' here (into the right eye);—with, 'For lustre thee!' here

[1] Viz. a he-goat, as the animal sacrifice to either Pragâpati, or (Vâyu) Niyutvat; see pp. 178, 184.

[2] See VI, 2, 2, 15.

(into the left eye), for bright and lustrous these two eyes indeed are;—with, 'This hath become the fiery spirit of all the world, and of Agni Vaisvânara,' here (into the right ear);—with (Vâg. S. XIII, 40), 'Agni, bright with brightness, the golden disk, lustrous with lustre,' here (into the left ear),—thus with two (formulas) containing 'all[1],' for the ear is all.

13. He then lifts up the human head—he thereby exalts it—with, 'Giver of a thousand thou art: for a thousand thee!' a thousand means everything: thus, 'the giver of everything, for everything (I bestow) thee!'

14. He then puts them (the heads) in (the fire-pan), first (that of) the man—having taken possession of the man by strength he sets him up;—the man in the middle; on both sides the other victims: he thus sets the man, as the eater, in the midst of cattle; whence man is the eater in the midst of cattle.

15. The horse and ram on the left (north) side: he thereby puts those two (kinds of) cattle in that region; whence those two (kinds of) cattle are most plentiful in that region.

16. The bull and he-goat on the right (south) side: he thereby puts those two (kinds of) cattle in that region; whence those two (kinds of) cattle are most plentiful in that region.

17. The (head of the) man he places on the milk[2],—milk means cattle: he thus establishes the Sacrificer among cattle,—with (Vâg. S. XIII, 41), 'With

[1] Only the first of the two formulas, however, contains the word 'visva,' all.

[2] The pan was partly filled with sand and milk, see VII, 1, 1, 41. 44.

milk anoint thou Âditya, the unborn child!' that unborn child, the man, is indeed the sun: thus, Him anoint thou with milk!—'the all-shaped maker of a thousand,' the maker[1] of a thousand is man, for to him belong a thousand;—'spare him with thy heat, harbour not evil thoughts against him!' that is, spare him with thy fire, do not hurt him!—'make him live a hundred years, while thou art built!' he thereby makes man the one among animals (capable of) living a hundred years; whence man, among animals, lives up to a hundred years.

18. Then on the left side (he puts the head of) the horse, with (Vâg. S. XIII, 42), 'The speed of the wind,'—this one, the horse, is indeed the speed of the wind;—'Varu*n*a's navel'—for the horse is Varu*n*a;—'the horse, born in the midst of the flood;' the flood is the water, and the horse is indeed the water-born;—'the tawny, rock-founded child of rivers;' rock means mountain, and the waters are indeed founded on the mountains;—'harm him not, Agni, in the highest region!' the highest region means these worlds: thus, do not harm him in these worlds!

19. Then on the right side (the head of) the bull, with (Vâg. S. XIII, 43), 'The imperishable, red drop,' the drop doubtless is Soma; and that bull is the same as the imperishable Soma;—'the eager one (bhura*n*yu),' that is, the bearer (bhart*ri*);—'Agni, the forward-striving, I glorify with homages;' for

[1] 'Pratimâ' is perhaps taken here by the dogmatic expositor in the sense of 'likeness, counterpart;' in which case one would have to translate, 'the counterpart of a thousand, the all-shaped one.'

the bull is sacred to Agni; and 'the forward-striving,' he says, because forward (towards the east) they hold up Agni[1], and towards the front[2] they attend upon him;—'duly fitting thyself by limbs,' when he is built up, then he does indeed duly fit himself limb by limb;—'harm not the inexhaustible, wide-ruling cow[3],' the cow is indeed wide-ruling (virâg), and the wide-ruling is food, and accordingly the cow is food.

20. Then on the left side (he puts the head of) the ram, with (Vâg. S. XIII, 44), 'The defender of Tvash*tri*, the navel of Varu*n*a,' for the ewe is sacred both to Varu*n*a and to Tvash*tri*;—'the ewe born from the highest sphere;' the highest sphere doubtless is the ear, and the ear is the regions,—(thus[4]) the highest sphere is the regions;—'the mighty, thousandfold artifice of the Asura,' that is, the great, thousandfold artifice of the Asura[5];—'O Agni, harm it not in the highest

[1] See VI, 4, 3, 10.

[2] Or, 'they attend upon him (Agni, the fire-altar) who tends towards the front (east);' inasmuch as the altar is built in the shape of a bird flying eastwards.

[3] Or, harm not the cow, the wide-ruling (or wide-shining) Aditi!

[4] After the two premises (with 'vai') the inference seems here to be introduced without any particle. Similarly in paragraph 24; while in paragraph 19 the particle 'u' is used to perform that office. Cf. however VII, 4, 2, 1, where a third parallel clause (which logically might have been the inference) is introduced by 'u vai.'

[5] Sâya*n*a refers to the legend in Taitt. S. II, 1, 2, 2, here alluded to:—Svarbhânu, the Âsura, struck the sun with darkness. The gods sought an expiation for that (darkness): the first darkness of his which they dispelled became a black ewe, the second a red one, the third a white one; and what they cut off from the surface of the bone (?) that became a barren sheep, &c.

region!' the highest region are these worlds: thus, do not harm him (the ram) in these worlds!

21. Then on the right side (he puts the head of) the he-goat, with (Vâg. S. XIII, 45), 'The Agni who was born from Agni,' for that Agni was indeed born from Agni[1];—'from the pain of the earth or also of the sky;' for what was born from the pain (or heat) of Pragâpati, that was born from the pain of the sky and the earth;—'whereby Visvakarman begat living beings,'—the he-goat (or, the unborn one) is Vâk (Speech)[2], and from Vâk Visvakarman[3] begat living beings;—'him, O Agni, may thy wrath spare!' as the text, so the meaning.

22. These are the victims; separately he puts them down, separately he 'settles' them, and separately he pronounces the Sûdadohas on them; for separate from one another are those animals.

23. He then offers on the human head,—sacrifice is offering: he thus makes man the one among animals fit to sacrifice; whence man alone among animals performs sacrifice.

24. And, again, why he offers thereon:—he thereby lays vigour into the head. He offers with ghee,—ghee is a thunderbolt, and the thunderbolt means vigour: he thus lays vigour into it. With 'Hail' (he offers),—the 'Hail' (svâhâkâra, m.) is a male, and the male means vigour: he thus lays vigour into it. With a trishtubh verse (he offers);—the Trishtubh is a thunderbolt, and the thunderbolt

[1] Viz. inasmuch as the fire to be ultimately deposited on the fire-altar was taken from the original (hall-door) fire.

[2] See VI, 1, 1, 9.

[3] That is, Pragâpati, the lord of procreation; see VI, 1, 2, 6 seq.

means vigour; the Trish*t*ubh is vigour: with vigour he thus lays vigour into it.

25. Having run through[1] the (first) half-verse, he pronounces the Svâhâ;—the *rik* (verse) is a bone: having cleft asunder that skull-bone which is here inside the head, he there lays vigour into it.

26. Having then run through the (second) half-verse, he pronounces the Svâhâ,—having joined together that skull-bone which is here on the top of the head, he there lays vigour into it.

27. [Vâ*g*. S. XIII, 46; *Ri*k S. I, 115, 1] 'The brilliant front of the gods hath risen,' for that man is yonder sun, and he indeed rises as the brilliant front (face) of the gods;—'the eye of Mitra, Varu*n*a, and Agni,' for that (sun) is the eye of both gods and men;—'he hath filled heaven, and earth, and the air,' for when he rises he indeed fills these worlds;—'Sûrya, the soul of the movable and immovable;' for that (sun) is indeed the soul of everything here that moves and stands.

28. He then stands by (the heads, revering them) with the Utsargas[2]. For at that time when Pra*g*âpati wanted to slaughter the victims, they, being about to be slaughtered, were distressed (or pained); and by these Utsargas he drove out their distress[3], their evil. In like manner does this one, by these Utsargas, now drive out their distress, their evil.

29. Now some remove the distress of whichever (head of a) victim they put down, thinking lest they might put distress, evil, thereon; but it is they that

[1] That is, having rapidly muttered it.

[2] That is, (means of) deliverance or removal, a term applied to the next five mantras.

[3] Lit. their burning heat (*suk*); cf. par. 32 seq.

put distress, evil, thereon; for the distress they remove from the preceding one, they put on (the altar) with the succeeding one.

30. And some revere (the heads) whilst moving round them, thinking, 'we remove distress upwards;' but these indeed follow the distress, the evil, upwards; for upwards he (the Sacrificer) goes by this performance[1], and upwards they remove the distress.

31. Let him remove it outside the fire (-altar); that fire (-altar) being these worlds, he thus puts distress outside these worlds;—outside the Vedi; the Vedi being this earth, he thus puts distress outside this earth;—(he does so) standing with his face towards the north; for in that region those animals are, and he thus puts distress into them in the region in which they are.

32. He first removes that of the man—for him he puts down first—with (Vâg. S. XIII, 47), 'Harm not this two-footed animal!' the two-footed animal doubtless is the same as man: thus, 'do not harm that one!'—'(thou) the thousand-eyed, being built for pith;'—the thousand-eyed he (Agni) is on account of the chips of gold; 'for pith,' that is, 'for food.'—'Graciously accept thou, O Agni, the sham-man, the victim, as pith!' a sham-man is a kim-purusha (mock-man)[2]: thus, 'accept graciously the kim-purusha, O Agni!'—'Building up therewith thy forms, get thee settled!' the form is the self: thus, 'Building up

[1] The Sacrificer builds the fire-altar with a view to his securing for himself a place in heaven.

[2] It is doubtful what is meant here by this term, unless it be a monkey, or a counterfeit human head; cf. p. 197, note 4.

therewith, perfect thyself[1]!'—'Let thy burning heat reach the sham-man! let thy burning heat reach him whom we hate!' he thereby lays burning heat into the sham-man, and into him whom he hates.

33. Then that of the horse, with (Vâg. S. XIII, 48), 'Harm not this one-hoofed animal!' the one-hoofed animal doubtless is the same as the horse: thus, do not harm that one!—'the racer neighing among the racers;' for neighing indeed he is, and a racer among racers;—'The wild fallow (beast) do I assign unto thee,' he thereby assigns to him the wild fallow (beast)[2];—'building up therewith thy forms, get thee settled!' that is, 'building up therewith, perfect thyself!'—'Let thy burning heat reach the fallow beast! let thy burning heat reach him whom we hate!' he thereby lays burning heat into the fallow beast, and into him whom he hates.

34. Then that of the bull, with (Vâg. S. XIII, 49), 'This thousandfold, hundred-streamed well—,' for a thousandfold, hundred-streamed well he, the bull (cow), indeed is;—'extended in the middle of the flood,' the flood doubtless are these worlds: thus, subsisted upon in these worlds;—'the inexhaustible, milking ghee for man,'—for ghee this inexhaustible (cow) indeed milks for man;—

[1] This paraphrase does not make it clear how the author construes and interprets this part of the formula; especially in what sense he takes 'nishîda.'

[2] Thus Mahîdhara (gauravar*n*a*m* m*ri*gam). In the St. Petersburg dictionary 'gaura' is taken here in the sense of 'buffalo, bos gavæus.' The parallelism in the next two formulas might indeed seem to point to that meaning.

'harm not, O Agni, in the highest region!' the highest region doubtless are these worlds : thus, do not harm it in these worlds!—'The wild buffalo do I assign unto thee,' he thereby assigns to him the wild buffalo (gavaya);—'building up therewith thy forms, get thee settled!' that is, 'building up therewith, perfect thyself!'—'Let thy burning heat reach the buffalo! let thy burning heat reach him whom we hate!' he thereby lays burning heat into the buffalo, and into him whom he hates.

35. Then that of the sheep, with (Vâg. S. XIII, 50), 'This woollen—,' that is, 'this woolly,'—'navel of Varu*n*a,' for the sheep is sacred to Varu*n*a;—'the skin of animals, two-footed and four-footed,' for that (sheep) indeed is the skin of both kinds of animals[1], two-footed and four-footed;—'the first birth-place of Tvash*t*ri's creatures,' for Tvash*t*ri indeed fashioned this as the first form; —'harm not, O Agni, in the highest region!' the highest region is these worlds: thus, 'do not harm him in these worlds!'—'The wild buffalo do I assign unto thee,' he thereby assigns the wild buffalo (ush*t*ra) to him;—'building up therewith thy forms, get thee settled!' that is, 'building up therewith, perfect thyself!'—'Let thy burning heat reach the buffalo! let thy burning heat reach him whom we hate!' he thereby lays burning heat into the buffalo, and into him whom he hates.

36. Then that of the he-goat, with (Vâg. S. XIII, 51), 'Verily, the he-goat was produced from Agni's heat;'—that which was produced from

[1] Viz. inasmuch as its wool serves as a cover for man and beast.

Pragâpati's heat, was indeed produced from Agni's heat;—'he saw the progenitor at first,' the progenitor doubtless is Pragâpati: thus, 'he saw Pragâpati at first;'—'thereby the gods at first (agre) went to the godhead;' the he-goat[1] doubtless is speech, and from speech the gods doubtless first went to the godhead, to the summit (agram);—'thereby they went to the height, the wise;' the height doubtless is the heavenly world: thus, 'thereby they went to the heavenly world, the wise;'—'The wild sarabha do I assign unto thee,'—he thereby assigns the wild sarabha[2] to him;—'building up therewith thy forms, get thee settled!' that is, 'building up therewith, perfect thyself!'—'Let thy burning heat reach the sarabha! let thy burning heat reach him whom we hate!' he thereby lays burning heat into the sarabha, and into him whom he hates.

37. As to this they say,—The pain (heat), the evil of these animals, which Pragâpati drove out, became these five animals; they, with their pith (sacrificial essence) gone out of them, are pithless, unfit for sacrifice; a Brâhmana should not eat of them: he consigns them to that region; whence Parganya does not rain in that region where these are.

38. He returns (to the offering-fire) and stands thereby worshipping it;—for when he goes outside the Vedi, whilst Agni (the fire-altar) is only half built up, he does what is improper; he now makes amends to him to prevent his doing injury. With

[1] 'Aga,' he-goat, is here again taken in the sense of 'a-ga,' unborn. As to the gods having sprung from Vâk, see VI, 1, 2, 6 seq.

[2] A fabulous animal with eight legs.

a verse to Agni (he worships): it is to Agni he thereby makes amends;—with an undefined one; the undefined means everything: by means of everything he thus makes amends to him;—with (a verse) containing the word 'youngest:' this indeed, to wit, the youngest, is his favourite form;—inasmuch as when born he took possession (yu) of everything here, he is the youngest (yavish*th*a).

39. [Vâg. S. XIII, 52; *Ri*k S. VIII, 84, 3] 'Shield thou, O youngest, the men of the liberal worshipper!' the liberal worshipper is the Sacrificer, and the men are the people;—'hear thou the songs!' that is, hear this hymn of praise!—'protect thou kin and self!' the kin (race) means offspring: thus, 'protect both (the Sacrificer's) offspring and himself.'

40. Having stepped on the altar and walked round behind the naturally-perforated (brick), he lays down the Apasyâ*h* (water-bricks);—now the Apasyâ*h* are the same as water, and the water has gone out of these victims: he thus puts water into these victims, when he lays down the Apasyâ*h* (bricks). He lays them down close to the (heads of the) animals: he thereby puts the water together with the animals. He lays down five (bricks) in each quarter, for five are those victims. He lays them down in every (quarter): everywhere he thus puts water into them.

41. Now the first fifteen are the Apasyâ*h*,—water is a thunderbolt, and the thunderbolt is fifteenfold;—hence wherever the waters flow, there they destroy evil; and verily the thunderbolt destroys the evil of this place: hence, when it rains one should go about uncovered, thinking, 'May that thunderbolt remove evil from me!'

42. And the last five are the *Kh*andasyâ*h* (the metres' bricks);—the metres are cattle, and cattle is food; or rather the flesh of cattle is food, and the flesh has departed from these victims: he therefore puts flesh on those cattle when he lays down the *Kh*andasyâ*h*. He places them close to the victims: he thereby puts the flesh close to the (bones of the) cattle. The Apasyâ*h* are inside, the *Kh*andasyâ*h* outside; for the water is inside, and the flesh outside.

43. As to this they say, 'If there are that water and that flesh, where then is the skin, and where the hair?' Well, the skin of cattle is food, and the hair of cattle is food; and when he lays down the *Kh*andasyâ*h*, that is the skin of the victims, that is their hair. Or, again, those goats' hair which are in the fire-pan [1], they are hair. The fire-pan is outside, and the victims' heads are inside, for outside is the hair, and inside is the body. 'Whether in the one way, or whether in the other,' so *S*â*nd*ilya was wont to say, 'in any case we make up the victims wholly and completely.'

44. And, again, why he lays down the Apasyâ*h*. When Pra*g*âpati was disjointed the water went from him; that being gone, he sank down; and because he sank down (vi*s*), therefore there are twenty (vi*m*-*s*ati, viz. such bricks). It flowed from his fingers,—the fingers being the end, it (the water) went from him in the end.

45. Now the Pra*g*âpati who became disjointed is this very Agni who is now being built up; and the water (âpa*h*) which went from him is these very

[1] See VI, 4, 4, 22; 5, 1, 4.

Apasyâh;—hence when he lays them down, he thereby puts back into him that very water which went from him: therefore he now lays these down.

46. [Vâg. S. XIII, 43] 'In the way of the waters I settle thee!' the way of the waters is the wind; for when he blows hither and thither then the waters flow: in the wind he 'settles' this (first brick).

47. 'In the swell of the waters I settle thee!' the swell of the waters is the plants, for wherever the waters keep swelling there plants grow: in the plants he settles this (brick).

48. 'In the ashes of the waters I settle thee!' the ashes of the waters are the foam: in foam he settles this one.

49. 'In the light of the waters I settle thee!' the light of the waters is the lightning: in the lightning he settles this one.

50. 'In the path of the waters I settle thee!' the path of the waters is this earth, for on the earth the waters flow: on this earth he settles this one. Whatever water flowed from those (five) forms of his, that water he now (by these five formulas) puts back into him; and those forms themselves he thereby restores to him.

51. 'In the flood, the seat, I settle thee!' the flood is the breath: in the breath he settles this one.

52. 'In the ocean, the seat, I settle thee!' the sea is the mind; from the mind-ocean, with speech for a shovel, the gods dug out the triple science. Thereto this verse applies,—'May the true god know this day where the gods placed that offering, they who dug it out from the ocean with

sharp shovels;'—the ocean is the mind, the sharp shovel is speech, the offering is the triple science: it is thereto this verse applies. In the mind he settles this (brick).

53. 'In the stream, the seat, I settle thee!' the stream is speech: in speech he settles this one.

54. 'In the abode of the waters I settle thee!' the abode of the waters is the eye, for there water always abides: in the eye he settles this one.

55. 'In the goal of the waters I settle thee!' the goal of the waters is the ear: in the ear he settles this one. Whatever water flowed from those (five) forms of his, that water he now (by these five formulas) puts back into him; and those forms themselves he thereby restores to him.

56. 'In the seat of the waters I settle thee!' the seat of the waters is the sky, for in the sky the waters are seated: in the sky he settles this one.

57. 'In the home of the waters I settle thee!' the home of the waters is the air: in the air he settles this one.

58. 'In the womb of the waters I settle thee!' the womb of the waters is the sea: in the sea he settles this one.

59. 'In the sediment of the waters I settle thee!' the sediment (purîsha) of the waters is sand: in the sand he settles this one.

60. 'In the resort of the waters I settle thee!' the resort of the waters is food: in food he settles this one. Whatever water flowed from those (five) forms of his, that water he now (by these five formulas) puts back into him; and those forms themselves he thereby restores to him.

61. 'By the Gâyatrî metre I settle thee!—

By the Trish/ubh metre I settle thee!—By the Gagatî metre I settle thee!—By the Anush/ubh metre I settle thee!—By the Pańkti metre I settle thee!' Whatever water flowed from those metres of his, that he now (by these formulas) puts back into him; and those metres themselves he thereby restores to him.

62. These (bricks) are fingers (and toes): he puts them on all sides[1], for these fingers (and toes) are on all sides; he puts them at the ends, for these fingers (and toes) are at the ends; in four sets he puts them on, for these fingers (and toes) are in four sets; five he puts on each time, for there are five fingers (or toes) at each (limb); separately he puts them on, for separate are these fingers (and toes); only once he 'settles' each (set): he thereby makes (each set) one and the same, whence they have a common connecting-link.

[1] The four sets of bricks are placed in the middle of the four sides of the square 'body' of the altar-site, or at the ends of the two 'spines' intersecting each other.

CORRECTIONS.

Introduction, page xii, line 33. Read,—the day preceding the Soma-day, the animal offering to Agni-Soma being indeed a constant feature of that day's proceedings at every Soma-sacrifice; whilst the slaughter of the special victim, or victims, of the respective sacrifice takes place during the morning service, &c.

P. 5, last line of text. Read,—therefor.

P. 6, note 2, l. 3. P*ri*sh*th*ya sha*d*aha, see Introduction, p. xxi.

P. 8, last line of notes. For 'II, 665' read 'II, 663, in a different tune again.'

P. 9, l. 5 of notes. Read,—II, 720–22.

P. 34, l. 21. Read,—B*ri*haspati consecration.

P. 41, l. 14. For 'offering' read 'offspring.'

P. 104, l. 2. For 'truth' read 'law;' (cf. VI, 7, 3, 11.)

P. 146, l. 23. For 'become' read 'became.'

PLAN OF FIRE-ALTAR (AGNIKSHETRA)

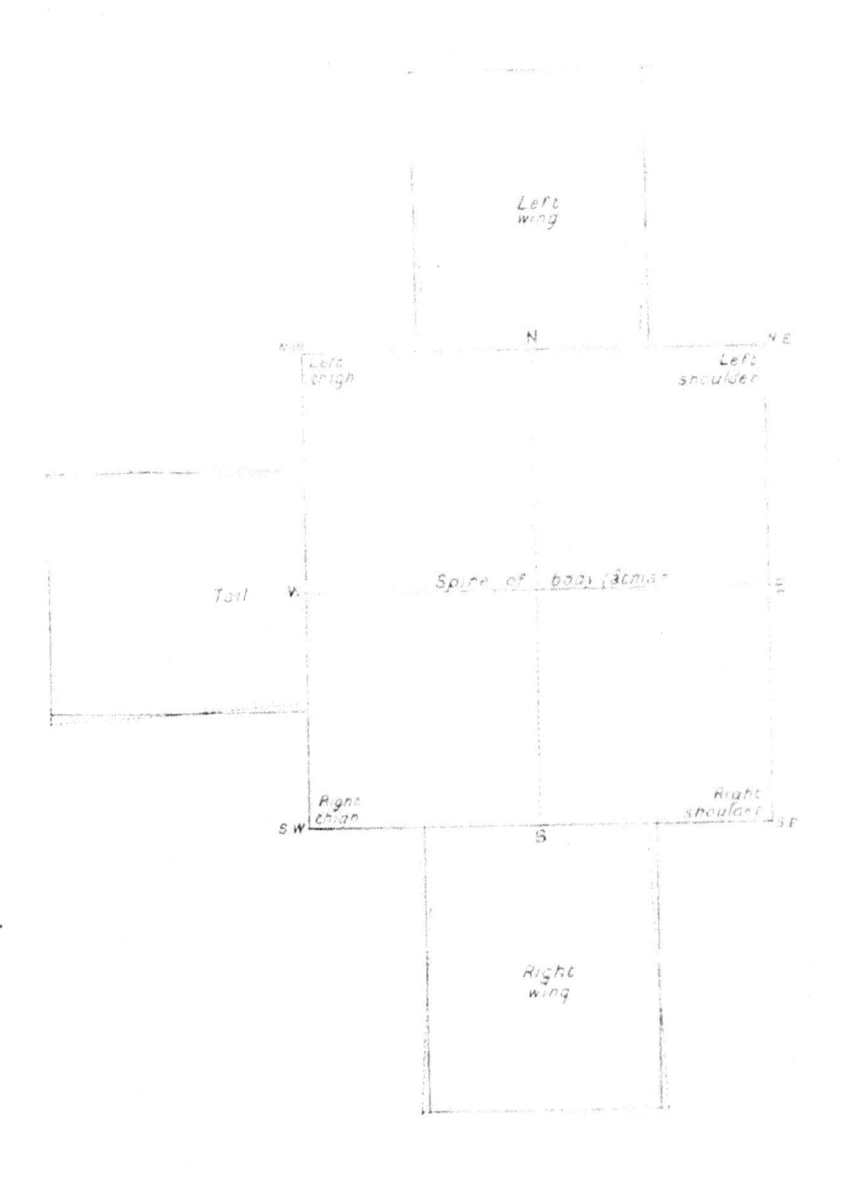

TRANSLITERATION OF ORIENTAL ALPHABETS ADOPTED FOR THE TRANSLATIONS OF THE SACRED BOOKS OF THE EAST.

CONSONANTS.	MISSIONARY ALPHABET.			Sanskrit.	Zend.	Pehlevi.	Persian.	Arabic.	Hebrew.	Chinese.
	I Class.	II Class.	III Class.							
Gutturales.										
1 Tenuis	k	...	....	क	𐬐	[illegible]	ک	ك	כּ	k
2 „ aspirata	kh	...	....	ख	𐬑	[illegible]	...	...	כ	kh
3 Media	g	...	....	ग	𐬔	[illegible]	گ	...	גּ	...
4 „ aspirata	gh	...	....	घ	𐬖	[illegible]	...	...	ג	...
5 Gutturo-labialis	q	...	....	...	....	...	ق	ق	ק	...
6 Nasalis	ṅ (ng)	...	....	ङ	{𐬢 (ng) / 𐬣 (N)}	...	...	...	...	...
7 Spiritus asper	h	...	....	ह	𐬵 (𐬓 *hv*)	[illegible]	ه	ه	ה	h, hs
8 „ lenis	’	...	....	...	....	...	ا	ا	א	...
9 „ asper faucalis	‘h	...	....	...	....	...	ح	ح	ח	...
10 „ lenis faucalis	‘h	...	....	...	....	...	ع	ع	ע	...
11 „ asper fricatus	...	*‘h*	....	...	....	...	خ	خ	ח	...
12 „ lenis fricatus	...	*‘h*	....	...	....	...	...	...	...	...
Gutturales modificatae (palatales, &c.)										
13 Tenuis	...	*k*	....	च	𐬗	[illegible]	چ	...	...	*k*
14 „ aspirata	...	*kh*	....	छ	....	...	...	...	...	*kh*
15 Media	...	*g*	....	ज	𐬘	[illegible]	ج	ج	...	...
16 „ aspirata	...	*gh*	....	झ	....	...	غ	غ	...	...
17 „ Nasalis	...	*ñ*	....	ञ	....	...	...	...	...	...

CONSONANTS (*continued*).	MISSIONARY ALPHABET. I Class.	II Class.	III Class.	Sanskrit.	Zend.	Pehlevi.	Persian.	Arabic.	Hebrew.	Chinese.
18 Semivocalis	y	...	...	य	[illegible] init. [illegible]	[illegible]	ي	ي	י	y
19 Spiritus asper	...	(y̔)	...	...	...	...	...	...	...	...
20 „ lenis	...	(y̓)	...	...	...	...	...	...	...	...
21 „ asper assibilatus	...	*s*	...	श	[illegible]	[illegible]	ش	ش	...	...
22 „ lenis assibilatus	...	*z*	...	...	[illegible]	[illegible]	ژ	...	...	*z*
Dentales.										
23 Tenuis	t	...	...	त	𐬙	[illegible]	ت	ت	תּ	t
24 „ aspirata	th	...	...	थ	𐬚	...	...	...	ת	th
25 „ assibilata	...	...	TH	...	...	...	ث	ث	...	...
26 Media	d	...	...	द	[illegible]	[illegible]	د	د	דּ	...
27 „ aspirata	dh	...	...	ध	[illegible]	...	...	...	ד	...
28 „ assibilata	...	...	DH	...	...	...	ذ	ذ	...	...
29 Nasalis	n	...	...	न	[illegible]	[illegible]	ن	ن	נ	n
30 Semivocalis	l	...	...	ल	...	[illegible]	ل	ل	ל	l
31 „ mollis 1	...	*l*	...	ळ	...	...	...	...	...	...
32 „ mollis 2	...	...	L	...	...	...	...	...	...	...
33 Spiritus asper 1	s	...	...	स	𐬯	[illegible]	س (ث)	س	שׁ	s
34 „ asper 2	...	...	s (ʃ)	...	...	...	...	...	ס	...
35 „ lenis	z	...	...	...	𐬰	[illegible]	ز (ذ)	ز	ז	z
36 „ asperrimus 1	...	...	z (ʒ)	...	...	...	ص	ص	צ	ʒ, ʒh
37 „ asperrimus 2	...	...	ẓ (ʒ)	...	...	...	ض	...	...	...

Dentales modificatae (linguales, &c.)										
38 Tenuis	...	*t*	...	ट	...	...	ط	ط	ט	...
39 " aspirata	...	*th*	...	ठ	...	...	ظ	ظ	...	...
40 Media	...	*d*	...	ड	[illegible]	[illegible]	...	...	...	...
41 " aspirata	...	*dh*	...	ढ	...	...	...	ض	...	...
42 Nasalis	...	*n*	...	ण	[illegible]	...	...	...	...	...
43 Semivocalis	r	...	...	र	[illegible]	[illegible]	ر	ر	ר	...
44 " fricata	...	*r*	...	...	...	...	...	...	...	*r*
45 " diacritica	...	...	R	...	...	...	...	...	...	...
46 Spiritus asper	sh	...	...	ष	[illegible]	[illegible]	...	...	...	sh
47 " lenis	zh	...	...	...	...	...	...	...	...	...
Labiales.										
48 Tenuis	p	...	...	प	[illegible]	[illegible]	پ	...	פּ	p
49 " aspirata	ph	...	...	फ	...	...	...	...	פ	ph
50 Media	b	...	...	ब	[illegible]	[illegible]	ب	ب	בּ	...
51 " aspirata	bh	...	...	भ	...	...	...	...	ב	...
52 Tenuissima	...	*p*	...	...	...	...	...	...	...	...
53 Nasalis	m	...	...	म	[illegible]	[illegible]	م	م	מ	m
54 Semivocalis	w	...	...	...	[illegible]	...	...	...	...	w
55 " aspirata	hw	...	...	...	...	...	...	...	...	...
56 Spiritus asper	f	...	...	...	[illegible]	[illegible]	ف	ف	...	f
57 " lenis	v	...	...	व	»	[illegible]	و	و	ו	...
58 Anusvâra	...	*m*	...	अं	[illegible] ã	...	...	...	...	...
59 Visarga	...	*h*	...	अः	...	...	...	...	...	...

VOWELS.	MISSIONARY ALPHABET.			Sanskrit.	Zend.	Pehlevi.	Persian.	Arabic.	Hebrew.	Chinese.
	I Class.	II Class.	III Class.							
1 Neutralis	0	...	....	...	....	...	...	...	ְ	ă
2 Laryngo-palatalis	ĕ	...	....	...	....	...	...	...	...	...
3 „ labialis	ŏ	...	....	...	....	ا fin.	...	...	...	...
4 Gutturalis brevis	a	...	....	अ	𐬀	𐭠 init.	ـَ	ـَ	ַ	a
5 „ longa	â	(a)	....	आ	𐬁	𐭠	ـَا	ـَا	ָ	â
6 Palatalis brevis	i	...	....	इ	𐬌	...	ـِ	ـِ	ִ	i
7 „ longa	î	(i)	....	ई	𐬍	𐭩	ـِي	ـِي	ִי	î
8 Dentalis brevis	*li*	...	....	ऌ	....	...	...	...	...	...
9 „ longa	*lí*	...	....	ॡ	....	...	...	...	...	...
10 Lingualis brevis	*ri*	...	....	ऋ	....	...	...	...	...	...
11 „ longa	*rí*	...	....	ॠ	....	...	...	...	...	...
12 Labialis brevis	u	...	....	उ	𐬎	...	ـُ	ـُ	ֻ	u
13 „ longa	û	(u)	....	ऊ	𐬏	ا	ـُو	ـُو	וּ	û
14 Gutturo-palatalis brevis	e	...	....	...	𐬈(e) 𐬉(e)	...	...	...	ֶ	e
15 „ longa	ê (ai)	(e)	....	ए	𐬆, 𐬇	𐭩	...	...	ֵ	ê
16 Diphthongus gutturo-palatalis	âi	(ai)	....	ऐ	....	...	ـَيْ	ـَيْ	...	âi
17 „ „	ei (ĕi)	...	....	...	....	...	...	...	...	ei, êi
18 „ „	oi (ŏu)	...	....	...	....	...	...	...	...	...
19 Gutturo-labialis brevis	o	...	....	...	𐬊	...	...	...	ָ	o
20 „ longa	ô (au)	(o)	....	ओ	𐬋	ا	...	...	וֹ	...
21 Diphthongus gutturo-labialis	âu	(au)	....	औ	𐬈𐬎 (au)	...	ـَوْ	ـَوْ	...	âu
22 „ „	eu (ĕu)	...	....	...	....	...	...	...	...	...
23 „ „	ou (ŏu)	...	....	...	....	...	...	...	...	...
24 Gutturalis fracta	ä	...	....	...	....	...	...	...	...	...
25 Palatalis fracta	ï	...	....	...	....	...	...	...	...	...
26 Labialis fracta	ü	...	....	...	....	...	...	...	...	ü
27 Gutturo-labialis fracta	ö	...	....	...	....	...	...	...	...	...

SACRED BOOKS OF THE EAST

TRANSLATED BY

VARIOUS ORIENTAL SCHOLARS

AND EDITED BY

F. MAX MÜLLER

*** *This Series is published with the sanction and co-operation of the Secretary of State for India in Council.*

REPORT presented to the ACADÉMIE DES INSCRIPTIONS, May 11, 1833, by M. ERNEST RENAN.

'M. Renan présente trois nouveaux volumes de la grande collection des "Livres sacrés de l'Orient" (Sacred Books of the East), que dirige à Oxford, avec une si vaste érudition et une critique si sûre, le savant associé de l'Académie des Inscriptions, M. Max Müller. . . . La première série de ce beau recueil, composée de 24 volumes, est presque achevée. M. Max Müller se propose d'en publier une seconde, dont l'intérêt historique et religieux ne sera pas moindre. M. Max Müller a su se procurer la collaboration des savans les plus éminens d'Europe et d'Asie. L'Université d'Oxford, que cette grande publication honore au plus haut degré, doit tenir à continuer dans les plus larges proportions une œuvre aussi philosophiquement conçue que savamment exécutée.'

EXTRACT from the QUARTERLY REVIEW.

'We rejoice to notice that a second series of these translations has been announced and has actually begun to appear. The stones, at least, out of which a stately edifice may hereafter arise, are here being brought together. Prof. Max Müller has deserved well of scientific history. Not a few minds owe to his enticing words their first attraction to this branch of study. But no work of his, not even the great edition of the Rig-Veda, can compare in importance or in usefulness with this English translation of the Sacred Books of the East, which has been devised by his foresight, successfully brought so far by his persuasive and organising power, and will, we trust, by the assistance of the distinguished scholars he has gathered round him, be carried in due time to a happy completion.'

Professor E. HARDY, Inaugural Lecture in the University of Freiburg, 1887.

'Die allgemeine vergleichende Religionswissenschaft datirt von jenem grossartigen, in seiner Art einzig dastehenden Unternehmen, zu welchem auf Anregung Max Müllers im Jahre 1874 auf dem internationalen Orientalistencongress in London der Grundstein gelegt worden war, die Übersetzung der heiligen Bücher des Ostens' (*the Sacred Books of the East*).

The Hon. ALBERT S. G. CANNING, 'Words on Existing Religions.'

'The recent publication of the "Sacred Works of the East" in English is surely a great event in the annals of theological literature.'

Oxford

AT THE CLARENDON PRESS

LONDON: HENRY FROWDE

OXFORD UNIVERSITY PRESS WAREHOUSE, AMEN CORNER, E.C.

FIRST SERIES.

VOL. I. The Upanishads.

Translated by F. MAX MÜLLER. Part I. The *Kh*ândogya-upanishad, The Talavakâra-upanishad, The Aitareya-âra*n*yaka, The Kaushîtaki-brâhma*n*a-upanishad, and The Vâgasaneyi-sa*m*hitâ-upanishad. 8vo, cloth, 10*s*. 6*d*.

The Upanishads contain the philosophy of the Veda. They have become the foundation of the later Vedânta doctrines, and indirectly of Buddhism. Schopenhauer, speaking of the Upanishads, says: 'In the whole world there is no study so beneficial and so elevating as that of the Upanishads. It has been the solace of my life, it will be the solace of my death.'

[See also Vol. XV.]

VOL. II. The Sacred Laws of the Âryas,

As taught in the Schools of Âpastamba, Gautama, Vâsish*th*a, and Baudhâyana. Translated by GEORG BÜHLER. Part I. Âpastamba and Gautama. 8vo, cloth, 10*s*. 6*d*.

The Sacred Laws of the Âryas contain the original treatises on which the Laws of Manu and other lawgivers were founded.

[See also Vol. XIV.]

VOL. III. The Sacred Books of China.

The Texts of Confucianism. Translated by JAMES LEGGE. Part I. The Shû King, The Religious Portions of the Shih King, and The Hsiâo King. 8vo, cloth, 12*s*. 6*d*.

Confucius was a collector of ancient traditions, not the founder of a new religion. As he lived in the sixth and fifth centuries B.C. his works are of unique interest for the study of Ethology.

[See also Vols. XVI, XXVII, XXVIII, XXXIX, and XL.]

VOL. IV. The Zend-Avesta.

Translated by JAMES DARMESTETER. Part I. The Vendîdâd. 8vo, cloth, 10*s*. 6*d*.

The Zend-Avesta contains the relics of what was the religion of Cyrus, Darius, and Xerxes, and, but for the battle of Marathon, might have become the religion of Europe. It forms to the present day the sacred book of the Parsis, the so-called fire-worshippers. Two more volumes will complete the translation of all that is left us of Zoroaster's religion.

[See also Vols. XXIII and XXXI.]

VOL. V. Pahlavi Texts.

Translated by E. W. WEST. Part I. The Bundahis, Bahman Yast, and Shâyast lâ-shâyast. 8vo, cloth, 12*s.* 6*d.*

The Pahlavi Texts comprise the theological literature of the revival of Zoroaster's religion, beginning with the Sassanian dynasty. They are important for a study of Gnosticism.

VOLS. VI AND IX. The Qur'ân.

Parts I and II. Translated by E. H. PALMER. 8vo, cloth, 21*s.*

This translation, carried out according to his own peculiar views of the origin of the Qur'ân, was the last great work of E. H. Palmer, before he was murdered in Egypt.

VOL. VII. The Institutes of Vishnu.

Translated by JULIUS JOLLY. 8vo, cloth, 10*s.* 6*d.*

A collection of legal aphorisms, closely connected with one of the oldest Vedic schools, the Kathas, *but considerably added to in later time. Of importance for a critical study of the Laws of Manu.*

VOL. VIII. The Bhagavadgîtâ, with The Sanatsugâtîya, and The Anugîtâ.

Translated by KÂSHINÂTH TRIMBAK TELANG. 8vo, cloth, 10*s.* 6*d.*

The earliest philosophical and religious poem of India. It has been paraphrased in Arnold's 'Song Celestial.'

VOL. X. The Dhammapada,

Translated from Pâli by F. MAX MÜLLER; and

The Sutta-Nipâta,

Translated from Pâli by V. FAUSBÖLL; being Canonical Books of the Buddhists. 8vo, cloth, 10*s.* 6*d.*

The Dhammapada contains the quintessence of Buddhist morality. The Sutta-Nipâta gives the authentic teaching of Buddha on some of the fundamental principles of religion.

VOL. XI. Buddhist Suttas.

Translated from Pâli by T. W. RHYS DAVIDS. 1. The Mahâ-parinibbâna Suttanta; 2. The Dhamma-*k*akka-ppavattana Sutta. 3. The Tevigga Suttanta; 4. The Âkaṅkheyya Sutta; 5. The *K*etokhila Sutta; 6. The Mahâ-sudassana Suttanta; 7. The Sabbâsava Sutta. 8vo, cloth, 10*s*. 6*d*.

A collection of the most important religious, moral, and philosophical discourses taken from the sacred canon of the Buddhists.

VOL. XII. The *S*atapatha-Brâhma*n*a, according to the Text of the Mâdhyandina School.

Translated by JULIUS EGGELING. Part I. Books I and II. 8vo, cloth, 12*s*. 6*d*.

A minute account of the sacrificial ceremonies of the Vedic age. It contains the earliest account of the Deluge in India.

[See also Vols. XXVI, XLI.]

VOL. XIII. Vinaya Texts.

Translated from the Pâli by T. W. RHYS DAVIDS and HERMANN OLDENBERG. Part I. The Pâtimokkha. The Mahâvagga, I–IV. 8vo, cloth, 10*s*. 6*d*.

The Vinaya Texts give for the first time a translation of the moral code of the Buddhist religion as settled in the third century B.C.

[See also Vols. XVII and XX.]

VOL. XIV. The Sacred Laws of the Âryas,

As taught in the Schools of Âpastamba, Gautama, Vâsish*th*a, and Baudhâyana. Translated by GEORG BÜHLER. Part II. Vasish*th*a and Baudhâyana. 8vo, cloth, 10*s*. 6*d*.

VOL. XV. The Upanishads.

Translated by F. MAX MÜLLER. Part II. The Ka*th*a-upanishad, The Mu*nd*aka-upanishad, The Taittirîyaka-upanishad, The B*ri*hadâra*n*yaka-upanishad, The *S*vetâ*s*vatara-upanishad, The Pra*s*ña-upanishad, and The Maitrâya*n*a-brâhma*n*a-upanishad. 8vo, cloth, 10*s*. 6*d*.

VOL. XVI. The Sacred Books of China.

The Texts of Confucianism. Translated by JAMES LEGGE. Part II. The Yî King. 8vo, cloth, 10*s*. 6*d*.

[See also Vols. XXVII, XXVIII.]

VOL. XVII. Vinaya Texts.

Translated from the Pâli by T. W. RHYS DAVIDS and HERMANN OLDENBERG. Part II. The Mahâvagga V–X. The *K*ullavagga, I–III. 8vo, cloth, 10*s*. 6*d*.

VOL. XVIII. Pahlavi Texts.

Translated by E. W. WEST. Part II. The Dâ*d*istân-î Dînîk and The Epistles of Mânûs*k*îhar. 8vo, cloth, 12*s*. 6*d*.

VOL. XIX. The Fo-sho-hing-tsan-king.

A Life of Buddha by Asvaghosha Bodhisattva, translated from Sanskrit into Chinese by Dharmaraksha, A.D. 420, and from Chinese into English by SAMUEL BEAL. 8vo, cloth, 10*s*. 6*d*.

This life of Buddha was translated from Sanskrit into Chinese, A.D. 420. It contains many legends, some of which show a certain similarity to the Evangelium infantiae, &c.

VOL. XX. Vinaya Texts.

Translated from the Pâli by T. W. RHYS DAVIDS and HERMANN OLDENBERG. Part III. The *K*ullavagga, IV–XII. 8vo, cloth, 10*s*. 6*d*.

VOL. XXI. The Saddharma-pu*nd*arîka; or, The Lotus of the True Law.

Translated by H. KERN. 8vo, cloth, 12*s*. 6*d*.

'The Lotus of the true Law,' a canonical book of the Northern Buddhists, translated from Sanskrit. There is a Chinese translation of this book which was finished as early as the year 286 A.D.

VOL. XXII. *G*aina-Sûtras.

Translated from Prâkrit by HERMANN JACOBI. Part I. The Â*k*ârâṅga-Sûtra and The Kalpa-Sûtra. 8vo, cloth, 10*s*. 6*d*.

The religion of the Gainas was founded by a contemporary of Buddha. It still counts numerous adherents in India, while there are no Buddhists left in India proper.

Part II, *in preparation*.

VOL. XXIII. The Zend-Avesta.

Translated by JAMES DARMESTETER. Part II. The Sîrôzahs, Yasts, and Nyâyis. 8vo, cloth, 10*s*. 6*d*.

VOL. XXIV. Pahlavi Texts.

Translated by E. W. WEST. Part III. Dînâ-î Mainôg-Khirad, *S*ikand-gûmânik Vigâr, and Sad Dar. 8vo, cloth, 10*s*. 6*d*.

SECOND SERIES.

VOL. XXV. Manu.

Translated by GEORG BÜHLER. 8vo, cloth, 21*s*.

This translation is founded on that of Sir William Jones, which has been carefully revised and corrected with the help of seven native Commentaries. An Appendix contains all the quotations from Manu which are found in the Hindu Law-books, translated for the use of the Law Courts in India. Another Appendix gives a synopsis of parallel passages from the six Dharma-sûtras, the other Smr*i*tis, the Upanishads, the Mahâbhârata, &c.

VOL. XXVI. The *S*atapatha-Brâhma*n*a.

Translated by JULIUS EGGELING. Part II. Books III and IV. 8vo, cloth, 12*s*. 6*d*.

VOLS. XXVII AND XXVIII. The Sacred Books of China.

The Texts of Confucianism. Translated by JAMES LEGGE. Parts III and IV. The Lî *K*î, or Collection of Treatises on the Rules of Propriety, or Ceremonial Usages. 8vo, cloth, 12*s*. 6*d*. each.

VOL. XXIX. The G*ri*hya-Sûtras, Rules of Vedic Domestic Ceremonies.

Part I. *S*ânkhâyana, Â*s*valâyana, Pâraskara, Khâdira. Translated by HERMANN OLDENBERG. 8vo, cloth, 12*s*. 6*d*.

These rules of Domestic Ceremonies describe the home life of the ancient Âryas with a completeness and accuracy unmatched in any other literature. Some of these rules have been incorporated in the ancient Law-books.

VOL. XXX. The G*ri*hya-Sûtras, Rules of Vedic Domestic Ceremonies.

Part II. Gobhila, Hira*n*yake*s*in, Âpastamba. Translated by HERMANN OLDENBERG. Âpastamba, Ya*gñ*a-paribhâshâ-sûtras. Translated by F. MAX MÜLLER. 8vo, cloth, 12*s*. 6*d*.

VOL. XXXI. The Zend-Avesta.

Part III. The Yasna, Visparad, Âfrînagân, Gâhs, and Miscellaneous Fragments. Translated by L. H. MILLS. 8vo, cloth, 12*s*. 6*d*.

VOL. XXXII. Vedic Hymns.

Translated by F. MAX MÜLLER. Part I. 8vo, cloth, 18*s*. 6*d*.

VOL. XXXIII. The Minor Law-books.
Translated by JULIUS JOLLY. Part I. Nârada, B*ri*haspati. 8vo, cloth, 10*s.* 6*d.*

VOL. XXXIV. The Vedânta-Sûtras, with the Commentary by *S*ankarâ*k*ârya. Part I.
Translated by G. THIBAUT. 8vo, cloth, 12*s.* 6*d.*

VOL. XXXV. The Questions of King Milinda. Part I.
Translated from the Pâli by T. W. RHYS DAVIDS. 8vo, cloth, 10*s.* 6*d.*

VOL. XXXVI. The Questions of King Milinda. Part II. [*In the Press.*]

VOL. XXXVII. The Contents of the Nasks, as stated in the Eighth and Ninth Books of the Dinka*r*d.
Part I. Translated by E. W. WEST. 8vo, cloth, 15*s.*

VOL. XXXVIII. The Vedânta-Sûtras. Part II. [*In the Press.*]

VOLS. XXXIX AND XL. The Sacred Books of China.
The Texts of Tâoism. Translated by JAMES LEGGE. 8vo, cloth, 21*s.*

VOL. XLI. The *S*atapatha-Brâhma*n*a. Part III. Translated by JULIUS EGGELING. [*In the Press.*]

VOL. XLII. The Buddha-*k*arita. Translated by E. B. COWELL. The Sukhâvatî-vyûha. Translated by F. MAX MÜLLER. [*In the Press.*]

VOLS. XLIII AND XLIV. The *S*atapatha-Brâhma*n*a.
Parts IV and V. [*In preparation.*]

VOL. XLV. The *G*aina-Sûtras. Part II. [*In preparation.*]

VOL. XLVI. The Vedânta-Sûtras. Part III. [*In preparation.*]

VOL. XLVII. The Contents of the Nasks. Part II. [*In preparation.*]

VOL. XLVIII. Vedic Hymns. Part II. [*In preparation.*]

Anecdota Oxoniensia.

ARYAN SERIES.

Buddhist Texts from Japan. I. Vagrakkhedikâ; *The Diamond-Cutter.*

Edited by F. MAX MÜLLER, M.A. Small 4to, 3*s.* 6*d.*

One of the most famous metaphysical treatises of the Mahâyâna Buddhists.

Buddhist Texts from Japan. II. Sukhâvatî-Vyûha: *Description of Sukhâvatî, the Land of Bliss.*

Edited by F. MAX MÜLLER, M.A., and BUNYIU NANJIO. With two Appendices: (1) Text and Translation of Saṅghavarman's Chinese Version of the Poetical Portions of the Sukhâvatî-Vyûha; (2) Sanskrit Text of the Smaller Sukhâvatî-Vyûha. Small 4to, 7*s.* 6*d.*

The *editio princeps* of the Sacred Book of one of the largest and most influential sects of Buddhism, numbering more than ten millions of followers in Japan alone.

Buddhist Texts from Japan. III. *The Ancient Palm-Leaves containing the* Pragñâ-Pâramitâ-Hridaya-Sûtra *and the* Ushnîsha-Vigaya-Dhâranî.

Edited by F. MAX MÜLLER, M.A., and BUNYIU NANJIO, M.A. With an Appendix by G. BÜHLER, C.I.E. With many Plates. Small 4to, 10*s.*

Contains facsimiles of the oldest Sanskrit MS. at present known.

Dharma-Samgraha, *an Ancient Collection of Buddhist Technical Terms.*

Prepared for publication by KENJIU KASAWARA, a Buddhist Priest from Japan, and, after his death, edited by F. MAX MÜLLER and H. WENZEL. Small 4to, 7*s.* 6*d.*

Kâtâyana's Sarvânukramanî of the *Rig*veda.

With Extracts from Shadgurusishya's Commentary entitled Vedârthadîpikâ. Edited by A. A. MACDONELL, M.A., Ph.D. 16*s.*

Oxford

AT THE CLARENDON PRESS

LONDON: HENRY FROWDE

OXFORD UNIVERSITY PRESS WAREHOUSE, AMEN CORNER, E.C.

Milton Keynes UK
Ingram Content Group UK Ltd.
UKHW012026110124
435898UK00003B/51